MEANS OF
ESCAPE

Also by Philip Caputo

A RUMOR OF WAR

HORN OF AFRICA

DELCORSO'S GALLERY

INDIAN COUNTRY

EQUATION FOR EVIL

EXILES

THE VOYAGE

GHOSTS OF TSAVO

IN THE SHADOWS OF THE MORNING

MEANS OF ESCAPE

PHILIP CAPUTO

THE LYONS PRESS
Guilford, Connecticut
An imprint of The Globe Pequot Press

FOR GEOFFREY AND MARC

The Lyons Press is an imprint of The Globe Pequot Press

Originally Published by HarperCollins

Printed in the United States of America

10 9 8 7 6 5 4 3 2 1

Design by Alma Orenstein

ISBN 1-58574-737-8

Library of Congress Cataloging-in-Publication data is available on file.

CONTENTS

AUTHOR'S NOTE

Some time ago, Philip Roth commented that what the innocent take for "naked" autobiography is "more likely mock-autobiography or hypothetical autobiography, or autobiography grandiosely enlarged."

Some readers may accept a degree of artfulness in autobiographies claiming to be straightforward. This note is for those who do not. I don't want to hoodwink them into thinking they've bought one thing, only to find it's another. This book is not a hypothetical or "grandiosely enlarged" self-portrait; indeed, it's only a partial autobiography, as well as a picture, often highly impressionistic, of events I lived through as a foreign correspondent in the Middle East, Vietnam, Afghanistan, and other places between the late sixties and early eighties.

It wasn't my intent to make a documentary record of those times, but to capture something of what they felt like, their anguish and dread, that is, their emotional truth. The sketches entitled "Disasters of War," which come between the autobiographical chapters, were inspired by Francisco Goya's drawings and paintings of the same name. I first saw them in the Prado in Madrid in 1967, when I was newly discharged from a tour of duty in Vietnam, and traveling through Europe to sort a few things out. I was mesmerized by Goya's ability to communicate the emotions of war with pen and ink and oils, and wondered if the same could be done with words. The sketches are my attempt to achieve that, and achieving it, I discovered, required a measure of inventiveness. My "Disasters of War" are, therefore, fictional re-creations of actual experiences, either my own or someone else's. Uncovering their inner truth as gracefully and economically as possible demanded a reassembly of their outward facts, sometimes the inter-weaving of two or three incidents, separated in time but united by a common theme, sometimes the creation of fictional characters, based on real persons.

In the autobiographical passages, however (to quell any anxieties on the reader's part), I have remained faithful to the facts of the events, as well to the facts of my own actions in them. These chapters are "naked autobiography," or, more properly, personal memoir—the tale that memory tells—and the reader can be assured that they are as accurate and honest as my memory could make them.

—PJC
JUNE 2002

DISASTERS OF WAR

White against green. The contrast was beautiful, thought David Victor Jones, resting on a hill above the rice paddy. The paddy was bright jade, the trees around it emerald, and the ducks were white.

"They look like egrets," he said to his friend Tom Lockhart.

"What's an egret?"

"A shorebird."

"Those are ducks, Deevee."

That's what everyone called him, Deevee. Sometimes they called him Davy Jones and asked what was in his locker at the bottom of the sea.

"I know they're ducks," he said. "They just look like egrets. Egrets are white like that. I've never seen a pure white duck before, never seen so many of 'em in one place."

"Lotta things in this place nobody ever seen before."

The ducks were in the tree line, which formed an "L" around the paddy. There must have been five hundred of them, waddling and quacking. Now and then some rose a foot or two in the air, wings beating, then dropped suddenly, as if they were tethered.

"Wonder what they're all doin' in there?" Jones wondered aloud.

Lockhart shrugged.

"Maybe they're migrating and resting up. I wonder if the ducks in this country migrate the way they do back home."

Lockhart rubbed a speck of rust on his rifle.

"Probably not," Jones said, answering his own question. "Climate doesn't change enough. They're probably some farmer's ducks. You seen 'em, Tom. They raise 'em like chickens."

"Yeah," Lockhart said, concentrating on the rust.

"They probably can't fly. That's why they're hopping up and down, like they're trying to fly but can't. They've probably been bred so's they can't fly. At least not far. You couldn't raise ducks if they could fly away any damn time they wanted to."

Lockhart looked at the ducks, which were about two hundred yards away, and said he could not see what Jones was talking about.

"The way some of 'em hop up, flapping their wings, then fall down. See, there's a couple of 'em doing that now. Like they're tied down. They're trying to fly, but it's been bred out of them."

"When the hell did you get to be this big expert on ducks?"

"I'm not. Just wondering."

"You're a weird one, Deevee. You've always been a little weird."

"I don't think I like that, Tom."

"It ain't a insult. You just see things funny. You look at 'em from weird angles."

"I still don't like it."

"Hey, forget it, okay? So now you seen somethin' nobody else ever seen. Ten zillion white ducks that can't fly. Let's leave it at that."

The order to move out came down the column. Twenty-one men, with Lockhart and Jones as tail-end Charlies, stood and started marching down a dike that ran straight as a road across the middle of the rice paddy. Jones glanced toward the ducks, pleased by the beauty of the contrast between their white wings and bodies and the deep rich green of the trees. Did that make him weird?

"Hey," said Lockhart, looking at Jones over his shoulder. "What do them farmers raise the ducks for?"

Dumb, thought Jones. He's so dumb he can't figure what the ducks are raised for, but he calls me weird.

"To eat. What else? They bring 'em to the markets in these cages made out of twigs and sell 'em live."

"So if we shot a few, we could have us a duck dinner, right?"

"No," Jones said, thinking, What a dummy.

"Roast duck. Duck stew. Duck alley orange."

"No way. One round out of these pieces would blow a duck to bits."

"Then maybe we could grab us a few. They can't fly, right?" Lockhart paused, squinting toward the birds. "Hey, know what, Deevee? I think they are tied down. I think I just seen a rope or somethin' on one of their legs."

Jones stopped to look as several ducks leapt into the air, but he could not see anything tied to their legs. He wished he had the el-tee's binoculars. Why would a duck farmer tie his ducks down? Maybe they could fly, and maybe tethering them was a way to train them not to.

Lockhart was twenty yards ahead of him, the rest of the platoon well ahead of Lockhart. Jones walked at the double to catch up. Lockhart stepped off the dike and started to slog across the paddy toward the trees.

"Pass the word to hold it up a sec, Deevee. I'm gonna snatch us some."

"You goddamned idiot, Lockhart, get back over here."

"Hey, they're sittin' ducks," Lockhart said and laughed; then he fell hard, facedown. Jones heard the shot in the same instant and saw a muzzle flash. It came from the tree line, in the middle of the ducks. In the next moment, bullets were spraying across the paddy. It looked like a hailstorm, and three or four men on the dike ahead fell the way Lockhart had. The ducks were quacking like crazy. Jones dived behind the dike. All he could hear was gunfire, explosions, and quacking. He crawled toward the platoon, looked up once and saw men running, falling as they ran. Four or five fell in a row, one right after the other like … like ducks in a shooting gallery. Others, just a few, were lying behind the dike, firing at the ducks.

Muzzle flashes blazed among the birds. Jones fired back. He saw feathers flying, white against green. He saw no men in the trees, only ducks.

The platoon's firing grew sporadic. A lot of men were down. Jones emptied one magazine after another, but the incoming fire never slackened. Shooting ducks? It couldn't be, yet it was. He heard the clang of an empty magazine, raised his head slightly to load another, felt a blow to his skull, and then saw nothing at all.

When he came to, blood was running down his face. His helmet was gone. No one was shooting at the ducks anymore, but the ducks hadn't ceased fire. The bullets snicked and cracked overhead, then stopped. Jones glimpsed, through blood-blurred eyes, the ducks flying toward him, low over the waist-deep rice. For a moment, he thought he saw men under them, running in a low crouch. He blinked, but couldn't clear the blood from his eyes. No, there weren't any men, just birds, skimming over the rice shoots, white against green. Hundreds of ducks, coming to finish off the wounded. He crawled toward the platoon, slithered under a pile of dead men, and lay still.

Quack quack quack—that was all he heard beneath the stacked corpses, his face half buried in the mud. Quacks and an occasional shot. The ducks were getting closer. Jones burrowed deeper, smelling sweat, paddy slime, and the salty sweet odor of blood. He could hardly breathe. He hardly dared breathe. Quack quack quack, another shot. He felt cold webbed feet crawl over his lower legs, which were sticking out from the pile of bodies. He felt the rough scrape of a bill. It was too late to move his legs now. If he did, the ducks would know he was still alive. The quacking was very loud. Another shot, very close. Oh please please please God don't let them kill me. Two more shots. One blasted through the body atop Jones's and struck him in the back. He felt the bullet slam into his flak jacket, but didn't know if it had gone through.

The quacking grew fainter, and the gunshots stopped.

Jones lay in the mud-stinking darkness for a long time. It was so hard to breathe he blacked out once or twice. He felt as if he were drowning, Davy Jones at the bottom of the sea. When he could not stand it any longer, he began to slither out from under, but the corpses pressed on him with their full, truly dead weight. He had to crawl out inch by inch, and each inch seemed to take five minutes. He thought he would go crazy, buried alive in a tomb of corpses. Another inch, another. He was getting weaker. He passed out, came to again, and gained another inch.

Suddenly the weight grew lighter. Someone was pulling the bodies off. Jones heard voices ... American voices. "Anybody alive? ... No, sir ..." His ankles were grabbed, and with a hard tug, he was pulled free.

"We got a live one, skipper!" someone shouted, turning him over. "It's Jones! Get a corpsman up!"

He forced his lids to open against the caked blood and saw three or four dim figures standing over him. Someone patted his cheeks.

"Deevee? Where you hit? ... Where's that goddamned corpsman ... Hey, Deevee, say somethin', man. Hey, talk to me. Davy Jones."

He opened his mouth, lips pulling against the dried blood around them. He tried to speak, but couldn't.

"C'mon, Deevee ... corpsman's comin' up now ... Talk to me ..."

He had to say something so they wouldn't think he was dead!

He licked his lips and tried once more.

"Quack," he said.

David Victor Jones, the sole survivor of his platoon, was hospitalized for wounds to his head and back. The bullet in his back lodged in his shoulder blade. It was very painful, and the one in his skull gave him migraines. He was given frequent doses of morphine, which made him feel wonderful, like he was a bird flying on the ceiling. He was addicted when he was discharged from the service four months later.

His papers said he was discharged for psychiatric reasons. Early in his hospitalization, his commanding officer interviewed him to learn how the platoon had been wiped out. Jones answered that it had been ambushed by a battalion of enemy ducks, and if the captain thought he was a weirdo who saw things funny, then all the captain had to do was take a look at the tree line. There he would find thousands of beautiful feathers white as an egret's, and many dead ducks.

"We musta killed a hundred of 'em, sir, but there was just too many for us."

The captain left. Jones knew he had not believed him, but he wasn't upset. After all, this country was full of things no one had seen or heard of before. Jones then called for a corpsman, complaining that his back wound was causing him a great deal of pain. Could he have an extra shot of morphine? Actually, the pain was no more severe than usual; David Victor Jones just wanted to fly on the ceiling like a bird. In a place where men were ambushed by killer ducks, it seemed the only sensible thing to do.

ONE

Escape Velocity

It started with trains and fanciful flights to the moon.

I am talking about restlessness, go-fever—call it whatever you like. It afflicted me most of my life, coming and going like chronic malaria. I still suffer recurrences, although the intensity of the episodes has diminished and the intervals between them have lengthened. It was a simple malady in my boyhood, easily diagnosed: I wanted to wander the great world. Later on, as I see it now, it became a symptom of a deeper, more complicated disease: a phobia of everyday life, with its ruts and routines, its predictability that seemed first cousin to death. Whenever I went to sleep knowing I would wake to a day without surprises, whenever a familiar voice, of a wife, child, parent, or friend, made me grind my teeth, or a domestic Sunday stretched before me as long and dull as all eternity, the season in my soul changed to late autumn and a voice cried in my head, "This is it, this is how it'll be for the rest of my life!" My remedy was to pack a bag and head for the nearest airport or train station, or for the open road. If that sometimes led me to the wrong places, it was an improvement over neighborly adultery, alcoholism, drug addiction, and most of the other means people use to escape the desperation of their clock-wound lives, including a bullet in the temple.

Where I went was not always important, as long as it was There and not Here. Of course, if I stayed long enough, the most remote, exotic There became a humdrum Here, compelling me to move on. That was why the journey mattered more than the destination. I was a pilgrim for whom the pilgrimage was the shrine.

I had never gone on the bum, except for a brief period when I hitchhiked and rode the rails through the Southwest and Mexico, but I was only a dilettante hobo. Most of my rovings were as a middle-class nomad, gainfully and more or less respectably employed. I would not be ashamed to admit that to the most sunburnt knight of the road. The hobo is not a superior breed of wanderer simply because he travels without money or knowing where his next meal is coming from. Refugees do that all the time. Anyway, the self-portrait I wished to paint was not of a tramp but of a romantic figure taking risks in far-off places, and that seemed to require some form of employment. If I had been born in Melville's or Conrad's day, I would have signed on board a whaler or tea clipper, but the sea had ceased to be a calling and sailors had become little more than hourly laborers on oceangoing warehouses.

And so I joined the marines and went to war. After I'd recovered from that experience, I took up a foreign correspondent's itinerant trade and spent five years vagabonding through lands with intemperate climates and politics. Those two words, "marine" and "foreign correspondent," bore a powerful magic. They signified the glamour I was after, shouted above the noise of commuter traffic, TVs, and weekend lawn mowers—the whole quotidian racket—that it was still possible for an adventurous young man to live out a myth. There were other reasons for choosing those professions, if that's what they were. They took me into the blank spots of the human interior, which I was also curious to see. Carrying a rifle in Vietnam or a portable typewriter in the Middle East and Africa, I explored extraordinary situations as well as extraordinary places. Journeying into those states of extremes that lay people bare and force them to reveal the secrets of their minds and hearts was another way of escaping the everyday.

My geographical wanderings showed in my passport, thick as a paperback from the extra pages stapled into it by gray-faced consular clerks, the pages filled with stamps and visas written in the tongues of some thirty-six kingdoms, republics, and dictatorships. The stamps did not reflect every place I'd been; I'd slipped over a border or two without telling the authorities I was visiting.

There were no documents for my travels into the psychological Theres. The record of those border crossings was written in my dreams, and most of them were not good dreams. Oh, I saw courage, saw kindness in the meanest circumstances, saw a few people rise above the muck to show the angel that should be in us all, but I'm afraid I saw more of the devil that is definitely in us all. I saw him in the grin of a Chinese Nung who was making a fashion statement with a necklace of human ears, in the eyes of teenage apprentice terrorists who couldn't wait to blow up their first airliner, in the violent gestures of a Zionist fanatic outlining his plan for a Final Solution to the Palestinian problem. One or two times—and it was one or two times too many—the Dark One gave me a red-eyed wink in the mirror.

I am nearing fifty now, and I'm not looking for any more visas except the tourist kind, nor do I seek terra incognita. There are no terrae incognitae left, at least not in the world that appears in atlases. These days, you'll hear transistor radios around the bedouin fires instead of the songs of Harun al-Rashid, and you'll find the natives upriver wearing souvenir T-shirts. As for those terrae incognitae of the human interior, well, there's no end to them, but I've visited enough to know that you don't have to steam up the Congo to find the heart of darkness—it's probably right in your own backyard. The world, which seemed in my boyhood full of beauty and mystery spiced with a bit of danger, has in my manhood lost most of its beauty and mystery while gaining more than a seasoning of danger. I don't know if this represents a change in the world or in my perceptions. I do know that the glamour's gone. I have been wounded by gunfire, captured by terrorists, knocked flat by unknown fevers, and I now think Pascal might have been on to something when he said that the unhappinesses of men are caused by their inability to be at peace in a room. In short, I have settled down, which doesn't mean I've lost all curiosity and wanderlust. There remain moments when I cannot stand by a shore without wanting to cross the water, or hear a plane without wishing I were on it, or look at a highway without wondering where it goes.

I was six weeks past twenty-eight when I heard his voice crackle from the Sea of Tranquillity, his words converted to radio signals shot across a quarter million miles of space to be captured and restored to words by the television set in my parents' suburban basement, its screen showing a blurry Neil Armstrong climbing down the *Eagle's* ladder to make a footprint on the printless lunar dust.

"What did he say?" my grandmother Rose asked. She was seventy-five years old, her hearing wasn't what it used to be, and she had missed Armstrong's message.

"He said," I told her, "'That's one small step for a man, one giant leap for mankind.'"

She glanced at me from the leather easy chair usually occupied by my father, then turned back to the TV. Buzz Aldrin descended the ladder and pogoed against a backdrop of ice-castle mountains to join Armstrong beside a plastic American flag flying stiffer than a flag in a thirty-knot wind.

"Men on the moon! I don't believe it!"

My grandmother's expression of disbelief was no figure of speech. She remembered wagon clatter on the cobblestoned streets of Chicago, where she was born in 1894, the news of the Wright brothers and of Geronimo's death, the day when she was a young bride and workmen came to her flat to pull out the gas lamps and install electricity.

My father, half prone in the recliner alongside the easy chair, was not as awed. He had been a machinist and was now a technical troubleshooter for Continental Can Company. He had worked with machinery all his life and knew that achievements that struck his mother as miraculous were really matters of understanding certain principles and physical laws, then translating those understandings into a design, design into test model, model into prototype, and so on. This is not to say he was blasé about the scene unfolding before him. He was mightily impressed because he had at least a glimmering of how difficult a feat it was. The know-how that must have gone into it! The engineering! The sheer elegance of a rocket burn timed to deliver the precise thrust needed to reach escape velocity, the graceful calculus that sent the command module on a 250,000-mile parabola to intersect the moon's trajectory at the one point where its gravity would snare the module and sling it into lunar orbit as smoothly as an outfielder catching a pop fly and tossing it home.

My father had gone to college to study engineering, but had dropped out after only six months; my grandfather's business had failed, a Great Depression casualty. College was out of the question for my father. He had to look for work. There wasn't much in the 1930s; he dug ditches for the Public Works Administration, then found a construction job, and was delighted when the company gave him a nickel an hour raise. Those experiences so early in life had made him a cautious, pragmatic man, as well as one who revered education. I suppose it is a law of human nature that fathers always seek to live through their sons, fulfilling vicariously ambitions thwarted by circumstance or their own limitations. Mine wanted me to be an engineer, and though he was never pigheaded about it, he had made it clear that he would be very pleased to see me one day design the machines he could only repair.

I wanted to be an engineer, and not just because it was what my father wanted. I truly wanted it. My main ambition in grammar school and high school was to become a test pilot. Take the stick of some jet-powered, rocket-assisted needle-nosed bird, ram the throttle to the fire wall, and blast off through ozone and stratosphere to realms where blue sky darkened into black. I knew all about Chuck Yeager long before a book and a movie made his name as common as household detergent. I believed in manned space flight long before men flew there. Believe is the proper verb; in the early 1950s, only a handful of specialists like Yeager and Werhner von Braun, rocketry's high priest, had the facts, knew where the technology was headed. For them, the idea of sending human beings into orbit or of landings on other planets was not science fiction. For most everyone else it was little more than a Ray Bradbury fantasy.

But I kept the faith. I not only believed men would one day walk on the moon; I believed *I* would. That was why I felt only envy as I sat in a pine-paneled basement in Westchester, Illinois, watching Armstrong and Aldrin bounding across the Sea of Tranquillity. A waterless sea on an airless world more silent than the Antarctic, and whiter, and colder, and emptier, a *virgin* world where not even a single cell had wriggled and divided in primordial slime. It should have been I up there out there, free from earth's gravity and all the powers binding me to the suffering blue sphere shining in the lunar sky.

I had flown to the moon and beyond years before Armstrong, the engine of my imagination fueled by early television series like "Captain Video" and "Tom Corbett, Space Cadet" and by two books, *The Conquest of the Moon* and *Across the Space Frontier.* I loved those titles. The words "conquest" and "frontier" rang like gongs in the temple of my American soul. If I had been born in the past century, I would have gone up the wide Missouri with Lewis and Clark, or into the Rockies with Jim Bridger and Kit Carson. I regretted that I had come along much too late for such adventures. One of my great-grandfathers had emigrated to America in the early 1880s and laid track for the Great Northern across the Dakotas and Montana. He had seen buffalo, Indians, and the last of the Old West.

I wished I had. I wanted to make tracks on the trackless, chart the uncharted. I wanted to light out for the territory, but the territory was gone. The vast plains where my great-grandfather had drilled spikes were vacant of buffalo and Sioux and filled up with farms, ranches, towns, and shopping centers. So I looked to the sky, the high frontier. My eyes were literally on the stars.

Often I tried to picture what it looked like up there out there. Chesley Bonestell showed me. Chesley Bonestell did the illustrations for *The Conquest of the Moon* and *Across the Space Frontier.* What illustrations! Beautiful, beckoning artist's conceptions of white, wheel-shaped space stations twirling far above a haloed earth, of the moon's surface shaded in subtle pastels of cream and green, of interplanetary ships voyaging to Venus and Mars, with cutaway drawings to show the crews floating weightless through passageways, peering at distant constellations through Plexiglas domes. To hurtle through the black unknown in such a shell would be thrilling.

I couldn't wait to go. With Bonestell's illustrations for blueprints, I built my own spaceship. The place of its construction was the same basement where I would watch Armstrong and Aldrin many years later; the date was several months after we moved to Westchester, late in the fall of 1951.

Westchester was a suburb of people dead in the middle of the middle class—skilled tradesmen, office workers, housewives, young couples starting off. I am convinced my parents' decision to move there made all the difference in my life. The town was the manger of my restlessness.

It had begun as a dream of Samuel Insull, the London-born utilities king whose holdings were worth three billion dollars in a time when billionaires were almost unheard of. One of his companies was Chicago's Commonwealth Edison, and he decided to use some of his vast fortune to build a replica of an English country village on the prairies west of the city. It was incorporated as Westchester, the streets plotted and given British place-names. A few houses went up, most conforming to Insull's architectural tastes—square Georgians, counterfeit Tudors, ersatz Stratford-upon-Avon cottages—but Insull never fulfilled his vision. Construction stopped in the early 1930s, when his financial empire collapsed and he was indicted for mail fraud and embezzlement. Six years later, the billionaire from Dickensian London died broke. There were then more rabbits and pheasants than people living in his fantasy village. Weeds and brambles overtook the sidewalks, the lampposts tumbled, knocked down by storms or by the weight of the wild grapevines that had coiled around them like strangler figs.

Westchester did not revive until the postwar housing boom, a land rush that changed the face of America almost as radically as the settling of the frontier. The new communities bore no resemblance to the upper-class bedroom suburbs established earlier in Winnetka, or Scarsdale, or on the Main Line. The residents of those places had been insulated by social position and old family money from the worst effects of the Depression. The suburbanites of the fifties were mostly working stiffs who had been at the epicenter of that economic temblor and had no sooner crawled out of the rubble, dusty and bruised, than they were thrown into World War II. Now that they had a leg up on life, they flocked to the Westchesters of America with low-interest loans from the Veterans Administration or, if they weren't veterans, with down payments carefully hoarded over the years. Theirs were not the big dreams of a Sam Insull. They were modest people with modest means and visions to match. A home of their own with a garage, appliances, and the proud green badge of a lawn were all they wanted, along with good schools for the kids.

It was the era of the Organization Man and the cold war, conservative suits and backyard bomb shelters. Security was the watchword of the day. Military security for the nation, job and financial security for ordinary men and women. After what they had been through, from Black Friday to V-J Day, they did not want adventure, nor did they have hearty appetites for risk. They welcomed the calm of the Eisenhower era. They helped create it.

And calm was the atmosphere in Westchester in the years I grew up there, from 1951 to 1959, when I left for college. Westchester lounged like a man on a lawn chair on Sunday afternoon, in what I have seen described as "drowse of the accustomed." And that stifling drowse eventually awakened in me a hunger to live intensely. Instead of the accustomed, I sought the unaccustomed, the strange instead of the familiar, the extremities of experience instead of the middle ground.

In a phrase, I was bored. So were most people my age, for most were raised as I was. If our parents' generation welcomed and helped create the tranquillity of the Eisenhower years, we their children welcomed and helped create the turmoil of the sixties. Vietnam. How we needed it, patriots and protesters alike, warriors and antiwarriors. It gave us the conflict and drama so absent when we were growing up. In *Dispatches,* Michael Herr wonders if "Vietnam was what we had instead of happy childhoods." I don't think so: Vietnam was what we had *because* we had happy childhoods. Certainly that was true of me. It took a war to get me out of the suburbs and keep me out.

Our house, a buff-brick trilevel with pecky cypress trim, stood at 1947 Suffolk Avenue. It was brand-new when we moved in, the basement where I would build my rocket ship an unfinished cavern. Just about everything in the house and around it looked unfinished in those days. Our front and back yards were raw dirt patches rutted from the contractor's trucks. Suffolk Avenue itself was largely fictitious—an unpaved lane of yellow clay that turned to gumbo whenever it rained, its future route marked by surveyor's stakes and not a tree on it. We had no immediate neighbors; our house was the only one on the block. The others were in various stages of construction, some mere foundations, some with roofs and chimneys and doors installed, waiting for their owners to claim them. Eastward and northward, an embrowned prairie somber as a moor reached to two railroad lines, the Illinois Central and the Indiana Harbor Belt. Southward, the prairie jumped across Cermak Road, today a four-lane highway but then a rural road, and met the Salt Creek woods. Ancient oak and sycamore shaded the dark creek and harbored raccoon, possum, rabbit, red fox, and an infrequent deer. The woods were a last remaining slice of an older America. One of my fifth-grade classmates showed me the flint arrowheads he had found there. At Wolf Road, the town's western limit, a one-room schoolhouse and a small country church, both long since closed, stood like empty sentry booths against the encroachment of split-level suburbia. Beyond stretched a pure Mid-western countryside of cow pastures and cornfields, where pioneer farmhouses crouched behind cottonwood windbreaks. Some were abandoned, the farms sold off to land developers who had not yet begun to subdivide them. Spared the bite of plow and bulldozer, the fields had reverted to wild prairie, high yellow grass weaving through the rusted wire of derelict fences.

Westchester was a lonesome place, especially for a ten-year-old. It wasn't really a place at all, and it wasn't lonesome in the way a wilderness cabin would be. Although phrases like "sense of communi-ty" and words like "identity" were not in my vocabulary, I felt the absence of those qualities. In their place was a vacancy that I could see when I looked out the back windows at the mile of brush and weeds between us and the Harbor Belt tracks, that I could smell in the new wood and fresh plaster of our house—the odors of a house without a history. My parents had picked the right month to move in: November. As Westchester was neither town nor country, November was neither autumn nor winter, a month of low skies too warm for snow and too cold for rain.

The house seemed chilly the day we moved in, despite its mod-ern oil furnace. My mother sat my sister and me down on the untrod carpet and played a game to amuse and distract us because she knew we felt uncomfortable in our strange surroundings, I more than my sister. I complained that I was cold. My mother stood and turned up the thermostat, which was a real novelty. My grandparents' bungalow, where we had lived before, had been heated by a coal furnace that had to be stoked several times a day. Now all we had to do was turn a knob to the desired temperature and the oil burner would start push-ing hot air through the vents. I stood over one of them and let the fur-nace's breath blow on me, but I could not get warm. It was a cold that had nothing to do with the temperature, and it got into me and stayed there for a long time.

I remembered the furnace in my grandparents' place and help-ing my grandfather shovel coal into its cast-iron belly on the days when the Chicago wind felt like a Siberian express. The volcanic blaze inside was frightening and cheery at the same time, and it could thaw a cold boy's numbed feet and fingers in five seconds flat. Just the memory of it warmed me up. That was *heat*—not the pallid whisper of forced air, but real fire that made the steam pipes boil and the radiators bang and thump like a marching band.

The bungalow was at 1414 Ridgeland Avenue in Berwyn, less than ten miles from Westchester. It seemed a lot farther. Berwyn, whose streets merged seamlessly into Chicago's, was the bluest of blue-collar towns, a rung or two up the socioeconomic ladder for the Czech, Polish, and Italian immigrants who had come from crowded tenements in the city's heart. My grandparents, Fiore and Enricetta Napolitan, moved in 1925 from Chicago's Little Italy. The bungalow was large by the standards they were used to, and there my grandparents raised their four children—my mother, Marie, and her three brothers. There I spent the first decade of my life, and how I missed that life.

We were all together under one roof. Our family occupied the attic flat; my grandparents, uncles, aunts, and cousins lived on the floors below. It was an Old World way of life, clannish and patriarchal. I missed the tribal sense of belonging, of knowing who I was and where I fit in and where I came from. I missed the smells—no sterile odor of new wood and fresh plaster in that house, which was steeped in the aromas of savory sauces, fresh bread and pasta baked by my grandmother, sausages and salamis and provolone hanging in the wine cellar, where jugs of Italian red and muscatel were racked like torpedoes along a cool concrete wall. I missed the sounds—Caruso singing arias and aching Neapolitan ballads on my grandfather's RCA Victrola, the kind you had to wind up; bachelor uncle Fred, a part-time musician, playing scales hour after hour on his accordion; the clop and rattle of the black junkman's horse-drawn wagon in the alleyway, the junkman crying out, "rags and old iron" in a Deep South accent that made it sound like "ragsalarn"; the men in the family whooping around the radio when the Cubs scored a run or Marciano another knockout. I missed the holiday feasts, when the front two thirds of the basement would become a kind of banquet hall for the fifteen of us and half a dozen or more relatives. Everyone sat at two cafeteria tables laid end to end and covered with dishes that celebrated our dual heritage—plates of antipasti, lasagna, and ravioli sharing space with sweet potatoes, pumpkin pie, and a roast turkey that looked as large as an ostrich. It would be skilfully carved by my grandfather, who was the head butcher at the old Stevens Hotel in downtown Chicago. He approached the carving as he did almost everything, with the utmost solemnity. He was a grave, puritanical man. Completely bald except for a gray fringe above his ears, with thin lips, a sharp nose, and pale eyes covered by wire-rimmed glasses, his face was a monk's, his bearing a warrior's. He had been a sergeant in a cavalry regiment before he'd emigrated from Italy in 1908, and he still carried himself with a cavalryman's pride and authority. It gave him a presence that could fill a room and made him appear six feet tall, though he was only five-eight. Once I had asked him what he did in the army, and he'd told me in his broken English, "First the cannons fire, then the infantry attack, then we take out our sabers and ride in"—he paused, giving a thin, cold grin as he flourished his arm—"and cut 'em to pieces." Actually, he had never seen action, but when he stood at the head of that long table, his face pulled into its usual severe expression as he stropped a carving knife, I would imagine him astride a horse, whetting a saber while the cannons fired and the infantry attacked.

Of course, I had a life outside his house, and I missed that, too. It was a city kid's life. There were alleys where I played a version of stickball with my cousins and my classmates from the Karel Havlíček grammar school, a block from where I lived. On the sidewalks, we younger kids played hopscotch, while older boys with an aura of incipient delinquency pitched pennies and girls skipped rope, high voices calling out syncopated chants to which their feet and the twirling ropes kept rhythm: *Down in the valley where the green grass grows, there lived an American beauty rose.* Corner grocery stores sold candy and ice cream and baseball cards that we traded and collected. On Saturday afternoons, I would walk with my friends to the Ritz Theatre on Roosevelt Road and watch matinee serials: westerns with Tom Mix and Lash LaRue, mysteries starring Charlie Chan and Bulldog Drummond.

My parents were less enchanted with life in Berwyn. Where I found our extended family warm and close, they found it claustrophobic. It was most cloying for my mother. My father escaped to the plant every day, but she was housebound with her mother and all those kids and relatives. Not long ago, while I was rhapsodizing about those days, she told me, "I couldn't wait to get out of there. I could hardly breathe." Her only exit, and it wasn't much of one, was in the summers, when Continental Can sent my father to Wisconsin, Michigan, or Minnesota to service the canning factories it supplied with closing machines—the machines that vacuum-sealed the tins of corn, peas, and sugar beets. He was on the road from May to October. As soon as school was out, he would drive down to bring us north and spend the summers with him. It was an adventure for my sister and me, living in one-horse towns or in backwoods cabins without running water or indoor plumbing, places where you had to truck your garbage to the town dump to keep the bears away. But exchanging the crowdedness of the Berwyn bungalow for such rustic isolation was no adventure for my mother. She wasn't charmed by the antique woodburners she had to cook on, or by the smelly well water she had to pump by hand when she washed dishes.

She wanted, as the advertising slogans put it, a home of her own with all the modern conveniences. So she and my father saved every spare dime from the day they were married. After twelve years, they had enough for a down payment. They hired a contractor, and in the spring of 1951, ground was broken on the Westchester house.

We visited it often, accompanying my father when he drove out in his 1941 maroon Oldsmobile to inspect the house's progress. We watched it grow, and whenever some significant plateau was reached—completion of the floor, or the roof, or the plumbing—I would be told, "This is going to be our new house, Phil, this is where we're going to live." I did not believe it. I refused to. I could not imagine living in a wasteland where there were no candy stores, movie theaters, or sidewalks to pitch pennies on.

Throughout that summer and fall, I pretended that my life would never change. I pretended until I could not pretend any longer. One day, movers emptied our attic flat and transplanted the furniture and appliances to the new house. Then the same thing was to be done to me, but I was not some dumb chair to be picked up from one place and dropped in another without a peep. After our suitcases had been loaded in the Oldsmobile and we had said our good-byes, my mother turned to my sister and me and said, "Okay, kids, it's time to go."

"No!" I shouted. "No!"

And ran up the stairs into the hollow kitchen and locked the door. How strange to see the chairs and tables gone, the stove and refrigerator missing, their old places marked by patches of linoleum lighter than the rest of the floor. I claimed the deserted room for my own. I was going to stay there by myself. On Monday I would go to my classes at Havlíček and play stickball in the alley after school. Next Saturday, as ever, I would go to the Ritz to watch Lash LaRue disarm gunslingers with his black whip.

The door handle turned violently.

"Phil, open this door, open it right now!"

It was my father.

"No!" I yelled. "No!"

"Damnit! I said to open this damn door!"

"Joe! Stop swearing!" It was my mother. "Don't lose your temper."

There was an interval of silence, followed by the sound of my grandfather's slow, deliberate footsteps on the stairs. A key clicked in the lock, the door swung open. My father's face was flushed, my mother looked as if she were going to cry, my grandfather was staring through his wire-rimmed glasses with an unfamiliar expression, one I could not read.

"Now let's go," my father said, moving toward me. I could tell he was struggling to keep calm. "It's time to go, son."

"No!"

I ran and grabbed the stove's gas pipe, protruding about a foot from the wall. It was anchored solidly, and I clung to it as hard as I could. My father took me by the waist and began to pull. He was a strong man then, not gymnasium strong but hard-work strong, forearms like oak table legs. With a tug, he broke my grip.

I was crying so hard it seemed I would turn myself inside out. I knew then the meaning of the word "uprooted," for I felt like a sapling that had been ripped out of the ground.

"We've got to go, son. That's it."

My father held me tight in an embrace that combined love and anger, that was somehow tender and violent at the same time.

"No!"

I turned to look at my grandfather. Normally behavior like mine would have moved him to put me over his knee and give me a whack with the thick garrison belt that was his instrument of discipline. But all he did was stare with that peculiar expression, peculiar because it was gentle. In a moment, I recognized it as sadness and knew he was my ally. He did not want me to go either. He did not want any of us to go, to see his clan broken up. Somehow I wriggled out of my father's arms and ran to him and held him by the waist.

"Grampa, I'm not going. I wanna stay here with you and Gramma."

He put his arm around me, said something in Italian. I did not understand it. No matter, he was my ally, and a powerful one. He was the ultimate authority in that household. His word was the last word, and if he said, "My grandson stays here," then I would stay.

He reached down and did something extraordinary, unprecedented in fact. He kissed me on the cheek. I had never seen that old cavalry sergeant kiss anyone. I thought I had won, but he gently pushed me toward my mother.

"Grampa?"

"*Figlio mio,*" he said in a sorrowful undertone. I understood what that meant—my son—as I understood that it was also his way of saying good-bye.

He gave me another gentle push, and my mother took me by the hand. I could not believe it. My grandfather had surrendered. I lost my awe of him in that moment, not my love or respect, but my awe. His power was not absolute after all, and that realization took the defiance out of me. I followed my parents down the stairs and into the '41 Olds, as dumb and unresisting as the chairs and rugs the movers had loaded onto the van.

Ours was no merry Oldsmobile as we drove west on Cermak Road. I sulked in the backseat, acting as if I were being kidnapped by my own parents. We crossed Harlem Avenue out of Berwyn into North Riverside. A huge TB sanitorium glowered on one side of the road. I always covered my nose and mouth when we passed it, but I didn't that trip. Feeling enormously sorry for myself and seeking revenge on my father and mother, I took deep breaths, hoping to infect myself. Boy, wouldn't they regret what they'd done when I started coughing up blood.

After North Riverside came Broadview, which bordered Westchester on the east. The Indiana Harbor Belt marked the city limits of both towns. As we approached the tracks, the warning bells began to ring, the gates swung down beneath flashing red lights. My gloom lifted a little; trains thrilled me. I sat up and looked out the window. There it was, bearing down from the north under a long mane of smoke, the headlamp growing larger and larger; then came a blast from the whistle, rising, falling, oh what a sound that was. In a moment, the engine thundered through the crossing, its bells chiming, drive-wheel pistons churning, coal tender trailing, and behind the tender a line of freight cars a mile long.

My father pulled the hand brake and muttered a curse, drawing another rebuke from my mother. The train was not only long, but slow. As far as I was concerned, it could not be long and slow enough. I hoped the caboose was somewhere in Milwaukee. I sat reading the names on the boxcars. There were plenty because the Harbor Belt was a connector railroad that handled the rolling stock of a dozen other lines. *Chicago and Northwestern ... Atchison, Topeka & Santa Fe ... Erie-Lackawanna ...* The rush of the train and the hypnotic rattle of steel on steel blew the clouds from my soul ... *Illinois Central ... New York Central ...* The names, as I whispered them to myself, sounded as stirring as epic verse ... *Union Pacific ... Great Northern ... Chesapeake & Ohio ... Lehigh Valley ... Rock Island ...* I wondered where each boxcar had been and where it was bound.

More than half the train had gone by when I saw him for the first time. He was riding an empty, sitting in the open door as casually as another man would sit on a park bench. He wore a beat-up leather jacket and blue jeans, a greasy fedora covered his head. I could not see his face clearly—the train wasn't that slow—but I did see him wave as his boxcar clickety-clacked past the gates. It was a good long wave, and I was sure he was waving at me. I quickly rolled down the window for a clearer look.

The empty had gone down the track, but I saw the man craning his neck to look back at me as he waved, waved not at my parents, nor at any of the people in the automobiles lined up behind ours, but at me and me alone. And the same sure instinct that told me that also told me what he was saying: *I'm a free man, boy, nobody tells me where I can live or can't live, I go where and when I damn well please, so whatchya doin', a red-blooded American boy, sittin' in that car with your mommy and daddy, come on with me, come on and ride the high iron ...*

"The window," my mother said. "It's cold."

I rolled it up and sat quietly, keeping my secret. The hobo had called me to join him as he headed God knew where. After another minute or two, the caboose passed by. Soon it banged over the Salt Creek trestle, and all that was left of the train was a trail of smoke the wind stretched thin and pushed across the fields and over the leafless woods.

The gates went up. We continued down Cermak, turned onto muddy Suffolk Avenue, and parked in front of the trilevel with the buff-brick walls and pecky cypress trim. The sight of it did not depress me. Why should it have depressed me? I wasn't going to live there. While my parents unloaded the luggage, I sneaked around to the back, pretending to be exploring our new grounds. The coast looked clear, so I started across the prairie toward the railroad tracks. I did not run, afraid of drawing attention, just walked as if I were exploring. If I was going to be uprooted, I'd decided, then I was not going to settle for any half measures. I was going to become truly uprooted by answering the hobo's call. I was going to hop a freight.

A pheasant spoiled my plans. I had gone some distance, could see the tracks shining up on the roadbed, when the bird exploded almost from beneath my feet. I let out a yell. My father, who had been looking for me, heard me. His voice came thinly over the prairie. "Get back here ..." I turned and saw him, between me and the house. He was waving. I took off running. He came after me. He was still a young man, only thirty-six, he didn't smoke, and had played a lot of ball and run track in his youth. He caught me in no time, scooping me up in midstride.

"Where do you think you're going?"

"Tracks," I gasped, my lungs burning. "Train tracks. I'm running away."

"The heck you are." He spun me around and gave my backside a whack. "You stay away from those tracks, do you hear? They're dangerous."

We started walking, my father holding my hand tightly to make sure I didn't bolt. All the way back, I kept looking over my shoulder toward the tracks. I had been taken from my true home, that was how I felt. I didn't have a home, just like the man who had waved to me from his perch up on the high iron.

In the years ahead, I would see him again and again. Eventually, I would get to know him quite well. As a matter of fact, I still run into him, though nowhere near as often as I used to. Oneway, short for Oneway Ticket, is the name I have given him. As far as I know, he has none of his own; he's as unchristened as a bastard raised by wolves. He does, however, go by a number of aliases, more than I can remember, and he's got as many disguises as a pulp-fiction private eye. Hobo is the least clever of them. He has appeared to me over the years dressed as a fighter pilot, a merchant sea captain with a Scottish brogue, a trench-coated foreign correspondent, a ... well, no sense in cataloguing them all. At a vulnerable point in my life, he materialized resplendent and bemedaled in a marine recruiter's dress blues. In whatever getup he's appeared, he has always beckoned me to leave Here for There, promising that There is the place I will find adventure, excitement, true love, knowledge, fame, glory, riches, escape from the humdrum. All that is never Here; it's always There, over the hill and around the bend.

That year's winter, a rough one even by Midwestern standards, made it easy to obey my father's prohibition against playing by the railroad tracks. With no natural obstacles to impede them, Arctic fronts swept across the prairies with the ease of Panzers blitzing through Poland. I had no desire to ride boxcars in such weather. Just walking the six blocks to school, a parochial elementary called Divine Infant Jesus, was adventure enough.

Delivering the morning papers was an ordeal. It had not been my idea to take on a paper route but my father's. He believed in Work and the Value of the Dollar the way the nuns like Sister Maria-Theresa, my fifth-grade teacher at Divine Infant Jesus, believed in the Holy Ghost and the Communion of Saints. He saw in me a streak of inherited impracticality, a natural inclination toward daydreaming, indiscipline, and irresponsibility. I think he was afraid I would turn out to be like his father if I did not learn the Value of Work and a Dollar early in life.

My paternal grandfather was also named Joseph. His story was an all-American saga: a rise from immigrant poverty to success and riches, followed by a rapid plunge into failure and then an early death. He was not a practical man, "just a real happy-go-lucky guy," my father would say in a tone of loving disapproval, as if he were speaking about a charmingly mischievous child.

Joseph Caputo, Sr., landed at Ellis Island in 1902, a fourteen-year-old orphan with a heart damaged by a childhood bout of scarlet fever. A *paesano*—a relative from his native Calabria—brought him to Chicago and got him a job as a water boy on the railroad. He must have learned something about Work and the Value of a Dollar, humping water buckets for thirsty section gangs. But he must have learned another lesson as he watched the 20th Century Limited roar by on its way to New York, portly gentlemen sipping whiskeys in the club car, their bustled ladies raising coffee cups in the dining car. He must have realized that he was not going to get anywhere in America simply by working hard. As he might have said, "You gotta have an angle."

He laid his water bucket down and went to work as a waiter and bartender. That served as his apprenticeship. Sometime during World War I, he found his angle. He and three other men formed a partnership and went into the bar and restaurant business. Their place, the name of which has been lost, was at 808 West Madison Street, in what was then a high-rolling nightclub district. The restaurant, on the second floor, was an intimate spot that served Italian food, of course. An excellent chef, my grandfather cooked some of the dishes himself. The bar, on the first floor, looked like a men's club: paneled walls, leather booths, a mirror-backed mahogany bar that shone richly in soft lights. The Star and Garter burlesque was across the street. It was no grungy strip joint, but more the way a Las Vegas lounge would be today. The Star and Garter girls were among my grandfather's most faithful customers. After the show, they would come in to dine with their escorts, usually respectable businessmen taking brief holidays from their respectable marriages. The restaurant's most famous patron was Enrico Caruso, who stopped in for a plate of pasta whenever he gave a concert at the Civic Opera House. My grandfather had a fine voice and sometimes accompanied Caruso in impromptu serenades.

When the Volstead Act was passed, the bar became a speakeasy, where ward bosses and ordinary citizens bellied up with bootleggers to guzzle illicit whiskey and gin.

Zealous federal agents now and then raided the place (the city cops had been paid off), confiscated the liquor hidden between the floor joists, and hauled my grandfather and his partners off to jail. The raids were largely cosmetic, intended to keep up appearances, and it usually took only a discreet word or two from a local politician to have the charges dropped.

But the raids persuaded two of the partners to try some other venture. Joe and Charley bought them out. The business prospered. With profits split two ways instead of four, Joe and Charley grew rich. My grandfather moved his small family from the city to the middle-class suburb of Bellwood. Their new house was a fine place, a four-bedroom white colonial with a portico and pillars, a wide lawn, and a garage in which my grandfather kept his new black Pontiac sedan. He'd paid almost a thousand for that, even though he did not know how to drive. My father became the family chauffeur.

My grandfather would not have been considered rich by the stout gents he had seen on the 20th Century Limited, but in his own eyes he was a long, long way from the orphan who'd toted water for gandy dancers. The kid with the damaged heart. It was damaged only in the physical sense; he was a soft touch for any kind of sob story. His generosity had made him a legend in his native village, where immigrants bound for America were told, "If you're going to Chicago, see Joe Caputo. He'll help you out." They would show up at 808 West Madison dressed in their steerage rags and ask him for a little something to help them get on their feet in the New World. The green-horns would give my grandfather an IOU if they could write; if not, he would write it for them. He stuffed the notes in a velvet-lined box where he kept the nickel-plated .32 caliber revolver he carried when he delivered the day's receipts to the Mid-City Bank down the street. In a few years, there were so many slips of paper in the box it looked like a lottery jar. He found other ways to dispose of excess income. Sometimes, in the early-morning hours, he came home tipsy on wine or bootleg whiskey and, singing arias from Rossini and Verdi, tossed his pocket change into the air. The house had a gravity furnace. Much of the change, from pennies to silver dollars, fell through the grates into the boiler below. The furnace became a treasure chest. In warm weather, my grandmother, as frugal as her husband was profligate, sent my father into the basement to retrieve the previous night's take from the ashes.

Then came the Crash of 1929, followed by the repeal of Prohibition. Joe and Charley's place did not survive those twin catastrophes. Drinking had lost its outlaw appeal, now that it was legal again, and with people lining up at soup kitchens, few could afford to eat out anymore. The Star and Garter girls stopped coming in; their sugar daddies couldn't pay for romantic dinners with worthless stock certificates. West Madison began to decline into a skid row. Joe and Charley hung on long after they should have but finally closed their doors in 1933.

My grandfather was too proud to go on relief, too proud to ask his creditors to repay their loans (they were all broke anyway). He signed up with the Public Works Administration but never worked for it because his faulty heart could not have withstood hard physical labor. I don't think his soul could have withstood it either. To go from what he had been to ditchdigger would have crushed him. My father, bearing the same name, dropped out of Crane Technical College and went to work in his place, and that ended my father's dreams of becoming a mechanical engineer. My grandmother, who had been living the life of the leisured suburban matron, found menial labor in a biscuit factory so the family could meet the interest payments on the house. In time, Joe Caputo, Sr., was working again, hired as a singing waiter and bartender at the Blue Ribbon Spa on posh Michigan Boulevard. He had been a free-spending freewheeler, a one-man bank for the poor, a pal of ward bosses and big shots and the great Caruso, and now he was forty-five years old, mixing drinks and singing for strangers. Three years later, he was dead, the stress of poverty and the years of abuse finally telling on his heart.

Naturally, he had not saved a dollar. All the money he'd made had been plowed back into the business, and the rest had gone into immigrants' pockets or down the grates into the furnace. Not long after he was buried, the bank foreclosed on the Bellwood house. A moving van came and carted the furniture to a flat my grandmother had rented in Berwyn. She and my father then packed their clothes and passed under the pillared portico for the last time, my father carrying their luggage to the Pontiac sedan, my grandmother a velvet-lined box that contained a pair of pearl cuff links, the nickel-plated .32, and a pile of IOUs from people she had never seen.

If my father saw hints of his father in me, his perceptions were dead on. I was fascinated by the man and delighted in the stories my grandmother told about him and the times he lived in (enough years had passed for her to look back on all that with nostalgia, even the bad parts). Often, when we visited her on Sundays, I would ask to see photographs of him. One, taken in the 1920s, showed him in a natty topcoat, spats, and a Borsalino rakishly cocked, its brim shadowing a face across which a grin flashed an intimate knowledge of a world filled with glamour and romance. I would never see him as a bent old man with quivering hands but always as he was in the picture, young and dashing and surrounded by the halo of a roguish era. Showgirls. Bootleggers. Raids by G-men. The Roaring Twenties. If I could not have been born early enough in history to have gone up the wide Missouri with Lewis and Clark or shipped out on a whaling voyage, whyohwhy, I asked myself, could I not have lived in my grandfather's day and rubbed shoulders with Eliot Ness and Al Capone? Whyohwhy had God punished me by bringing me into the world just in time to grow up in a suburb in I-like-Ike, Ozzie-and-Harriet America?

Feeling doomed to the commonplace, the moral of my grandfather's story—a fool and his money are soon parted—was utterly lost on me. It was not lost on my father, the victim of that foolishness. He took steps to impart the moral. When he saw an advertisement for carriers for the Chicago *Tribune,* he, shall we say, strongly suggested I take the job and save every dime earned. Learn the Value of Work and a Dollar.

The *Tribune,* then the somber voice of Colonel Robert R. McCormick, the publisher whose views on labor unions, the Social Security Administration, and other subversive organizations were to the right of King George III, called itself the "World's Greatest Newspaper." I didn't know if it was, but it must have been the World's Biggest. The daily editions were as thick as its three competitors—the *Sun Times, Herald-American,* and *Daily News*—put together. The Sunday edition resembled a piece of furniture. An Olympic shot-putter could not have tossed those monsters with accuracy, so I lugged them to the subscribers' porches, setting them down as if I were leaving a parcel.

A news-agency truck delivered the papers to our house before sunrise. Envying my sister, Patricia, as she snoozed cozily under warm covers, I would reluctantly crawl out of bed, dress, and join my father in the kitchen for breakfast—bacon and eggs in those happy days before the discovery of cholesterol. Dressed in Sears Roebuck work clothes, he was the incarnation of the salt-of-the-earth American workingman. Looking at him made me feel a rush of love, pride, and security; if he were to die suddenly, for sure he would leave his family with more than a cheap pistol and a pile of uncollectable IOUs. Still, I wished he were more like his father. I wanted to come down to breakfast and find him dressed in spats and a borsalino, ready to drive off to a rendezvous with bootleggers instead of to a machine shop. Then we would be rich and I would not have to go out into subzero temperatures to learn the Value of Work and a Dollar.

After breakfast, I folded the newspapers, which was as easy as folding the Chicago yellow pages, and packed them into the basket of my Schwinn. Bundled up, I pedaled off into the dark and the cold, except on Sundays, when I made my rounds by sled because the basket could not accommodate more than three or four of the huge editions.

On my bike or pulling the sled, I was usually attended by a great deal of self-pity and resentment. Seditious thoughts stole into my head. As soon as spring came, I was going to run away, preferably to some place where it never snowed.

There were things I liked about the paper route, such as watching the sun rise on clear mornings over the railroad tracks, the snow changing color from white to rose, the shadow of a tree falling on a fresh drift with the definition of a line drawing on a tablet. I also liked being in the know before everyone else. Before television imposed its moronic reign on the information industry, people got their news in print, and I was the first in the neighborhood to see the print. When I folded the papers, I always took a few moments to scan the headlines and read a paragraph or two from the front-page stories. YANKS, CHINESE REDS BATTLE IN N. KOREA. GOP PICKS IKE. HORSEMEAT SCANDAL ON WEST SIDE. It gave me a sense of satisfaction and superiority that I knew what had happened in the world while my customers slept in ignorance. That, more than any lessons about the Value of Work and a Dollar, made the route worthwhile, or at least bearable. I dramatized myself, saw myself as the plucky little messenger, braving blizzards and frost to bring people the news of the day.

A false spring came in mid-January, a freak but welcome pause in winter's tale. The balmy weather led me to break my father's rule. I had an accomplice in my forbidden excursions to the Harbor Belt tracks. He had moved into the house next door. His name was George Weidenfeller, a red-haired, freckled kid and a fifth-grade classmate. George shared my fascination with trains, but where I was capitivated by their romance—Casey Jones dying at the throttle of Old Ninety-Nine—he was a railroading pedant. He had a wonderful picture book that explained the classifications of steam locomotives. Each type was distinguished by three numerals that designated the number of its wheels: leading truck, drive, and trailing truck: 4-6-2s, 2-8-0s, and so forth. George could also recognize the major lines by their colors, from the Union Pacific's red on yellow, to the Milwaukee Road's orange and black, to the silver and red of the Santa Fe. He gave me tutorials on the names of long-distance passenger trains. Some had a folkloric ring, like Orange Blossom Special and Hiawatha; others were as proud and stirring as the mottoes of royal heraldry—Empire Builder, Colorado Eagle, California Zephyr.

One afternoon during the spell of fraudulent April, I let George in on my secret: when the true spring came, I was going to hop a freight and become a hobo. We were in his basement, looking at the locomotive picture book.

"What freight?"

"The Indiana Harbor Belt."

"That won't take you nowhere. It just goes around the bottom of Lake Michigan. To Gary, I think."

"Well, that's somewhere."

"There's trains that go way farther than Gary. I'll show you."

We rode our bikes east to Gardner Road, then pedaled north, past the Wilbert Burial Vault Company—a gloomy reminder in optimistic 1950s suburbia of where we all end up in time—then past a succession of boxy houses separated by vacant lots turned into ponds by melting snow. After we'd gone a little more than a mile, we stopped beneath an iron bridge with the words ILLINOIS CENTRAL painted on it in white. We hid our bikes in the tall weeds beside a creek and climbed the slushy embankment to the I.C.'s single track.

I had never been up there before. Thirty-odd feet above the road, I looked out across prairies and fields and shingled roofs, their chimneys smoking. To my Middle Westerner's eyes, the embankment seemed like a mountain; the view from it was a panorama. But the most enticing perspective was the one offered by the track, running ruler-straight to the horizon.

"We're gonna hafta wait," George said.

"For what?"

"Wait'll you see it," he answered mysteriously.

We killed time by tightrope walking on the rails, or hopping from tie to tie, counting them and wondering how many it would take to go around the world. Bored with that, I sat down. In a little while, I felt a slight vibration in the rail. George looked eastward and said, "Here she comes!"

Away off, a headlamp glowed like a solitary star.

"Know what she is?" George asked rhetorically. His freckles seemed to pulse. "The City of New Orleans! She goes from Chicago to New Orleans. That's in Louisiana."

Mentally, I projected an image of Sister Maria-Theresa's map of the United States, my mind's eye tracing the Mississippi southward.

"That's *really* far."

"A thousand miles!" George said, as if it were the distance to another galaxy. "And she'll make it by sunrise. She's really fast, a streamliner."

The diesel's horn groaned.

George hopped off the tracks to lie on the embankment. I did not move, as transfixed as a deer by the oncoming light. I could see the locomotive now. In no time, it seemed to loom like a moving cliff.

"Phil! Get off! You'll be splattered!"

I leapt and landed beside George. In five seconds, the engine highballed past in a shock of wind, the horn blasting like Joshua's trumpet. I had never been so close to a fast train. It was at once terrifying and exhilarating, the exhilaration somehow arising from the terror. The wheels did not make the monotonous clickety-clack of the lazy freights on the Harbor Belt but an almost solid crack, like a lightning bolt's. Dining cars and dome cars and passenger cars shot by in a streak of gleaming stainless steel. Suddenly, the track was clear again. I jumped back onto it and looked. The baggage car was a diminishing rectangle, and then the City of New Orleans was gone, so swiftly gone it was if she had been an illusion. I felt changed, graced, if you will, to have been so near so awesome and beautiful a creation. I wished I could have snatched the wind of her passage and hung on and ridden her all the way, a thousand miles before the next day's dawn.

"Wasn't she something?" George asked. "Wasn't she fast? Betcha she was doing a hundred easy."

I did not say anything. I looked down the track to where the rails' shimmer hung like a dancing curtain, a curtain I might pass through to another life, another world far from Westchester and the buff-brick trilevel. *There.*

Spring's coup was short-lived; within a week, winter recaptured its seat of power. Inches of new snow fell to replace the snow that had melted. When I pulled my *Tribune*-laden sled on Sunday mornings between the high drifts piled up by the plows I could not wait to return to the house and its forced-air heat. I felt trapped, by the weather and by my own need for warmth and comfort.

The nuns at Divine Infant Jesus imposed additional restrictions on my freedom of action. The school where they taught was a two-story L-shaped building attached to the parish church. It had large windows and red-brick walls, across one of which stainless steel letters spelled the words "Gloria in excelsis Deo." Inside, the halls smelled of scrubbed tile and floor wax, like the halls at Havlíček School, but they were strangely quiet. The nuns were strict disciplinarians, who kept youthful rambunctiousness well in check. They had more rules and regulations than the army. Girls had to wear drab, dark-blue uniforms to class, boys dress slacks, dress shirts, and ties. One hour a day was devoted to memorizing the Baltimore Catechism, and woe to the student who did not know its questions and answers by heart. *Who made us? God made us. Why did God make us? To know, love, honor, and serve Him.* The Sisters marched us through the Stations of the Cross on the first Friday of every month and made sure we attended Mass on holy days of obligation. I was overdosed on religion. As I knelt in church listening to gloomy Latin chants, I thought about Oneway and wondered where he was. Probably riding the Orange Blossom Special through Florida citrus groves, free as the wind.

Restless as I was inwardly, I was outwardly a diligent, well-behaved student, not by choice, certainly not by inclination. Fear made me complete my homework and stopped me from acting up in class. The nuns belonged to the Order of the Blessed Virgin Mary, B.V.M. for short. The students at Divine Infant had their own interpretation of the initials: Black-Veiled Monsters. The Sisters were dedicated to making their pupils docile by periodically beating them across the knuckles or over the head with metal-edged rulers, often for infractions that would have rated no more than a scolding at a public school. The beatings were applied only to boys; girls were exempt, for some reason. Most of the nuns were the kindest of women, but their gentleness was overwhelmed by the others, who seemed to embody an ancient Greek dramatist's conception of the Furies.

To avoid the dread ruler, I became a model of deportment in class, a bookworm outside it. As a result, my life became even more confined. When other boys came to our house and asked me to play, I pleaded that I had to do my homework.

Finally spring came, bringing with it a flurry of lawn-creation among Westchester's new residents, for what is a suburb without lawns? After my father and I cleared the construction rubble from the muddy swales in the front and the back of the house, a dump truck rumbled up our new street (road crews had paved it and put in sidewalks with the first thaw), backed into our new driveway, and unloaded a small mountain of rich black earth. My father rolled a wheelbarrow from the garage and handed me a shovel. We spent all that day and the next spreading the dirt.

When the topsoil had been spread to a thickness of several inches, we leveled it with a lawn roller. Pushing and pulling it hour after hour, I would have felt like a Russian serf if I had known what one was. Certainly I felt as dirt-bound as the farm boys of old when I took a break and, looking past the fixed skeletons of new houses rising on the prairie, saw the moving steel of a locomotive on the Harbor Belt.

The boxcar was one of a line parked on a siding next to the brick factory just south of Cermak Road. A switch engine idled a distance down the track, bleeding steam. Engineer and fireman were in the cab. The boxcar's door was open.

"Boost me up," I said.

"I don't think we better go in there," George said, glancing toward the engine.

"Hurry up before somebody sees us. Gimme a boost, then I'll pull you up."

George hesitated. Squatting, I sprang straight up, pulled myself inside and, lying on the wooden floor, held my hands down to George. With a worried look, he grabbed them and clambered in beside me.

We inspected the steel cavern, empty except for a few shipping tags lying around. The other door was also open. If we looked straight through, it boxed a view of the Salt Creek woods; if we changed angle by moving to the left, we could see our houses, almost a mile away. I imagined my father, trudging behind his seeder across the pitchy soil I had helped make as flat as an outfield. I had done my bit. I had been a good boy, but I would do no more yard work, deliver no more *Tribunes*, and never again recite the Baltimore Catechism for Sister Maria-Theresa.

"Boy, this is really going to be great!" I said.

George nodded without conviction. He looked down at the roadbed's tar-blackened gravel.

"Hey, y'know, we shoulda brought something to eat."

"We'll eat at a hobo camp," I said. "Hoboes have camps. They eat beans outta cans. Beans, beans, the musical fruit …"

"The more you eat, the more you toot," said George, picking up the limerick.

"The more you toot, the better you feel …"

"So eat beans at every meal!"

We laughed.

"But we oughta have something just in case," George said, turning serious again. "Peanut butter sandwiches." He looked toward his house. "This car ain't going anywhere for a while. S'pose I go back and get some peanut butter and a loaf of bread?"

It seemed like a good idea. I told him to go ahead, warning that he had better make it fast if he did not want to miss the train.

He nodded solemnly, lowered himself to the ground, and ran

across the fields. When I heard the sound of a man's footsteps draw-ing close, I went into a corner of the car and curled up in a ball, trying to make myself invisible in case it was a railroad detective. The man walked past. I crept back to the door and peeked out; it was the brakeman, heading toward the end of the line of boxcars, a flare siz-zling redly in his hand. I ducked my head inside when he turned and signaled, moving the flare back and forth on a horizontal. From up ahead came a loud cough, followed by a succession of quieter coughs that fell to a whisper. There was a second loud cough, then another succession of quieter ones merging straight into a third loud one, and a fourth, the number of quiet coughs between the loud ones growing less and less until there were none, only one loud cough after another, not like coughs any longer but like deep, rhythmic drumbeats. I was nearly knocked to the floor when the boxcar lurched backward. All down the train, drawbars and couplers banged like iron bells. The car jerked forward a few feet and stopped, the engine hissing and wheez-ing. I dared another peek toward the rear of the train. The brakeman was leaning way out at an angle from the last car, one hand on a grab iron, the other circling the burning flare round and round. The engine got up a head of steam. The car lurched forward again, soot rolling into the door, the train moving with a series of bumps and jerks, then smoothly. It wasn't going any faster than a walk, but I sat down, holding on tightly with sweating palms, my throat feeling nar-row as a straw. The brick factory slowly slipped from view. Trees took its place, then they vanished, and I saw the girders of the Salt Creek trestle flickering by and the creek below, showing as slats of brown water through the spaces between the ties.

I had hopped a freight!

I stood up, wishing there were people I could wave to, people who would envy me. The train picked up a little speed. The woods on the far side of the creek went past. Outside was a strange landscape—fields, houses, buildings I had never seen before. I panicked. Through some reverse emotional alchemy, the gold of my high excitement instantly turned into the basest fear. Where were George and the peanut butter sandwiches? What indeed would I eat? What if there were no hobo camps where friendly knights of the road would allow me to share their cans of bubbling beans? What if they were child killers and kidnappers? My parents would be worried about me. I could almost hear my mother, frantically calling missing persons. Where would I sleep? In the boxcar without a blanket?

All these thoughts rocketed through my young head in the time it took to go a hundred yards. I looked down at the roadbed, passing beneath about as fast as I could pedal my Schwinn at top speed. I tensed to jump, my fear of breaking a leg or ankle warring with my dread of hunger and hard cold beds, of being lost in the lonely unknown. Dread won. I took a deep breath and jumped, my legs running under me at the train's speed for a second or two before they crumpled and I rolled sideways down the embankment into a dry culvert.

I stood up, shaking all over, and checked myself for broken bones. I was intact except for skinned hands and a couple of scratches on my face. On the roadbed above, the last car clattered by, the brakeman sitting on the catwalk atop it, smoking a cigarette. I climbed to the clear track and saw the trestle, only a city block away. Altogether, I had journeyed half a mile. I headed down the track, forced into a goose step by the spacing of the ties, and, after crossing the trestle, cut through the woods toward home, drawn there by a force as invisible and inescapable as the gravity that had clutched me when I jumped.

I was vastly disappointed in myself. The difference between what I was, a well-loved suburban kid unwilling to surrender his real comforts for an abstract freedom, and the adventurer I wanted to be was no mere gap; it was a Grand Canyon.

It was, that is, until the day my mother returned from shopping with a book she had bought for me on impulse. It was a children's condensation of *Treasure Island*. I found a way across the chasm, though it turned me into a recluse. My friends nicknamed me "Hermit" because I seldom left the house to play ball or ride bikes with them. I preferred to remain in my room in the company of books, for I had discovered the power of imagination and of words. They magically flew me out of my banal existence to heroic times and far-off places and made me a bold doer of bold deeds. It wasn't Jim Hawkins who buccaneered with Long John Silver, or Huck Finn who rafted the Mississippi with Nigger Jim, or young Kim who spied for the

British in the Khyber Pass. It was I. I did all those things and more without ever leaving my room except to go to the library to check out the books.

I took breaks from reading only to watch the weekly episodes of Tom Corbett and Captain Video. Television did not excite my imagination as much as books, but with a little extra effort I could transport myself into the tube and battle reptiles in Venusian swamps with Tom Corbett, sit between Captain Video and his copilot, Ranger, as they played dodge-em with asteroids.

The idea of space travel intrigued me. After I picked up *The Conquest of the Moon* and *Across the Space Frontier,* it captivated me. I think I know some of the reasons. Because space travel did not exist at the time, my fantasies could range unhindered by reality. I could walk on a moon made of green cheese if I wished, or explore a Mars populated by a menacing race of superior intelligence and technology. Mostly, though, space travel represented the ultimate escape. I was afraid that the apron strings that had yanked me off the boxcar would tug at me no matter where I went in the world. The solution was to leave the world altogether. If I were on Mars, I might yearn to return to my warm bed and Mom's home cooking, but I would not be able to do anything about it. But Wernher von Braun's books said such voyages would not become reality until 1990. 1990! I would be an old man. And so I decided to leave imaginatively, on a lunar flight of fancy.

I began to build my spaceship out of used bed sheets, which became the cockpit's bulkheads. I cut a round hole in two of them and taped wax paper over each hole. Now I had the side bulkheads, complete with portholes. The forward one presented more of a challenge. It needed a big observation window, like the ones in the ships Chesley Bonestell had drawn, but the wax paper was not wide enough. When I pasted sheets of it together, the paper buckled at the seams, a definite design flaw in a rocket that would have to go 25,000 miles an hour to break gravity's chains (a fact I had culled from *The Conquest of the Moon*). I resolved the problem by reinforcing the seams with cardboard strips, glued by their ends to the rim of the window. Black construction paper became the space my ship would travel through. Playing God with my paint set, I filled the empty heavens with stars, planets, and galaxies, then pasted the construction paper across the backs of the side portholes and the observation window.

When that was done, I hung the bed sheets from the clotheslines in the basement, fastening the front one to the sides with safety pins, leaving the rear one free so I could enter the cockpit. It now needed furnishing. A folding card table made the console. Scrap lumber retrieved from the basement crawl space became the control panels, onto which I pasted dials cut out of shirt boxes and nailed knobs made of empty spools dyed with shoe polish. A sawn broom handle became my flight stick.

When I was finished, I brought my sister to the basement to show her my creation. She looked puzzled by the square of bed linen, hanging like a huge garment bag.

"It's a rocket," I explained authoritatively. "We're going to fly it to the moon."

"I can go?" asked nine-year-old Patty, wide-eyed.

"Sure, but you can't be a girl."

"Okay."

"Girls can't be copilots."

"Okay."

"You have to wear these."

I rolled up her long curls under one of my winter caps and gave her a pair of carpenter's goggles purloined from my father's workbench, explaining that she had to wear them so she would not be blinded by extraterrestrial radiation. I then strapped on my flight helmet, an old leather cap that, with imagination, resembled the hats worn by World War II aviators. A pair of swimming goggles went over my eyes.

"We're ready to blast off!"

She wanted to know what that meant.

"It's what Captain Video *always* says to Ranger before they go to another planet," I said, annoyed by her ignorance. "Ready to blast off."

"Okay."

"Okay, then. Let's get on board!"

With the ceremony of an actor pulling back a stage curtain, I opened the rear bed sheet and ushered Patty into the cockpit. She looked with wonder upon the knobs and cardboard dials, at the painted cosmos showing through the wax-paper portholes.

"That's the copilot's seat," I instructed, gesturing at one of the two folding chairs in front of the card table. She took her seat, and I took my mine.

"Now when I say something, you say, Check. Okay?"

"Okay."

I paused, trying to remember the crisp orders Captain Video issued to Ranger.

"Mommy!" my sister called to my mother upstairs. "Phil and me are going to the moon!"

Interested by our novel travel plans, my mother came down the basement steps. She peeked inside and laughed affectionately.

"Oh, how cute," she said, and told us to wait while she got her Kodak.

I pretended to be irritated by the delay, but I secretly enjoyed having our picture taken in *my* rocket. Also, the interval had given me time to think up authentic-sounding commands.

After my mother left, I turned one of the knobs and said something like, "Begin hydrazine flow." Hydrazine was one of the fuels used in the rockets in *The Conquest of the Moon* and *Across the Space Frontier.*

Patty smiled at me. I reminded her to say "Check."

"Are we going to the moon now?"

"You have to say 'Check' first."

"Check!"

"Begin liquid oxygen flow."

"Check!"

"Uh ... fire the ... uh ... thruster boosters."

"Check!"

"Five ... four ... three ... two ... one ... Blast off!"

I pulled back the broom handle, took a deep breath, and mimicked a rocket engine, beginning with a low growl, like a watchdog's, then increased the volume until it reached the sublime roar of full thrust. I shook the card table and rocked back and forth in my chair to simulate the trembling of the ship as it rose on a pedestal of flame, rose on the bright fires of my imagination right through the roof of the buff-brick trilevel into the realms where blue sky darkened into black. Twenty-five thousand miles an hour! Escape velocity! We had broken the bonds of earth. I gazed out the portholes at ringed planets and pinwheel galaxies. Snug inside my small enclosure, I was sure I would journey out to the boundaries of the solar system and beyond. There seemed no limit to the places I would go, nor to the things I would do, none at all.

DISASTERS OF WAR

At noon, the radio announced that the cease-fire had gone into effect. The shooting never stopped, but the women came out of their houses and queued up in front of the bakery to buy bread. They were poor Moslem women with plump bodies and long, homespun dresses that resembled nuns' habits, and their families had not had any bread for a week. The bakery was on one of the streets in the souks off Martyrs' Square; it was so narrow a tall man standing in the middle with outstretched arms could almost touch the buildings on either side. When the mortar shell landed, a few yards from where the women stood, the confined space magnified the explosion so that three women were dismembered while five more lay dead in strangely contorted positions, their shattered bones and joints attaining in death a flexibility impossible in life. Another five were wounded, but they had been taken to the hospital by the time the correspondent got to the narrow street off Martyrs' Square. All he saw were the bodies, a lot of shattered glass, and round loaves of bread scattered here and there. Some loaves had been blown to fragments and the crumbs lay in puddles of blood, like croutons in a dark-red bisque.

Later, the correspondent sat in his office, trying to write. A week ago, his editors had told him to find a human interest story that would dramatize the suffering the civil war was inflicting on the ordinary, innocent people in Beirut. Now he had found one, but he could not write it.

Nothing came to him except the words "an even baker's dozen"—which made him want to laugh—and the image of the bread crumbs looking like croutons in a bloody bisque. He did not write that because it would never get into his newspaper—a family newspaper read by eight hundred thousand people at their breakfast tables. Still, he ought to have been able to write something. He knew the emotions he was supposed to evoke. He did not feel them, but he was a professional who knew how to manufacture emotions and express them on the page without making them sound faked, without any suggestion that they were anything other than what he himself felt, which, lately, was nothing. He knew all the tricks of his trade, but today his tricks failed him. Possibly he was tired of faking.

He wanted to tell the truth as he saw it. That was the trouble. The truth would not be acceptable to his editors, who would want to see a story about a tragedy. What happened to the Moslem women had not been tragic. Given some of the things that had happened in the war, it had not even been particularly horrible. A lot of the women in Beirut were not as innocent and ordinary as the correspondent's editors believed them to be. They praised their sons and husbands for fighting, which encouraged their sons and husbands to keep fighting. The correspondent had known of women who forced their men to fight when the men did not want to; in a war like this one, a man who failed to fight for his faith and family disgraced himself and them. Possibly the women at the bakery had been different and just as innocent and ordinary as the editors in America thought, but the correspondent saw no reason to think so.

He did know they had been stupid to think the cease-fire meant anything and to leave their houses; all the cease-fires before had broken down, some almost at the same moment they were declared. The women had been especially stupid to queue up. Everyone in Beirut knew that bunching up invited disaster. For all those reasons, the incident had not been tragic, outrageous, or pitiable, but ridiculous. Maybe that was why the words "an even baker's dozen" had made the correspondent want to laugh.

He let himself laugh now. It was not a big belly laugh, not a guffaw, not even a chuckle, but a short, sharp snort. He tore the blank paper from his typewriter and threw it in the wastebasket; then he went to the bathroom to wash up before going home. At least he had not lied or faked anything. He combed his hair, noticing how rapidly his hairline had receded in recent months. Thirty-four and growing bald already. Looking in the mirror, he knew the baker's dozen had not been the only casualties he had seen today.

TWO

City Room

I never came close to fulfilling my dreams of following Chuck Yeager's contrails into realms where blue sky darkened into black. I had no talent for designing airplanes, or for flying them. I lasted only three semesters at Purdue University's School of Aeronautical Engineering, where I'd earned D's and F's in calculus, physics, and thermodynamics. After I dropped out (dropping out had a certain flair, a suggestion of squandered opportunities, whereas flunking out connoted only stupidity), I hitchhiked up to Great Lakes Naval Training Center to enlist as a Marine Corps aviation cadet. I passed the flight physical but failed another exam, the flight aptitude rating, and failed it dismally, answering only a third of its questions correctly. My score indicated, said the officer administering the test, that I would likely fly a high-performance jet into the nearest hillside, assuming I was able to get it off the ground in the first place.

Grounded! I was almost in tears. My heart had been set on becoming a test pilot for so long I could not imagine doing anything else.

I stayed out of school for the next term, over my father's protests. He was worried he would not have a college graduate for a son, but I needed a respite from classrooms to find a new direction for my life, a new means of escape now that the wild blue yonder was closed to me. For the next six months, I lived at home, yes, in that very same house on Suffolk Avenue, earning my keep first as a driver for the U.S. Post Office, then as a brakeman for the Chicago and Northwestern railroad. If I could not sit in the cockpit of a supersonic fighter, at least I could renew my affair with my first love, freight trains.

I hoped for work as a road brakeman, riding a caboose on a cross-country highballer; lacking seniority, I was instead confined to the C&NW's Proviso Yards, a labyrinth of switch tracks and sidings where the romance of the rails quickly soured. The work was hard and monotonous except in the Hump Yard, where it was hard and dangerous. In the Hump Yard, road trains were assembled under the pressure of traffic managers' schedules. When a train had to be made up for a run to a distant city, a switch engine would pull at high speeds strings of rolling stock from the sidings to the main track. The brakemens' job was to cut out the boxcars, flatcars, and tankers marked for that train from those going to different destinations. That required them to hop the cars, unhitch them by yanking the drawbars, then jump off and signal the engineer with lantern or flare to shunt the cars back onto the sidings and, when that was done, to hop on again and stop them with the hand brakes.

The Hump Yard was no place for the timid, the unfit, or the slow, and the boss of that noisy, treacherous world was the yardmaster, Sam Sarkashian, Black Sam the Mad Armenian, as he was known. He stood five-nine and weighed two hundred and ten pounds, very little of it fat. For Sam, the title of yardmaster was not honorific; he was a master in the fullest, worst sense of the word, a slave driver proud that no train ever left a minute late if he could help it. He bullied the brakemen to make schedule, most often with his profane tongue, sometimes with a kick in the butt or crack in the head. He was universally hated and feared. In the Hump Yard office—a caboose shorn of its wheels—testimonials to Sam covered the walls: BLACK SAM IS A MOTHERFUCKER. NO HE'S NOT—HE NEVER HAD A MOTHER. BLACK + SAM = ASSHOLE. When the crews "tied up for beans"—broke for lunch—Sam would sit at his rolltop desk in the grounded caboose, his huge, furred hand wrapped around a greasy sandwich, and look at the commentaries unfazed, as if they were either compliments or invective directed at someone else. A brakeman named Billy French said Sam was not offended because he couldn't read.

Billy was about five-six, wiry, and wound as tight as armature coils. He hated Sam enough for the rest of us because Sam took a special pleasure in bullying him. One night, their conflict came to a head. Sam was cursing Billy for being too slow, and Billy swung his lantern at Sam's skull. Sam ducked and dropped Billy with a punch to the midriff. He could have kicked Billy half to death, but, in an unusually charitable mood, he walked away, leaving the little man on his knees, gasping for breath.

I was Sam's second favorite victim. He delighted in giving young, inexperienced hands a hard time (working a few shifts under him was considered a baptismal rite throughout the yards). Whenever a chance came to escape him, I took it. One night, I volunteered to go to a remote sidetrack to mark certain cars routed for a westbound train. The foreman handed me a schedule and a piece of chalk.

As I walked between the switch tracks, boxcars ranked on both sides like buildings on a narrow, unlighted street, I saw a few dim figures crouching in the shadows ahead. I stopped, my heart quickening: it could have been a gang of thieves, pilfering freight.

"It's okay, fellas," one of them said. "Ain't no bull, just a brakeman." He stood up, facing me. "Hey, you …"

I shined the lantern at him, illuminating a face covered with a stubble of beard. He made a visor with one hand, and I turned the light on the others, who did the same. They were a rough-looking bunch, but I did not see any weapons.

"Take it easy with the light," the man standing said. "We ain't trouble. We're travelin' men, lookin' for directions you might say. This here the westbound?"

"It is." I took a few steps toward him but was stopped cold by a rank odor, an invisible barrier of dried sweat, unlaundered clothes, and skin innocent of soap. "Where're you going?"

"Calarada to pick peaches."

He might have been thirty or sixty, his body lean, like a young man's, his face as creased as his rumpled shirt.

"Didn't know they grew peaches in Colorado," I said warily. "Thought it was all ski resorts and cattle ranches."

"Got peaches, too, and we're gonna pick 'em. You could save us a lotta time and trouble if you could tell us where there's an empty."

I relaxed, assured they were only hoboes. Brakemen were supposed to report them to security, but I had no intentions of doing so.

"This way," I said.

I led them to an unloaded boxcar and shoved the door open.

"We're going to make her up in a couple of hours," I offered. "So you can keep the door open till then."

The man doing the talking gave me a two-fingered salute. One by one, the others hopped on board.

"How far's she goin', d'yuh know?" the man asked, standing in the door.

"Galena. She'll be switched there."

"Galena? Birthplace of Gen'r'l Grant, remember my hist'ry right."

I nodded that he did. He stood up there on the high iron looking down on me, just long enough to allow me to recognize him and the invitation he was silently extending.

I did not accept it, only wished him luck and went on with my job because I did not want to disappoint my father more than I already had, because I did not want to worry my mother, because I was afraid I would never amount to anything if I answered to Oneway's wayward call. Two hours later, Black Sam shouting at me to throw this or that switch, I wished I had and, wishing, watched the train clatter down the main track, outward bound with its tramp passengers. The road engine would highball the car through the Illinois corn to Galena—old brick houses and white-steepled churches hugged by Mississippi River hills—and there would switch it to another locomotive that would haul it over the great river at dawn and all day across the flatlands of Iowa and east Kansas, following the iron trail rising westward with the land to the wide dun reaches of warrior-haunted plains, through old cow towns huddled against the long American night, westward always westward toward mountains reddening in another dawn, when the hoboes would pile out to make for orchards waiting swollen for the touch of their vagrant hands.

I went on working for Black Sam Sarkashian, who played a pivotal role in my life. He accomplished what my father had failed to do—convinced me to go back to college, which in time led me into a love affair with the English language and the newspaper business. Not that Sam had undergone a conversion from tyrannical yardmaster to kindly career counselor for a confused nineteen-year-old. His only intent, on the hot, humid night I quit the Chicago and Northwestern, was to break as many of my bones as possible.

We were making up another train. For more than an hour, I had been throwing switches, leaping on and off freight cars. I was worn out and pouring sweat by the time I gave the engineer the highball. He was cranking up the diesel for the run to the main line when Sam spotted a car routed for another train.

"You dumb son-of-a-bitch," he hollered. "Whazzat doin' there? Cut that car."

The train was rolling at a good ten miles an hour. I ran to catch up, lunged for the grab iron, caught it. My work boots, their soles slick with roadbed grease, slipped through the foot brace. One leg slid inside the brace and bounced against the flat of a truck while the other swung in midair and my hands clutched the grab iron. Terrified, I chinned myself, pulling my leg free. I jerked the drawbar, disconnecting the rear end of the car, then jumped off and flashed a signal to stop. When the train screeched to a halt, I popped the front couple and walked to a switch, my knees watery. Cursing Sam—he should not have ordered me onto a train moving so fast—I threw the switch and signaled the engineer to bump the car onto the sidetrack. The car was in motion when Sam yelled from behind me: "Not that one, you asshole!" He was pointing frantically. "*That* one! Move your ass! Get the lead out!"

Shaken and distracted by my close call with amputation, I had thrown the wrong switch. I ran to close it, but I was too late. The boxcar was rolling through it by the time I got there.

"Brake it!" Sam screamed. "Brake that car!"

I told him to commit an impossible act with himself. I could never stop the boxcar with the hand brake before it hit the line of rolling stock on the adjoining track; when it did, I damn well did not want to be on it.

A groan and then a shriek of rending metal, the boxcar smashing into an ore car, knocking it and a second ore car over, tons of taconite spilling with a tremendous crash and a loud pinging as spikes broke loose, popping like huge rivets, twenty or thirty feet of track ripped up, and the boxcar derailing, its rear trucks burying themselves into the roadbed so that it resembled a boat grounded on a reef.

"You stupid wop son-of-a-bitch!" Sam bawled like a bull with its testicles caught on a barbed-wire fence. "Look watchya done! I'll break your guinea neck, I'll bust you up worse'n you busted up them cars!"

He was coming at me, thick bandy legs seeming to move sideways as the giant torso moved forward, fists balled at the ends of his long arms, swinging at his sides. I had learned a lesson from Billy French—if you go to hit Black Sam Sarkashian, you had better hit him and hard, barroom brawl hard. I feinted a left jab, then whipped the lantern with my right into his forehead, putting all my one hundred sixty pounds behind it. The blow would have knocked an ordinary human being unconscious. Sam was merely stunned. Also blinded by the blood spilling from the gash above his eyebrows. I figured I had made my point and took off running before his head and vision cleared. I ran to the main office, turned in the bent lantern, told the clerk where to send my last paycheck, then sprinted to my car and sped out of the lot, my railroading days over and done.

In the fall, I enrolled at Loyola University as an English major. I was better at analyzing Melville and Shakespeare than physics problems. Books still held their power to transport me out of the ordinary. I did some work for the college newspaper, which gave me the notion to become a reporter. I took a creative writing course from a fine teacher and even better man named Stanley Clayes, who gave me the notion to become a novelist. Sometimes I had a notion to become both.

Somehow I got sidetracked. I was easily sidetracked—too restless, too eager to go everywhere and do everything. Oneway, disguised as a Marine Corps recruiting officer, convinced me that the Corps, not newspapering, would be the royal road to adventure. Marines went everywhere, did everything. I was commissioned a second lieutenant the day I graduated, February 2, 1964. I did not have to report for active duty until mid-May, and having fulfilled my filial obligation to get a degree, I felt I could do as I pleased with the three months of freedom.

Partly inspired by Jack Kerouac's ramblings, I took off for Mexico, stopping in New Orleans for a look at Mardi Gras, then rode a

Greyhound to San Antonio, thumbed south from there through dry mesquite country, and crossed the border at Laredo.

Mexico was the best traveling I've ever done because all I owned could fit in one small suitcase and all I needed was an open road, because I was young and still innocent of the bitter knowledge I would soon acquire in Vietnam. The world seemed wonderful, filled with discoveries, as new to me as it had been to Adam. The best traveling. There had been discomforts—the night of shivering half sleep on a windy beach near Guaymas, the flea-infested flophouse next to the train station in Mexico City—and a few brushes with danger—the two bad hombres, one fat, the other scrawny and toothless, who picked me up on the highway in Guerrero and had a notion to rob me at knife point of my last thirty dollars until I appealed to their sense of self-preservation by flashing a switchblade I'd taken along for such encounters. But the joys made a few fleas and amateur bandits worth the trouble: the way the Monterrey hills went from brown to copper in the sunrise; the fertility rite danced in Tehauntepec to celebrate the sea turtles that laid their eggs in the sands; the cheerful, reckless truck driver who gave me a ride out of Guadalajara, sharing his jugged tequila and declaring as he careened around mountain curves that we were *amigos de la carretera;* and riding in the back of another truck through the Sonora night, desert silence, and so many stars I might have been soaring above earth's soiled air. Back in the land of the gringos, I hopped a Southern Pacific freight in Arizona, the boxcar door open to the smells of sagebrush all the way into New Mexico. Riding the high iron at long last! I hopped out near Las Cruces to thumb again, and there was always the road, steel track or blacktop, four-lane or two, the road running crooked or straight from Here to There.

After my discharge, in May of 1967, traveling became an escape not from the commonplace but from the fits of depression and rage that were symptoms of Vietnam's inner wounds. I loved and hated the war, and hated myself for loving it, and sometimes could not distinguish which emotion was which.

When I returned to Westchester from Camp Lejeune, North Carolina, my parents threw a party for me. Twenty-five or thirty friends and relatives gathered in the buff-brick trilevel with the pecky cypress trim. For a long while after they arrived, feeling unfit for civilized company, I stayed in my room on the third floor, the door locked. It was the room my father had finished for me while I was still in grammar school, knotty-pine boards fitted tongue in groove, corners and joints morticed flawlessly, so that trim was not needed to conceal mistakes. A good carpenter doesn't hide his sins, my father used to say, because good carpenters don't commit any.

I needed to hide the sin of my knowledge, which was: it's very easy to kill a man. Five pounds of trigger pull was all it took, and if human life could be taken so easily, did it have any instrinsic value? That was a question I could not ask my friends and relations downstairs. I could not share my knowledge with them. The mere possession of it made me feel ashamed.

My hunting shotguns were racked on a wall above a portrait of the cavalry sergeant, standing in his blue uniform in stern Victorian pose, one hand on the back of a chair. The shotguns were loaded because I could not sleep without a loaded weapon nearby. If I were one of those psychopaths who make headlines in the long American night, I could go downstairs with both pumps blazing and wipe out half the guests. Did they know how tenuous was their grip on life? Five pounds of trigger pull. *Bangyerdead.* Did they know how easy it was to kill someone? A corollary lesson from the war: given the right circumstances, just about anyone is capable of just about anything. Our ethical values, which we think are as solid and incorruptible as brass, are really base metal that corrodes in intemperate moral climates—and more quickly than we care to believe. *Bangyerdead.*

I did not feel at home at home and left for Europe in the middle of June, with fifteen hundred dollars saved in the service and one hundred pages of *A Rumor of War.* I had begun the book about six months before, writing in my spare time in my room at the Camp Lejeune bachelor officers' quarters. The manuscript was a jumble of tortured syntax. I could hardly write a single declarative sentence, which told me more about the state of my mind and nerves than the best psychiatrist could have. I sought refuge from Vietnam in Europe and hoped the spirit of Hemingway (fellow war veteran, fellow child of the Chicago suburbs) would descend on me in some Paris café and give me the grace to write well or, as he might have said, straight and true.

The Paris of the sixties was not Hemingway's Paris. It was far more expensive, and it was a neighborhood in the Global Village. Mass communications, and France's history in Indochina, made the war almost as big an issue as it was in the States. It was in the headlines and on television. Graffiti covered the walls in working-class districts—U.S.A. OUT OF VIETNAM!

I found a cheap pension somewhere on the Left Bank and scribbled where Hemingway had, in the Café Deux Magots on the Boulevard St.-Germain, but the only spirit to descend on me was the spirit of the Black Beast: a sense of hope abandoned and a conviction that the war had not been an anomaly or any sort of exceptional experience but in truth the essence of the human condition, which was pointless dying and suffering, the essence purified of the illusions and self-deceptions people stir into the brew of ordinary life so they can drink it without becoming sick, blind, or crazy. Anger spun me out of that despair. Looking at the customers, complacent tourists and gabby students on holiday, and at the smug waiters bringing with the cups of *café au lait* little receipts bearing the pretentious slogan *Café Deux Magots—rendezvous des intellectuels élites,* I would wrestle with an urge to start punching people in the mouth or, if I were in a particularly bad mood, to machine-gun the lot of them. How easy.

It scared me to have fantasies so violent because I knew I was capable of acting on them. It made me feel like a psychological freak; if my mind had taken physical form, it would have been put in a sideshow with the geek and the alligator lady. Years later, those bloody thoughts and imaginings would serve a purpose: they would give me an insight into the terrorist's soul, empowered by rage and contempt for life to slaughter without discrimination or remorse.

I went to Spain and then to England, where I ran out of money. I returned to the States in the fall, without a single page added to the one hundred I'd brought to Europe.

Back in my room in Westchester, I immediately began typing résumés. I sent them to almost every large and medium-size newspaper in the country; journalism seemed to promise adventure and a chance to earn a living with whatever writing talent I had. The replies dribbled in during the next month. No training, no experience, sorry, no job. I turned to the want ads, desperate to do almost anything for an income and self-respect. After all, it was embarrassing for a twenty-six-year-old college graduate and ex-combat officer to be living off his parents.

For the next couple of weeks, I endured interviews with company personnel directors, who would inevitably ask, "Where do you think you'll be five years from now?" The first couple of times, I answered naively that I hadn't the foggiest idea where I would be five years from now, and then made things worse by explaining that I'd acquired the habit of not thinking about my future in Vietnam, where it had been doubtful I had one. The personnel directors shook my hand and showed me the door. I wised up and, in later interviews, gave more suitable responses. The idea was to appear sanely ambitious by forecasting a modest rise into middle management.

It was all a sham—the last place I wanted to be five years from now, or at any time, was in middle management—but I somehow passed myself off as an eager corporate beaver and was hired as an assistant sales promotion manager by the National Advertising Company. It was a subsidiary of 3M Corporation, the giant manufacturer of Scotch tape and, according to the brochure given new employees, thirty-five thousand other products. Thirty-five thousand! National Advertising played a small role in that orgy of production; it made and sold billboards. Its plant and offices were in Bedford Park, a drab suburb on the southwest side, where acres of factories, warehouses, and blue-collar cottages sprawled under industrial skies and the air stank from the Argo cornstarch plant.

Now that I had a regular income, I rented an apartment on the near north side, in a young singles neighborhood. Every morning, I made a long commute down smog-shrouded expressways to Bedford Park and then spent eight hours writing sales promotion copy, or speeches for the sales manager, or outlines for sales meetings, or schemes for sales contests, or exhortations to the firm's far-flung salesmen. *Latest studies show that x-thousand motorists travel major traffic arteries in your sales area EVERY DAY ... be sure to tell your prospects that that means X-THOUSAND POTENTIAL CUSTOMERS for them, using outdoor advertising ... x-percent MORE than they could reach through radio, television, and newspapers COMBINED ... at only A FRACTION OF THE COST!*

After three or four months, I knew in my very cells what Thoreau had meant when he talked about lives of quiet desperation. Once I had led thirty-five men into battle, in a jungle on the far side of the world. I had confronted the ultimates of life and death. Fifteen of my comrades had been killed in action. Had I survived while they had not just so I could promote the advantages of billboards over other forms of advertising?

Yes, I was having difficulties adjusting to civilian life and its everyday demands. I questioned whether I *ought* to adjust and wondered if a lot of the psychological problems suffered by returned warriors were truly signs of pathology or merely considered so by modern society, which could not function if everyone saw things with the warrior's clarity. Who was maladjusted, the warrior or society, which, if it were to continue manufacturing thirty-five thousand products, or thirty-five million, required its members to believe that the making and acquisition of those products were necessary to their happiness? The warrior knew mankind would get along fine without them because life and death, and courage in the face of death, were all that really mattered. Everything else, save for love, was nonsense. Who could blame him if, home from the war, he took off into the woods? Who could blame him if he fled through alcohol and drugs? Possibly all those addicted veterans I read about were not trying to forget the war but to remember it and the great truths it had taught them by making themselves useless to a society that valued them only as means of production and imbecile consumption.

I grew slightly deranged.

By the spring, I was seriously considering shipping over in the marines and volunteering for another tour in Vietnam.

Providence or blind luck saved me from making that suicidal move. I received a letter from the Chicago *Tribune*, belatedly telling me that my application had been given serious consideration. I was asked to stop in for an interview.

Harold Hastings, the executive editor, was a thin man with a thin mustache, dark hair graying at the temples, and a breezy friendliness that spoke of country-club locker rooms, congenial laughter over gin and tonics at the nineteenth hole. His manner was a welcome change from the stiff personnel directors, with their sterile textbook interrogations. Leaning forward in his high-backed chair, its tufted leather shining dully in the light of a brass desk lamp, Hastings wanted to know why I thought I would make a good newspaperman (a red-blooded term he said he preferred over the formal and anemic "journalist"). I did not have a good answer; I just thought I would, *knew* I would. *And, oh Christ,* I thought, *if I don't get this job, I'm going to do it, ship over.*

"Most of our applicants have journalism degrees," Hastings said, his arms and elbow making a bipod that supported his chin. "Or they've worked for a small-town weekly for a couple of years, gotten a bit of seasoning before they tackle the major leagues."

I glanced around the office and, drawing on my previous job-interview experience, told myself to sound confident but not cocky.

"I was a reporter and feature writer for my college newspaper."

"Saw the samples you sent. Not bad stuff ..."

My heart rose a floor or two.

"... but a school newspaper, well, that's not the same thing as getting out on the street and digging out a story, is it?"

My heart returned to the garage level.

"No. But I've also had a few years' experience free-lancing," I offered, bending the truth into a hairpin.

"Saw those samples, too. Fiction. We're not in the fiction business, and besides, you didn't say where your free-lance stuff's been published. Or has it?"

He asked the question in his congenial tone, but a rivulet of sweat coursed down my ribs.

"No, it hasn't. Free-lancing's a tough nut to crack."

Hastings bent his head to peer closely at my résumé, as if he were looking for something he might have missed, some shred of qualification.

"Maybe I should have asked you why you *want* to become a newsman," he said, raising his eyes.

I answered that it would be an exciting way to make a living, then blurted out that I hoped one day to become a foreign correspondent. It was as dumb as a kid trying out for junior league football saying he hoped to become a starting quarterback for the Forty-Niners, dumber, because a kid would not be expected to know better.

"Foreign correspondent?" Hastings appeared vaguely amused by my audacity. "They're the elite. Some of our correspondents had to work local and national news for years before they got sent overseas."

"Oh, yes, sir, I understand that, I was just ..."

"But you're right about this being exciting." The years dropped off his face in an instant, as he seemed to recall his days as a cub reporter. "I think it's the most exciting business in the world. Why don't I show you around our city room?"

I nodded, suppressing an impulse to ask if the tour meant he'd decided to hire me.

The advent of VDTs has sucked the glamour and individuality out of today's city rooms, turning them into generic copies of law and insurance offices. In the late 1960s, the *Tribune's* city room was still a place of noise and dirt and magic, as cavernous and exciting as a busy railroad station in the days of the great passenger trains. It could have served as a stage set for *The Front Page,* long as half a city block, almost as wide, its ceiling vaulting like a cathedral's. I could feel the voltage in the air the minute I stepped inside, smelled it in the odors of ink and pot paste and smoke from pipes, cigarettes, cigars. Hastings led me past ranks of battered gray desks, each one half buried under drifts of copy, newspapers, notes, and press releases. Some of the reporters sat idling over paper coffee cups, some pounded manual Underwoods and Remingtons like mad pianists, some were speaking into black telephones, plugging their opposite ears against the noise: ringing phones, hammering Teletypes, reporters and editors bellowing, "BOY! COPY! COPY DOWN!"

Hastings, plowing through the trash that overflowed the barrels and spread across the rubber tile floor, brought me to a big U-shaped desk. In the center of the U a stocky, dark-haired man sat by a bank of squawking police radios while the rim around him was occupied by copy editors and rewrite men, who wore headsets through which they communicated with reporters phoning in breaking stories: *Yeah, got it ... okay, got that ... give me the victim's name ... chief give you a damage estimate? ... how big was the crowd ...* a voice crackled through one of the radios: *This is twenty-six for the desk.* The man in the slot grabbed a microphone: *Twenty-six, it's about time. Whaddya think this is, a monthly? We need four grafs on that three-eleven for the first ... get to a phone and call rewrite ...*

I was looking at the city desk, Hastings explained. The man sitting by the radios was an assistant day city editor, sometimes called a "slot man." He was talking to a reporter-photographer team in a radio car.

Hastings pivoted, pointing to a cluster of desks where half a dozen young men and women stood fidgeting with the expectancy of people waiting for a stadium gate to open.

"And that's The Pit."

I gave him a questioning look.

"The general assignment pit. Where our new people start off. They're waiting for an assignment. Could be anything—a murder, a fire, a big political speech ..."

Just then, as if it were an act staged for my benefit, the slot man rose to a half crouch, jabbing his finger at one of the reporters.

"Nolte!" he yelled. "Hat and coat! That three-eleven's a four now. Take twenty-eight."

He flipped a set of car keys to the man called Nolte, who caught them in midair and made a dash for the door.

"That's how it's done," Hastings said with a smile. "And that's how those men over there started off. Some of them began as copyboys, probably before you were born. I call that Heavyweight Row."

He gestured across the room toward another rank of desks. Behind one sat a bald man, his tie loosened, his shirtsleeves rolled up, a roguish smile on his face as he spoke to a blocky man in a brown suit. The next desk was occupied by a reporter with thinning gray hair, who held a phone to his ear with a crooked shoulder while he took notes on his typewriter. Hastings let me know that I was looking at legends. The man with the smile was Jim Strong, the labor editor— he was on a first-name basis with every union boss in the country. The one in the brown suit was Joe Morang, ex-marine, ex-prizefighter, an old China hand who had been a cub reporter on the Shanghai *Express* back in the thirties and who was now a top police reporter—a call from him went straight to the superintendent. The reporter on the phone was George Bliss, also a former boxer, a navy hero in World War II, and today the best investigative reporter in the city, if not the country—Pulitzer Prize and so many lesser awards there wasn't a wall big enough to hold them.

It was as if Hollywood myth had come to life. Hard-living, hard-boiled, two-fisted newshawks. Even the newshens looked tough, with cigarettes hanging from their lips—no vapidly pretty anchorwomen with perfectly modulated voices and thousand-dollar designer dresses.

Hastings then guided me past a row of offices behind glass half walls—the lairs of the city, managing, and foreign editors—to the center desk. If, in the city room's anatomy, the city desk was the heart, the center desk was the brain. There, toward deadline, the managing editor, his assistants, and sometimes the editor himself sat and decided which stories would make front page, which would be entombed with the truss ads. Hastings pointed out the editor in chief—a portly man in a vest named W. D. Maxwell, successor to the deceased Colonel McCormick (and even more right-wing, if that was possible). Beside him was the managing editor, Tom Moore, a big ex-football player from Michigan State. Moore called out to the national desk, in a voice surprisingly soft for so large a man: "Hey, Spoke. Where's that Washington piece?"

The copy editor he'd spoken to was potbellied and sallow-faced, dressed in green trousers, a purple shirt, and a stained yellow tie. A stinking Italian stogie hung from his lips, the tobacco juice dripping to add new spots to his tie.

"I'm killing his darlings," he grumbled to Moore. "The guy thinks he's T. S. Eliot."

"Well, kill' em quick. We're close to lockup."

With a grin, Hastings ushered me over to the outlandishly dressed deskman.

"Phil, this is Roland Spokely. Spoke, this is Phil Caputo. We're thinking about hiring him. Not much experience, but he's a pretty good writer."

Roland Spokely made a grunting noise and did not look up from the copy, through which his pencil slashed like a scythe. He held the sheet up and growled, "BAAOOY—COP-PEEE!" Only then did he turn toward me, his puffy eyes squinting through the cigar smoke.

"Good writer, huh? So is this guy, damn good." He rattled the copy paper. "One of the best I've seen, and I've seen some."

I shoved my hands in my pockets, shuffled.

"Uh ... do you mind my asking ... if he's so good I mean ... why did you take so much stuff out?"

Roland Spokely gave me a good long squint.

"Because most places put up with mediocrity—the Chicago *Tribune* puts a premium on it."

And, a drop of brown saliva dribbling onto his shirt, he began to dismember another story.

"Character, isn't he?" Hastings asked, shaking his head as he brought me to the foreign desk, which bore the vestigial name of cables desk, although correspondents now filed by telex instead of telegram. The telexes, and the wire-service Teletypes, stood in a row in a long narrow room glassed in to muffle their racket. It was deafening when we entered the room—and thrilling, a sound that communicated the drama of far-off events, a sound that was the heartbeat of the news business. My own heart thumped in rhythm to that loud and urgent pulse when I glanced at the datelines on the paper rolling out of the machines—pronorlake (the *Tribune's* cable code, Hastings explained) exvesey/Saigon ... pronorlake exstarr/moscow ... exmorgan/paris ... exsiegert/bonn ... and Rome and Tokyo and Mexico City ...

The paper had a small foreign staff, Hastings shouted, only ten full-time correspondents.

"So anybody who wants to go overseas for us will have to spend a lot of time paying his dues," he went on, his voice dropping as we moved back into the city room. On the wall above the cables desk a dozen clocks ticked off the times from around the world. A rewrite man on the rim was talking to a stringer, phoning in from some far capital, and then the floor began to tremble.

For a split second, I thought it was an unlikely earthquake and wondered why everyone was going about his business, unalarmed.

"What is that?" I asked Hastings. "That shaking."

"Those are the presses. Five floors down. They're running off the bulldog now." The bulldog was the first edition. "We keep them idling twenty-four hours a day—it's cheaper that way—but when an edition's put to bed, we crank 'em up to full speed. Well, let's get back to my office."

Chill bumps rose on my forearms as I followed Hastings out. The floor, vibrating from the power of the presses thundering down in the building's guts, felt like the deck of a mighty ship getting under way. The whole building, all twenty-four stories of it, seemed *alive*, and I knew, not in my mind but in my blood and marrow, *This is it, this is where I belong*.

Hastings sat in his chair, hands locked behind his head.

"Know one of the things that drew me to your résumé?" he asked. "You were in the Corps. So was I. World War Two."

The old marine brotherhood. *Semper Fi*. I had wanted the job before I saw the city room. Now I lusted for it, but I said with assumed humility that all I'd learned in the marines was how to fire a rifle and dig a foxhole. Those were hardly qualifications for a reporter.

"Wrong. Sometimes it takes a bit of guts to be a reporter. You can wind up in dangerous situations, and that goes double for foreign correspondents." The chair creaked as he hunched forward. "And I like the fact that you were an English major. Assume you studied Shakespeare."

"Yes, sir. Two courses."

He rapped his knuckles on my résumé.

"That's the stuff! Shakespeare. Gives you a sense of the language, that and the King James Version. The trouble with these journalism grads we get is that they know how to do this or that but they can't make their stories sing because they don't have a sense of the language. Someone with the guts to get a story and the ability to make it sing, that's who we're looking for."

I couldn't restrain myself anymore.

"You've found him," I said, my voice almost squeaking.

He smiled faintly.

"I think so, too."

I very nearly leapt off the chair.

"Who knows, maybe you'll get to be a foreign correspondent someday. You'll become famous. We've had some famous ones—Dubois, Sheen, Jay Allen."

I very nearly leapt again, seeing in a kind of epiphany that fame was one of the things I wanted. To read my byline, front-paged in bold type above some exotic dateline.

"When can you start?"

"Tomorrow. Right now if you want."

"Ah, don't you think you should give notice to"—he glanced at the résumé—"National Advertising?"

"Oh, yes, sir," I said, embarrassed. "I'll give it tomorrow. Two weeks. I can start in two weeks."

"See you in two weeks, then," Hastings said, rising to shake my hand.

And so I became a newspaperman, only because I had been in the marines and had read Shakespeare.

He looked as bland and establishment as his name: clean-shaven jaw, thin lips, straight hair black as anthracite, the gray temples lending him the appearance of a mature authority beyond his thirty-six years. He favored horn-rimmed glasses, oxford shirts, and wing-tip shoes, and could have blended into the somber foliage of any blue-chip law firm or corporate boardroom. The zealotry in his nature wasn't apparent until you looked into his eyes, burning with a flame blue, clean, and concentrated, like a gas jet's.

Tom Smith was the editor of *The Trib,* a tabloid owned by the Chicago *Tribune,* with which it was distributed as an insert three times a week in the western suburbs. The paper was an experiment; devoted exclusively to suburban news, its purpose was to snatch a share of the market from the big suburban chains, like the *Pioneer Press.* If it succeeded, it would be expanded to the northern and southern suburbs. Toward that end, Smith had been given editorial freedom, making him the earl of a minor, semiautonomous province in the *Tribune's* vast media empire, which included the New York *Daily News,* the Orlando *Sentinel,* WGN—the largest broadcast system in the Middle West—tracts of Canadian forest, pulp mills, and a fleet of Great Lakes freighters that transported the newsprint from the mills to the pressroom whose rumblings and quakings had so awed me.

Like a young man sent out to the colonies for seasoning, I was sent to *The Trib* to acquire the experience I lacked. After a year or so reporting in the suburbs, I could move "city-side," better equipped to scramble for assignments in The Pit.

The Trib's newsroom, in a big, white colonial-style office building in Hinsdale, just a fifteen-minute drive from Westchester, could have fit into a corner of the one downtown. There was no atmosphere of smoky *Front Page* drama or grizzled legends who had won Pulitzers and written for the Shanghai *Express.* Every reporter—only a dozen-odd compared with the multitudes at the *Tribune*—was under thirty. But what the staff lacked in size and experience, it made up for in youthful enthusiasm and camaraderie. We were part of something new, in on the ground floor. We wanted *The Trib* to succeed; *we* wanted to succeed.

Probably I wanted to more than anyone else because my shortcomings were painfully obvious. Hastings could sing the praises of my liberal-arts education all he wanted. I found out right away that a few journalism courses would not have done any harm. I would watch the other reporters come in from an assignment, sit at their typewriters, and bat out leads in ten seconds flat while I chewed my nails and chain-smoked, staring at a sheet of paper as blank as my brain. I was all right at features and human interest stories, but hard news paralyzed me. Twenty-two-year-old Andrea Aleff, fresh out of J-school, gave me a crash course. The four W's, she instructed in her husky voice. What, where, when, who. It was simple. Yeah, sure.

Eventually, I got the hang of it and covered town council meetings, zoning board hearings, county courts, the police blotters, a fire or two, highway accidents sufficiently gory to rate a couple of paragraphs, even a sensational murder trial—an airline pilot had killed his wife and tried to make it look like suicide.

Cub reporter. *Newspaperman.* When I thought of the millions of people who got out of bed dreading their shops, offices, and factories, I realized how lucky I was. I woke up almost every morning impatient to get to work, eager to see what the new day would bring. Sometimes, after the things I'd done and the places I'd been, it bothered me to be working in the very suburbs I thought I had left forever, but by and large I had achieved escape velocity. No drowse of the accustomed in newspaper work. It was a perpetual adventure, a continuous education. I was happy, and able to keep the Dark Thing at bay most of the time.

One day, five months after I'd joined his staff, Smith summoned me into his office. I entered nervously. With the exception of Neil Mehler, the managing editor, Smith inspired uneasiness in everyone at the paper. There was something remote and cold about him, even a little cruel—that blue light in his eyes, the way his thin lips would curl into an expression between a smile and a sneer, the air of tension he gave off, as if he were waging a constant battle to keep strong passions in check: the Puritan's old war between desire and its repression, between appetite and a profound sense of sin. I sat in one of the chairs facing his desk, afraid he was going to fire me.

After some preliminary inquiries into my feelings about working at *The Trib,* he rolled his chair back and with uncharacteristic casualness flung his feet onto the desk.

"I'm not quite as happy with this paper as you seem to be," he said, the words wriggling through his half-clenched teeth. "It's a bulletin board. We report the news, sure, but it's bulletin-board journalism. Journalism should be more than a bulletin board."

His wing tips swung back to the floor, and he pushed his chair tight up against the desk, pitching his face forward.

"It should be an instrument. It is the best instrument—the best weapon—democracy has for effecting social and political change."

I had no idea what he was driving at, yet those words, an *instrument*, a *weapon*, bore into my mind like a diamond-bit drill.

He reached into a drawer and handed me a typewritten list of names: Accardo, Ricca, Alderisio, Cerone—the bosses of the Chicago family of the Cosa Nostra, Al Capone's successors. The list went on to their lieutenants and sublieutenants: Glimco, Aiuppa, Nicoletti, Buccieri. There were twenty altogether, and all of them, Smith said, lived in the western suburbs, *The Trib's* beat.

"They make fortunes off gambling and loan-sharking, prostitution, narcotics, every kind of racket, and then they buy big homes in places like River Forest and Oakbrook and hoodwink their neighbors into thinking they're respectable businessmen."

A note of indignant surprise sounded in his voice, as if he had just discovered an appalling fact of life. I could not quite understand his outrage, having grown up with the knowledge that gangsters bought big, expensive houses in classy suburbs. After all, to get rich and acquire the trappings of respectability were among the reasons they became gangsters.

"Another thing—they're trying to wash their filthy money in legitimate businesses in this area. We are going to put a stop to that. We are going to deny them their respectability. We are going to expose everything we can about them. They make huge profits by appealing to the basest appetites, and they're allowed to get away with it. We're going to change that. We are going to hit them where they live, literally."

Smith was as Midwestern as I, but as he spoke, I seemed to see him in Pilgrim black, flinging a sermon from a pulpit in a frame church encompassed by Massachusetts woods.

"We are going to publish photographs of their homes, quotes from their neighbors about what fine neighbors they make, and then we are going to show those neighbors of theirs exactly what sort of businesses they are in. We are going to make life difficult for them."

The pencil lines of his lips drew into their half smile, half sneer. "We'll run them out if we can. What do you think?"

I told him what I thought: Every law-enforcement agency in the country, from the FBI on down, had tried to run the Mafia out of somewhere. What made Smith think a small suburban paper could succeed where they failed?

"What have I said? The power of the press. An instrument, a weapon for change. It can make things happen, Phil. We are going on a good old-fashioned newspaper crusade."

And who were "we"?

"You and I. I as the editor, you as my investigative reporter."

He sat back, giving me a few seconds to absorb what he had told me. I was being promoted, not fired.

"Okay if I smoke?" I asked.

Smith did not touch tobacco or alcohol, but he gestured for me to go ahead. I lit up. Investigative reporter? It seemed I had just learned how to write obituaries.

"You won't be covering regular news from here on in. You'll be on special assignment until further notice. You'll report directly to me."

"Do you have an ashtray?"

He shoved an empty wastebasket from under the desk, never once taking his eyes off me. Those eyes told you he wasn't all WASP suburban gentility. There was something of the killer in him.

"We're going to start with Joseph Aiuppa. I want you to find out everything you can about him, about him personally and the rackets he runs. Dig out information about his house, interview his neighbors, find out if he's involved in any legitimate businesses in this area."

Smith continued to outline the strategy for his crusade. I only half heard him; the phrases *special assignment, report directly to me, an instrument, a weapon* were cracking inside my head like billiard balls on a hard break.

Peculiar how we deceive ourselves, how we don't know we are looking for something until we find it. I had been sincere when I'd told Smith I loved my job, but when I left his office, not so much walking as levitating, I realized I'd been lying through my teeth. I had grown bored, covering the pedestrian events of the suburbs. A debate on a sewer bond issue did not stir the blood. I needed a challenge, the stimulus of danger—not for its own sake because that was cheap thrill seeking. I wasn't the type to take up mountain climbing or big-game hunting to massage my adrenal glands. If I was going to take risks, it had to be in the service of a cause. I wanted a mission but hadn't seen that until Smith gave me one.

It took me on another trip, not so much geographical as moral, into a world I had heard about but had never seen from the inside. Clip joints where the B-girls hustled the conventioneer for five-dollar drinks, promising lurid thrills he couldn't get from his old mama back in Hicksville, but never delivering, and if he objected too vigorously, there was always a big boy with brass knuckles to persuade him to leave quietly with his empty pockets. Bars with names like the Paddock Lounge—twenty phone lines running into the back room to handle the bets. The tawdry, secondhand Frank Sinatra glitz of mob-run nightclubs. It could be a Runyonesque world some of the time, full of racketeers with colorful nicknames like "Icepick Willie," "Milwaukee Phil," "Jackey the Lackey," but for the most part it was sordid, corrupt, and violent—the bought cop, the bent politician, the numbers runner who tried to cheat his bosses hung from a meat hook and tortured with cattle prods for three days before he was taken down and shot through the head.

A journalistic gumshoe was the last thing I had expected to be, but I discovered that I made a pretty good one. I loved the independence of working the street alone, following trails of fact until they led to something. I was willing to put in twelve-hour days, to stay up till all hours to go on vice-squad raids or to spend days examining, with the myopic persistence of a scholar studying medieval texts, tax records, trial records, arrest records, the records of real estate transactions. I developed sources in the Illinois Crime Investigating Commission, the State Liquor Control Commission, and—a real coup—the organized crime squad of the FBI. A special agent, John Dahlman, opened his files for me, and it gave me, a twenty-seven-year-old cub, a buzz greater than any drug to walk into the FBI's offices in downtown Chicago and have Dahlman drop his reports in my lap. We had an arrangement of mutual exploitation, a quid pro quo of sorts. I used him for information I could never have gotten on my own, he used me to publish evidence that would have been inadmissible in court.

Oh, I was zealous, as zealous as Smith. We made a great team, two wires running off the same current. He was the Puritan who needed to fight Satan and Sin, and I had to be at war with the unambiguous Wrong denied me by the complexities of Vietnam, where the White Hats and Black Hats changed headgear so often you could not remember which side you were on, or were supposed to be on, and after a while, it didn't make any difference. The Outfit, as the crime syndicate was called in Chicago parlance, became my Nazis, Japanese, and Chinese Reds all wrapped up in one unquestionably villainous package.

The primary villain, Joseph Aiuppa—dumpy and bald, with a hooked nose so big and black-rimmed glasses so thick his face reminded you of a party gag—ran all the gambling, prostitution, and loan-sharking in Cicero, the Vatican of the Chicago Outfit. His headquarters were the same Capone had used: the Towne Hotel, a gloomy brick building on Cermak Road, half a block from where Cicero's streets dipped under rusting viaducts into Chicago's westside slums. In the Towne, Aiuppa kept his accounts, assigned the hits, conferred with his soldiers and button men. Along Cermak and up and down Cicero Avenue were the bars and bust-out joints where the girls fleeced the conventioneers, the bookies took the bets, and collectors with names like Jimmy "The Turk" Torello unwound after a hard night cracking the kneecaps of debtors late in their payments.

Aiuppa was the sort of mobster who aspired to WASP refinement and the obsolescent gentility of the country squire. He lived in Oakbrook, a preserve for surgeons, lawyers, and corporation presidents. Aiuppa's ranch house sprawled at the end of Yorkshire Drive in the fashionable subdivision of Yorkshire Woods, its trees and split-rail fences bestowing a rustic atmosphere appropriate to its British-sounding name. He owned a hunting reserve in southern Illinois, the Yorkshire Quail Club, its clubhouse graced by a stone fireplace above which hung a portrait of Aiuppa, a paunchy gangland parody of the sporting gentleman in Abercrombie & Fitch hunting garb, English pointers at his feet.

For a reporter, his story was an embarrassment of riches and heavy-handed ironies. His aspirations to country-club class began early in his criminal career, when he broke into country clubs for sporting equipment, which he then fenced, using the proceeds to purchase machine guns for the Dillinger gang. At one point, I interviewed the supervisor of Illinois shooting preserves, asking why the state allowed a known mob figure to own and operate one. He told me, "Because Mr. Aiuppa is very interested in the propagation of quail." Aiuppa might have been, but he had acquired his syndicate nickname "Joey the Doves" by showing a passionate interest in the annihilation of another game bird, the mourning dove. On a Kansas hunting trip, Aiuppa and a dozen mob cronies were caught blasting the birds from speeding automobiles off telephone wires, like Hollywood hoods tommy-gunning rivals. Altogether, fourteen hundred mourning doves became victims of underworld violence, one of the largest slaughters in the history of the Federal Wildlife Service.

Two wires running off the same current. Smith and I were both ambitious. He was a rising star among Tribune Company executives, but it was a crowded field. A campaign against Aiuppa and organized crime might give him a boost. It might do the same for me, speeding the day when I could move into the big leagues downtown. I took chances I did not have to take.

Peter Kotsos, chief of enforcement for the State Liquor Control Commission, phoned me one day: Aiuppa was using his Oakbrook home to meet with his top lieutenants. That was standard cop and newsman shorthand—top lieutenants. The sit-downs usually started around ten in the morning. Kotsos said I could take his word for it, but if I wanted to give the story added punch, it would be better to see for myself, take pictures of the cars pulling into the drive. He would make the tag numbers for me. Be careful, he warned. Aiuppa had a vicious temper; once he had tried to run down a federal agent on a stakeout.

Freddie Klinger, my photographer, rolled the window partway down to use as a support for his long lens. We were parked half a block from the house, near a grove of oaks. It was mid-October and the leaves looked splendid. A midnight-blue sedan turned into Aiuppa's driveway, followed by two more cars. *Whirrrclickclickclick* went Klinger's motor drive. He and I waited, talked football. The oak leaves fluttered past the windshield like dying embers.

The sit-down was over by one in the afternoon. The automobiles left. Aiuppa rode in the passenger seat of the last one, a Chrysler.

Klinger was a veteran street photographer. He followed with skill, hanging a discreet distance behind, timing the lights perfectly. Once I saw Aiuppa's driver take a long look in the rearview mirror. A squeeze in my lower intestine, a little clutch of excitement and dread.

"No sweat," Klinger said. "If he thought he was being followed, he'd speed up or slow down to check out what we'd do. See? He's maintaining the same speed."

We tailed the car to the Towne Hotel. There were no oak woods around there, just a tyranny of warehouses, storefronts, and vacant lots. We had lagged too far behind to get a picture of Aiuppa going inside.

The clutch of excitement and dread.

There was an outside chance I'd see him; if not, I would have a little color to add to the story.

"Do we do one of those movie-type things?" Klinger made a circle with his thumb and finger, flipped his cigarette out the window. "You know, if you're not out in ten minutes, I call the cops?"

"I'll be right out."

The lobby had the shadowy, dusty look of an aging widow's parlor, except for the heads mounted on the walls. A cape buffalo, a rhino, a lion, a kudu—some of the three thousand pounds in trophies Aiuppa the sportsman brought back from a safari he'd taken with Accardo, the boss of all bosses in Chicago.

I went up to the front desk and asked the clerk the rate for a single. He told me, in a voice that suggested he had not been trained in hospitality.

"I'd like one for one night."

"We got no vacancies."

I gestured at a board with about twenty keys hanging from it.

"What about all those?"

"Reserved."

"All of them?"

"What did I just say?"

"Who for?"

"You a cop?"

"No. Just a salesman, looking for a room for the night."

"Reserved."

"I'd like to talk to the manager."

"He ain't in."

"When he is in, where can I find him? Upstairs?"

"Get the fuckatta here."

Outside, Klinger asked if I had seen him. I shook my head.

"You shouldn't have gone in there. The guy can be a bad actor."

"I got some color. The lobby's full of mounted heads he brought back from Africa."

"Take care yours doesn't end up there."

Around two, we trailed Aiuppa to the Luxor Baths, a Russian steam room in what had been a Jewish neighborhood on the west side. Two hours later, he returned to the Towne. An hour after that, he went to Nicky's MGM Lounge, a syndicate restaurant on Cicero Avenue. By ten o'clock, he was back on Yorkshire Drive, holding another sit-down.

That was his schedule—as busy and bourgeoisie-regular as any other executive's.

I phoned Kotsos with the tag numbers. He did not have to call vehicle registration; he knew the license numbers by heart. (The Liquor Control Commission had been on Aiuppa's case for weeks because of its campaign to shut down his vice dens.) The men Aiuppa met with at his house were Simone Fulco, an armed robber who was also his nephew; Larry Rassano, his driver and a convicted felon awaiting deportation to Italy; and his college-educated accountant, Anthony Ortenzi.

When Smith was pleased, his lips slanted like a hypotenuse.

"Great stuff. So we've got it confirmed? He's using his *Oakbrook house* to hold meetings with syndicate thugs? Great stuff. Now interview his neighbors. See what they say about that."

They said Joey the Doves made a wonderful neighbor. He was quiet. Helped maintain the parkway. Supplied the beer. Gave candy to kids on Halloween.

⋄   ⋄   ⋄

"Great stuff. Just what I figured they'd say. We'll run every quote."

In late October, we broke a three-part series with sidebars, maps showing the location of the house, mug shots, photographs of the cars in the driveway.

MEET CICERO AND OAK BROOK'S JOE AIUPPA

"THE DOVES" MAKES MONEY OFF NIGHT OWLS

AIUPPA'S BARS SERVE BOOZE, BRASS KNUCKLES

We won a partial victory. We did not run Aiuppa out, but the county state's attorney vowed to investigate the Oakbrook meetings for criminal conspiracy, the Liquor Control Commission, encouraged by the publicity, closed down every clip joint in Cicero, and the vice squad raided several bookie parlors. The big coup was scored without help from the law. I received an anonymous tip that Aiuppa was acting as an intermediary for a developer in a multimillion-dollar real estate deal. I worked ten-hour days to pin the information down, discovering that the developer, whose name was Robert Brugh, had purchased an exclusive option to buy a fourteen-acre tract owned by the widow of Robert Ansani, who had been Aiuppa's partner in a company that manufactured illegal gambling equipment. Brugh planned to build a seven-million-dollar townhouse project on the land, which was going for sixteen thousand an acre, and had petitioned the Du Page County Zoning Board to rezone it for commercial use. Informational doors opened. It turned out that Brugh had once been a member of the Yorkshire Quail Club, where he had hunted with Aiuppa. He had also enlisted Aiuppa's aid in purchasing the option on the Ansani property. When I had all that locked up, I telephoned Brugh at his office and could almost see him squirming as he admitted, denied, then admitted again that he and the gangster had discussed the deal.

The story made the front page:

DEVELOPER ASKS PROJECT OK FROM DU PAGE
FOR SYNDICATE-OWNED TRACT NEAR HINSDALE

It led to another discovery: Aiuppa, his income pinched from the loss of his Cicero vice operations, was trying to sell twenty acres he owned for half a million dollars.

2d SYNDICATE-OWNED TRACT PUT ON MARKET

Information is light, and its glare was too much for Brugh. He withdrew his petition to the zoning board and dropped his purchase option the next week. Real estate brokers said the gangland taint on both pieces of property would make them almost impossible to sell.

SYNDICATE ACRES FOR SALE—WILL THERE BE A TAKER?

Smith was ecstatic.

"Now you can see what I meant," he said, his gas-jet eyes burning. "A weapon for change! A newspaper can make things happen! We've shut down a mob-money laundry!"

The next day, he posted a notice on the office bulletin board: I had been awarded a one-hundred-twenty-five-dollar bonus—a lot of money for a cub earning a hundred and fifty a week.

During the fifteen months I worked for *The Trib,* Martin Luther King and Robert Kennedy were assassinated. All the mythmakers were dead, and the myths died with them, and the serpents that had been estivating in the mud of the American id ever since Oswald ended the New Frontier with three shots from a mail-order rifle hatched on the streets of Chicago during the Democratic National Convention. Weathermen ran down Michigan Boulevard wearing football helmets and smashing windows with baseball bats. Their mirror image, Chicago cops in blue riot helmets, cracked undergraduate skulls in front of Hubert Humphrey's campaign headquarters, swatted whoever stood in their way—newsmen, bystanders, ministers. Sirens whooped and howled, gas grenades popped, radicals chanted, *What do you want— revolution—when do you want it—now!* The sounds of a lunatic America that had lost its bearings with its legends. My apartment was near Lincoln Park, where Yippies frolicked around tribal bonfires. I had to move out for a night; the apartment was filled with tear gas.

With all that going on, crusading against the Mafia seemed

quixotic and old-fashioned. Chasing antiquated bad guys whose evil was almost attractive because it was familiar beside the new and nameless demon loose on the streets, Smith and I might well have been characters in a rerun of "The Untouchables," black-and-white anachronisms in wide-brimmed hats and padded suits. Walter Winchell, speaking in the staccato of a thirties gangster flick, would narrate:

> After they were shut out of Cicero, the mob moved their vice operations into the suburb of Lyons ... Smith sent Caputo to check out a tip that gambling and prostitution were running rampant on Ogden Avenue.

And the show would end with front pages spinning into full-frame close-ups of the headlines:

FIND PROSTITUTION, GAMBLING IN LYONS ... SYNDICATE
PINBALL RACKET IN LYONS ... LEARN LYONS MAYOR INSURES
HOODS' NIGHTCLUBS

Smith gave me another bonus.

The same current. I, too, had a sense of sin. It was not like Smith's Protestant sin, which could be expiated through faith alone, but Catholic sin, dark and baroque, absolved only through confession and penance.

I was no longer a practicing Catholic but remained Catholic in my soul. I was atoning for a sin. I have described it at length in *A Rumor of War*, so I'll just summarize it here. One hot night during my eleventh month in Vietnam, I sent five men on an unauthorized mission to capture two men a villager had identified as Vietcong sappers—booby trap and demolition experts. If the Vietcong caused any trouble, they were to be killed, I said. The patrol went out, shot one VC to death while he lay on his bamboo bed, captured another man, and then executed him with a shotgun when they were halfway back to the platoon's outpost.

Those were the surface facts, but surface facts seldom explain anything. Surface facts cannot tell you that there was murder in my heart that night, that the command to capture was silently counter-manded by an order to kill, delivered in a voiceless, primal language of expression and gesture. The surface facts cannot tell you how we laughed when the patrol returned with the body of the second man, one side of his head shattered by the shotgun blast, how we laughed and kicked the corpse and mocked it, mocked it because there he was at last, the phantom enemy who had shot us from ambush, who had sniped at us from the trees, who had wired the booby traps that blew off our feet and legs and testicles, there he was where he belonged, lying dead at our feet. How easy. Five pounds of trigger pull, a load of double-O buckshot at point-blank range. *Bangyerdead.* We laughed and put our boots to his ribs until I shined a flashlight in his face and saw that he was not one of the VC but the villager who had informed on them. A kid—sixteen years old. The patrol had mistakenly killed the wrong man. I compounded my complicity with an act of moral cowardice: I tried to cover up the horror with a story that the patrol had set an ambush, which the Vietnamese boy had walked into.

The investigation lasted five months. All six of us were charged with murder. One of the men, the one who had fired the shotgun, was court-martialed and acquitted. The charges against the rest of us were dropped. Our military counsels told us we were legally innocent, though I was given a commanding general's letter of reprimand for the attempted cover-up. A letter of reprimand is little more than a judicial scolding. Mine was written in the same stilted boilerplate as medal citations, an official language that means almost nothing, yet each phrase stung like a cat-o'-nine-tails: *compromised your integrity as an officer ... seriously called into question your fitness for future command ... betrayed the trust and confidence reposed in you.*

Oh, in time I partly redeemed myself in Marine Corps eyes. At Camp Lejeune, I demonstrated my fitness by successfully command-ing an infantry training company and left the service with an honor-able discharge. But I was unredeemed in my own eyes and in the eyes of the boy we had butchered. I saw them quite a bit, sometimes in my dreams, sometimes awake and drenched in clammy sweat in the mid-dle of the night, sometimes in broad daylight. I would see the flash-light shining down on that ruined head like the radiance on the head of some martyred saint in a Renaissance painting. I mean the light, not the head—I'd never seen one of those saints with his brains leaking out of a gash in his skull. The eyes weren't saintly either. They would have looked as wide and startled as the eyes of a jacklit deer but for the accusation in them: *I am the man you killed.* The image had a sound track, too: our laughter. Talk about a hyena chorus! I could hear it in my memory but never could have reproduced it with my voice, which was a good thing, because you had to have surrendered to the savage in yourself to laugh like that, and surrendered unconditionally. I'll tell you, it was a laughter that howled straight out of the earliest ages of man.

Whenever I heard it and saw those eyes, I knew the Dark Thing was going to pay me a call. I guess the Dark Thing was a guilt that somehow got twisted into a black anger. *You may be legally innocent,* it would whisper, snuggling up to me, *but you have a helluva debt to pay.* It never told me how, never gave me my penance. In time, I understood why. I had condemned myself, and having done that, it was up to me to forgive myself by making a penance that would necessarily have to be of my own devising.

That explained the nearly fanatical way I fought Tom Smith's crusade against organized crime. In Vietnam, I had fallen in with the Forces of Darkness; now I was enlisted in the Forces of Light. Each ten- or twelve-hour day I worked, each risk I took, all in the name of a social and moral Good, was both a suffering and a joy, a joy because it was suffering. Each became a bead on a metaphorical rosary, though I didn't know how many rosaries I would have to say before those eyes stopped staring into mine and that barbaric laughter fell silent.

Somehow or other, a bit of Calvinism got mixed in with all that Catholic guilt, or, to turn the idea around a little, my guilt was the wellspring of my ambition. I felt I had failed as an officer, betraying not only the "trust and confidence" reposed in me by my commission but my own best image of myself. I desperately wanted to succeed as a journalist, for success would be a sign of grace. And it was a sign of grace whenever I took a chance and got away with it.

The risks were not all that great, nowhere near as great as those taken today by Colombian journalists exposing cocaine kings whose minimum-wage hit men from the scrapwood slums don't give warnings before they empty their Uzis into you. The narco-terrorists of

South America have learned what the political terrorists of the Middle East found out twenty years ago: all the barriers have fallen. You can assassinate anyone, kidnap anyone; you can blow airliners out of the sky, gun down innocent bystanders, set off bombs on crowded streets, and no one will stop you. The world may even respect you, grant you observer status at the United Nations. The Mafia antedated the Age of Terrorism. An Old World concept of honor and the more pragmatic notion that publicity was bad for business restrained its members from harming legitimate newsmen, cops, or judges. If you were straight, they wouldn't touch you, even though in their goriest wet dreams they saw you hanging from a meat hook, twitching from the shock of cattle prods.

But every organization has its rogues.

"The receptionist said you're Mister Caputo. You Mister Caputo?"

Standing beside my desk was a gray-haired man in his middle fifties, with black eyebrows and thick lips that suggested a sensual nature.

"Who're you?"

"You do not recognize me? You been writing all these stories about me and you do not recognize me?"

Both hands were in his jacket pockets.

"You look better than your mug shots."

"You have a sense of humor."

I rejected as melodramatic nonsense the thought that he had a gun in one of the pockets.

"I would like to talk to you. In private."

Smith was not in. We went to his office. I sat on the desk, next to a photograph of Smith's wife and children. Mario DeStefano took one of the chairs, still with both hands in his pockets. Convicted murderer, loan-shark racketeer, hit man, DeStefano was a psychopath with a reputation for working the far edges of the Mafia's field of permissible conduct.

"So what do you want to talk about?" I asked, feigning a certain sangfroid.

"You're young."

"Twenty-seven."

"A boy."

"Did you come here to discuss my age?"

"These stories you've been writing about me, they are not true. But they are not hurting me. This is who they are hurting."

His hand moved inside his pocket.

"My granddaughter made this."

He pulled out a crayon drawing. A house, a tree, a stick figure, a bright-yellow sun.

"She is only six. The other kids in her school make fun of her. Your grandpa's a gangster."

Brutal people are often given to sentimentality, and the fraudulent appeal to my compassion for his granddaughter disgusted me.

"Isn't that what you are, Mario?"

He raised his hand as if swearing an oath.

"On my mother's grave, I am not a syndicate man. I did my time, and I have been legitimate ever since. I run a legitimate business."

"The Bella Rosa pizzeria."

"Right. Best in Cicero."

"What is Leo Manfredi doing there every afternoon?"

"I grew up with Leo. And he is not there every afternoon."

"Every afternoon, just before post time, the Feds watch runners going back and forth between the Bella Rosa and the factories on Cicero Avenue. They're carrying bets and money between you and the bookies you have soliciting in the factories. If some stiff on a punch press can't cover, you'll loan him the money at one hundred percent interest per week, and if he misses an installment, you send Leo to convince him of the virtue of making timely payments."

"The Feds say that? The Feds are persecuting me. They are persecuting all Italian-Americans.

I reminded him that the head of the FBI's organized crime squad in Chicago was Italian-American. *I* was Italian-American.

"Then what is wrong with you, writing these things? This is who you are hurting, a little girl."

He waved the picture in my face.

"I'd say you're the one hurting her."

His eyes went cold and level.

"You think so, hah? You come work for me at the Bella Rosa. See for yourself. Pizzas, that is what you will see. No bookies, no runners, no Leo Manfredis. Pizzas."

"I have a job."

He shoved his hands back into his pockets and shook them. In each, a pile of coins jangled like Christmas bells.

"You come work for me for a month, say. Any shift you want. I will work your tail off, but you'll see. Pizzas."

"Thanks, Mario, but I don't think so."

He jangled the pockets again, making the noise a little louder.

"A month. Talk to your boss. Get him to give you a month off. You come work for me and see."

"I don't think so, Mario."

"It is her you are hurting, not me." His eyes moved to the photograph on the desk, his lips parting in a half smile. "How would you like it if I did something that hurt your family?"

"That's not my family."

"But you have got a family, don't you? What would you do if I did something to hurt them the way you are hurting mine?"

He was building a case to justify doing whatever he had in mind. I could almost hear Aiuppa or some other boss telling him, *Who gave you the green light to hit a reporter?* And DeStefano answering, *The man was a reporter, sure, but he was hurting my family.*

"Good talking to you, Mario."

I moved to the door and showed him the way out.

"You are ruining my life. How would you like it if I ruined yours?"

"Good talking to you."

I was in my car, a Triumph Spitfire, driving back to *The Trib's* offices from the Du Page County Courthouse in Wheaton. Kathy Burns, a new reporter on the staff, was in the passenger seat. She had been covering the courts and had asked me to give her a lift. The area around Wheaton was rural in those days, the road wide open, and I had the sports car up to sixty-five, twenty over the limit. Another car shot past us in the opposite lane.

"He lost a wheel!" Kathy yelled.

It was rolling down the middle of the road, as if it were still attached to the car; then it veered across our path, just long enough for me to see that it was a racing tire, mounted on a wire wheel with a spinner hubcap. I watched it wobble and bounce into a weedy culvert and somehow had the presence of mind not to hit the brakes or jerk the steering wheel. I slowly let up on the gas, easing the car toward the shoulder.

The speedometer dropped to forty, to thirty, to twenty-five. The car lost the momentum that had held it level, its left front end dipping. The needle fell to twenty, to fifteen. The car plowed into the dirt, bumped once, then came to a jarring stop.

My heart was not in my throat but somewhere behind my eyes, drumming like a grouse's wings.

"I thought it was their wheel," Kathy said in an involuntary whisper. There was no color in her face.

We climbed out. The axle was buried two or three inches, and I thanked my luck, God, and anything else that needed thanking that I had been speeding. That had kept us on an even keel long enough for me to slow down and pull over. If I had been going at the limit or slower, the axle would have pitched into the pavement and we would have flipped.

"How did that happen?" Kathy asked.

"Don't know. Wait here."

I walked back fifty yards or so, found the wheel in the ditch, and checked the spinner cap. They had been crude about it, using a hammer they had not bothered to wrap in a towel or cloth to conceal the dents it would make in the cast-aluminum cap. Maybe, in case I survived the wreck, they wanted me to see the dents, which spoke volumes. Not a bad idea, though—quicker and easier than other methods of arranging accidents, like draining brake fluid.

I rolled the wheel back to the car and broke out the jack and the rubber mallet used to tighten the cap.

"Let's hope we didn't bend the axle or the frame."

"I can't figure out how that happened."

"Spinner cap worked loose somehow."

I looked up and saw she did not believe me. Kathy was new but had been at the paper long enough to have heard about Mario DeStefano's visit some weeks before.

"It happens sometimes," I said, seeing no sense in alarming her further by confirming her suspicions. I jacked up the car and remounted the wheel, then drove off, more exhilarated than frightened by the close call. It had been another sign of grace. I could not be harmed because I was a soldier in the Forces of Light, with a special destiny.

DISASTERS OF WAR

The road was empty, sticky asphalt shimmering in the heat so that the shell casings, the empty ammo cans, the fragments of concertina wire, the helmets and canvas bandoliers thrown away in the retreat looked like trash floating in a stagnant, black canal. The road led down a gentle hill and through some rice paddies into a village, where, a little over a quarter of a mile away, the North Vietnamese were dug in. The South Vietnamese were shelling the village. An artillery spotter, crouched in a foxhole atop the hill, looked through binoculars and gave fire-correction orders to his radioman, who called them into the battery in a quick, too excited voice. Left so many meters. Drop so many. Fire for effect. Add so many meters. Repeat fire for effect. In a short while, no one on the hill could see the village for the smoke and dust. Sometimes a shell's shock wave tore an opening in the cloud, and the skeleton of a house, a patch of roof, or a clump of palm trees with shorn leaves showed for a moment or two before the smoke and dust closed in again.

It was through one of the momentary openings that the American photographers on the hill, squinting into their telephoto lenses, saw the two boys on the bicycle. The smaller one rode on the handlebars while the bigger boy pedaled in a strange way. He pushed the pedals two or three times with one foot, jumped off to walk the bike with an odd, hopping gait, got back on, pedaled a short distance more, and then jumped off to walk the bike again, hopping like a bird. The Americans watched for several seconds, marveling that anyone would try to get through such intense fire on a bicycle.

A shell burst, and the two boys vanished in the smoke, and one of the Americans said, "Well, I guess that's that." None of them made any moral judgments. Behind the hill were a company of Rangers, waiting in armored personnel carriers. As soon as the artillery lifted, they were going to try, once again, to retake the village. The Rangers needed the artillery to soften up the North Vietnamese, who had beat them back earlier in the day. So the Americans did not judge or condemn the spotter for continuing to call in fire.

"Holy shit!" said the same photographer who had earlier said, "Well, I guess that's that." The two boys had reappeared, the small one still on the handlebars, the other still pedaling one minute, walking the next with his funny little hop. They made it to the edge of the village and then were on the road.

Someone wondered out loud why the bigger kid did not pedal as fast as he could, why he kept jumping on and off the bike. Three or four shells ripped through the air, with a sound like a knife slicing through taut canvas, and exploded in the paddy fields at the edge of the village. They threw mud and water and more smoke across the road, and the Americans saw the bigger boy fall hard, the bike and the smaller kid falling on top of him. "That's that this time," the Americans all said. "For sure this time." A few seconds later, the boys were back up on their bicycle. The Americans started to cheer. "C'mon, kid! Pedal that sucker! C'mon, c'mon, you can do it! Attaway!" they yelled and cheered because they were in a war that offered few triumphs and even fewer reasons to cheer. Behind them, the armored personnel carriers were grinding slowly forward in a squeal and clatter of metal treads. The spotter called in a barrage to cover the advance. Fire for effect. The shells exploded almost as one, in a line all along the edge of the village. It looked like the eruption of a vast geyser and the boys vanished again, but the Americans knew they had survived even before they saw them emerge from the pall of dust and smoke.

They were coming up the hill now, well out of danger. The small boy had got off the handlebars because the incline made it hard for the other boy to push the bike. He pushed it steadily up the hill, hippety-hopping. One of the photographers raised his long lens to his eye.

"He's just got one leg!" he shouted.

Sure enough, the boy's right trouser leg was flapping like a ribbon in a wind. The Americans cheered louder.

They cheered and cheered, and when the boys finally made it to the top of the hill, they crowded around the one with the missing leg, slapping him on the back, shaking his hand. They patted him and the small boy up and down, checking for wounds.

"Not a scratch on 'em. Not a mark. Charmed, man, in a major way," a photographer said.

He and the others continued to touch the boys' arms and backs and faces, as if hoping some of that grace would rub off on them.

They asked the older one when and how he had lost his leg, but he did not understand them. They asked how far he had come. He didn't understand that either. All he said was, "Di-di Say-gone," meaning that he was going to Saigon, where, for now, there was no war. He laughed hysterically while the other boy just stared, in the way children do when they have been so afraid for so long they don't know how to be any other way.

The APCs were clanking down the road, crushing the helmets, flattening the ammo cans left behind in the morning's failed attack. The spotter was shifting the barrage backward in hundred-meter increments. Drop one-zero-zero. Fire for effect. The one-legged boy picked up his bike. "Di-di Say-gone," he said again. Saigon was over forty kilometers away. He threw his good leg over the seat and, giving the pedal one quick turn, coasted down the back of the hill with the smaller boy perched on the handlebars. One of the Americans said it was a damned shame it could not be downhill all the way.

"Kid earned it, y'know? Just coast the whole rest of the way."

"The whole rest of his life," said another.

Then they turned and, raising their binoculars and long-lens cameras, went back to watching the war.

THREE

The Desert

We were driving across the top of Sinai, along the road between El Arîsh and Suez, a saltwater sea to the north, an arid sea to the south, its dunes peaked or rising in long, curved ridges, still against the sky, like breakers arrested the instant before they curl and crash against the shore. I had been staring at that unpeopled desolation for a long time when he suddenly materialized, as if he had been exhaled by the desert. Mounted on a camel, he was riding along the crest of some dunes only a hundred yards away. A baggage camel carrying wooden poles and hide tents plodded behind him, amid a flock of goats that hung on its flanks and rear, like a fleet of small craft escorting a cumbersome ship into port. A couple of shrouded women and several children followed the goats on foot.

"Bedouin," said Elias, the driver and escort the Israeli army had assigned me. "You would like to take a photograph?"

He pulled over, and I got out with my camera. In the past month, on assignment in Israel and its Occupied Territories, I had met Arab peasants on the West Bank, Arab refugees in Gaza's squalid camps, Arab lawyers, merchants, and politicians in the bazaars of Nablus and East Jerusalem, but of the legendary nomads who had spread Muhammad's faith from Spain to Samarkand, I had seen nothing until now. As I focused and fumbled with the speed and shutter settings, the bedouin reined in and turned to face us. He was probably curious about who we were and what we were doing, but it was as if he were posing for the shot. He looked mythic against the backdrop of sand and sky, and I was thrilled, too far away to see the flies that probably made a whining halo around his head or to hear the hack of the tuberculosis that probably inflamed his lungs. I snapped a frame or two before he rode slowly away, vanishing over the dune with goats and wives and children, but he had captured my imagination in a way the Palestinians and the Israelis had not, could not.

It was early in 1973, and I was suffering from informational shell shock, stunned by a monthlong bombardment of data, facts, and arguments. Israeli officials like Jerusalem's mayor, Teddy Kollek (a stocky *mensch*, with the moxie of the professional pol, he could have been a ward boss in Mayor Daley's Chicago machine), had battered me with statistics purporting that the annexation of Arab East Jerusalem was good for the Arabs—more indoor plumbing, more jobs at higher wages, an improved diet and medical care and sanitation. Kollek said Jerusalem had the potential to become another Belfast, but he had studied the situation in Belfast and had concluded that if the Protestants had given the Catholics a bigger slice of the welfare-state pie, the British would not have needed to send paratroopers to Northern Ireland. He was not going to make the same mistake but would make sure the Arabs got a better life, a fair deal. I was there to listen and take notes, not offer opinions, so I refrained from telling Kollek that I heard in his philosophy an echo of those Yankee Rotarian nation builders in Vietnam—all we gotta do is show these people how to dig a good communal latrine and give 'em some chemical fertilizer to increase their yield and maybe set up a dispensary and they'll tell the Vietcong to go to hell. It was no use to tell the nation builder, All due respect, sir, but these people don't want latrines and fertilizer and dispensaries, what they want is to see our white Yankee faces out of here forever. Likewise, it was no good to tell Kollek that the Palestinians did not want flush toilets and TV sets but citizenship in a land of their own. They wanted an Arab East Jerusalem with an Arab mayor.

In Nablus, the center of Palestinian resistance, a PLO sympathizer, over cups of Turkish coffee served in his dim parlor, discoursed with angry eloquence against the injustices of Israeli rule, conveniently forgetting that the Israelis would not have been there if Jordan's

King Hussein had not launched his Arab Legion from the West Bank in the '67 war. He shook his fist, shouted impotent slogans about self-determination, and painted lurid pictures of the great jihad that would one day push the Jews into the Mediterranean.

The refugees were quieter and more poignant because their grievances were more authentic. There was something both pathetic and unsettling about the way they clung to their UN refugee cards—their claim tickets to lost lands that would be restored to them when (next year, ten years from now, a hundred, a thousand) the great jihad swept the Jews into the sea. I filled a notebook with their tales of eviction and exile, their accounts of the idyllic, fruitful lives they claimed to have led before the Israelis seized their farms and villages during the Israeli war of independence. Though the Arabs had started the war, the refugees' stories were heartbreaking. Yet I caught the ring of falsehood in some of them. They were not deliberately lying to me so much as unconsciously lying to themselves about their old lives. Over the years in the dreary camps, they had transformed memory into myth, their selective recollections making of their former homelands a paradise that, probably, had never existed. It certainly did not exist now. The villages had become Israeli suburbs; factories smoked where oranges and olives once had grown. The refugees would not recognize their lost Eden even if every tree and field were exactly as they had left it, for the pastures could not be as verdant, the orchards as bountiful, the waters half as clear and sweet as those that bloomed and flowed in that part of their minds where memories and dreams converged.

And all those voices, of Israeli and Palestinian alike, had been the voices of people entrapped by history as old as the Old Testament. Listening to them had been instructive, at times exciting—I was just thirty-one years old and on my first major foreign assignment—but ultimately confusing. In my room at the American Colony hotel in East Jerusalem, I would read over my notes and try to make sense of it all. Sometimes I would hear a figurative Jew shouting in one ear while a figurative Arab yelled in the other and would feel tempted to wish a plague on both their houses, the children of Isaac and Ishmael. So I decided to go into the Sinai, ostensibly for a story on Israel's Suez Canal defenses but really to mute those contentious voices and listen for a while to the vast silences of the desert. I think that is why the bedouin took hold of my imagination. He did not ride up to us and begin making speeches. He seemed to possess a wisdom that needed no words. He was outside of history, outside of time itself, like the desert. I wondered what his wandering life was like and promised myself to find out first chance I got.

Maybe I identified with him. I had become a bedouin myself, one who rode commercial airliners instead of camels.

It had started with an accidental meeting at a bus stop on one of those August days when Chicago steams like Rangoon. I left Tribune Tower intending to walk to the Elevated station for the ride to Oak Park, where Jill and I rented an attic flat. Walk to the El, ride to the Ridgeland Avenue stop, walk another five blocks home, eat dinner, read or watch television, help Jill, my wife of two years, put our infant son, Geoffrey, to bed. That was my routine after work. Now and then, when my wife and son were asleep, I went to the kitchen and tried to make some headway on *A Rumor of War.* I was in a rut, but a happy rut. Work provided enough adventure.

I had moved up to the city room from the suburbs in 1969. After a little more than a year on general assignment, covering the police beats, fires, and such sixties-era mayhem as antiwar demonstrations and a shoot-out between police and the Black Panthers, I was picked to join the paper's newly formed Task Force, a team of investigative reporters. There were four of us: Bill Jones, who led the team; Bill Currie, who had covered the invasion of Cambodia earlier that year; Pamela Zekman, just twenty-five years old but brilliant and driven; and, finally, myself, not as driven as Zekman but driven by the old demons of guilt and ambition.

Clayton Kirkpatrick, an innovative man who had replaced the paleolithic William Maxwell as editor and who had wrenched the *Tribune* out of the Stone Age in two years, conceived of the Task Force and gave it its mission: in-depth investigations of the city's social and racial problems, as well as its political corruption (and corruption in Chicago was a Comstock Lode for a reporter). We were released from hourly and daily deadlines, could take as long as we needed to pin down a story.

We were the glamour kids of the city room (Jones was the only one over thirty, and he was thirty-three), the envy of the staff. Our first series broke in early 1971—an exposé of the hideous conditions in Cook County nursing homes. TELL NURSING HOME ABUSES, the first headline thundered. SOME ELDERLY PREFER DEATH.

We got the story by working undercover as maintenance men and nurses' aides. Currie even managed to land a job as the *administrator* of one nursing home in a South Side slum. I got a deeper inside look by spending twenty-four hours in a home, posing as a mental patient (the usual jokes afterward about typecasting), who had to be kept overnight while his family—Zekman and Jones posing as a married couple—went out of town for a funeral.

Story after story filled the front pages for ten days: of old people beaten and neglected by callous staffs, strapped to their beds for days because the homes received higher Medicare payments for patients with bedsores.

In the following months, we fired salvos at the criminal courts system in Cook County; at crooked real estate brokers, subverting the fair housing laws to block-bust all-white neighborhoods; at the city's hospitals and blood banks for peddling tainted blood drawn from the arms of skid-row drunks and drug addicts. In a series on gun control, we took on the most formidable lobby in the country, the National Rifle Association.

It was heady stuff, muckraking journalism in the two-fisted, red-blooded style of Upton Sinclair and Lincoln Steffens. We were all young and passionately committed children of the sixties, with social consciences and low thresholds of outrage. We wanted to change things for the better, and that's what we were doing. We didn't mind, though, the more vulgar rewards that accrued: prizes, bonuses, and raises.

In the summer, we began our grand effort: an investigation of how the Daley machine got out the vote. The 1972 elections were coming up in the fall, and we intended to show that the electoral process in Cook County was a sham, about as free and honest as elections in a banana republic. The investigation would take five months. It would lead to the biggest exposé of vote fraud Chicago, or any other city, had ever seen, bring a blizzard of indictments, and win the Task Force a Pulitzer Prize.

We were three months into it on that broiling afternoon when I left the city room for home. Bill Currie and I, working undercover as vote canvassers, had spent all day pounding the streets to document what everyone in Chicago knew but had never proven: thousands of loyal Daley Democrats lived in cemeteries and vacant lots. Having done enough walking in the ninety-plus heat, I decided to take an air-conditioned bus to the Elevated station. Jim Yuenger, the foreign editor, was waiting at the stop, his tie pulled down, his suit jacket hooked over his shoulder.

Looking back with the creativity of hindsight, I now see that it wasn't Yuenger at all but that masculine siren, the crafty Oneway Ticket. Oneway must have been upset with me. I was a little too happy and settled to suit him. It was time to shake things up.

After an exchange of small talk, Yuenger-Oneway, in the most casual, offhanded tone, mentioned that Mike McGuire, the Rome bureau chief, was being transferred to Moscow in the fall.

"So we're going to have a bureau open," he continued. "You still interested in going overseas?"

I do not recall what I said, and for some reason my imagination fails me as much as memory; I can't make up what I might have said. All I can recall, or imagine I do, is the way the sunlight glinted off the microscopic particles of glass in the concrete, making Michigan Boulevard blaze as if it had been inlaid with ten million tiny rhinestones. I hear, though I can't be sure if this is also fanciful, Yuenger-Oneway telling me to talk things over with Jill. The Rome bureau chief was a roving correspondent who covered everything from the Strait of Gibraltar to the Persian Gulf. I could expect to be on the road six to nine months a year, and my wife might object to that.

Roving correspondent—Oneway knew which buttons to press, he was a regular aluminum-siding salesman. As the bus pulled up, the doors opening with a wheeze, he said, "Well, if it's okay with Jill and you want the job, you've got it."

Memory continues to fail. I can't be sure what my thoughts and emotions were as I rode homeward on the El. The car must have been crowded—it was rush hour—and rank with sweating bodies pressed into an unwanted intimacy. I see, in my imagination, a collage of gray commuters' faces with empty, exhausted stares and picture a grin stealing across my face, the sly grin of a truant schoolboy. *They're going to have to do this the rest of their lives, but I'll be escaping it. Rome bureau chief. Roving correspondent.* Imagination's eye also shows me the west side slums through which the rumbling train bears its passengers on tracks fifty feet above the street, the cars' windows level with the boarded or broken windows of tenements. The train passes factories and warehouses, abandoned relics heavy with the iron history of smokestack capitalism, walls smeared with street-gang graffiti.

The next image is of North Elmwood Avenue, the street where we lived: frame Victorians gazing with middle-class gentility across the lawns, planes of sunlight, like sheets of amber glass, angling through the tall trees that gave Oak Park its name. Usually, I enjoyed strolling up Elmwood after the stink and jostle of the El. I may have enjoyed it on that afternoon. I don't remember, but the Philip Caputo in my imagination sees the houses as dull and smug, the tree-lined street as a benign illusion, like a Norman Rockwell cover. It occurs to him that in many parts of late-twentieth-century America, the choice is between the horrors of the inner city and the suburbs' "drowse of the accustomed." But in Rome ...

He climbs the stairs to the top-floor flat, afraid his wife will offer powerful objections to moving abroad with a small child and another baby on the way, to her husband's taking a job that will keep him away at least half the year. He is afraid because he's too restless and too selfish to let this chance pass. He knows he'll go without her if he has to.

Now memory returns.

I told Jill after dinner, as we sipped coffee at the big round table in the dining room, the day's last glimmers pressing through the skylight to tint her blond hair a coppery red.

Jill had grown up in Oak Park, had gone to high school there and to college in neighboring River Forest. But she shared with me an itchy foot, a curiosity about the world. When she was a young girl, she wrote to travel agencies asking for brochures, which she stared at for hours, dreaming of seeing distant places. She didn't get her chance until after she'd taken her master's degree. The Defense Department hired her as a teacher for its overseas-dependent schools and sent her to an air force base in England, where she taught elementary English and ran the school library. She explored London on weekends, roamed the English countryside on school vacations. When her nine-month contract ended, she crossed the Channel, bought a Volkswagen in Germany, and spent the next three months on her own grand tour of Europe, traveling from Norway to Italy, Austria to France. It had been the one great adventure of her life, and she often spoke wistfully about the fun and freedom of it. Her wanderer's spirit was one of the things that had drawn me to her, but now she seemed to relish our settled life. We had been house hunting on weekends because the flat would be too small once the second baby arrived. We were on our way to becoming a married couple with a capital "M."

After I'd given her the details of Yuenger's offer, I braced for an argument. When, instead of objecting, she threw her hands over her head and exclaimed, "Thank God, we're saved!" I was thrown off balance, like a man shouldering into what he thinks is a bolted door only to have it swing wide open.

"Saved?"

"All those weekends we've been house hunting? Do you know what I was thinking? 'Now he'll go to work every day and I'll take care of the children, and we'll just live the way everyone else does.'"

"Thought that's what you wanted."

"The last thing. Call Jim now and tell him you'll take the job before he changes his mind."

I did, thinking how odd it was to be married to a woman for two years, convinced I knew her every thought and wish, and end up completely wrong.

We hired a language tutor (the only Italian I knew was a few words of the Calabrian dialect spoken by my maternal grandparents) and left the States in September.

We did not live in the heart of Rome, but above it, on Monte Mario. The *Tribune* rented a spacious apartment there for its correspondents, in a new building that had somehow escaped the ugliness of mass man and his mass modern architecture. It was near the steep, winding Via Trionfale, down which Caesars returning from Gallic victories rode into the city, surrounded by their legions. I followed the same route to work every morning less augustly—on a crowded bus surrounded by legions of Fiats and motorbikes. From my stop on the Via del Corso a short walk past the Trevi Fountain brought me to the *Tribune*'s bureau, which was in an ocher-walled building on the Via della Dataria. Once a Vatican palazzo, it had been bought by ANSA, the Italian news agency, and stood below the Quirinal, highest of the seven hills, where the Fountain of the Dioscuri splashed and six-foot guardsmen in knee-length boots rode their horses to the Presidential Palace, the plumes on their polished steel helmets tossing.

At first it seemed odd—delightfully odd—to pass such sights on my way to work every day. The Trevi and the Quirinal weren't all. In the course of a working day, I might take in St. Peter's Square, the Forum, the Coliseum, or the Baths of Caracalla, have lunch at a four-star restaurant like Al Moro or Il Buco, and then, on my way to an interview, pass through the Borghese Gardens, or walk by the Pantheon, or see enough Renaissance statuary to make an art historian dizzy.

I'm getting paid to be here! It was downright sinful. My American work-ethic conscience told me that commuting was supposed to be a necessary ordeal, not a tour of sights the average traveler might spend his life savings to see. But Rome's greatest charm was the way it wove the threads of the present into the tapestry of the past, juxtaposed the ordinary and the exceptional. Because its great art and architecture were not in a museum but a part of the city's daily life, it became commonplace, while the commonplace, because it was set against such an astonishing background, became extraordinary. I might see a vendor selling ice cream from a cart in the shadow of Trajan's Column or teenagers necking on the steps of the Pantheon, its pillars and dome, which once arched over sculptures of emperors and gods, elevating the lovers' banal caresses into the embraces of a grand passion. Rome was a constant escape from the everyday.

But it was also the capital of a foreign correspondent's wasteland. Covering Italy was a little like covering Canada or Zaire: things happened, but they didn't mean much. The Italians, who had seen so much history, took a long, happy walk to history's margins after World War II. Content to be junior partners in the Common Market, citizens of a third-rate military power, they had said good-bye to the dictators and the revolutionaries, with their visions of utopias and of building new Roman empires. Sometimes the country seemed an example of the warning (I think it was Rilke's) to beware casting out your devils because you might expel your angels with them. The Mussolinis were gone, but so were the Garibaldis, replaced by a succession of clerkish premiers whose coalition governments rose and fell, on average, every nine months. Because the governments collapsed over squabbles among the politicians, not conditions in the country, it seldom made any difference which one was in power. Italy ran just as inefficiently under the center-right as under the center-left. Few paid a lot of attention, least of all the Romans.

Other Italians called them *menefreghisti Romani*—I-don't-care Romans. The politicians played musical chairs, and the Romans went to their jobs and shops and markets; they filled the streets and side-walk cafés in the evenings, sipping espressi; they strolled hand in hand through the Piazza Navona, where street artists painted beside Bernini's Fountain of the Four Rivers; they cheated on their wives; they ate fusilli arrabbiata in the trattorias of Trastevere; they called each other *stronzo* or *cretino* in traffic jams; they clung to the straps of the buses reading in folded copies of *Il Messaggero* stories about the latest Mafia vendetta in Sicily or Calabria; in August, they drove their little Fiat *cinquecenti*—the Ford of Italy, within the means of the humblest laborer—to the seashore on vacation; they cheated on their husbands; they cheered their soccer teams and, if the team won, drove their *cinquecenti* through the streets, waving banners from the windows and shouting so joyously a stranger might have thought they were celebrating a victory in war; they went into the army but did not go to war; Communists marched now and then to protest one thing or another, banging little tin drums and singing the Italian party's stirring anthem, the *"Bandiera Rossa,"* but that was all they did. If they worked for the Anagrafe—the repository of civic records—they recorded births, deaths, and marriages in cloth-bound ledgers, and the recording went on, as regular as the cycles of nature, no matter who sat in the Presidential Palace on the Quirinal Hill where the Fountain of the Dioscuri splashed and the plumed guards-men rode, wearing sabers that needed no sharpening.

Now and then, representatives from the Age of Terrorism—usu-ally young crazies from the Red Brigades or the maniac fringes of the Fascist party (it was still around, dreaming dark dreams of a new *il duce* who would make the trains run on time)—broke the torpor by setting off a bomb or shooting a policeman or kidnapping someone of note. They dressed up their crimes as actions taken to combat some injustice or conspiracy (which was always a creation of their fevered imagina-tions), but their real purpose was to relieve boredom. *Enough of this bourgeoisie happiness,* was the subtext to the statements and ransom demands they phoned into the wire services. *Enough of these cheap Fiats for the proletariat, enough vacations, enough of these monotonous, benign governments.* Basta! *Let's get back into history.* How do I know this? Because there is a spiritual kinship between the terrorist and the journalist: both are incapable of coping with normality.

So after Christmas 1972 I went to the Middle East, which was interesting because hate and conflict are always interesting. The Middle East—so mired in history no one knew how to pull it out. After a week in Cairo and another in Amman, I crossed the Allenby Bridge into the occupied West Bank, then drove to East Jerusalem.

The American Colony hotel, a wonderful old place, once the palace of an Ottoman bey, was my base camp for the next two weeks, as I ranged out to the refugee camps and the West Bank towns with Israel Stockman. He was a bearish man in his late thirties, with a head and a chest full of rust-red hair that curled like the shavings of scrap iron and pale eyes that twinkled with irony one moment but turned hard and flat as buttons the next. I had met him through Charlie Weiss, the Voice of America correspondent in Jerusalem and also a *Tribune* stringer. Stockman was something of an enigma. He lived in Ramallah, an Arab suburb of Jerusalem, spoke several Arabic dialects as well as Farsi, and knew the Koran better than he did the Torah; yet he was a Jew, born to German and Russian kibbutzniks who had come to Palestine with the early Zionist settlers. He had an aura of mystery, which he cultivated by revealing as little as possible about himself. No one knew exactly what he did for a living. He had once been a professor of Arabic studies at Tel Aviv University but was now, he said, on leave to make a study of West Bank Arabs, among whom he had become a familiar sight, shambling down dusty streets in his rumpled khaki trousers and leather sandals or chatting with farmers and shepherds in the shade of olive groves. The press corps in Jerusalem had him pegged as a deep-cover agent of the Mossad, but I could not get a fix on him. Unlike most Israelis, who wore their emotions and opinions on their sleeves, Stockman kept his to himself. Sometimes he seemed scornful of his own society, jeering the new émigrés from Russia and Europe as "condominium Zionists" because the government was housing them in apartments beyond the reach of Sephardic and Palestinian Jews like himself; but he was equally contemptuous of the Arabs, whom he saw as hopelessly fractious and backward. Nor was he above the bigot's stereotyping. "Ha! look at him," he said one day as we passed a man shepherding his flock to pasture. "Do you know why anthrax is endemic among those men? Because they fuck their goats and then they fuck each other!" The closest he came to revealing his true feelings was on an afternoon while we sat in a field interviewing a farmer over a lunch of olives, pita, and hummos. In the midst of the conversation the farmer's son came running across the field hollering, "Stockman! Stockman!" He handed Stockman a worn gold coin he had found in a new-plowed furrow.

"Look at this," Stockman exclaimed. It was hexagonal, with a Hebrew inscription on one side, Roman numerals on the other.

Stockman translated the writing. The Jewish coin had been minted during the reign of Vespasian. He held the origins of the Middle East conflict between his thumb and forefinger. Might as well trace it back to the burning of the temple by Titus's legions, the beginning of the Jewish diaspora.

"Do you know what this means to me? It means I have my place here. I have a *right* to be here, as a Jew. It doesn't mean I have a right to kick this man off his land, but I do have my place here."

Magari, I thought. Would that it were. Would that the Arabs see the boy's discovery of the coin as proof Stockman had his place in Palestine. Would that the Israelis could see their belonging did not have to mean a diaspora for the Palestinians. But not far away, in the Kidron Valley, they were bulldozing Arab houses to make room for apartment buildings for Soviet immigrants.

I filed a four-part series on the West Bank and returned to Rome, anxious to be home after six weeks away, anxious also because Jill's pregnancy was nearing term. The baby arrived on February 12, and we christened him Marc Antonio in St. Peter's basilica.

I returned to my Rome routine: combing the newspapers in the morning for a lead, writing features to make up for the lack of hard news. The series got quite a response. Tearsheets of letters to the editor arrived in the mail. Those condemning me as pro-Zionist roughly equaled those accusing me of being pro-Arab. There was something to the charge of a pro-Arab bias. It wasn't that I found the merits of their cause greater; instead, I found them exotic and more fascinating than the Israelis. In Tel Aviv, I had often felt that I was in a Jewish neighborhood in New York or Chicago, but on the West Bank or in Old Jerusalem, where men in kaffiyehs sipped Turkish coffee in the shops near the Damascus Gate and the muezzins wailed and moaned from the Mosque of Omar, I felt very much abroad. The Israelis spoke English as a second language, some with a Brooklyn accent, the Arabs a strange, lyrical tongue hypnotic in its rhythms, its most banal greetings rolling from the lips like poetry: *Sabâh ilkhair´ kifhâlak? Quois, alhamdíllah.*

The Israelis were Here, but the Arabs were There, and the most There of them all were the bedouin. In April of that year, I went into the Sinai to find them.

The Sinai, jabbing like a spearhead between the Great Arabian desert of Egypt and the Negev of Israel, the waste-howling wilderness where the biblical Hebrews wandered and Moses received the Ten Commandments. The pharaoh's chariots had crossed it to the Battle of Megiddo (we call that place Armageddon), and Nasser's tanks had crossed into it in 1967, intending to sweep the Jews out of Palestine. You could not see the chariots, sunk beneath the oceans of sand, but the tanks, trucks, and armored personnel carriers were still above-ground in the Jidi and Mitla passes, all their hard proud steel twisted and whorled, so that the passes looked like galleries in an open-air museum of postmodern sculpture. One day all of that would be buried, too, would become part of the desert's invisible history.

The Jidi and the Mitla were in the north. Israel Stockman, Charlie Weiss, and I were going into the mountains in the south. Stockman, who wanted a chance to study the bedouin, would be the expedition's interpreter, of the language as well as the nomads' customs. Weiss would take pictures, and I would pay the costs or, rather, the *Tribune* would. We were going to the mountains because the recent wars had not touched them. The last desert ibex in the Middle East were there, and the last Sinai leopards, and the last of the pure bedouin. All would be gone soon; if the war had not touched the mountains, the Israeli occupation had. Graders and bulldozers were turning the wadis into roads for four-wheel-drive vehicles, irrigation engineers laying pipe in the big oases, encouraging the nomads to settle down to farming. It was sad. The only bedouin who kept the old, wild, warlike spirit were the hashish smugglers, whose camels trekked the stuff down secret mountain trails to the Gulfs of Suez and Aqaba.

Stockman had drawn up our itinerary: two days to drive by four-wheel from Jerusalem to Wad el-Tur, on the Gulf of Suez; there we would hire camels and drivers for the trip into the mountains by way of Wadi Hibran, one of the few that could still be traversed only on foot or camelback. If we did not find any uncorrupted bedouin there, we weren't going to find them anywhere in Sinai.

There were none at Dahab oasis, our first night's camp. The landscape was Scheherazade's Arabia. Eastward, date palms crackled in a wind off the dark-blue Gulf of Aqaba, across which the high dunes of the Saudi Arabian coast were the color of burnt butter in the lowering sun; westward, the Sinai mountains rose, barren as volcanoes on a dead planet, the clear air showing their every crease and fissure in stark relief. The bedouin encampment was not so picturesque. The nomads had exchanged their goat-hair tents for shacks built of driftwood and cast-off lumber, some roofed with palm thatch, some with rusting corrugated tin. The place resembled a Latin American slum. Four or five wretched-looking men squatted around a campfire. We parked the jeep and walked up to them, Stockman in the lead, the wind-whipped lengths of his hair like flames leaping from his head.

An old man stood up. He had a face as dark and wrinkled as a dried date and was dressed, like the others, in a filthy gelibya, over which he wore a threadbare suitcoat. Rubber shower clogs did for sandals. He reminded me of photographs of Indians in the frontier's twilight, buckskins and feathered bonnets cast aside for Indian agency flannel shirts and secondhand ten-gallon hats.

"Salaam aleikum—peace be unto you," the old man said.

"Wa aleikum as-salaam," Stockman replied with flawless pronunciation. "And unto you, peace."

The old man shuffled into one of the shanties and came out with a tattered carpet, which he laid next to the fire. We sat down, instructed by Stockman not to show the soles of our feet.

"That's an insult to bedouin," he explained. "Although I don't think it would bother these fellows. They're degenerate."

We sat in uncomfortable silence for a few minutes, our bellies rumbling. We were traveling light. Each of us had brought a sleeping bag and a two-gallon canteen but no rations. We'd expected to be fed because hospitality is an important bedouin virtue—a host would be offended by guests who ate their own food and drank their own coffee or tea. But these bedouin had long forgotten the rules of desert etiquette.

"Pardon me, O hosts," Stockman said, reminding them of their manners. "But may we have some coffee?"

The old man tried to put the best face on the breach of custom. He made excuses, fussily inquired about our health, and finally dispatched one of the others to make coffee. It came in a long, thin, brass pot and was poured into little cups without handles. After we had drunk the customary three cups, we were brought to the encampment's guest "tent"—a shack cobbled together out of driftwood logs, with a small window with a crude counter nailed beneath it. Inside, thatch mats covered the dirt floor and a big soft-drink cooler stood braced against a wall like a household god. Our hosts, it turned out, were M'zina tribesmen who had come out of the mountains to settle in Dahab after the Israelis began to run tourists into the desert in air-conditioned buses. Dahab oasis had become a stopover, a tourist trap, and the guest tent a beach house, from which the M'zina peddled soft drinks to thirsty sunbathers. It was easier than herding goats in hundred-degree heat.

We spread out sleeping bags as the old man lit a couple of kerosene lamps. He and the others sat down and struck up a game of gin rummy. While they played, they complained that Sheikh Abreik, ruler of Sinai, had failed to make a fair distribution of the monthly welfare payments of food and clothing the Israeli government gave to the various tribes. Stockman was incensed.

"A bedouin is supposed to amuse his guests, not play cards and complain. They're degenerate, absolutely degenerated from the contact with foreigners, with tourists. God, isn't there someplace in the world that's safe from tourists?"

He interrupted the card game, asking if anyone knew "The Lemon Is Bitter, but the Date Is Sweet," an ancient song as familiar to bedouin as "Oh Susanna" is to Americans.

One of the M'zina, a man who looked to be in his twenties, reached behind the soda cooler and pulled out a homemade, three-string harp. He braced it on his knee, strummed a few bars, and began to sing, as halting and self-conscious as a kid soloing at a school recital. He hadn't sung half a dozen words before he stopped. He could not remember the tune or the lyrics and passed the harp to the old man, who gave it a try. He couldn't remember either, so Stockman asked for the harp, and amazed everyone by singing the song all the way through.

"How do you like that?" he said with a nasty laugh, his eyes taking on their button-hard look. "I, a Jew, am the only one who knows their song."

The young man stashed the harp behind the cooler and then took out the chief artifact of the Global Village—a transistor radio. He tuned it to a popular music station in Cairo.

I checked my sleeping bag for scorpions and lay down. Outside, the date palm scratched in the wind, the surf struck the beach and withdrew with a sound like a breath, like a sigh. A love song moaned on the transistor. The old man slapped his cards on the mat.

"Gin!" he said in English.

"What do you think?" Stockman asked me.

"It's not what I expected."

We made Sharm el-Sheikh, near the tip of Sinai, before noon the next day. The storm started about an hour later. At first, it showed as a thin band on the horizon, as if someone had drawn a bead of brown joint compound between the weld of sky and desert. In less than ten minutes it grew into an immense, onrushing cloud, and the black line of the road, which we had been able to see for miles ahead, grew shorter and shorter until only a few hundred yards of it were visible.

"Roll up the windows, Young Winston." Stockman called me that for the wide-brimmed hat I wore; it reminded him of the one Churchill wore in his correspondent days.

I said we had better switch the wheels to four-wheel drive in case the sandstorm ran us off the road. Stockman got out on his side, I on mine, and it struck while we were turning the hubcaps. A million particles of sand smacked into us like birdshot. We jumped back into the jeep. The road was gone now. I drove slowly, gripping the steering wheel against the buffet of gale winds. When I could no longer see past the hood, I stopped. We were going to have to wait it out. The wind, now almost at hurricane force, shrieked and roared. Sand smashed against the windshield; pebbles the size of marbles pinged against the doors and hood, and the storm discovered cracks and openings we could not have seen with a magnifying glass. In a quarter of an hour, the inside of the jeep was as misty as a steam room, except that the mist was an ashen beige.

"Holy Christ, this is something!" I shouted over the noise.

"This? It's nothing compared to a real sandstorm. Some of them go on for days."

"What if we get caught in one of these when we're out there on camelback?"

"You make for the lee side of a dune or a hill and sit it out."

"And if there isn't a hill or a dune?"

"You kneel the camel and get on the lee side of it, and hope you are not both buried."

"Now just where and how, Israel, did you acquire this knowledge of desert craft?" Weiss asked from the back seat.

Whenever he was displeased, angry, or annoyed, Stockman crinkled up his nose, as if against a foul smell, and that was his expression as he turned and looked at Charlie through the dry khaki fog.

"In the Negev, when I was just a boy of twelve. Nineteen forty-seven, before independence, before *you* came here."

Stockman was establishing his sabra credentials. Sabras, named after a prickly cactus, are native-born Israelis, and they generally consider themselves superior to immigrants. The American-born Weiss let Stockman know he was no desert tenderfoot either. Something about coming to Palestine after World War II, a deckhand on an illegal immigrant ship. Something about giving the British the slip and going out to a pioneer kibbutz. Something about being on the Negev, carrying a Lee-Enfield against bedouin raiders. Stockman grunted, but I could not tell if he was expressing indifference to Charlie's adventures or if Weiss had won his begrudging respect. The storm did not care one way or the other. It hissed and bellowed for another half an hour before blowing itself out.

Our search for authentic bedouin, if there were any, began at Wad El-Tur, an oasis on the Gulf of Suez. We got there as the sun was dropping over Egypt, turning the gulf the color of a crushed plum. It was a remote and lonely place, seldom visited by the pink-faced gawkers who rode the air-conditioned tour buses: half a dozen mud-brick huts shaded by date palm and overlooked by a rickety windmill that pumped water to the gardens behind the huts. Up a hard-packed lane filled with bleating goats we found the village headman, hoeing a patch of beans. He was in his thirties, dark-skinned but without the high, sharp cheekbones and hawkish nose of a typical bedouin; in a suit instead of gelibya and turban, he could have passed as a Greek or Italian.

The usual greetings were followed by the usual trip to the guest tent—a hut with mud walls, a roof of sewn goatskins, and a mud floor smooth and hard as a cement slab, neatly swept and covered with tribal carpets. We drank three cups of coffee. Only when that ritual had been fulfilled could Stockman state our business: we were looking for camels and drivers to take us into the mountains. (Oh, I liked the sound of that.) The headman, who had a name befitting a royal sheikh, Subhi Salem el-Huebi, smiled apologetically and said it would not be easy to find camels and drivers.

Stockman nodded, knowingly and sadly.

"Just what I was afraid of," he said, and gave me another lesson in the changes that had come with Israeli occupation. Before the Six-day War, the twelve thousand bedouin in southern Sinai owned three vehicles; now they owned over three hundred. Breeding fine riding camels was becoming a lost art, good drivers going the way of the mountain man and the cowboy. To the bureaucrats in Tel Aviv and Jerusalem, that was progress. Stockman saw it differently: "Now the camels are degenerate and so are the drivers, most of them."

He pulled a pipe from his shirt pocket and, after taking a few thoughtful puffs, asked Subhi Salem el-Huebi if he knew of any good drivers. Yes, he did. He promised to send word out in the morning. But before we went anywhere, it would be a good idea to inform the sheikh of the southern Sinai, Rabiah Abu Atig, about our travel plans.

"And where do we find him?" asked Stockman.

"He will find you," replied Subhi Salem el-Huebi.

He did around noon the following day, as we were talking in the guest tent with el-Huebi's wife and mother-in-law. Coffee steamed on the embers of a cooking fire, the tent smelled of smoke, and the two women were straight out of a Roberts pencil sketch of nineteenth-century Arabia. Black shawls covered their heads, black ankle-length dresses their bodies; bracelets of hammered silver hung from their wrists, silver amulets from their necks, and their veils were made of coins sewn into the fabric: Egyptian piasters, British shillings, Saudi riyals, even an American half dollar or two—a numismatist's delight. Whenever the women moved, even slightly, they jangled and tinkled like wind chimes.

Bedouin women—Stockman was giving another of his lectures—were probably among the most exploited and oppressed on earth. Pledged to a man at eight or nine, subjected to clitoridectomies at puberty, they were married off by age thirteen, were dried-up, work-worn grandmothers by thirty-five, and generally dead at fifty-five.

"Some time ago," Stockman recalled, "a bedouin woman told me, 'Our men work us like beasts all day, and after we are married, they mount us like beasts at night.' Not even ten years ago, it would have been unthinkable for these women to be sitting in here with three strange men. This tells me that change is coming even here."

"So they're degenerate, right?"

"No. Just different."

The wife of el-Huebi demonstrated how different when she asked me for a cigarette. I glanced at Stockman.

"Go ahead. I've never seen this before," he said with an anthropologist's excitement at making a new discovery.

As she reached across the coals of the fire to take the cigarette, she looked directly at me over her coin-jeweled veil, the sleeve of her dress rising to expose her forearm; and that glimpse of nutmeg-colored skin, ringed to the elbows in silver, and the dark, oval eyes, staring with suppressed fire though the source of passion had been cut from her even before she'd known what sexual passion was, made me feel that in the small harmless gesture of handing her a cigarette I was breaking a powerful taboo. It occurred to me that the veil, accentuating the beauty of her eyes by concealing the distractions of her other features, had the opposite effect from the one intended. It made her more alluring, giving her an air of barbaric mystery.

El-Huebi's wife pulled a stick from the fire and, without raising the veil, stuck the cigarette in her lips and lit it. She exhaled. It was a weird sight—all that smoke pouring through a curtain of international pocket change.

Her husband came in with three or four other men from the village, curious to meet the strangers who wished to hire camels for a ride into the mountains. Suddenly, el-Huebi's wife tossed her half-smoked cigarette into the fire, everyone stopped talking, and, with expressions of fear, stared at the doorway. In it, dramatically backlit by the sun, stood a lean six-footer who bore an astonishing resemblance to Omar Sharif. He swaggered in, dressed in a spotless, slate-gray gelibya set off by a black cloak trimmed in gold. On his head, held by an embroidered band, was a kaffiyeh white enough to be used as a napkin, on his feet a pair of Gucci loafers instead of sandals. He was trailed by two thuggish-looking bodyguards, each armed with a revolver and a khanjar—the curved Arabian dagger.

Sheikh Atig glared at the two women: "You! Where is your shame? Get out of here."

Then, as they left in a jangling of silver, at el-Huebi's friends: "And you, get out of here and see to your goats."

And, as they walked out, at el-Huebi: "You leave, too. Go on, tend to your fields."

With everyone gone except us, Atig's manner turned charming. He sat down, crossing his legs, pulled a pack of Marlboros from his pocket, and offered it to us. We shook our heads. He took a cigarette, making sure, as he stuck it between his straight white teeth and flicked his Dunhill lighter, that we saw the gold Rolex gleaming on his wrist. Atig, king of hashish smugglers in Sinai, combined the dash of an old-time desert pirate with the hard business sense of a modern-day gangster. By tribal law, he should not have been a sheikh. When the former ruler died, Atig's uncle was the rightful heir, but Atig gathered a band of goons (like the two guarding the doorway) and made his uncle an offer he could not refuse: "Either I get the sheikhdom or you will die."

He and Stockman exchanged salaams, and then he asked what we were up to. We told him.

"And what route do you plan to take?" Atig asked, his eyes as black and steady as bench-rested rifle sights.

"Wadi Hibran to Wadi Salaaf, then to the oasis at Wadi Firan," Stockman answered.

"Very good. You will be under my protection. You will have my promise of safety on your journey."

"For your graciousness, we thank you," Stockman said, and it was plain he did not like having to say it, didn't think that he, citizen of the nation that now ruled the Sinai, should have to say it. But a lot of nations had ruled the Sinai at one time or another. All were gone. One day, the Israelis would be gone, too, and Atig knew it.

He stood abruptly, crushing the cigarette under his Guccis.

"But see that you do not stray from that route."

"He means," Stockman whispered to me in an aside, "to stay away from his smugglers' routes. We'd get a bullet for that."

"*Allâh yisal'limak*—God be with you," Atig said, and strode outside, his cloak bellying in the wind like a spinnaker, his bodyguards walking on either side of him. I expected him to leap onto a camel or an Arabian stallion. Ten years earlier, he might have, but a lot had changed since the Israelis took over. Sheikh Rabiah Abu Atig, the desert buccaneer, climbed into a new Dodge pickup and sped away in a grinding of gears.

Somehow, without telephones or telexes or a postal service, Subhi Salem el-Huebi's call for camels and drivers was spread. A bedouin rode into Wad el-Tur the next day on a big, muscular camel the color of a cigarette filter. He reined up. Flapping its lips and showing the big cubes of its teeth, the beast dropped to its haunches, collapsing like an enormous card table, the hind legs folding first, then the fore. Its rider swung off. He had looked regal in the saddle, nearly seven feet off the ground, but he was not so impressive on foot: no more than five-feet-six, with a sullen expression, a scrawny chest, a brushy, soot-black mustache, and a dingy kaffiyeh, one end hanging down the side of his face like a used dish towel. He coughed and spit, gave us his name, Suleiman, and offered his services. Stockman asked his qualifications. He said he'd been a camel driver the past ten years, but, things being the way they were, he had to supplement his income as a road-construction worker for the very highway engineers who were making his kind a vanishing breed.

He sat down, tucking his feet beneath his knees, and opened the bargaining: two drivers and four camels for four days at one hundred and thirty Israeli pounds a day. That came to thirty-two dollars, which seemed reasonable to me, but Stockman, his pipe crunched between his teeth, made a counter.

"It was one hundred and fifteen pounds just a few months ago."

Suleiman coughed and spit again, eyeing Stockman. He could neither read nor write, but when it came to money, he knew his arithmetic.

"You must understand. One hundred and fifteen was last year's price. It is more expensive to live now. One hundred and thirty pounds."

Stockman did not budge, nor did Suleiman, who, after an hour's haggling, walked off in a huff.

"Is that it?" I asked, seeing the whole thing end over a few dollars.

"It's just a ploy," Stockman said reassuringly. "He'll be back, I promise you."

Suleiman returned an hour later, this time with reinforcements: an older man, around sixty, with a clean-shaven, cinnamon-brown face. He wore a white gelibya and a dark-red vest, the ornamented hilt of a khanjar sticking out from the red sash cinched around his waist. Small as a jockey, he had a jockey's light-footed walk and carried a riding crop with braided tassels hanging from the knob at its tip. He took a seat outside the guest tent and let us know that he was Muhammad Abu Awaeid, for twenty years a driver and breeder of the best camels in all Sinai and part owner of a racing camel, and the price would be one hundred and thirty pounds a day for four days.

The bargaining went on till late afternoon, when Stockman gave in, agreeing to one hundred and thirty pounds a day for three and a half days.

"In addition," Muhammad said, waving his riding crop, "you must pay us twenty-six pounds for fodder."

Fodder?

"The camels should have one day off to graze, but since you insist on pushing for three days without stopping, then we must have fodder for them."

"All right," Stockman said wearily. "You shall have your fodder. I give in, but now our bargain is final."

They shook on it. A short while later, herdsmen brought the animals in, riding camels all, lithe and stately. The one in the lead was especially handsome: cream-colored, high-legged, as lean and nervous as a greyhound.

"Ya, Stockman! How do you like her?" Muhammad asked,

pointing with his crop. "The white female. That's mine. Is she not a beauty?"

Stockman agreed. Muhammad strode up to her with his cocky walk and to demonstrate his prowess as much as the camel's fine qualities did not kneel her to mount but leapt and grabbed the front saddle horn in both hands, swinging his sixty-year-old bones into the saddle. He tapped her neck, and she raced off in a stiff-legged run for perhaps fifty yards; then he turned her sharply and galloped back, pulling her up to a sudden halt. He flipped off, agile as an athlete half his age, and handed the reins to one of the herdsmen, who walked the camel toward a watering trough, the others plodding behind. Looking at them and knowing we would be riding them into the mountains, I felt the trip would have been worth any price.

We woke to the sound of them—a hollow gurgling, like bad plumbing. They were kneeling in a row beside the guest tent, noses in the fodder bags. We rolled up our sleeping bags and lashed them to the backs of the saddles with the sacks of flour, olives, sugar, and tea.

Muhammad took off the feed bags and handed Stockman the reins of the second camel, a pale, haughty-looking animal. He hauled his bulk into the saddle, and the camel rose with that two-part movement.

"Well, Young Winston, are you ready to tackle the Sinai?"

I wrapped a kaffiyeh around my head—might as well try to look the role—and stood beside my camel, Suleiman holding the rope reins to keep it on its knees while I mounted. Feeling a little nervous, feeling, I would say, rather small and fragile—you have no idea how big a camel is until you try to ride one—I clutched the saddle horn and swung aboard. Suleiman passed me the reins. I held them tightly, and then it was as though I were riding an unstable tectonic plate. The beast heaved, thrusting up its hind legs, pitching me forward, then rocking me backward when its forelegs rose and straightened. I was amazed and pleased not to have fallen off, an achievement that, combined with the altitude, made me feel superior to lesser beings like Suleiman, who now appeared as small as a toddler.

Muhammad tucked his khanjar in his waist, mounted, and gave a wagonmaster's wave. We started off, rocking slowly in our saddles, except for Suleiman, who, hacking and spitting, walked beside my camel with a yardlong stick in his hand. A great treeless plain reached before us for twenty miles, ending where the mountains punched abruptly into harsh, unclouded sky.

You cannot understand the bedouin and their ritualistic way of life, their unquestioning faith in a God both fierce and generous, their pride that is born of a humility, their patience and endurance, without confronting the desert on the desert's terms. Except for us, the camels, and the flies, there wasn't a living thing on that rocky plain. I had never experienced such stillness. No rivers ran, no birds sang. Even the wind blowing across all that desolation blew silently. It was a place as devoid of distractions as any on earth, timeless and awesome. I could understand how the idea of a single, abstract God was born out there. In the diverse and polychromatic landscapes of Europe, man's imagination created a multiplicity of deities, but on the desert, where nothing was ever sown or reaped, no such theological miscellany was possible. There could be room for only one God, without form or face, Arab Allah or Hebrew Yahweh—He Who Is.

Around noon, we came to a clump of leafless, stunted acacia, which threw their sparse shade over a dune and clumps of thorny brush. The thorns were as long and hard as roofing nails, but the camels crunched them as if they were cornflakes. We dismounted, gathered brush for a fire, and had a bit of lunch ourselves. My legs and back ached from the ride, and the rear saddle horn, rubbing against my buttocks, had raised a huge, painful blister at the base of my spine. Everyone had a good laugh when I dropped my trousers and asked Charlie to pop the blister and dress the exposed skin with a bandage from our first-aid kit.

After the break, we rode for another hour, beneath a sky that seemed a dome of scorching, polished steel, then stopped in another acacia grove to give Muhammad time to say his afternoon prayers (Suleiman, for some reason, did not bother). The old man unraveled his kaffiyeh, uncovering a head of sparse gray hair, and spread it on the ground; then he knelt, chanted "*Allahu akhbar*" in a low voice, and bowed. When he prostrated himself, flinging his hands and forehead down to touch the baked earth, he seemed to be humbling himself before the desert as much as before Allah. Who could say— maybe they were the same to him.

When he was finished, we pushed on toward Wadi Hibran, Muhammad and Suleiman crying "Hut-hut-hut" to the camels picking their way with spread toes over beds of shale. The bab el wad, or gate to the wadi, lay some three or four miles away. It was a wide opening in the wall of mountains. We were following a branch of the Darb al-Haj, an ancient caravan track once used by pilgrims making their way to Mecca. It was about twice the width of a city sidewalk, and Muhammad, in the lead, never deviated from it, though it wound and twisted, doubling the distance we had to travel. That was typical of a bedouin's hidebound ways, Stockman said, turning in his saddle to deliver another lecture. They generally knew one or two routes and kept to them steadfastly. The trails were their lifelines. To wander away from one was to risk getting lost, putting yourself at the mercy of the desert, which had none.

We rounded a hill and entered the wadi, winding off into the parched heart of the mountains. Each peak was sharp and grooved, like a flint arrowhead made by a race of titans. We had ridden about eighteen miles—no distance in space, but an immense one backward in time. At the wadi's gate stood a cone-shaped rock etched with Nabatean petroglyphs twenty-two centuries old. The almost rainless climate had preserved them so well they looked as if they had been put there the day before. The sight of them made me philosophical. All that remained of the Nabateans were a few inscriptions on a desert rock. And what remained of the ancient Egyptians, who had ruled Sinai before them? Of the Ottomans? Of the British? Nothing. Now history had come full circle—the Egyptians and the Jews had returned to Sinai, each claiming it for a possession, claims that sounded plausible and worthy of consideration in Cairo and Jerusalem. In Wadi Hibran, they sounded absurd. I preferred Muhammad's outlook: "No one owns the desert. It belongs to Allah."

Scrape of hooves, saddles creaking, Muhammad singing a camel driver's song that kept time to the slow swaying of the caravan. The rocking back and forth had proved too much for the tall Weiss, whip-sawing his long torso. He dismounted and went on foot. I would have liked to have joined him—the egg-size sore on my tailbone was an agony—but a stubborn and idiotic notion that I had to prove myself kept me in the saddle. Suleiman had corrected my riding style, telling me not to sit as on a horse, but with one leg hooked around the front saddle horn. It helped the pain, but not much.

Nearby, a flock of goats scampered down a mountainside, herded by two young girls in dark dresses. Suleiman stopped them and asked to buy a kid, and we knew we were in the backcountry when the girls refused to speak to him because he was a M'zina and they were from another tribe, the Eleigat.

An hour before dusk, we came to a dense grove of date palm arranged around a well, a welcome sight that explained better than any textbook why the Moslem image of paradise is of a boundless oasis. Two bedouin, naked to the waist, were hauling up leather skins of water and lashing them to a donkey.

Suleiman knelt my camel—I didn't have the hang of it yet—and I swung off, sunburnt and saddle sore. We filled our canteens and goatskin water bag in the well after the two bedouin had gone off with their donkey. In a little while we were lazing on our blankets and sleeping bags, heads against our saddles as Suleiman baked a loaf of pita on a crackling fire. I took notes while I had the light to do it. Muhammad looked at me out of the corner of his eye.

"You, el Agnabi," he said, addressing me by my nickname, "the stranger," "Whatever you are writing, be sure to write that I, Muhammad Abu Awaeid, am the sheikh el kara."

That meant the sheikh of the caravan, and I assured him he would be so identified. He turned to Stockman.

"And you, Stockman, when we come to Wadi Firan, you be sure to tell the people there that I, Muhammad, am the sheikh el kara, not you."

Stockman promised.

It looked as though Muhammad would be the only bedouin I would interview that day, so I asked what kind of living he made as a driver and breeder of camels.

He pointed toward the dimming sky.

"Business, income, and riches are just like poverty. All come from heaven and Allah."

But hadn't he taken this job to make some money?

"Of course. But I am also seeking a wife."

It turned out that both his sons had died, and, his first wife being too old to bear children, he hoped to find a good bedouin girl in the mountains who could give him a new son.

I laughed quietly to myself—you old goat—and closed my note-book.

"You rode well, el Agnabi. We came a long way. You are tired?"

I said I was, but it was a good tiredness.

"So you are happy?"

"Very."

"Good. I am the sheikh el kara and I am happy only if you are happy." He paused, turning his seamed face to the mountains, red-dening in the falling sun. "I am happy here. Out here is where I am content."

And I looked around, at the mountains, the date palm, the kneeling camels, the blankets and saddles arrayed around the fire, and felt the same contentment, a peace that settled into my marrow. I have always loved the lonely, wild places of the earth, what's left of them, and it was good to be in one with a few trusted friends, a fire burning, and a whole day's ride and new country to look forward to in the morning. And this, too: I had come out to the desert to reconnect myself to the authentic and the essential, to stay in touch with the only good thing I had brought out of Vietnam: the knowledge that life and death were all that mattered.

I got in my sleeping bag, zipped it against scorpions, and slept without dreaming.

We woke when it was still dark and rode through the morning cool, hoping to make the Hibran Pass—the midpoint of the jour-ney—by noon. The wadi was now not much wider than the trail. By midmorning, you could have baked bread in that narrow canyon with-out a fire. We stopped at a place that looked like a little chunk of Mars. Up near the head of a ravine, a wisp of campfire smoke rose like a fakir's rope.

"Maybe they have a well, inshallah," Muhammad said. "We need to water the camels in this heat."

Stockman laughed.

"It's not water he wants, but a woman. Our sheikh el-kara is going courting, Young Winston. Do you care to observe this native ritual?"

I did. Weiss, who had found a little shade under an overhang, elected to stay behind with Suleiman and the camels. I borrowed his camera, but Muhammad objected to my going along. El Agnabi was a stranger and might frighten whoever was up there. Stockman pointed out that I looked more like an Arab than some Arabs. Muhammad gave in, but instructed me to stay some distance behind, until he and Stockman had entered the encampment and made sure everything was all right.

Apparently, things might not be: Stockman pulled a nine-millimeter automatic pistol out of his saddlebag and jammed it in his back pocket.

"What's that for?"

"You never know. Could be some of Atig's hash smugglers. They might not take kindly to our intrusion and start shooting."

"Hash smugglers carry Uzis, right? What good is a pistol?"

"Would you prefer I throw rocks back at them?"

I could not argue with his logic, and we started up the ravine. It was not marked on the Israeli army map I carried with me, and I felt a little pressure just below my navel: a blank spot on the map and no idea if we were going to run into a potential fiancée for Muhammad or a gang of desert outlaws.

After climbing in the heat for a quarter of an hour, we saw a pair of goatskin tents pitched near a natural limestone cistern. It was almost dry. A woman in black was walking toward us. Excited, Muhammad gestured for me to crouch behind a rock. I guess he was afraid I might cramp his style. He and Stockman went ahead to greet the woman and smooth the way, and I almost spoiled it when I stood up to photograph their meeting.

"Get back down, you idiot!" Stockman growled, waving.

I ducked. He signaled me to come forward a few moments later. I made my salaams to the woman, and she to me. All I could see of her were eyes, peering blackly over her veil. We shook hands. Muhammad scowled and muttered something.

"Now what the hell did I do wrong?"

"One of the ways you express interest in a bedouin girl is to run your fingers gently across her palm."

"Thanks. You're the Pearl Mesta of the desert. That isn't what I did."

"But Muhammad thinks you did. They follow the old ways out here, Young Winston."

"They're not degenerate?"

"No. I'll assure the sheikh el kara that your intentions toward this woman are honorable."

"Fine." The heat and the flies—hundreds of them buzzed around the camp—were making me irritable. "And I'll thank you not to call me an idiot again."

"I won't if you don't behave like one."

We sat by the smoldering fire on a threadbare carpet the woman fetched from one of the tents. She followed traditional bedouin custom by baking us a loaf of pita and serving coffee, and Muhammad smiled. Her hospitality showed her to be a fine woman who respected the ancient codes; better yet, she was of childbearing age. He started to talk to her—chatting her up, I supposed. While he did, Stockman climbed to his figurative lectern and explained that the serving of bread and coffee—the equivalent of a T-bone and vintage wine for a woman as poor as she—was part of a rigid protocol.

"She is expected to treat us like guests, and we are expected to act like guests. Without that, there would be no peace or security on the desert. If there were no unwritten code of behavior, we could have walked in here and raped or robbed this woman, but we are expected to act in a certain way, just as she is."

And if we broke the rules?

"The men in her tribe would find out and we would leave these mountains feet first."

Just then, Muhammad abruptly fell silent, his expression souring when he saw a small, half-naked boy toddling out of one of the tents.

"Ah, so you have a husband?" he asked tentatively, and when the woman nodded, he looked as disappointed as a high school boy turned down for a date. He swigged the last of his coffee and stood.

"We must be pushing on, Stockman. There is no water here."

"Ha! You mean, O sheikh el kara, there are no single women here."

"Nor any water."

I asked Muhammad to hold off for a while; I wanted to ask the woman some questions.

"What for? You can't marry her any more than I. Less. You are an unbeliever."

"I don't want to marry her. It's my job to ask people questions."

Muhammad sniffed, as if to say, "What kind of work for a man is that?" and sat back down. The small boy sat in the dust beside his mother. It was hard to interview her because I could not take my eyes off him; flies, drawn by the dried goat's milk on his face, clustered around his mouth like gazelle around a waterhole. They crawled up his nose, flitted around his dirty hair, but he didn't try to brush them off. A little awkwardly, I turned to the woman and asked her name and age. Salama, she answered, and as for how old she was, she had been married in the year of the war. I understood that to have been the Suez War of 1956. Most bedouin girls marry at thirteen, so that would have made Salama about thirty. She told me her day began at dawn, when she rose to cook for her husband and three young children (the other two were sleeping in the tent). She spent the rest of the morning and afternoon following her goats as they searched for graze, walking for miles in blistering heat before returning to camp at dusk to bake bread and brew tea for dinner.

"And from where have all of you come?" she asked.

"Wad el Tur."

"Where is that?"

"On the sea, about sixty or seventy kilometers from here."

She gave me a blank look.

Stockman explained that Salama hadn't the vaguest idea where the sea was or what a kilometer was, so I said that Wad el Tur was a day and a half's ride to the south.

"I have never been that far. I have never been beyond the bab el wad."

That was less than fifteen miles away.

Salama reached for the long, brass pot simmering on the coals and offered me another cup of coffee, my third. Stockman grabbed me by the wrist as I raised it to my mouth.

"Before you drink that you should know they have a saying out here. 'The first cup is for the guest, the second for the host, the third for hospitality, but the fourth is for the sword.'"

"How about de-crypting that for me."

"It means that if you drink a fourth cup you have overstayed your welcome and have come to fight. So this one will be your last."

After I drank it down, I wanted to resume the interview, but I was so intimidated by all the complex rules that I decided against it.

"You are finished now with asking her things?"

I nodded to Muhammad.

"Then we must be pushing on. There is no water here."

As we stood to leave, Stockman offered Salama four Israeli pounds—less than a dollar but a fortune to her.

"I refuse it if it is in payment of my hospitality," she said.

"No, it is a gift, an offering."

She took the coins, kissed them, then pressed each one against her forehead—the highest form of thanks a bedouin can give. The little boy sat passively in the dust, half his face hidden by flies, and then we said good-bye to Salama, leaving her alone in the wilderness but protected by the desert's unwritten laws.

The trail too steep for riding, we had to walk the camels up to the Hibran Pass. The sun was a penance, and when we filed into a tight corridor between two sheer rock faces, the farting camels nearly asphyxiated us. We whispered thanks when we came out onto a wide, windy plateau.

All around it cairns of flat stones stood like truncated termite mounds. They were more than ten thousand years old, Professor Stockman informed us, probably built by a race of neolithic moon worshippers whose lunar god, Sin, had given Sinai its name. Like the Nabatean inscriptions back at the wadi's entrance, they looked as if they had been made only yesterday. No one knew what they signified, if they were altars, burial mounds, or memorials to some Stone Age king. It chilled me to file past them, imagining prehistoric tribesmen piling those stones so carefully atop one another, for reasons no one would ever know. But, I reflected, if the buttons were ever pushed and the Global Village went up in a blast of fissioning atoms, people ten thousand years from now might poke in the radioactive rubble and find the McDonald's golden arches and ponder what manner of men had made them and why.

The trail rose gradually now, and then we crested the pass, and it was as if we had reached the edge of the known world. Wherever we looked there were mountains and buttes and towering chimney rocks wind-carved into surreal forms and not a sign of human life in all that red and beautiful vastness. I caught a movement on a ledge more than a thousand yards off, asked Stockman to pass me his binoculars, and saw a pair of ibex the instant before they leapt across a chasm onto another ledge as easily as man would jump a rain puddle. One more quick leap and they were gone, and I thanked whatever god ruled that lonely place for letting me see them.

We walked the camels down the other side of the pass into the sandy avenue of Wadi Salaaf and stopped to rest through the blaze of early afternoon. Two Eleigat, double-mounted on a lumbering baggage camel, rode up, stopping just long enough to tell us we could spend the night with some Ulat Said tribesmen, camped in the Umm Taha valley.

Muhammad spat. "Ulat Said. Men without honor."

The valley was lipped by jagged, oblong peaks, like the mouth of a volcano squashed slightly out of shape. The domes and bells of goat-hide tents, with awnings stretched out from their entrances, made patches of black and dark brown against the valley floor, blushing a faint pink in the sunset. Half a dozen women, hauling up hide buckets by a crude block-and-pulley, hovered around a well. A flock of goats were trotting down the face of a mountain, hurried along by a boy blowing tunelessly on a shepherd's flute, each disconnected note hanging momentarily in the air before the next rose to take its place.

We stopped a discreet distance from the camp. In a few moments, a delegation of three or four tribal headmen came out to see what our business was. Weiss, Suleiman, and I stayed with the camels while Stockman and Muhammad greeted them. They kissed each headman three times on both cheeks, then touched foreheads, intoning, "Salamat, salamat, salamat." Other formalities followed, and Weiss said it was a good thing bedouin did not lead busy lives because it took them half an hour just to say hello. After a lot of palavering, Stockman and Muhammad called us over.

"They say there are too many women in their camp for us to stay in their guest tent," Stockman explained. "We'll have to pitch our camp at least two hundred meters away, and we must not have any contact with their women, not even visual."

"We've already seen some of them," Charlie said. "Around the well. They didn't look like anything I'd leave home for."

"They're serious about this, Charlie. They follow ..."

"Yeah, yeah, yeah, I know. They follow the old ways out here."

"At least they're not degenerate," I said.

Maybe they weren't, but that didn't make them admirable in Muhammad's eyes.

"These people are shameless buggers," he said, and spat. "They should have invited us into their guest tent and *kept* their women out of our sight." He spat again. "These Ulat Said lack honor."

The large gathering of Ulat Said—some twenty or thirty families altogether—had stripped the valley of deadwood and brush. Weiss and I, sent out to forage, had to walk better than a mile, picking up a twig here, a clump of thornbush there before we found enough. We started back, our haul cradled lovingly in our arms. A flock of goats passed by, flanked by another shepherd boy blowing a flute, more melodiously than the first. I paused, taking it all in—the goats trotting toward the tents pitched in the distance, fires glowing beside the tents, the boy and his piping flute, Muhammad and Suleiman bedding down the camels by our camp, the encircling mountains shading to a gray-blue in the twilight—and felt the old thrill of reaching escape velocity, escape this time from our ugly and graceless century.

After we got the fire going, Muhammad found a new reason to curse the Ulat Said. It is traditional, near the end of a caravan ride, to treat your drivers to a feast of roasted goat. We sent a shepherd boy to the camp with word that we wished to buy a kid. Muhammad's eyes twinkled and he smacked his lips, and even sullen Suleiman managed a smile. The boy came back with an old man with skin like rhinoceros hide. He was carrying a small, brown goat and he wanted eighty Israeli pounds for it.

Stockman, shaking his head, told him it wasn't worth half that much.

"Twenty pounds, no more."

I could tell he was working himself up into a fit of stubbornness, and after six days of bread and tea, I damned well could have done with a bit of goat myself, so I tried to break the impasse by offering forty. Muhammad begged me to withdraw the offer: if we bought the kid for that much the old man would tell his friends how easily he had cheated us. We would be "blackened," lose face.

Stockman upped his offer to twenty-five pounds; the old man countered with seventy-five.

"You must understand," he added politely, "in such conditions as this, everything is according to the seller and not the buyer. Why, people come here all the way from El Arîsh and pay that price."

"Then the people from El Arîsh must be very hungry or very rich or very stupid," said Muhammad.

The goat wriggled in the old man's arms. It looked cute. The hell with it, I thought, I don't want goat anyway.

The old man then came up with a novel suggestion.

"If you buy it now for seventy-five, but you eat only half tonight and the other tomorrow, then you will have paid only half as much."

Stockman bit down on his pipe.

"What kind of fools do you take us for?"

"Why, no fools at all."

"That's right, but, you, sir, are an idiot. You will please leave our camp and not insult us any longer."

The old man bowed graciously and went off, Muhammad cursing him to his back as a shameless bugger, without honor and of dubious ancestry. So far, except for our fee, he had got nothing out of the trip: no wife, no roasted goat.

We had to make do with bread, olives, and tea, but when the stars lit up, the whole sky seemed like a benediction.

I woke up suddenly, a cold tingling in my scalp. Had I only dreamed it? I looked around. The others were asleep, but the camels were standing stock-still in their hobbles, their heads raised and alert. Their wariness told me I had not been dreaming. I must have heard the sound in a half sleep. Half scream and half hiss, it had come from somewhere in the dark crags far above. I moved closer to the fire's embers, stirred them with a stick, and wondered if I should wake Stockman. I decided against it. He probably would think I had had too much sun because only a handful were left in Sinai and the chances of hearing one so close to a crowded camp would have been ten thousand to one. I looked at my watch—a little after four—and sat listening until my eyelids felt as if sash weights had been tied to them.

An hour or so later, Stockman shook me awake. The fire was burning brightly against the early-morning blackness, tea bubbling in the pot. We drank it down, then rose stiffly to saddle the camels. They were skittish; even Muhammad, who could control them with a mere click of his tongue, had to struggle to make them kneel.

I hefted my saddle, but before I could toss it over my camel's back, he whipped his long neck around to bite me. I jumped away just in time, snatched Suleiman's walking stick, and cracked the animal hard across the nose.

"That's the way, Young Winston. Don't take insolence from him. What the devil is wrong with them this morning?"

I flung the saddle on, tightened the cinches.

"I heard a leopard about two hours ago."

"Bah!"

"I was going to wake you up and tell you, but I figured that's what you'd say, 'Bah.'"

He mounted, his camel jacking up beside mine.

"Let's get going. It's thirty kilometers to Wadi Firan."

We rode the length of the valley and filed through a notch in the mountains into a wide bowl that looked like a vast rock quarry. My camel was balky and nervous. I had to tap his neck constantly with a crop to keep him moving, and when that failed, Suleiman would smack his haunches with the walking stick. Even so, I fell a hundred yards behind the others.

The camel stopped again, stretching his neck and raising his head. I tapped his withers, kicked his flanks. He wouldn't move anything except his head, which turned one way, then the other, seeking a scent. Stockman, Muhammad, and Weiss were well ahead, figures in the morning mirage.

"Hut-hut, haddee," I said, digging my heels into the camel's sides. He ambled ten yards, then lowered his head toward a thornbush, as if to eat. I saw a pile of droppings in the bush.

"Goddamn you, move."

He twisted suddenly to one side, all six or seven hundred pounds of him, and almost threw me. I jerked the reins, but he twisted again in the opposite direction, then bent himself into a bow, straightened, and went off, plunging and bucking, with me hanging on to the saddle horn. He made another twist, that crane of a neck bending back so far his nose almost touched his tail; then his whole body whipsawed and I was flung sideways like a stone from a slingshot. I was high enough and in the air long enough to have a coherent thought: "Jesus Christ, I'm going to hit headfirst." I saw the boulder—it was about twice the size of a basketball—and then did not see anything for several seconds.

When I came to, I rolled to my stomach and stood shakily, tasting blood in my mouth. It was pouring down a gash in my forehead. Through multicolored spots, Stockman and the others were trotting toward me. Suleiman had the camel under control and was giving him a thrashing.

"What the hell happened?" Stockman knelt his camel and swung out of the saddle to look at my skull. "That's a bad one. Get the first-aid kit, Charlie. What happened?"

"Smelled something ... went nuts ... threw me ..."

"Your leopard?"

"Ask the camel."

"Don't have to. It *was* a cat of some kind. Leopard or a bobcat. Muhammad heard it, too. Let's get you fixed up and get out of here. That was an omen and I believe in omens."

"Three days and you're bedouinized already?"

"You don't have to be bedu to believe in omens."

Weiss patched me up, and I tested myself for skull fracture by touching my toes to see if I lost my balance. I was all right and climbed back in the saddle. Muhammad said something to me, of which I understood only my nickname—el Agnabi.

"What's he saying?" I asked Stockman.

"He admires the way you got back on right after you fell. He called you 'The brave stranger.' You've won his respect."

Muhammad turned his camel and led us off. Looking at him, straight-backed and graceful in his seat, holding his tasseled riding crop like a scepter, I could not have thought of another man whose respect I'd rather have.

The oasis at Wadi Firan was a national forest compared with the one at Wad el Tur—acres of date palm broken by small, irrigated fields and clusters of mud-brick houses. The green was a pleasant change from the barren reds and browns, but the thud of generators and the sound of trucks and jeeps grated after the desert's immense silences, and how tame and domesticated the walled houses looked compared to the hide tents of the Ulat Said. The bedouin who lived in them looked tame. They were not really bedouin anymore, but fellaheen, like their cousins in the Nile Valley. They moved across their fields and garden plots, some on foot swinging hoes, some on growling Israeli tractors, and they seemed a little envious when they stopped work to watch us ride past, Muhammad in front, his erect posture expressing pride in his wandering brotherhood and scorn for those dirt-bound farmers, who did not share in it. The sheikh el kara.

We dismounted beside a big, cement-lined pool where a small caravan of about ten camels were taking on water. Their four riders were M'zina, and Muhammad greeted them warmly, happy to be among his own people. They had come to the oasis for supplies of flour, coffee, and tea, which they would soon carry back into the mountains by the same route we had followed. They asked Muhammad about trail conditions, and in the course of telling them he related the tale of the leopard and my accident. One of the M'zina, a youngish man with a mustache shaped like a croquet hoop, grasped my hand and said something.

"You're getting a lot of mileage out of falling on your ass, el Agnabi," Stockman said.

"I fell on my head, not my ass."

"Some would say there's no difference. Anyway, this fellow's telling you that you are now true bedu because you weren't afraid to remount."

I basked in the compliment, although a three-day ride through a mere sixty miles of Sinai mountains did not make me a T. E. Lawrence, much less an authentic bedouin. Also, I had had no choice but to remount; it was either that or walk all the way.

We had come to the end of our ride (though not the journey— we had to go another thirty miles to the coast road, which would take several hours by vehicle, then drive back to Jerusalem, another two days), so Stockman suggested that we send Muhammad and Suleiman off with full bellies by giving them the feast of roasted goat denied us by the greedy old man at Umm Taha. He knew just the spot, and Muhammad's fellow M'zina were welcome to join us.

We rode to the edge of the oasis and dismounted near a six-hundred-year-old monastery built by Greek Orthodox monks. An old caretaker came out, smiling toothlessly. *"Ahlan, wasahalan—*welcome. *Ahlan washalan mit ahlan wasahalan*—a thousand welcomes. A thousand welcomes to you, O riders."

He brought us to a field out back, where grape arbors offered shade and olive trees marched up the hillside. The caretaker produced a fine kid in about half an hour. Muhammad called for God's blessing: "*Bismillah ar-rahmam ar-rahim*—in the name of Allah, all merciful, all loving-kind." As Suleiman held the kid down, he drew his dagger and slashed its throat to the neckbone, the dry soil drinking the hot blood.

They had it skinned and gutted in no time, chunked the meat, the organs, the windpipe, even the eyes, mixed them with a pot of steaming rice, and made a bedouin pilaf. We wolfed it with our fingers or with hunks of pita. The young M'zina with the curved mustache provided dinner music, pulling a harp from his saddlebag. He knew the words to the "The Lemon Is Bitter, but the Date Is Sweet." Stockman and Muhammad sang with him. When they finished, another M'zina took out a small, crude drum and began to beat a harsh, rapid rhythm. His voice went up in a chant that sounded eerily like a flamenco, the others and Stockman coming in on the chorus. I caught only one familiar word—"hashish." It was a smuggler's song, and I'll never forget that moment, the smells of wood smoke and roasted meat in the air while those men of the desert sang an outlaw ballad and the wind moved through olive trees planted a hundred years before Columbus sailed from Spain.

It was late afternoon by the time the feasting and singing were done. The M'zina and Muhammad and Suleiman wanted to put on some miles before dark.

The good-byes, like the hellos, took a long time. "*Allah yisal'limak, Allah yifazdak.*" Embraces. Handshakes.

"We will ride together again if you return to Sinai, inshallah," Muhammad said to me.

"Inshallah."

The bedouin mounted up, then rode at an easy pace up the hill behind the monastery. Muhammad and Suleiman brought up the rear, leading our two riderless camels. They followed the caravan around a bend and were gone, and with generators thumping and tractors growling only a hundred yards away, it was impossible not to see them as two of a breed as threatened as the Sinai leopard. I thought of Muhammad's invitation and hoped I would ride with him again through the great lonely places, where we would sleep beneath the stars and rise to watch dawn light the wadis and ibex jump the ledges of the desert mountains.

Maybe I would, inshallah, and yet, somehow, I knew He didn't.

Three days later, Weiss and I were back in his century-old stone house in Jerusalem. I phoned Jill to tell her I would be home in another day or so. She said Yuenger had been trying to reach me. It was urgent, something about some troubles in Beirut. I was to call him as soon as I got back.

Because it was three in the morning in Chicago, I went to the press center to see if the foreign desk had telexed me any messages. They had.

HEAVY FIGHTING BETWEEN FEDS AND LEBANESE ARMY. PROCEED BEIRUT ASAPEST. REQUIRE 600 WDS FOR SUNDAY FINAL. TWX WHEN U ARRIVE. RGDS. YUENGER.

"Feds" was shorthand for "fedayeen," and "require" meant that the paper had damned well better have the six hundred words, and "proceed asapest" meant I should have been in Beirut yesterday, if not sooner.

That night, with the camel-jockey saddle sore still burning my backside, I landed in Cyprus and boarded a Middle East Airlines plane for Beirut. Just before getting on, I ducked into the men's room to make sure I had nothing on me that showed I had been in Israel. Like most correspondents who covered both sides of the Middle East conflict, I carried two passports, one for Israel only. That was to avoid Israeli entrance and exit stamps in my regular passport. Those could get you expelled from an Arab country or, worse, an extended stay in a prison cell. I stashed the restricted passport in a secret compartment a tailor in Rome had sewn into my luggage. My phone book, containing the numbers of both Israeli and Arab sources, had to stay on me. I reminded myself to transfer the Israeli numbers to another book first chance I got. I went through my wallet, made sure it had no Israeli currency, then cleaned out Israeli business cards. A voice announced that my flight was in final boarding. In my rush to make the plane, I failed to see that I'd left two cards in my wallet.

An hour later, the plane was coming in for a landing. Pools of darkness blotted the expanse of lights stretching from the harbor toward the heights of the Anti-Lebanon Range. Parts of the city had been blacked out. A nervous flickering, like heat lightning, showed over West Beirut, where most of the Palestinian camps were. Flares were pinned to the sky like sparkling carnations, and tracers made red scratches above the rooftops.

Shellfire. Flares. Tracers.

Welcome back, pilgrim, to the twentieth century.

DISASTERS OF WAR

The American rammed his shovel into the soft dirt, his arms sore from hours of digging. He lit a cigarette, smoking it through the big kerchief that covered his face. As he smoked and watched Mehmet count the corpses, the lyrics to a silly rock-and-roll tune from his high school days ran through his brain: "Gonna take my problems to the United Nations, doo-doo-do-doot, doododoo …" Who sang it? Bobby Darin? By the time the American finished his smoke, Mehmet had finished the count. The American went down the line of bodies and tallied them himself to double-check: he prided himself on the accuracy of his reports to the commission and on their unbiased nature. "Gonna take my problems to the United Nations …" Maybe it was Bobby Vinton.

The Turkish flag fluttered over the empty village, where a platoon of soldiers waited to rebury the ninety-six people. Odd how the village showed hardly a sign of what had happened: a few bullet holes in the walls, that was all. The Greek Cypriot militia had been methodical and efficient. Hardly a wasted round.

"Ninety-six!" Mehmet said, when the American came to the last corpse. "Almost all of them women and children."

"I can see that."

"So that is all of them. Except for him." Mehmet gestured at the sole survivor, a fourteen-year-old boy, lying on a stretcher nearby with a festering leg wound. "The entire village!"

"When is the ambulance going to come?"

"Soon, soon." Mehmet looked at the line of corpses. "You should send to the commission photographs of this. This is why the Turk army had to invade. This is what the Greeks have been doing to us for eighteen years—discriminating against us, murdering us. This is why Cyprus must be partitioned."

Mehmet was taking his problems to the United Nations. (Fabian? Ricky Nelson?) The American raised his palm to tell Mehmet to save the propaganda. He, the American, only made reports; others acted on them, or failed to act, as the case might be. Besides, he had helped dig up the mass grave of massacred Greeks just a few days ago. He had been in the Greek refugee camps in the south—sixty thousand homeless people without shelter against the July sun, without blankets against the night's chill. He had interviewed a Greek girl who had been raped by a squad of Turkish soldiers. He had reported all that to the commission, as he would report these killings, accurately and without bias.

The ambulance arrived. The wounded boy was put inside. Afterward, the American escorted the army ambulance, which bore the Moslem red crescent, through the Kyrenia Pass. There was little likelihood of any Greek snipers or guerrillas lying in ambush, but just in case they were, the American figured they would be less likely to shoot when they saw his white car flying the pale-blue flag of the United Nations from its radio antenna.

"Gonna take my problems to the United Nations ..." Dion and the Belmonts?

In Kyrenia, empty now except for Turkish soldiers, some patrolling the streets, some sitting in the seaside cafés, rifles in their laps, the ambulance brought the boy to an evacuation point on the beach. Abandoned yachts rode on the gentle harbor swells. Beyond, freighters off-loaded supplies under the guns of the Turkish fleet. The American waited for the helicopter that was to take the boy to a hospital ship. His leg was twice normal size and blue-black, and there was no possible way the doctors could save it.

A younger boy sat fishing off a jetty, casting his line between two moored sailboats. The boy reeled in, changed bait, and cast out again.

"How's the fishing?" the American asked.

He smiled and shrugged.

"No good. No perch today."

The helicopter landed and the stretcher bearers turned their faces away from the sand and dust blasted by the rotor blades. The wounded boy, staring glassily at the sky, refused with a slow shaking of his head the cigarette the crew chief offered him. Then he was lifted up and strapped inside.

"And the world calls us Turks barbarians!" the crew chief shouted at the American. "Why don't you show the world what the Greeks have done!"

The American said nothing. Everyone was taking his problems to the United Nations.

The chopper rose with a slapping sound, its nose down, tail rotor up, before it straightened and flew over the harbor and the white yachts toward the hospital ship.

The American walked back to the jetty to see if the young angler's luck had changed. The boy shrugged and smiled once again.

"No perch," he said, but did not ask the American to do anything about it.

Doo-doo-do-doot, doododoo ... Bobby Darin, the American was sure that's who it was.

FOUR

The City

"Aw, Jeeeezus, not another goddamned Nam story," moaned Barry Came. "Can't you ever tell a story that's not about the goddamned Nam?"

"Cork it," said Nick Proffitt. He was *Newsweek*'s Middle East bureau chief, Came his number two. "It's not my fault you missed out on the biggest story of the decade."

"The goddamned Nam. Jeeeezuz Christ."

Proffitt, tallish and beefy, with a shock of thick brown hair combed straight back, pulled his glasses low on his nose and glared at the slight, dark-eyed Came.

"I said to cork it. I'm your boss, remember?"

"Oh, the boss says cork it."

"This story has a moral."

"What moral?"

"If you fucking cork it you'll find out," Proffitt said and, pushing his glasses back up to his eyes, turned to his audience.

We were gathered around one of the big tables in the bar at the St. Georges, the best hotel in the Middle East before it became a charred casualty of the Lebanese lunacy. Not plushly modern, like the Vendome or the Phoenicia, both across the Rue Corniche, it was a grand old place whose wood-paneled lobby and bar gleamed like staterooms in a presidential yacht. I can't remember how many of us were there that night, the night after I arrived in Beirut. I'm not sure *who* was there, so I'll give myself the license to people the table with some of the correspondents covering the fighting between the army and the Palestinian guerrillas. I'm taking the liberty because I do recall that the presence of so many big press guns affected an impulsive and nearly fatal decision I was to make later that night. Peter Jennings, then ABC's Middle East correspondent, might have been there, along with Juan DeOnis, the *New York Times's* Beirut bureau chief, AP's Holger Jensen, and Georgie Anne Geyer, roving correspondent for the Chicago *Daily News,* my chief competition. Geyer, with her pageboy haircut, quiet voice, and girlish nickname, Gee-Gee, seemed out of place in what was then the almost exclusively male world of war correspondents. But she belonged in it as much as the most grizzled macho man, and if you were covering the same story as she, you were likely to find yourself bombarded by rockets—urgent messages about your lousy performance sent by your foreign editor.

Another reporter was there—seated not at the table but in my mind. Don Kirk, the *Tribune's* new Far East bureau chief, had burned up the track with story after front-page story from the previous year's Easter offensive in Vietnam. He had been nominated for both the Pulitzer and the Overseas Press Club Award, and rumor had it that he would win at least one of the prizes. He was considered a star of the first magnitude in the paper's heavens.

I had been a luminary on the suburban beat, on general assignment, and on the Task Force, but as a foreign correspondent, I cast a fainter light. In nine months, I had not covered a major story; there had been none to cover. Beirut was my first, and I was determined to add some candlepower to my star. (Correspondents, no less than ambitious generals and admirals, need wars to advance their careers.)

"She wanted to go to Khe Sanh," Proffitt was saying as he began his story about a famous woman war correspondent. (I'm concealing her name and fuzzing the details of the story to avoid embarrassing her.) "She pulled all the strings and finally got herself on a C-130 resupply flight. The plane comes in. Mortar fire on the airstrip, so the plane doesn't shut its engines down when it off-loads. It hardly *stops.* Open the cargo door, keep taxiing, and push all the shit out—C-rats, ammo—and she gets pushed out with it and runs across the airstrip to a bunker. She's there. Storied Khe Sanh. She spends the day there, trying to get a story, but the marines won't talk to her. What's this chubby chick doing at Khe Sanh? Pretty soon, *she* starts to wonder what she's doing there because she has to take one helluva leak and there's nothing there but open latrines and those heads they had over there, y'know, a four-holer with some chicken wire around it. And six thousand marines who can't remember the last time they saw round-eye ass. Only thing she can do is wait till it's dark. By this time, her kidneys are as big as footballs, her back teeth are floating. She sneaks into one of the officer's heads, drops trou, and squats. She has a little smoke—she smoked like a fiend—and then she drops the cigarette down the hole. What she doesn't know is that the marines are going to burn out the head the next day. They've already poured about five gallons of diesel fuel down there." Proffitt paused for effect, pursing his lips as if he were going to blow a kiss. "*Whomp!* It goes off. Talk about getting a fire lit under your ass! She stumbles out with her trou and skivvies down around her ankles and the whole head's burning. Marines to the rescue. What do they see? Her standing there bare-assed, looking at the officer's head going up in flames."

Came slugged his drink and gave Proffitt a pinched look.

"So what's the moral?"

"The moral is—the final indignity is that there is no final indignity."

If this book were a novel, now would be the moment for the bomb to explode, but my memory whispers that things did not happen with such neat, dramatic timing. The explosion came later, after I had listened to more war stories, from Proffitt, from Holger Jensen, who had also covered Vietnam, and from whoever else might have been there. I had begun to feel like the outsider I was, a green lightweight among seasoned heavyweights. I wasn't even yet accredited with the Ministry of Information (that day, a Monday, had been Martyrs Day, the Lebanese equivalent of Independence Day, and all government offices had been closed). With no one to interview, I did not have a very clear idea of what the fighting was about, and I had been too embarrassed to ask people like Proffitt and Geyer to fill me in. I had glanced at a few stories at Reuters, through which *Tribune* reporters filed their copy, but there was little background in the terse wire service dispatches. Something about the Palestinians taking over the neighborhoods around the camps, turning them into states within a state. Something about the presence of ten thousand well-armed guerrillas, mostly Moslem, tipping the country's oh so delicate balance of sectarian power in favor of its Moslem population. Something about the Christian leaders and military officers deciding to move against the PLO and reassert the authority of the army and government.

The bomb went off in the street, in front of the Phoenicia Hotel. Not much of a blast—just enough to rattle windows and nerves in the St. Georges. We ran outside for a look, found a small hole gouged in the pavement, some broken glass. One of the taxi drivers hanging around the St. Georges said it had been tossed from a car and might have been a hand grenade. Everyone filed back inside, but I hung behind, glancing at the drivers, who leaned against one of the beat-up Mercedes cabs, smoking and talking. Bursts of automatic rifle fire came from the camps, three or four miles away, and spent tracer rounds floated lazily into the dark sky, like embers from a fire. Winston Churchill had once written that the war correspondent's job is to go as far as he can as fast as he can. I don't know if I was thinking of his comment at that moment; I might have been. For sure a hotel bar was no place from which to cover a war. That wasn't what Don Kirk had done in Vietnam. Let my competitors drink and tell war stories. I was going to get one and beat them all. Go as far as I could as fast as I could. I didn't know that you could go too far too fast, but I was about to become educated.

I hired a driver named Zouhair Fakhreddin: dark-haired, lean, and about thirty years old. He'd told me he knew the location of a Lebanese army position near the airport. The troops were shelling Palestinian guerrillas in Sabra Camp, a few hundred yards away. My plan, if the cockeyed scheme could be called a plan, was to talk my way into the position, get a firsthand look at the fighting, interview a few soldiers and officers—Zouhair would act as my translator—and be back in a couple of hours with an eyewitness dispatch.

Things started to go wrong almost from the start; Zouhair could not find the position and began driving aimlessly down blackened streets made sinister by their complete vacancy, their atmosphere of silent expectancy.

"Got any idea where you're going?"

"Oh, yes, yes," Zouhair answered.

We came to an intersection. Zouhair pointed to the left, at a block of dark buildings, and said: "Fedayeen. We can't go near there. You are American and the Americans support Israel. They would hold you for ransom or kill you if they caught you. Kill me, too. They are murdering cutthroats."

I listened to him with one ear and out the open window with the other for a sound, any kind of sound—a voice, a radio, a barking dog, the evil metallic click of a rifle bolt jacking a round into the chamber.

We drove several more empty blocks. I had a sense of not seeing something that could see me. Fear must have shown on my face like a neon rash.

"What is the matter?" asked Zouhair. "Are you scared? I'm not."

He muttered to himself that the army position was somewhere nearby, but after we had gone another block or two, he stopped and said we should walk; a lone car moving at night would be prime target for a sniper or ambush.

We had been out of the car only a minute or two when three teenage boys materialized. They weren't armed, so I told Zouhair to ask them where the fighting was. They wanted to know who we were and asked for some identification. I showed my Rome press card, the only piece of press identification I had.

"This way," one of them said in Arabic, gesturing for us to follow him and his friends.

We walked behind a short distance, walked in a darkness as deep as any I had seen in the jungle on moonless midnights. I almost bumped into the muzzle of an automatic rifle, its bipods resting on the parapet of a sandbagged bunker. The outline of a man's head and shoulders showed behind the rifle, pointed at my head. The three boys shouted into a tangle of low walls and buildings. Voices shouted back out of the darkness, and Zouhair whispered in my ear: "Oh, my God, they're fedayeen."

He had whispered, but he might as well have howled.

Two more youths materialized, tall and thin, with shoulder-length hair. They looked like hippies, but they weren't, not with magazine pouches girdling their waists and AK-47s in their hands. One took hold of my wrist, not roughly but firmly enough to let me know he wouldn't tolerate any attempts to run away. The other man held Zouhair. They led us into a narrow passageway between a building and a wall about five feet high. A dozen armed men crouched behind the wall, some with faces swaddled in kaffiyehs. A hundred and fifty yards from the wall, a mound of earth rose, the silhouettes of bunkers and dug-in armored cars scalloping its crest. The army post—we had missed it by a block.

A muzzle flash from the mound, a burst of machine-gun fire, bullets cracking into the front of the wall.

"Get down and run!" someone shouted in English, and we were all bent over, running. The guerrillas stopped and let loose over the wall, a dozen AKs on full automatic, rock and roll, and the Lebanese troops answered with mortars and armored-car guns, shells whooping overhead, crashing into buildings less than a hundred yards away. Children started to wail, women were screaming. The long-haired guerrillas prodded Zouhair and me out of the passageway, past a line of shacks, and into a courtyard, well out of the line of fire.

"Squat!"

The command came in English from a third guerrilla, his rifle trained on us. A fourth appeared from out of the shadows—tall and fair for a Palestinian, maybe twenty-five years old, dressed in a nylon windbreaker.

"Who are you and what are you doing here?" he asked in good English.

"I'm a correspondent for the Chicago *Tribune*."

"Identification?"

I again produced the Rome press card. He glanced at it under a penlight, then slipped it into his pocket.

"Okay, Mister Journalist, you wait right here until this shooting is over. Then you can write your story."

He walked off. A man came out of a house.

"*Marhaba*," he said. "Hello."

"*Marhaba*."

"You like tea or coffee?"

"Coffee."

"Bitter or *masbut*?"

Masbut meant "just right" and, when applied to coffee, "medium-sweet."

"*Masbut*," I answered.

"Yes, *masbut* for me, too," Zouhair said.

In a few minutes our coffee came, in two little cups. We sat sipping it while a block away shells exploded and rifles crackled and the children cried. Now and then shell flashes illuminated our guard, sitting with his back to the coffee man's house, his rifle still on us.

The noise fell off. The sound of a car came from somewhere. Voices cried out, first in Arabic, then in English, "Stop! Stop!"

We heard the car gun its engine, then a long burst of automatic fire. The engine stopped suddenly. The mortars and armored cars opened up again, the racket amplified by the crowded streets and buildings of the refugee camp.

The young man in the nylon windbreaker reappeared, walking casually. He handed my press card back to me.

"Okay, Mister Journalist. Come with me. You are a journalist with the fedayeen. We are comrades now."

I believed him because I wanted to. My audacity had paid off, aided by blind luck. Now, instead of a report from the army side, I would come back with an exclusive from behind guerrilla lines. But in that premier seat of knowledge, the gut, I knew I was not a correspondent with the fedayeen; I was their prisoner.

We wound through a labyrinth of dirty streets and passageways, hugging the walls of concrete and mud-brick hovels. A hand clasped mine—Zouhair's. He might not have been scared out on the street, but he was plenty scared now. Somehow, I could not let his hand go.

We were led into a low cement building. Roaches scampered across the floor, away from the light of the single, naked bulb hanging over a metal desk. A short, thickset man sat behind it, feet propped up, an AK in his lap. A second man, thin to the point of emaciation, lounged on a beat-up sofa, under a boarded-up window; a third, two or three inches over six feet tall, stood in a corner, slouching insouciantly while explosions shook the building and spent shrapnel pattered against the walls like a light rain. The man in the windbreaker gestured to Zouhair to sit on the sofa, to me to sit in a chair in front of the desk; then he left.

For the next several minutes we sat under the silent stares of the three other men, stares that were a little curious, a little suspicious, a little hostile. The tall one's eyes had a look of sullen menace. I stared back at him, convinced that if I showed the least sign of nervousness or fear, he would take me for a spy and shoot us both. He smiled derisively.

"Tonight you sleep with us."

All right, I thought, act calm, act like a correspondent. Start asking questions.

"So what are you fighting for?"

The thickset man behind the desk answered, stilted phrases rolling off his tongue as off a mimeograph machine.

"Our movement is national and revolutionary. We have many enemies—Israel and the Zionists, who took our land, the reactionary Arab regimes allied to Israel, and"—he paused, giving me a good long look—"the American imperialists."

A student well drilled in the radical catechism.

A guerrilla came through the door and hurriedly gave him an order in Arabic. He stood up, buckling his ammunition belt. The peace symbol was painted onto one of the magazine pouches and under it the words "Peace and Love." He saw me glance at that bit of heavy irony and threw a wicked look over his shoulder as he went out the door.

"Peace and love, hah!" he said with a kind of snort.

The man who came in after him was of medium height, paunchy and bald. He could have been a carpet salesman in one of the bazaars, or a shopkeeper, some petit bourgeois with a fat wife and a brood of squalling kids at home. The belt of an automatic pistol made an olive-green stripe beneath the round eaves of his belly. He sat down behind the desk and stared at Zouhair and me with large brown eyes that should have been soft but instead clamped on me like handcuffs.

"Empty your pockets and give me all your papers," he said quietly in English.

We did, placing our wallets, keys, and small change on the desk, along with my pocket phone book, passport, notebook, and pens. Zouhair burst out in a stream of Arabic. I guessed he was declaring his innocence. The man listened with the bored patience of a desk sergeant to a stale alibi. Then he turned to me, asking in that quiet voice of his: "What were you doing in our positions at night?"

I explained: correspondent, wanted to report on the fighting, stumbled into their positions by accident. If he was a shopkeeper or carpet salesman, it was for sure he never gave his customers the wolf's grin he gave me.

"And why do you not have a press card from the Ministry of Information?"

For someone who was fighting the Lebanese government, he showed an unusual respect for its authority. I explained the absence of the press card: the Ministry of Information was closed because of the holiday.

"Where did you come to Beirut from?"

"Rome. I'm based in Rome. There's my press identification from Italy."

The man was not impressed. He flipped through my passport, noting the date of my entry into Lebanon.

"I don't see any stamps from Israel," he said.

"No."

"You're an American. How many times have you been to Israel?"

My heart started beating so hard I was sure everyone in the room could hear it.

"Just once. Three years ago. As a tourist."

He opened my wallet and spread its contents. It was only then I saw my oversight. The two Israeli business cards, one from the Information Ministry in Jerusalem, stood out like the hands of a luminous watch in a pitch-black room.

"You have been carrying these for the past three years?"

"I guess I must have."

"Unusual."

"Yes, I guess it is."

He gathered our documents, put them in two plastic bags from the desk drawer, and walked out.

Time warped as we waited with the two guerrillas, the tall one standing, the thin one on the sofa beside Zouhair. Ten minutes might have passed, or an hour, or three hours.

A shell or rocket burst nearby. The house trembled. Shrapnel crackled against the walls outside. The tall man stared with his sullen, half-closed eyes. *These are the men who fill the ranks of Black September,* I thought, *and they think I'm a spy for Israel.* Gut knowledge and brain knowledge were one. *It's just a matter of time till I die.*

The tall man was called outside. He was back five minutes later and told us to follow him. We did. The thin man walked behind. Again, the warren of hovels and narrow streets, men crouching against walls, bullets cracking in the air like invisible whips. *Marhaba,* the men said as we passed, *marhaba, marhaba.* And I answered back, *Marhaba, Ahlan,* Hello, Hi. *Act calm, act friendly, and surely someone will see that you are just a correspondent.* We jogged across a field filled with rubble. *Is this where it'll come?* I wondered. *Out here in this field? They'll tell us to stop, to kneel, and then press the muzzles against the back of our heads and ... bangyerdead.*

We reentered the maze, coming finally to an abandoned apartment house. I made a mental note that it was six stories high, the highest building in the neighborhood. The tall man led us up a darkened staircase. "Slowly, slowly," advised the thin one from behind. He was wary that we might try to run, but I wasn't about to give him an excuse to shoot us. Besides, where would we run to in that maze outside? Still, I was thinking of how to escape, making mental notes of small details that might help us when we tried.

On the fourth floor, the tall man opened the door to what had been a tiny kitchen and was now a prison cell. Steel bars crossed its single window. The stench from an adjoining squat toilet was strong enough to make our eyes water. Zouhair started to protest, shouting at the guards in Arabic. I grabbed his arm.

"Don't," I said. "Don't piss them off."

"Sorry for the conditions," the tall man apologized in his listless voice. "But this is all we have."

"Don't worry," said the other. "You'll be out of here in two hours. At dawn."

I knew he was lying, as the guerrilla in the nylon windbreaker had lied. Lulling us with false hopes so we would cooperate in our own imprisonment and, maybe, execution.

The guards produced two clean blankets from somewhere, told us we could keep our cigarettes, instructed us to knock if we had to use the toilet, then asked for our belts and shoes.

Zouhair's face collapsed.

"But why?" he asked.

"The shoes to make it harder for us to run, the belts because we might use them to strangle one of them. Or hang ourselves." I turned to the man with the sullen, half-closed eyes. "Isn't that right?"

"Yes."

The two men went out with our belts and shoes. The door shut behind them, the lock snapped, and a sense of helplessness coiled around me like a chain. Already, gray was bleeding into the sky. In the twilight falling through the barred window, I looked at Zouhair, sitting slumped in a corner.

"Zouhair, I got you into this. I'm sorry. That's all I can say."

He made a dismissive gesture.

"You did not force me."

"Still, it's my fault. But we'll get out of this all right," I said, with more confidence than I felt.

"Yes. In two hours they'll let us go. They'll let us go at dawn."

"No, they won't. Not then. We'll go nuts if we start believing everything they tell us. They'll let us go eventually, if we play our cards right, but not in two hours."

A few minutes later, as if to remind me that the guerrillas weren't the only hazard, the army started to bombard the camp with roof-busting 120-millimeter mortars. Zouhair and I lay flat, listening to the shells, now louder, now softer, like the footfalls of some monster pacing back and forth through the early-morning dark.

In the middle of all that, exhausted, I fell asleep.

Dawn. Roosters crowed, children shouted and cried, the muezzin or, rather, a tape recording of the muezzin, called the faithful to prayers they would not say in mosques they could not get to because of the shellfire.

A one-twenty hit a building half a block away. Smoke fingered through the window bars.

Zouhair and I lit our last cigarettes, puffed them down to the filters.

Another one-twenty close by. The building rocked. Plaster dust sifted down in a dry mist. Zouhair shouted through the door to the guards to move us to a lower floor.

"We'll be killed in here!"

"Many people are dying," one of the guerrillas yelled back. "What are two more?"

We lay tight against the floor, arms wrapped around the backs of our skulls, waiting for the mortar that would drop two stories of concrete and steel on top of us.

Later in the morning, after the shelling lifted and we had smoked several butts picked off the filthy floor, two air force jets whined in circles over the camp. I stood and watched them through the window. High up and silver against the hot pale sky, the French-built Mirages circled like hunting eagles.

Four stories below, a jeep with a heavy machine gun mounted on its rear sped up and stopped at an intersection. A guerrilla swung into the seat behind the gun and opened up on the planes. In no time, it sounded as if everyone in the camp with a gun was firing. Thousands of bullets flew skyward and fell, useless as stones; the planes were way beyond machine gun and small-arms range.

"All those crazy assholes are going to do is draw fire!" I yelled.

They kept shooting, and I wondered if they were trying to draw the planes into range. But that tactic required a deliberateness, and the Palestinians' fire was wild and random. It had a quality of ecstasy that told me the guerrillas *wanted* to force the planes to attack them. To die in action would fulfill their loony dreams of a fiery martyrdom. Fedayeen, after all, meant "self-sacrificer."

The planes responded to the invitation. Firing rockets, they came in low with a deafening techno-howl. One or two rockets crashed into the backside of the building. It shook like a toy in the hands of an angry child but somehow stayed upright. More rockets struck a row of houses across the street. I was down on my belly, trying to make myself thin as a sheet of paper. The room was cloudy with smoke and cement dust and Zouhair was shouting, "Allah deliver us! Allah deliver us!" Somehow, we miniaturized ourselves, bent our bodies into tiny balls, and squeezed into a cupboard under the sink. On the bottom of the sink were the words "Made in Romania."

"Will we be safe now?" Zouhair asked.

"Unless we take a direct hit," I lied, thinking, *Am I to be killed here, in a Palestinian refugee camp, under a Romanian sink, by Lebanese pilots flying French-built jets?*

A loud whoosh, rockets bursting in the street, the building swaying, Zouhair crying out "Allah deliver us," then people screaming in the street, deep animal screams of pain that drowned out even the roar of the jets as they flew off. I crawled out from the cupboard and looked down at a lump of bloody matter that might once have been a human being (high explosive tends to transform all living creatures into generic tissue). A man, with his shattered leg dragging, was being led away by two guerrillas. An ambulance came up. Three or four dead and wounded were thrown inside. The ambulance raced off, squalling like a demented gull. Jet howl, rockets and bombs, human screams, and now ambulance sirens. Overture to finale, the whole symphony of a berserk century had been compressed into five or ten minutes.

The mortars resumed and machine-gun rounds crackled past the window.

"Allah deliver us!"

There were no atheists in foxholes, or in kitchens with Balkan plumbing. I prayed, too. All the prayers the nuns taught me at Divine Infant Jesus School in Westchester, Illinois. The Mirages did not return, the mortars and gunfire fell off. A logician would have disputed me, but I saw cause and effect between my orisons and the sudden, blessed lull.

The door opened. In it stood the dayshift guard—a pudgy young fedayee with a three-day growth of beard and a rifle. He looked like a young Yasir Arafat.

"You can go to the toilet."

Zouhair answered that we did not have to because we had not eaten or drunk a thing since before midnight.

"No food," the guard said. "Even we don't have any."

"How about cigarettes?" I asked.

"I don't smoke. It's bad for the health."

He locked the door again.

We ate two moldy pieces of pita we found in a cabinet and washed them down with tap water.

We topped off our meal with more cigarette butts.

The guard started to pound on the door with a hammer. Zouhair asked what he was doing.

"Putting on a second lock to make sure you don't get out."

"In the name of Allah, why are you doing this?"

The hammer kept the beat to the guard's words:

"I spit"—bang-bang—"on Allah"—bang-bang—"Everything I get"—bang—"I get with"—bang—"my own hands"—bang-bang—"and my gun"—bang-bang. "Don't talk to me"—bang—"of Allah"—bang—"You are both spies"—bang-bang-bang.

Zouhair slumped again in a corner, eyes on the floor.

"He's a blasphemer. We are the captives of blasphemers. They must be Communists, from the PDFLP."

The Popular Democratic Front for the Liberation of Palestine was a militantly Marxist faction of the PLO, and so independent of Arafat's central command it was the next thing to renegade.

"These are men without God, Philip. Men without God can do anything. I think they are going to shoot us."

He started to cry. I sat next to him, hugged him close.

"C'mon now ... c'mon ..."

His head fell against my shoulder.

"We are in the hands of men without God."

"C'mon, Zouhair ... We can't ... C'mon ..."

I told myself that I had been a lieutenant of marines, a combat veteran who had to be strong in this crisis, strong enough for the two of us; but as I clasped the back of Zouhair's head and felt his tears soaking into my shirt, a memory came to me, so powerful and vivid it was almost a hallucination. Zouhair's head became the tiny head of my infant son, Marc, snuggled against my shoulder, Zouhair's tears his tears, and that half memory, half delusion brought the terrible thought that I might never see him, or Geoff, or Jill, or anyone again. The thought mothered a vast pity, for my family and for myself.

"C'mon, Zouhair ..." The pity rose in my throat, bitter as bile. I started to choke, my eyes grew damp. "C'mon, we've got to be strong ... Can't let them ..." With an enormous effort, I rammed the pity and self-pity down into my gut, where, suddenly, it coagulated into a rage. "Can't let the *motherfuckers* get to us. C'mon, c'mon ..."

At noon, the guard opened his new lock and brought in a pot of sweetened tea and two packs of cigarettes. I reached for them with such desperation that, a second later, I was disgusted with myself.

He returned in an hour with two more armed men. He called one of them "Erebia," a strongly built man with a neatly trimmed beard and thick glasses that would have made him look professorial if the eyes behind them had not been so cold and dead. A killer's eyes. I was to go with him and the other man.

Following the expressionless Erebia down the stairs, I decided that if I was being led to my execution, he would be the shooter.

We crossed a street, hopping over an open sewer, and entered a large, dilapidated room with boarded windows and a squad of guerrillas, two sleeping on canvas cots, six more eating or cleaning their rifles. Erebia gestured to me to sit on a straw mat in the middle of the room. The fedayeen did not say a thing, staring as if I were some rare kind of animal captured after a long and difficult chase. Who were they—my firing squad?—and what were they thinking? Were they thinking anything? I had an instinct that my life depended on how I acted, but I had no idea how I should act. I felt outraged—who the hell did these Palestinians think they were to imprison a legitimate newsman and treat him like a spy, what authority did they have in this country?—but was afraid to let my outrage show. It might have incited them. I was also terrified but afraid of letting my terror show; the guerrillas might have mistaken a display of fear as an admission of guilt. How did innocents behave? Calmly. But how to act calmly with nine armed men around me and mortar shells exploding outside? In the desert, Israel Stockman had guided me through the bedouin's ritualistic codes of conduct, but there was no guide to the rules of the world Zouhair and I had fallen into. I wasn't entirely sure it had any.

How to behave? When in doubt, do nothing. I sat like a buddha. I didn't move my eyes. I hardly breathed.

"Where is the prisoner?"

The question came from a man who could have played an RAF pilot. In his middle or late thirties, with light-blue eyes, short black hair salted with gray, and a clipped mustache, he was neatly dressed in a cotton shirt and pressed trousers. A small leather case was tucked under his arm.

The guerrillas laughed at his question and pointed at me.

"He looks like an Arab," he said, sat in front of me, and then, with an arctic smile, fixed his pale eyes on me.

I could hear my heartbeat, the blood thudding in my veins, but I began to feel a little less confused: there *was* a chain of command and Mr. Blue Eyes was a big link in it. He and nobody else was the one I would have to convince, he was in charge, he was *The Man*.

He opened the leather case and took out my passport, press card, wallet, and phone book.

He held the passport up to my face.

"Is this yours?" His English was almost flawless.

"Yes."

The wallet next.

"Is this yours?"

"Yes."

The phone book—yes—the press card—yes.

His smile thawed a little as he gave me a cigarette. The worst enemy of the prisoner, whether he's a pilot downed over enemy lines, a dissident voyaging in the Gulag Archipelago, or the victim of terrorist kidnapping, is hope. The prisoner can be tied blindfolded to a post, can hear the firing squad loading its rifles and the commands to "readeee ... aim ..." and will continue to hope for a last-minute reprieve or rescue. Hope is his greatest torment, yet he will grasp at any straw to support it; and when the reed snaps the agony of his despair is all the greater than it would have been if he had abandoned hope from the beginning. The warming of Mr. Blue Eyes' smile and the offer of the cigarette were the reeds I grasped. He sees that they've made a big mistake! He's going to give my papers back and tell me I'm free to go!

When, instead, he told me to give him a brief autobiography, I felt a sickening drop in my stomach.

"What do you want to know?"

"The important things about your life."

"Beginning when?"

"When you were born."

I told him. He turned and translated my birth date to a young man, a kind of recording secretary who sat behind him with a tablet of paper in a clipboard.

"Where were you born?"

"Chicago."

"And how long did you live in Chicago?"

I explained that I had lived in two suburbs. What were their names? Berwyn and Westchester, I answered, and my brain split like an overgrown amoeba. Half swam in the present, half far in the past, where I saw my grandparents' bungalow and the buff-brick trilevel with the pecky cypress trim. I could not reconnect the two halves, the past with the present. How did someone raised by ordinary people in such ordinary places end up a prisoner in an Arab guerrilla camp? *This is what you wanted,* answered a voice in my head. *You wanted to*

escape the middle grounds of experience for the extremities. Well, here
you are.

In the next hour, I took my interrogator through my life to college graduation.

"And after university, what?"

I paused, giving myself a second or two to think, to think as fast
as a chess player at a critical point in the match. Should I tell him I
had been in the Marine Corps? The U.S. Marines—what, in the
minds of most Asians, Latins, and radical Arabs, could be more
emblematic of what they viewed as Yankee imperialism? I considered
omitting all mention of military service, but then I thought, "Who the
hell is this guy with his blue eyes, his British officer's mustache, his
impeccable English? What access does he have to what information?
Maybe he already knows you were a marine officer in Vietnam and is
just waiting to catch you in a lie."

I opted for a defensive move.

"I went into the service."

"You mean military service?"

"Yes."

"Go on."

"I was discharged after three years, and then ..."

"Which years?"

"Nineteen sixty-four to sixty-seven."

Here it comes.

"What did you do in the military?"

You've still got some maneuvering room.

"I was in the infantry. A foot soldier."

"And you never did any intelligence work?"

"No."

"What happened after your discharge?"

I breathed a silent sigh of relief and went on, Mr. Blue Eyes
translating my answers phrase by phrase, the recording secretary's
pen flying over the paper, his Arabic script as opaque as the faces of
the young fedayeen all around me.

What with the painstaking translation, my autobiography took
two hours. When I was done, the interrogator rewarded me with
another smoke.

"Okay, Philip," he said, lighting my cigarette, then his. "You've been very cooperative so far. From now on I want you to continue that way."

He seemed pleased, and hope—stupid, tormenting hope—rose in me again. I realized that I wanted to please Mr. Blue Eyes. I was disgusted with myself. The issue still was: how to behave. I don't mean demeanor, but doing the right thing. If I had fantasized a situation like the one I was in, I would have been an exemplar of courage. As soon as the questioning began, I would have said, "You have no authority in this country, you have no right to detain and question an accredited, legitimate correspondent. I demand that you release me immediately."

The extremities of experience. Hadn't I learned in Vietnam that people on the outer edges seldom fulfill their ideal images of themselves, that they never are half as brave, compassionate, or wise as they imagined? The few who are become heroes and heroines, but I was no hero. I hadn't groveled, I hadn't begged. All I had been was cooperative, but what a vapid word, with its suggestion of bland accommodation. Shouldn't I at least try to be the courageous man in my fantasies? But for what purpose? Wasn't my first obligation to stay alive for the sake of my wife and sons? Yes, but at what cost? Another thing I had learned in Vietnam was that there are worse things than death, such as not being able to look anyone straight in the eye, especially the man in the mirror. How to act. I saw that I was going to have to walk a narrow path between kamikaze bravery and craven surrender. I was going to have to draw a line for myself. I decided I wasn't going to sign anything, like, say, a phony confession admitting that I was a spy for the CIA or Israel.

"Now all I want from you are the facts, Philip, the facts," Mr. Blue Eyes was saying, cigarette smoke puffing out of his mouth with each word. He sounded like a parody of Jack Webb on the old TV series, "Dragnet." "If you don't tell the truth, things will not stop with me. You'll go higher, and things could get worse. So, are you ready to begin, Philip?"

"I'd like to know something first. Are you going to shoot me no matter what I say? If that's it, then you might as well do it now."

His smile turned a little wistful.

"Despite what you may have heard about us, we are not murderers."

I thought: we'll see about that. Mr. Blue Eyes' eyes, tiny arctic seas to accompany his frosty smile, latched onto mine.

"What were you doing inside our lines last night?"

"For one thing, I wasn't inside your lines ..."

The smile vanished.

"You were *caught* inside our lines by our men."

"I was *taken* inside your lines by your men."

He had all the cards, he was willing to concede minor points of semantics and geographics.

"Then let us say you were very near our lines late at night. What were you doing there?"

"I'm a correspondent ..."

"What else are you?"

"That's all."

"Agents use journalism as a cover, don't they?"

It was more accusation than question. I answered that I didn't know any correspondents who moonlighted in espionage. A mortar barrage crashed close by and the fighting started again, machine guns and automatic rifles sounding like two dozen jackhammers.

"What else are you?" the interrogator shouted, both to make himself heard over the noise and to establish that he could be very unpleasant when necessary.

"Nothing else!" I shouted back.

"*What else?*"

"*Nothing! I'm not anything else, goddamnit!*"

We were like two men trying to hold a conversation in the middle of a construction site. Deconstruction site would have been more like it. The sounds outside were the sounds of things blowing up, flying apart, fragmenting.

"Very well, Philip!" Mr. Blue Eyes yelled. "I hoped we could do this quickly, but now I see we must do it the slow way!" He picked up my phone book. "We are going to go through this! I am going to ask you about each and every name in this book, and you will answer!"

"There must be two hundred names in that book!"

"We have lots of time!"

I felt myself falling, falling. At least twenty of those names were Israeli. Almost that many were names of prominent Arabs on the West Bank. If he asked, I would have to admit that I had lied the night before and had flown to Beirut from Israel. That alone, I thought, would be sufficient fare for a ticket to the courtyard wall, but I drew another line for myself: if, to save my skin, I had to lie about anyone in the book, I would not do it. It would be tempting to lie just to please Mr. Blue Eyes, to say, yes, so and so is an agent for the CIA or the Mossad, but that sort of false witness could be a death sentence for someone like Israel Stockman or Charlie Weiss.

The interrogator began, and we went through the book name by name, the shellfire adding to the terror of execution the fear that a mortar would make a firing squad unnecessary.

The fedayeen in the room joked about the different sounds—whines of ricochets, crackle of AKs, the wall-shaking blasts of rockets. During a break in the middle of the questioning, a guerrilla I nicknamed "The Happy Warrior" came in, snapping his fingers and dancing in what looked like a mimic of a Southside Chicago ghetto strut. He was a sniper who carried a long rifle with telescopic sight.

"*Marhaba*, Mister," he said, twirling around me, fingers going *pop-pop-pop*. "How are you, how are you, brotha?"

He jived his way to a cot, where he flopped down and dug into a plate of bread and olives. When he finished eating, he jumped up and spun around me again, laughing, fingers cracking.

"Back to business, Mister. Good-bye, good-bye."

And he pirouetted out the door.

Mr. Blue Eyes went back to his business: my source book. Who is this person? Who introduced you? Why is this name in your book? When he came to an Israeli name, he did not demand that I confess it was the name of a secret agent. I was almost disappointed. I wanted to find out if I would cross my self-drawn line, but the interrogator only listened to my answers and translated them for the secretary, filling page after page with his calligraphy.

After seven or eight hours, we reached the W's ...

Charlie Weiss ...

Tribune stringer in Jerusalem. Also Voice of America correspondent in Israel ... What is a stringer? ... A part-time correspondent.

Mr. Blue Eyes closed the book. Hope leapt again, against my will.

"We will continue tomorrow, Philip," he said, and went out. I saw that it was dark.

*   *   *

Zouhair came in, led by two fedayeen. One was tall, with powerful forearms, short black hair, and close-set, cretinous eyes divided by a hooked nose.

Zouhair practically fell on me.

"*Alhamdu i'llah!* You are alive! I thought they had killed you."

"Not yet."

"What were they doing?"

"Interrogating me."

"Did they beat you?"

"Not yet."

Dinner arrived—bread, olives, and tea. With Mr. Blue Eyes gone, the guerrillas seemed to relax. They peppered me with friendly questions about life in America. I, ever the journalist, made some attempts to interview them, to discover what motivated them. I guess I was playing a game with myself, trying to transform my disaster into an opportunity: my capture was giving me a rare, inside look at a world few people had seen, a kind of terra incognita that spawned the young men who made lurid headlines with their hijackings and bombings, their cross-border raids to shoot up Israeli kibbutzim and seize hostages. What were they thinking? What map could I draw of the insides of their minds? Now *there* was the real terra incognita. Their mental interiors were hidden behind an insurmountable range of political cant. All I got in answer to my questions were the standard, stilted phrases about the revolution and the Zionist entity.

The Happy Warrior, sniper rifle slung, bopped in and made a few jokes. There was a lot of bantering back and forth, none of which I understood. Western rock played on a transistor: the Beatles or the Stones or the Doors, I can't remember which. I had read somewhere that hijack victims sometimes identified with the hijackers—an odd phenomenon for which the usual suspects in the think tanks and universities had a dozen different theories. Something like that seemed to be happening to me, eating under fire and listening to the radio with the fedayeen. A feeling of camaraderie seemed to grow between us, even, I would say, a certain bonhomie. I suppose the think tankers could have supplied several explanations: I *wanted* to identify with the guerrillas, thinking that would help them identify with me and make it more difficult for them to shoot me, or I might have been suffering from an extreme case of the tourist's See-Ethel-These-Folks-Are-Just-Like-Us Syndrome because it was just too awful to think that my life was in the hands of people utterly alien and unknowable. On a more basic plane, we were bonded by shared dangers—if a mortar crashed through the roof it would not distinguish between me and them.

I knew all the apologies, all the political and historical arguments for Palestinian terrorism. The Jews were terrorists first, remember Deir Yassin, the Arabs would say, naming the Palestinian village where over two hundred and fifty men, women, and children were massacred in 1947 by the Irgun. I had heard most of the rationalizations: one man's terrorist is another man's freedom fighter. Right. What interested me, though, were the psychological roots of terrorism, whether it was committed by Arabs or Jews or Christians. Was it just passionate conviction that powered a man to reach moral escape velocity and sent him beyond the tedious pull of man's laws, God's commandments, and even nature's inborn restraints? What would make some young Palestinian plant *plastique* in the restaurant of a neutral city like Paris, knowing it would kill and maim scores of people who had had nothing to do with the loss of his homeland? When did this notion that everyone and anyone was fair game get started? With Deir Yassin? The bombing of Guernica? With Frantz Fanon's *The Wretched of the Earth,* which had become the social gospel of Third World revolutionists? The oppressed had to liberate themselves psychologically as well as politically, and the means to that liberation was the collective catharsis of violence against the oppressor. The mere act of striking a blow freed you from degradation, Fanon had said. From there, it was not a big step to violence for violence's sake—hey, if it makes you feel better, do it.

Maybe it was the zeitgeist of the late twentieth century. One by one, the barriers to unacceptable conduct have fallen; yet I wondered if the late adolescents around me, joking and laughing, were merely products of their times. Memory, boosted by a little imagination, allowed me to leap into their minds and gave me a brief, dim glimpse of how someone could slaughter innocents without guilt or pity. I remembered those black rages that had come over me after Vietnam and the urge as I sat in Paris cafés to open up on everyone because they did not *deserve* to be so smug and comfortable while others were suffering and dying on the far side of the world. Possibly a fury like that burnt inside the fedayeen, a flame pure as the refiner's fire and hot with hate. And that, as much as anything, accounted for the strange feeling of brotherhood that seemed to have risen between us.

But I was not their brother. I was in the den of the Beast with the Children of the Beast.

The guerrilla with the idiot's eyes and the lumberjack forearms got a sudden inspiration: Zouhair and I should be tied up. The others agreed that that would be a good idea. Two lengths of rope were produced.

"This isn't necessary," I said. "There's nine of you with guns."

"My name is Mahmoud."

"This isn't necessary, Mahmoud."

"Lie down on your stomachs."

He tied Zouhair first, lashing his wrists behind him, then his wrists to his ankles.

"Hey, Mister, where are you from in the States?" he asked as he tied me.

"Chicago."

"Chicago? Hey, do you know my brother owns a grocery there? I am thinking of going there someday. If we let you go, maybe we can have dinner there. How about that?"

"Sure. We could talk over old times. What restaurant do you have in mind?"

He cinched the knots.

"Does that pain you?"

"No."

Actually, it did, but I was afraid that if I said so, the moron would only tie it tighter.

"If it starts to pain you, let me know and I fix."

Someone suggested it would be the decent thing to do to let us smoke.

"Hey, Mister, do you want to?" Mahmoud asked.

"It'd be a little hard like this."

"I help."

He lit a cigarette, stuck it between my lips, and withdrew it after I'd inhaled. I had never in my life felt so helpless and humiliated.

"Another?"

"No, thanks."

The building seemed to jump an inch from its foundations from the explosion of a one-twenty.

"Hey, Mister, what restaurant do you think we could go to?"

"Depends on what kind of food you like." (I ruled out kosher.)

"Any kind. Maybe my brother's wife could cook for us, with food from his grocery store. Of course, we have to let you go first."

I looked up at him, his eyes so close together they seemed to want to leap the bridge of his nose and fuse into a cyclops's eye. It was clear that he was not a cretin; he was crazy, Mahmoud the Mad.

Zouhair and I lay there, bent like rockers. A short, very thin boy came in. He was a walking lesson in the duality of man's nature: Kalashnikov in one hand, Shakespeare (in English) in the other. He lay down on a cot and, brushing back a shock of his long, black hair, started to read aloud by the soft light of a kerosene lamp.

"'In thy faint slumbers I by thee have watch'd ...'"

"'And heard thee murmur tales of iron wars,'" I said, finishing the line. I was looking to establish points of contact. *"Henry the Fourth."*

"Yes! You have studied Shakespeare?"

"Yes."

"When there is not fighting, I'm studying literature at A.U.B. My name is Tasin," he said, pronouncing it Tah-seen. "But I call myself 'The Chocolate Soldier.'"

"How old are you, Chocolate Soldier?"

"I am just this month eighteen."

He raised the book again to his face.

"'Speak terms of manage to thy bounding steed, Cry 'Courage! To the field!' And thou hast talk'd of sallies and retires, of trenches, tents, of palisadoes, frontiers, parapets, Of basi ... Of basi ...'"

"Basilisks," I corrected.

"What is that, Mister?"

"A big cannon."

"Shakespeare is very hard to understand."

Tasin set the book down and tuned the transistor. The rock music faded and the melancholy strains of "Danny Boy" flooded the room.

"Now we have background music," I said, but I was thinking of the rest of Lady Percy's speech: "Of basilisks, of cannon, culverin, *of prisoners' ransom ...*"

The building rocked again. Tasin laughed.

"Ah, my friend. War is a filthy business, merely a contest to see who is the stronger. Today the fedayeen are strong—we fought off the planes. But tomorrow more planes will come and we will all die."

The Chocolate Soldier threw his arms straight over his head and laughed, and laughed, and laughed.

Just this month eighteen.

We spent our second night in the stinking kitchen-prison, sleeping in fitful intervals between crescendos of gun and shellfire. The night was not murmuring tales of iron wars; it was shouting them. In the long spells of wakefulness, Zouhair talked about his family. He was divorced, had two daughters and a son. He asked about my family. I started to tell him about Jill and the boys, then cut myself off when the pity and self-pity gorged my throat again.

Don't talk about them, don't even think about them. You've got to act as if they don't exist because you could be dead before morning, and if you live, you might well be locked up here for months.

Another captive's dawn, sky and rooftops cross-hatched by the window bars, pale light of the Levant gilding distant mountains and glinting off two Mirages, strafing another Palestinian camp. Here and there, shells burst, the erupting smoke like flowers blooming in time-lapse.

A migraine drilled behind my eyes. I banged on the door. The locks clicked.

"What do you want?"

It was the day-shift guards: the pudgy, health-conscious one and Erebia of the killer eyes. I asked for four aspirins.

"No," said the health nut. "It's bad for you to take four at once. Take only two."

"Four! I've had these before, and four is what gets rid of them."

He pondered for a moment, locked the door behind him, and returned half an hour later with four aspirins.

"I will give you two now, two later."

"Four now."

He mused some more.

"Okay, but you have to promise me you'll take only two now."

"I promise."

He gave me the pills. I took two as prescribed.

"Good. Now I bring something to eat."

As soon as he left, I gulped down the other two.

He came back with a tray of pita, olives, and tea.

Zouhair wouldn't eat. I pleaded with him to take some food, remembering stories I'd heard from American POWs in Vietnam: when a man refused to eat, it was a sure sign he was losing his will to live.

I force-fed myself and threatened to do the same to Zouhair if he didn't at least try.

"All right! All right! All right!" he hollered, almost crying.

He ripped off hunks of bread and crammed them in his mouth until his cheeks bulged.

"Dere. Blu hoppy now?" he blubbered, spitting crumbs. "Eeening now, I eening now, blu hoppy?"

Half an hour later, we both had to use the toilet. We pounded on the door. No one came.

"WC! WC!" Zouhair shouted.

Still no one came.

"WC! WC!"

I remembered Nick Proffitt's moral from two nights and a hundred years ago as I hopped up on the counter and, straddling the sink (Made in Romania!), emptied my kidneys and bowels. Zouhair followed me. We washed the waste down the drain, used our underwear for toilet paper, and pushed them through the bars—a statement of sorts, and an emphatic one to anyone below.

Erebia and Mahmoud the Mad led me downstairs and across the street for a long afternoon's chat with Mr. Blue Eyes. He started off genially—had I slept all right? Did I get enough to eat?—then turned to the first topic of the day, which was, again, my pocket telephone book. He wanted to know why I had separated the six-digit number for Middle East Airlines' Rome office into pairs, with dashes in between.

I looked at him blankly.

"I don't understand the question."

"What do the dashes mean?"

"What do you mean, 'What do they mean'?"

"What is the meaning of these dashes?"

"They don't mean anything."

"If they mean nothing, why did you put them there?"

"I always separate phone numbers with dashes. Everyone does."

"Do you mean to tell me that it's your habit to put dashes in a phone number?" he asked, sounding like a cross-examining prosecutor closing in for the kill.

"Yes."

He flipped through the phone book, showed me a number with only one dash in it.

"Why only one?"

I was sitting across from him on the straw mat in the middle of the floor, the same squad of fedayeen lounging on the cots, a mute armed chorus to our little drama. I looked at them, then at Mr. Blue Eyes, and thought, *This is all a ploy to confuse me, Applied Kafka.*

"It's a seven-digit number," I explained, feeling a flush of anger. "With six-digit numbers, I separate the first three from the last four with one dash. With six digit numbers, I separate them into pairs, with two dashes. That's how they do it in Rome. When in Rome, do as the Romans do."

"If it's your habit to use these dashes, why are there some numbers in your book *with no dashes?*"

He triumphantly displayed an undivided phone number as if it were a photograph of me passing secrets to the Master Spy of the Universe.

I'd had enough.

"This is bullshit."

"Excuse me?"

"Bullshit!" I said, raising my voice. "You know I'm a correspondent, you know you shouldn't be holding me, and now you're trying to justify it with these bullshit questions."

He leaned toward me.

"Why are some numbers separated by dashes and others not? Answer me!"

"Look! These are just fucking phone numbers, all right? Sometimes I separate phone numbers with dashes and sometimes I don't, and anyway, what fucking difference does it make?"

The shooting had died down, but I was yelling at the top of my lungs. Behind me, Erebia subtly shifted in his chair so that his rifle pointed straight at me, the muzzle just a few inches from my ear. I got the message—don't forget who's boss around here—and reined myself in. *No groveling, Philip, but no kamikaze heroics, remember?*

The interrogator lit a cigarette and looked off as he smoked it. For five minutes, no one spoke a word. I squirmed, my folded legs growing numb, a young panic thumping in my chest.

Finally, Mr. Blue Eyes looked at me.

"Who were the two men who were with you Monday night?"

"What two men?"

"Stop lying to me!"

"Did you talk to the men who captured us? They'll tell you. We were alone."

"Stop lying! I want the truth! Give me the names of the two men in the car behind you!"

"No one was with us. We were alone."

He half rose, looming over me like an immense shadow.

"I want the truth! There were two men in a car behind you. They got away, but we got you. Who were they?"

I remembered the car we had heard speeding down the street, the burst of machine-gun fire ... But that had been half an hour after we were captured. Did Mr. Blue Eyes really suspect Zouhair and I were working with a team? Or was this line of questioning another ploy to confuse me?

"I have no idea who they were. We were alone."

He crushed his cigarette in a way that suggested he would have liked to have put it out in my eye.

"Yesterday, I told you I wanted only the facts. I wanted the truth. I told you it will go harder on you if you lied, and now you're lying. Now tell me ... *Who were the men in the car?*"

"I don't know. We were alone."

For the next quarter of an hour the conversation was repeated again and again. My voice developed a tremolo, from fear and frustrated rage. I wanted to grab the interrogator by the collar and shake him until his neck snapped. Again and again. "Who were the men in a car?" I began to doubt my own senses. Maybe two men had been with us, maybe I had forgotten who they were. "Who were they?" ... "We were alone ..." A conversational carousel, turning, turning, for fifteen minutes, then twenty, then twenty-five. I felt a powerful temptation to satisfy Mr. Blue Eyes by giving him a couple of names, the first to come into my head. I warred against it. No kamikaze heroics, no groveling, no lies either.

"We were alone!" I practically screamed. "Do you hear me? Alone! You can ask me from now till doomsday and you'll get the same answer. There wasn't another car, we were alone!"

The interrogator's lips turned into a bland quarter smile. He translated my answer to the secretary, then said something to Mahmoud the Mad, who went outside.

What next? A thought cried in my head: *he's going to come back with two more prisoners, two men they've broken, who are going to say, Yes, the American was with us, in a second car ...*

Instead, Mahmoud the Mad returned with a tray full of coffee, tea, and cigarettes. Mr. Blue Eyes turned genial again but switched back to his interrogator's mode after the break. The new topic was my business cards. The same routine as with my phone book: who are these people, how and when did you meet them, what is your relationship to them? When he came to the two Israeli cards, I braced for a savage grilling and was baffled when he treated them no differently than the others. My surprise must have showed.

"We know you were in Israel recently," Mr. Blue Eyes said. "These two were not the only people you saw, of course."

"No."

"We will discuss later who you saw and why." He turned another card, snapping it like a blackjack dealer. "Who is this person?"

I stared at the name but could not match it to a face.

"I don't recall."

"What do you mean, you don't recall? How did this man's card get in your wallet?"

"I'm a journalist. Meet a lot of people. They give me their cards, I put them in my wallet and then forget about them."

He gave me a skeptical look, but it was the truth: my wallet was a trash can. He went through two or three more cards, which I did remember, but I drew a blank on the next one. It had been given to me in Chicago and must have been two years old.

Mr. Blue Eyes let out a breath to tell me he was losing his patience.

"You say you are a foreign correspondent but that you are carrying business cards given to you two years ago in the United States? This is what you are trying to tell me?"

"Yes."

He slapped the cards on the mat.

"This is ridiculous! You can't convince me that you carry these cards for no purpose! Whenever I go anyplace, I always make certain I carry only what I need. How do you explain that?"

"We have different personality traits. You're an organized person and I'm not."

"You are a disorganized person. This is why these useless cards are in your wallet?"

"That's why, yes, but am I guilty of something because I'm not organized?"

"So, that's your explanation? That's your final answer? You're a disorganized person?"

"Yes, my final answer."

The interrogator shrugged, as if to say, "Well, if that's the way you want it," translated my answer for the secretary, then lit another cigarette and turned to look at some undefined point in space. I now recognized that pose as prelude to a tough barrage. While he mused and smoked, The Happy Warrior came in dancing, shuckin' and jivin', spinning his sniper rifle as if he were trying out for a drill team.

"*Marhaba,* my friend." He did a few fast steps around me. "How are you today, brotha?"

Mr. Blue Eyes told him to keep quiet and sit down, then turned to me.

"How many times have you been to Israel?"

Here we go.

"Twice."

"When?"

Should I tell him? What if he then asks, "Why did you tell our men you had been there three years ago as a tourist?" Ah, I was in a world where I could be condemned for a messy wallet, where the dashes in a phone number, or the absence of dashes, could be inter-preted as secret codes, where one thing was as bad or as good as another. I gave him the dates of my visits.

"For what reason did you go?"

Part of my answer was swallowed up by the screech of jets and the doom-doom-dooming of big antiaircraft machine guns. Rockets burst nearby, and, in the distance, I heard the bass roll of bombs.

Mr. Blue Eyes went back to shouting questions, I the answers.

The floor quaked. The fedayeen guards didn't budge or look in the least frightened. Terrorists or freedom fighters, murderers or guerrillas, say what you wanted about them, they were brave enough. I tried to copy their sangfroid, though a refrain was playing in my mind, *If the guerrillas don't kill me, if the guerrillas don't kill me, the bombs will, the bombs will ...*

"Who were you with on your last trip to Israel?" Mr. Blue Eyes hollered.

"Israel Stockman and Charlie Weiss!"

"Who are they?"

"I told you before!"

"Damn you, Philip! Answer my questions!"

A salvo of rockets exploded in the street. Shriek of shattering glass, a dull thud of a vehicle's gas tank bursting, shrapnel flung against the walls and door like stones hurled from a hundred huge slingshots.

Everyone hit the floor. Tasin, The Chocolate Soldier, dove under a metal cot with me and Mr. Blue Eyes.

"Oh, what a dirty business ... dirty, dirty business ..."

"You said they'd be back!"

"Yes! And here they are! We'll all die!"

And The Chocolate Soldier laughed.

When more rockets hit, their blasts and the jet roar and the anti-aircraft guns merging into a single noise, Mr. Blue Eyes pulled a long cushion over his head, then, in an oddly compassionate gesture, slid half of it over mine.

"Now, Philip, don't be frightened. This will protect your head."

From outside came the smells of burning gasoline and rubber, the screams of women, children bawling.

"What about them?"

"Well, Philip, they can kill our bodies with their tanks and planes and guns, but they can't kill our spirits."

I assumed that wasn't cant, that he believed it. I felt a little embarrassed because my expression of concern for the women and children had been fraudulent; I wanted Mr. Blue Eyes to think I was a decent guy so he would go easier on me.

The planes peeled off, we crawled out from under the cot, and the interrogation resumed, as if the air raid had been nothing more than an annoying interruption.

With one exception, the guerrillas were disciplined in handling their weapons: whenever they entered the room, they cleared the chambers and snapped the safeties on. The exception was Mahmoud the Mad, who always kept a round in the chamber and never put his rifle on safe. He was forever toying with it and pointing at people, giggling as he did. When he got bored with that, he would perform awkward karate kicks and punches, huffing and puffing and grunting like a character in some low-grade Hong Kong martial arts movie.

Zouhair and I, sitting in the kitchen-prison, heard him giggling in the room outside.

"A guest, my friends!" he called. "We have brought you a guest!"

The door opened. Mahmoud shoved a tall, fat man inside.

"Here he is, heh-heh-heh!"

The man pleaded with Mahmoud the Mad. Zouhair translated for me: the fat man had a night-shift job at the airport and had been on his way to work when, like us, he strayed too near the fedayeen positions. He was asking why the guerrillas had captured him, a poor working man.

"Standard procedure," was the answer Mahmoud gave.

The fat man sat down and, without speaking a word, stared at the opposite wall with dull eyes.

Now we were three in a room that was at best six feet wide by seven long and only six and a half feet high. It was hot, the stench of the blocked squat toilet was as powerful as ever. I wanted to move to the window for a breath of air, but twilight had brought a new hazard: a sniper. Every few minutes, a bullet would crack past the window, so we sat tight against the wall, shoulder to shoulder.

The Chocolate Soldier came by with dinner.

Number Three (he never told us his name) shoveled his down, smacking his lips as if he were eating the tenderest filet. When he was through, he belched loudly and lit a pipe, the stench of his strong tobacco only a little less noxious than the stink from the toilet. He belched again, then, raising his buttocks slightly, farted loudly without apology or embarrassment.

"A pig!" Zouhair hissed at me in English. "Why must we be imprisoned with a pig!"

"Because the final indignity is that there is no final indignity."

"What?"

"Nothing. Wisdom from a friend of mine."

Number Three's pipe had gone out. He relit it, emitting another belch. I wanted to grab him and smash his wide, jowly face. But no, no. We were all prisoners together, we could not turn on each other.

Sniper or no sniper, I went to the window to suck in some clean air. On the street, children, old men, and women with babies and bundles on their backs were scurrying out of Sabra as fast as they could. From the window of a building some thirty or forty yards away several fedayeen, one with binoculars, were scanning for the sniper. I caught a nanosecond glimpse of a puff of smoke before I hit the floor hard. The tank shell's blast sent a nail of pain through my eardrums. On quaking legs I stood to look. A huge hole was where the window had been. Smoke poured out of it and blast marks streaked from its rim like rays from some dark, smoldering, dying star.

I sat down again, sandwiching myself between Zouhair and Number Three, who asked something in Arabic.

"He wants to know what happened," Zouhair translated.

"Some fedayeen were just killed by a tank."

Number Three uttered a few words, then belched.

"He says, 'Good.' He hopes they all die. That is my hope, too."

"If they do, we're going to die with them," I said, and then, trying to make the best of things, quipped that all we needed now was a fourth for bridge.

Half an hour later, my joke became a prophecy fulfilled.

"Another guest, my friends!" Mahmoud cackled, prodding with his rifle a dark-skinned man dressed in a pin-striped suit and silk tie. With his curly black hair, long sideburns, and mustache, he looked like a Latin American matinee idol from the forties. His story was similar to Number Three's: worked at the airport, hadn't been able to get there for three days, but had left this evening because he thought the fighting was over (where he got that idea was a mystery; all he would have needed to do was stick his head out a window and listen).

Now we did not have room to stretch out our legs. If we stood, we stumbled over one another. Someone was always asking to go to the toilet, or for a cigarette, or for something to drink. Number Four had a special problem: an artificial kidney, for which he needed medicine three times a day. He would die without it, he said, and kept banging on the door, calling *"Hazibab, hazibab"*—"Hey you, hey you." No one came.

I had had enough. I just about smashed the door with my fists and bellowed for the guards. Now someone came: The Chocolate Soldier.

"This is crazy! This guy needs medicine or he'll die! Let him go, for Christ's sake!"

Tasin wanted to know what kind of medicine. Number Four told him. Saying he would see what he could do, The Chocolate Soldier left. He was back in an hour: no luck in finding the medicine.

Number Four groaned.

"For three years I have lived on an artificial kidney and now I must die like this."

"You're not going to die," I said.

"I think so. Without the medicine, I will be dead in two days, maybe less." He glanced up at the window, then ran his hand lightly over the wall. "But what is a man's life? Like this. Only a brush against a wall and then it is gone."

"Fuck your Arab fatalism. I'm only thirty-one and I'd like my brush to last a little longer."

I saw myself laid out, eyes wide and still, mouth ajar.

Our minds were wonderfully concentrated, focused as a martyr's when the lion's cage is opened. All we talked about was death, which, when you think it over, is probably the only subject worthy of conversation, all others being amusing games to distract us from the great conundrum that makes even the best of lives a tragedy. I don't recall that we arrived at any conclusions or obtained valuable insights that would have made dying any easier, although Zouhair received a faint revelation.

"All my life, Allah has not been good to me," he said, his dark eyes angry. "For three days I have been praying to Allah to deliver us, but he has not answered." He stood up and went to the window and stuck his fist through the bars. "I curse you Allah!" He spat and shouted again. "I curse you, Allah, I curse you!"

The sniper's bullet cracked past the window with a sound like a snapping rubber band, only louder.

The health nut and The Chocolate Soldier brought us eggs in the morning. Zouhair and Number Four wouldn't eat.

"I spit on their food," said Number Four, knotting his silk tie as if he were off to a business meeting. "I will die anyway without my medicine. Who do these people think they are? I am a Lebanese. Who do these people think they are that they can arrest me in my own country?"

Number Three slurped his fried eggs.

"There is just one way out," Number Four went on. "We must stop with these planes and mortars, killing only the innocent ones, the women and children. That's stupid. We should come in here with the army and fight the guerrillas man to man and kill them, one by one."

"You are right!" Zouhair brightened at the vision of a hand-to-hand wipeout. "All my life I have hated the Palestinians, and now I hate them even more. They think they are so brave. But why don't they fight their real enemy, Israel?"

Number Three wiped up his egg yolk with a slice of pita and let out a tremendous belch.

"When were you in Israel?"

"How many times do I have to tell you?"

"As many times as I ask."

The Chocolate Soldier lay on a cot, reading Shakespeare's sonnets, The Happy Warrior did a jig around me, Erebia stared with an expression so still he looked like a photograph of himself, Mahmoud the Mad toyed with the bolt and safety of his rifle, click-click, snick-snick, and Mr. Blue Eyes repeated my answers to the secretary, filling page after page, all to the usual percussive accompaniment.

"Why did you go to Israel?"

I told him again.

"Why don't you have a Lebanese press pass?"

"Look, you *want* me to tell you I'm a spy, right? Will that make you happy? Okay, I'm a spy."

"Is that the truth?"

"No."

"I want only the truth."

"That's what I've been giving you for the past three days."

"I don't believe you."

"Then why don't you take me out and shoot me now?"

"That would be crude. I told you, we are not murderers."

"I don't believe *you.*"

When I returned to the kitchen-prison, Messrs. Three and Four would not look at me.

I squeezed into my place against the wall.

"What's up?" I asked Zouhair.

"They are angry with you. They say they would be free by now if it wasn't for you."

I turned to them.

"Sorry, gentlemen. I didn't ask to come here either."

Mr. Four banged on the door.

"*Hazibab … hazibab …*"

The pudgy health nut answered. Mr. Four asked if he, a dying man, could have some tea.

The guard left. When, after more than an hour, he did not come back, Mr. Four banged on the door again.

The Chocolate Soldier opened it. Where was the man with the tea? we asked.

"I am afraid the sniper got him," Tasin said. He grinned at Mr. Four. "But we have just now been told you are free to go. There are some men coming who will take you out of here, so you can get your medicines."

Mr. Four, smiling like a kid at Christmas, shook our hands as he left with two fedayeen. He was in tears when they brought him back, less than an hour later, and shoved him into the kitchen and slammed the door after him.

He had no idea what had happened. The guerrillas had put him in a car, driven him to the edge of camp, and then turned around and brought him back, without explaining why.

"It was to torment me!" he cried.

I suspected it was for another, worse reason: no reason. The guards just got a sudden, demented inspiration.

Number Four lay down, whimpering like a hurt dog. I put a blanket over him.

Zouhair was crying and cursing God.

Number Three smoked his pipe.

"Put that fucking thing out!" I said savagely. "We can't breathe in here!"

Lice were crawling through my hair. The stink of my own body revolted me. I kicked the door.

"Let us out of here for some air."

"Stop all that noise and moving around!" It was Mahmoud. "I have orders to keep you quiet."

He relented eventually and opened the door. We staggered out, gulping the fresh breeze blowing through the window of the guards' room. With his rifle, Mahmoud gestured for us to sit on a cot. He sat in a chair across from us, staring. Through the peepholes of his close-set eyes, I could see the synapses in his brain making wrong connections, cranial electrons arranging themselves into bizarre configurations.

He giggled, chambered a round, and pointed the rifle at me.

"Tell me your opinion of the Arab-Israeli conflict."

"I've been answering questions for three days. I'm sick of answering questions."

"Tell me. I want to know if you are a friend or an enemy of the Palestinian people."

"Do you think I'm going to give you an honest answer with a loaded gun pointed at me? Point it somewhere else, Mahmoud."

"Tell me!"

I parodied the Third World catechism: *the suffering people of Palestine, in their just struggle against the Zionist entity, the U.S. imperialists, and the reactionary Arab regimes* ...

He stood up, the AK leveled at my chest.

"You work for the CIA, don't you?"

"That is absolutely ridiculous."

"You lie! You lie! You lie!"

The only defense against a crazy is to act crazier. I stood and pressed myself against the muzzle.

"All right, Mahmoud. You have your gun. Now ask me again."

He backed away. I moved a step toward him.

"Go on. Ask me the same question, and if you think I'm lying, blow me away. I don't care. Otherwise, stop pointing that thing at me."

He lowered the rifle.

"Okay, Mister. Okay."

He sat down. Synapses misfired again, electrons made designs like something out of a bad acid trip. He let out another giggle.

"What is your hotel room number?"

"What do you?" I interrupted myself. "You're thinking of breaking in there, right?"

"Yes. We want to see what else you've got in there."

I imagined the conclusions they would draw when they tore my suitcase apart and found the extra passport, with its Israeli exit and entry stamps, stashed in a secret compartment.

I gave him the room number anyway, figuring he was bluffing.

"Okay, Mahmoud, I've been honest with you. Now you be honest with me. When are you planning to shoot me? Tonight or tomorrow?"

I've had seventeen years to think about it, but I still haven't figured out why I asked that.

"Oh, no, Mister. You are our friend now, but if you are our enemy, then we'll shoot you."

"If I'm your friend now, why don't you let me go?"

"Do you have a family?"

"Wife, two children."

Sparks flew from his synapses, electrons whirled into a new pattern as Mahmoud the Mad became in a twinkling Mahmoud the Kind.

"Oh, my! Oh, my!" he said with genuine distress. "We have human feelings. We do, we do! We feel for other humans! For the sake of your wife and children, we would never shoot you. Don't worry. Go to sleep now."

"Sure, sure," I said, virtually certain it would take only another sudden change in his brain chemistry for him to kill us all.

In the morning, Mr. Four was curled up in the fetal position, crying softly to himself.

No one would do anything for him. We three prisoners and the guards had closed into worlds of our own. Forcing myself out of mine, I drew Mr. Four's blanket back over his shoulders and gave him some water. I was about to congratulate myself for being the only one who had refused to give up when a cloak of resignation dropped over me. What was the use? We were all going to die. So what? Jill and the kids would get a lot of money from the paper. Memories of them flooded into me, a flood I could not stop. The next thing I knew, I was sobbing uncontrollably. The others, whom I'd been trying to cheer up for the past day and night, now tried to cheer me.

The Chocolate Soldier gave me his book of sonnets.

"Read these. Maybe they will help you to forget," he said, then asked if I had read Sartre.

Yes, I had.

"Do you know what Sartre says?"

"A lot of things," I said, and got a grip on myself.

"He says when a man cannot control his destiny, he can only cry."

That day's interrogation lasted only an hour instead of the usual six or seven. Erebia and The Chocolate Soldier led me back to the cell. Zouhair and Numbers Three and Four were sitting on the cot in the guards' room, chatting affably with Mahmoud the Mad.

I sat next to Zouhair. He leaned over and whispered to me: "Try not to talk to Mahmoud. That man is not normal."

"No shit."

Mahmoud stuck out a foot and lightly kicked me in the shin.

"Hey, Mister. Do you know what we Palestinians are going to do someday? We'll come to America and kick Nixon."

"Watergate will do that for us," said The Chocolate Soldier, playing the political pundit.

Mahmoud opened two cans of beer and poured a glass for me. Then he, The Chocolate Soldier, and everyone else began talking in Arabic. I went into the kitchen-prison for the book of sonnets, returned to the guards' room, and read and sipped the warm beer. The poems were as welcome as the beer, both for themselves and for the escape they provided from the incomprehensible language swirling around me.

A guerrilla came in, whom I recognized from the night of our capture. He was the one who had "Peace and Love" painted on his magazine pouch. He was clean-shaven now, dressed in a battle uniform: camouflage shirt and trousers, short-billed cap. Very politely, almost with diplomatic formality, he shook hands with each of us, saying each time, "*Marhaba,* how are you?"

Idiotic hope leapt in me. They're letting us all go!

I was 25 percent accurate: Mr. Four was to be freed so he could get his medicine.

He gave the guerrilla a wary look but was assured his release was for real this time.

Four stood up beaming. He brushed off his suit and reknotted his tie, then turned to me and shook my hand.

"I wish I could stay here with you to see you through all of this, but if I do not get treatment, I will die."

"You don't have to kid me," I said. "You don't *really* want to stay here."

He laughed and walked downstairs to freedom as another guerrilla, also in full uniform, came up the stairs. He was tall, thin, and sallow and spoke five words that sounded like a death sentence: "We want the American now."

Mahmoud the Mad stood up quickly and waved his rifle at me.

"Let's go," he said.

I was led into the street. After more than three days in dim rooms, the afternoon light made me blink. Two armed, uniformed fedayeen came up, rolled a kaffiyeh into a blindfold, and tied it to my head. One man grabbed me tightly by each arm. Mahmoud poked me in the butt with his rifle.

"Walk."

We moved along for perhaps ten minutes. I lost all sense of direction. The fighting was over, at least for the moment; the street was jammed with people. I could hear men's voices, women's voices, children's voices. I stepped into a pothole or shell crater and fell. The two men jerked me up, then shoved me against a wall and let go of my arms. Voices, but now only male voices. I waited for the clattering of rifle bolts, and, as I surrendered all hope, my heart gave one last rapid flutter before it slowed almost to a stop. A strange tranquillity washed over me. It was the unknown I had feared all along. Now I knew what was going to happen and was at peace. Silently, I made an act of contrition, the old, sweet words coming back to me from those grammar school days in shadowed confessionals pungent with incense. *Oh, my God, I am heartily sorry for having offended Thee ...*

I waited. Nothing.

"Mahmoud?"

"Yes?"

He was standing in front of me.

"Am I going to be shot?"

"Why do you want to know?"

"Because it will be the last thing I ever do and I want to do it right. I want to die like a man."

"Don't worry. We won't shoot you."

The two guerrillas took hold of my arms again and led me a long, long way into what seemed to be a room. Several men were speaking. Mahmoud told me to sit, maneuvering me onto a bench. I was given a few sips of water and a cigarette. I had hope again, so my heart was pounding again.

When I finished the cigarette, I was guided through some sort of passageway, then down a steep set of stairs. The air thickened: the mustiness of old cellars, of abandoned cisterns, of crypts and catacombs. I felt gravel or cinders under my bare feet.

The blindfold came off. One of the guerrillas lit a candle and I saw I *was* in a cellar, a windowless pit. In front of me was a heavy wooden door with a thick bar resting in a cast-iron bracket. Mahmoud opened it.

"This is where you will sleep tonight."

It was a hole in the wall, a kind of alcove less than a yard deep, about five and a half feet high, and five feet long. The stone walls dripped. Roaches, scared by the candle, shot past our feet, making for their beloved darkness.

The uniformed guerrillas pushed me inside.

"Do I get a blanket?"

They threw me one.

I lay down on the blanket. In the fluttering candle, Mahmoud the Mad's face looked diabolical, the eyes like black buttons stitched too close together.

The molecules in his cranial chemicals shifted once more and formed one of their oddball patterns.

"Well, what do you think of your accommodations?" he asked with a giggle.

"It's definitely not first cabin."

"Is there anything you want?"

"To get out of here."

"Tomorrow, *inshallah.*"

The three shut the door and the click of the crossbar sliding into place was as loud as a tolling bell.

All became a darkness that was to light what absolute zero is to temperature. I held my hand to my eyes and could not see it. Though I am only five-feet-seven, I could stand only if I bent my knees, could lie down only by folding my legs into my chest or by bracing them up against the wall. I lay there, numb, for possibly half an hour. The hole became intolerably hot. The only ventilation was a crack, an inch or two wide, between the door and the cinder floor. Claustrophobia cinched around my chest like a tourniquet. I put my face against the crack and tried to suck in fresh air. Some cinders stuck to my lips. I pulled them off. They crumbled in my fingers, and the smell told me they were droppings. Shit.

Rat shit.

The final indignity is that there is no final indignity.

So this was how they were going to do it—no honorable, warrior's death by firing squad but slow suffocation in a hole filled with rat shit.

The darkness became palpable. It acquired a texture, a weight. It bore down on me, heavier than ten elephants. I started to choke. Voices came from beyond the door.

"Mahmoud!" I shouted.

He did not answer.

"Goddamn you! MAHMOUD!"

Someone, not Mahmoud, yelled in a mocking falsetto: "So sorry. We don't speak English."

I hammered the door with the edge of my fists. Two men, faces yellowed by a candle, opened the door. One had a kaffiyeh drawn across his mouth, the other wore a bushy mustache. He said, in the tone of a father speaking to a demanding child: "What is it you want?"

"This goddamned door opened. I'll go mad in here."

"Well, then, go mad."

"YOU SON-OF-A-BITCH!" I shouted as he slammed the door.

I slumped to the floor, self-pity flooding me once again. My family and friends were thousands of miles away, and I was imprisoned in a black hole in a strange land, lost to the world.

Lost to time as well, to man's calibrated time and to nature's time of light and dark. There was only dark and no sense of movement from one moment to the next. I thought I was getting a preview of what hell would be like: a constant and terrible *nowness*. I wanted to cry, but no tears came, only a choking, moaning sound, a kind of emotional dry heaves.

I stopped groaning. I was angry now. I decided to annoy my watchdogs by singing as loudly as I could. I sang "Oh, Susanna" and "Clementine" and "She'll be Comin' Round the Mountain" and every old American folk tune I could think of.

A voice came through the door: "Shut up! Any more noise out of you and I'll shoot you!"

"OH, MY DARLING, OH, MY DARLING, OH MY DARLING CLEMEN-TINE ..."

"I said to shut up or I'll shoot you!"

"IN A CAVERN, IN A CANYON, EXCAVATING FOR A MINE, WAS A MINER, A FORTY-NINER, AND HIS DAUGHTER CLEMENTINE ... OH, MY DARLING, OH, MY DARLING ..."

"I have orders to shoot you if you make trouble!"

"Then go ahead and shoot me. C'mon, *do it*. I want you to."

Get hold of yourself. Mr. Blue Eyes probably wants you to go insane, or half insane. He's put you down here to break your spirit, to make you pliable so he can get you to say whatever he wants you to say, confess to whatever he wants you to confess to. You must get out of here alive and sane. Think of how to do that.

I recalled a story from World War I, about a British officer who had kept from going crazy in the trenches by reciting the *Aeneid* to himself in Latin. All right, I had studied the *Aeneid* in Latin, long ago, in high school. Could I possibly remember it? What a fine mental discipline it would be to force myself to recite it, verse by verse. It would be a safety line to cling to in the pool of depthless dark.

Arma virumque cano ... Arma virumque cano ... What? ... *Troiae quo ... No, qui ... Troiae qui ... ab oris ... Italiam ... Italiam ... Italiam ...*

I fought for the next line.

Italiam fato profugos Laviniaque venit litora ... That was it! ... *Multum ille et terris ...* What? What next? Begins with "i" ... *Iactus?* No. *Iactatus ...* Yes! ... *Iactatus et alto ...*

There was a scratching at the door, a squealing, and more scratching.

Rats.

Soon, it sounded as if half a dozen were clawing at the door. I rolled up my blanket and plugged the crack that was my only source of fresh air. In no time the hole was stifling, was a hand clamping around my windpipe.

I pulled the blanket out. If the rats wanted to come in, let them.

I folded the blanket in two, spread it on the floor, and lay down again.

The rats scratched and squealed.

Iactatus et alto ... et alto ... etaltoetaltoetalto ...

It was no use. Could hardly expect myself to recite a Latin epic from memory with rats trying to get at me.

I had to try something simpler and more familiar, so I said a rosary, then recited the Twenty-third Psalm. I laughed, recalling a profane version from Vietnam: Yea, though I walk in the valley of the shadow of death, I shall fear no evil ... 'cause I'm the meanest son of a bitch in the whole damned valley ...

But I was in a black hole and I did not feel very mean, so I recited it straight: *The Lord is my shepherd, I shall not want. He maketh me to lie down in green pastures. He leadeth me beside the still waters ...*

I recited it over and over. It, and the rosary, became a kind of mantra. I hit on a way to mark the passage of time. Assuming it took five minutes to say the psalm and one rosary, reciting twelve sets would use up an hour. Assuming I had been put in the hole at about three in the afternoon and that it was now five, and assuming further that Mahmoud the Mad's promise that I would be let out the next day was not false, how much longer did I have to go? About fifteen hours, assuming they released me at eight in the morning. A lot of assumptions, but I had to have some sort of starting point.

I said the first set and, when I was done, pressed my finger to the dank wall, making a mark I could not see.

"That's one," I said aloud to help me keep track.

Over and over. Rosary and psalm, psalm and rosary.

The sound and rhythm of the words soothed me. After a while, the sheer repetition of them put me into a trance. At first, it was the words alone, and then something else: a *power* began to flow through me, a *power* that tranquilized and strengthened me at once.

One of the few advantages to being in extremis is that it grants you perceptions denied you in the middle grounds of experience.

Oh, blessed rage for order ...

As I lay there, wondering what that power was, I began to reflect on the Book of Job and the seemingly cruel and senseless afflictions he suffered. I asked the same question Job did: why has this happened to me? Why these unmerited sufferings?

Absurdists would have said, There is no reason, your blessed rage for order is all for nothing because the universe is without order, this is the age of quarks and quantum physics.

That sort of half-baked postmodernist babble would have done just fine if I had been back on the Boulevard St. Germain, sitting in the Café Deux Magots, the rendezvous of the intellectual elite, but it simply would not do in a rat-infested hole in a Beirut cellar with two men outside ready to blow out my brains if I gave them trouble.

Oh blessed rage for order ...

At first I concluded I was being punished for my pride and ambition. I'd gone too far, too fast, just to beat my competition.

But that wouldn't do either: the punishment did not fit the crime.

Then I concluded that I was being punished for my lack of faith.

That also would not do, but I was getting close.

Finally, I concluded—no, that's the wrong word, implying as it does the end result of a logical process—I *grasped* that God was manifesting himself to me. I did not see or hear Him; I felt him, in the tactile rather than the emotional sense. The *power* surging through me was God. He wasn't making any promises, or trying to extract promises from me because He knew I would not keep them. He wasn't there to bargain like some carpet peddler in a souk but was simply telling me that He did exist and that I needed Him. I had found in the city that encounter with the absolute I'd sought in the desert.

A brief flash-forward—some years later, I was talking to a friend on the paper, a hard-bitten newshawk as smug in his cynicism as certain kinds of churchgoers are in their piousness.

"You didn't really mean it," he said, referring to the series I had written about my captivity, "when you said you *found God* in a hole in a basement?"

"Yes, I did."

He looked deeply troubled.

I fell asleep on my back, legs propped against the wall.

When I woke up, the *power* was still in me. I felt strong and sure of myself and mentally prepared for the next interrogation. *If that blue-eyed bastard thinks he can make me go nuts or break me, he's got another think coming. I'll tell the truth, and if he doesn't believe me, then he can sentence me to death. I don't care. Death is better than this.*

I felt stronger still. I had conquered fear of death, the great dark mother of all other fears. Fear of madness—mental death. Fear of hunger or thirst or cold—the death of comfort. Fear of disgrace—the death of self-respect. Fear of fear—the death of courage. All those little fears of little deaths, children of the great mother fear of the great death. But how great would it be? Not very. *Many people are dying,* the guerrilla had told Zouhair, *what are two more?* Answer: not much, and one death only half that.

Oh, blessed rage for order ...

I decided to clean up my little home. I pushed the rat droppings through the crack, shook out my blanket, then stripped and dusted off my filthy, stinking clothes. Done with that, I began calisthenics to keep up my physical strength. The hole was too small for proper push-ups, so I did them on my knees, fifty altogether. By bending my knees a couple of inches, I was able to touch my toes. I finished with a few squats, then dressed and sat down to resume my prayers. I couldn't recall where I had left off before I'd fallen asleep. How long had I been asleep? Five minutes? Five hours? The *power* was draining out of me, God was forsaking me. Why? Why? The exercises had roused a terrible thirst; except for the few sips of water given to me before I was taken to the hole, I had not drunk anything for twelve or thirteen hours. I knelt, and putting my mouth to the crack, called out, "Mwai, mwai"—Arabic for water.

I must have called for half an hour, but no one answered.

I had to go to the toilet. Again I banged on the door, and again no one answered. Kneeling down, I pissed, aiming for the crack beneath the door. The urine puddled and soaked into my blanket. No final indignity.

Engulfed by fury, I hammered the door, very nearly springing one of the thick planks.

"You bastards! You lousy bastards! Hey, listen to this! I used to be sympathetic to you Palestinians, but you've lost me!"

Not that they should have cared, but they had lost my sympathies to the extent that I now saw why the Israelis behaved toward them with what we in the West criticized as "intransigence." What compromise was possible with the fedayeen? How could you talk reasonably with men so paranoid?

The door swung open. The same two men. I stood up and sneered at them, giving a mock bow.

"*Sabâh ilkhair*"—good morning. I wasn't as crazy as I was acting. If they responded with the same phrase, I would know what time of day it was. I grinned and sneered and spat at their feet. "*Sabâh ilkhair*—you sons-of-bitches!"

Without a word, they slammed the door in my face. All my wrath and bravado leaked out of me. I tried to get a grip on myself, to restore that tranquillity I had felt just—how long ago was it? I banged on the door again, and banged and banged, and then suddenly lost my senses of taste, smell, and touch. Only my hearing was left as the cinder floor gave way, and I became a disembodied consciousness, without eyes, hands, or tongue, plummeting like a free-falling parachutist into a bottomless black, faster and faster. I knew I had my hearing because I heard myself scream. It's a scream I can still hear in my memory, the scream a man would make if he were being gutted alive. The howl of a lunatic.

I snapped out of the hallucination and sunk to the floor. Well, I had gone crazy, if only for an instant. Next time it would be longer, and eventually I would not snap out of it. I had to escape. I saw that all my pounding had sprung the bottom of a plank. If I could do the same to two or three more, I could squeeze out and ... What? Run. To where? Into the blazing muzzle of an AK-47. I had been raised among workingmen, according to clear and simple codes, one of which was that a man never gave up in a fight. And to run into certain death would have been just a way of giving up.

The psalm and the rosary—go back to that, I commanded myself. But where had I left off? Who cares? Start over, from one. *The Lord is my shepherd ... That's one ... that's two ... three ...*

Oh, blessed rage for order.

The door opened again. The two men told me to stand. I managed to. When they blindfolded me and led me back up the stairs, I was giddy with joy. Outside, the air stank of the camp, but the odors of mud were as lilies, the reek of the open sewers as jasmine. I sucked in deep deep breaths, like a drowning man shot back to the surface.

The blindfold was removed in the interrogation room. I sat down on the straw mat, Mr. Blue Eyes gazing down on me with a certain softness.

"Well, Philip, I now believe you are a journalist."

I blew out my cheeks in relief.

"That's what I've been telling you all along."

The gaze turned pitiless.

"But what else are you?"

I'd dropped my left and walked straight into that one.

"Nothing else."

"I SAID, WHAT—ELSE—ARE—YOU!"

"Nothing else. Nothing. *Nothing.* Can't you get that through your skull?"

He bent down, shaking with a real or theatrical anger.

"I want the truth! You might be a reporter, but you are also an intelligence agent! That's what you were doing in our lines at night!"

"If I was an agent, do you think I'd be so stupid to be carrying a passport with my real name in it, a phone book, Israeli business cards?"

"That could have been just what you wanted us to think! That you're too stupid to be an agent ..."

I was so worn out I could hardly sit up straight, a limpness suggesting the transformation of my skeleton into cartilage. I pointed at one of the guerrillas.

"Tell that man to put his gun to my head and then you ask me if I'm a spy and if you still don't believe me, then tell him to blow my head off. I don't give a damn anymore."

But that bluff was growing a little stale.

Mr. Blue Eyes sat on the mat, folding his legs, his knees touching mine, intimate as a lover's. He rested his hands on my shoulders. He spoke softly.

"I have told you, Philip, we are not murderers. I have told you that what you propose would be very crude. We have other ways to get the truth. What happened to you last night is *nothing* compared to what we can do. Believe me, please, *nothing*. Now, I want you to convince me you are a journalist only."

I broke into sobs. A face leaned over me—the face of the man who last night had told me, "Well, then, go mad." Now he was almost in tears, watching me break down.

"Please," he said, "lie down, rest."

He pressed gently on my shoulders. Mr. Blue Eyes tore his hand away.

"No!"

He grabbed my chin and held my face close to his.

"We are going to get the truth, Philip. What I did to you last night is something I learned from the Israelis when they captured me on the West Bank. I had to live in a hole like that, I had to sleep in it every night for eighteen months, not eighteen hours ..."

I said I didn't believe him; no one could mentally survive such an ordeal.

"Oh, yes. I did. What you went through is nothing compared to what I went through. Now you listen to me. I cannot believe you are a reporter only. No intelligent reporter would have come toward our lines at the worst of the shooting, unless he had other business ..."

"You seem to want to believe I'm a spy," I blubbered. "You're my prosecutor, my jury, my judge. I'm going to die no matter what I say."

"First of all, I don't want to believe anything. If I think you are guilty, you will be referred to one of our courts. You will have a jury. If they find you innocent, you will be freed. If they find you guilty, then, Philip, then you *will* die."

"That would be cruel and inhuman," I said, picturing what that court would be like—some drumhead tribunal straight out of the Reign of Terror.

"Can't you understand that we are at war? When your country captured spies during the Second World War, it executed them. What's unnatural, what's so inhuman about that?"

"I'm no spy."

"Convince me, Philip. Carefully but quickly convince me you are a reporter only."

I composed myself and started talking, beginning with the moment I left the St. Georges to see about the bombing. I spoke for twenty minutes, possibly half an hour. I was Scheherazade, spinning a tale for my very life. If a lie repeated often enough begins to sound like the truth, the truth repeated often enough begins to sound like a lie. I had told my story so many times it sounded like a story. When I came to the end, I said: "That's it. You can send me to your court, you can stick me back in that hole for the next year and you'll never hear me say anything other than what I've just said."

I felt spent, exhausted, empty—and beaten. My tale had sounded false even to my own ears. Mr. Blue Eyes stared at me, expressionless.

"How would you like a shave?" he asked.

I scraped my bristly chin and nodded.

"Do you use an electric razor or a blade? Would you like hot water?"

I asked for a blade, hot water, and soap, struggling not to hope. A last shave for the condemned man? Or was Mr. Blue Eyes concerned about how I would look when freed?

A guard brought a pan of hot water, shaving lather, a straight razor, and a mirror. When I was finished, Mr. Blue Eyes told me I looked much better. A smile flickered under his mustache. He slapped me on the thigh.

"Philip. You are our friend. You have nothing more to worry about."

If I had been standing, my knees would have buckled.

"Ambassador Yezid—he is the Algerian ambassador to Lebanon—is to pick you up in his car in one hour's time."

I did not ask why I was being handed over to the Algerians. It could have been the Kalahari bushmen for all I cared.

For the last time, I was led back to the kitchen-cell. The door was conspicuously left open, and no armed guards were around. Nor were Zouhair and Number Three, who had been released the night before. I stood by the barred window, looking down at the mess shells and rockets had made of a building. Two boys were playing soldier, using sticks as rifles. They looked no older than twelve, but they ran zigzag and carried their rifles in the way that's taught in basic training. One boy made a John Wayne dash for a mound of bricks and hit the dirt, snapping his stick gun to his shoulder at the same time. *Bangyerdead!* His feigned fire streamed at the other boy, who fell acrobatically in feigned death. He got up, and the two exchanged roles for the next round of make-believe. It was not a child's game but a drill for the time when the rifles would be real and they would not get up when they fell.

"Hey, Mister Journalist!" It was The Chocolate Soldier, flanked by Erebia, Mahmoud the Mad, and The Happy Warrior. "Hello, hello. We knew it, we knew all along you were only a journalist."

"Well, you had me fooled."

They all shook my hand, except The Happy Warrior, who gave me a high five and a dap.

"Where did you learn that?"

"In the movies. *Shaft,* Mister Richard Roundtree. Hey, brotha ..."

Mahmoud the Mad's synapses were discharging normally and even the sphinx-faced Erebia wore a smile, though it was so vague you had to look hard to see it. They were all three Children of the Beast, but they seemed nearly as happy and relieved as I, which made me wonder if they had been picked as my firing squad in case things had gone the other way.

"Let's have some tea," The Chocolate Soldier offered.

We drank it in the guards' room.

"So now you have a great adventure to write about."

I said I didn't think it had been an adventure.

"But all you have lost is time," he said philosophically. "Please, the next time you want to visit the fedayeen, come by day through the front door, not the back door by night."

He laughed and laughed.

"Tasin, why are you always laughing?"

"What else can I do? Tomorrow they may send me on a mission to Israel and I will be killed."

"*Will* be?"

"Oh, yes. None of our fighters ever come back alive from Israel, so I live from moment to moment. It makes me sad at times, but I am committed to the Resistance. I will never have a wife, not even a good friend. So I just laugh."

Just that month eighteen.

Mr. Blue Eyes came up the stairs. He handed me my notebook and pen and, dismissing the others, sat on the cot beside me.

"Now I am ready to answer *your* questions."

I looked at him, baffled.

"You are a journalist, so now you can interview me."

What the hell, a little role reversal might do me good. The interview lasted forty-five minutes. I won't recount it now because most of Mr. Blue Eyes' answers were rote repetitions from the Third World Book of Common Cant. The only time he seemed to speak straight from the heart was when, with a pained, almost bemused expression, he shook his head and said: "We have nothing against the Jews or their religion, but I cannot understand why Palestinians like myself have been forced to pay for the Nazis' crimes against the Jews."

The phone rang.

"Well, you are officially now a free man, Philip," Mr. Blue Eyes said, hanging up. "Please come with me."

We walked back to the headquarters where I had been questioned by the bald man with the paunch and the pistol. He was there, with a few guerrillas. My money, wallet, passport, all my belongings were returned. Only my belt and shoes were missing, which seemed to trouble everyone. Mr. Blue Eyes promised they would be found and returned as soon as possible.

A Citroën limousine pulled up, the Algerian flag flying from its front fenders. Out stepped a portly six-footer, wearing glasses and a pale-blue poplin suit.

"Half the world has been looking for you," Ambassador Yezid said jovially, and shook my hand. "You've caused us all several sleepless nights." He paused, scrutinizing me. I must have looked like hell. "I hope you feel no bitterness toward these people."

I said nothing, my silence bringing an air of tension to the room.

"Please put yourself in their shoes."

"He can't put himself in his own shoes," Mr. Blue Eyes said, and everyone laughed.

Yezid asked my size. Nine and a half.

"Exactly mine. We'll stop at my residence and I'll loan you a pair."

We said good-bye, stepped into the air-conditioned, thickly carpeted limo, and drove out of the ruined and squalid camp, diplomatic flags snapping nicely above the headlights.

On the way to his residence, Yezid told me I could thank a lot of people for my release, but none more than Georgie Anne Geyer.

Gee-Gee?

"Oh, yes. What a tenacious woman!" said Yezid with mixed exasperation and admiration. This was what happened:

Three days after I had disappeared, Gee-Gee and several other correspondents were having lunch at the St. Georges, enjoying a brief caesura in the fighting. Someone at the table asked if anyone had seen me. At almost that moment, Gee-Gee got a phone call from the Chicago *Daily News* foreign desk. The *Tribune* had not heard from me since Sunday. Could she help find me?

She dropped everything she was doing and, working nearly round the clock for the next thirty-six hours, tapped all her best sources. Official sources, semiofficial sources, and sources in the Beirut shadow world, where spooks and scholars and scholar-spooks crept like cats between government and guerrilla authority. She went to the Lebanese Foreign Ministry and to the headquarters of Yasir Arafat himself, where she was told that the fedayeen were not holding me or anyone. About the same time, the man I called Number Four telephoned the foreign ministry to say that he had just been released from the camp, where the guerrillas were holding an American reporter for the Washington *Post,* a man named Caputo. Gee-Gee went to Yezid with these two bits of information because the Algerians had close ties to the PLO. He began phoning his contacts, who made ritual denials. The PDFLP was the most independent and uncontrollable of the factions. Geyer figured the guerrilla command did not want it known that they had balky groups in the resistance, so she rather bravely went to the Democratic Front itself—and got the same denials. She phoned the Foreign Ministry once again. Partly at her urging, they sent a team to the guerrillas to find out who was holding whom where. On Friday, Zouhair and Number Three called the U.S. Embassy and confirmed Number Four's report, correcting the name of my employer. Gee-Gee took that scrap to the Foreign Ministry, where she was told their negotiators were hard on the case and that I would be released within hours.

"And today at lunch, the Front called me and told me to come to Sabra. When we get to my house, I will call Miss Geyer and tell her to order drinks for three."

I did not say anything, feeling gratitude and shame. Christ, beating her to the punch was one of the reasons I'd gone winging off without a second thought.

"Ah, the world is all upside down these days, Mr. Caputo," Yezid said. "Isn't it supposed to be the knight who rescues the damsel?"

However it was supposed to be, I said, I did not feel very knightlike.

The ambassador crinkled his nose.

"I am afraid you don't smell like it either."

With Yezid's shoes on my feet, I stepped out of the limousine in front of the St. Georges. I had to face a battery of cameras and microphones. I was a newsman who had made news, and I was embarrassed.

"Now you are going to learn what it's like to be on this side of the camera," Yezid said with a wicked chuckle.

I looked away from the cameras a moment, out across the hotel's graceful terraces toward the Mediterranean, the same Mediterranean I had looked upon five days ago, spread beneath the same skies; but never I had seen skies so clear, nor a sea so blue.

"Hey, Phil ... Phil ... Congratulations ..."

It was Peter Jennings, from ABC. I nodded to him, and then he said something that left me speechless.

"And congratulations on the Pulitzer."

I stared, uncomprehending.

"You were on an investigative team in Chicago, weren't you?"

I nodded. He said the team had won the prize. The committee had made the announcement on Tuesday, my first full day in captivity.

"Could you give us a few minutes?"

And I stepped up to the mikes to accept an unearned and transient celebrity.

Postscript ...

In the Middle East, it is very difficult to maintain a balanced view of the conflict between Palestinian Arab and Israeli Jew. Each side is so passionate in its convictions, so able to persuasively argue the justice of its cause, that the neutral observer often becomes embarrassed by his or her neutrality and gives in to the temptation to choose one side over the other. It makes things simpler.

The day of my release, I hated the Palestinians with such fervor that I was ready to enlist in the Israeli army. But the next morning, as I sat in my room in the St. Georges struggling to write an account of my capture, I was interrupted by a knock at the door. It was a bellboy, holding a brown paper bag.

"Some men left these for you at the front desk," he said.

I opened it . . . and felt the hatred drain out of me like poison from an abscess. Inside were my shoes, brightly polished, with a note from my captors apologizing for misplacing them.

DISASTERS OF WAR

The driver parked alongside a small pagoda with a curving tiled roof, a stone altar, and an urn of joss sticks burning under a smiling buddha, its round face and belly chipped by bullets. Khanh, the interpreter, hopped out of the jeep and passed the word that the bac-si had arrived in the village.

In a short time, people began to line up beside the jeep. Most were old men and women, but a few were younger women with small children. The old people complained of headaches or stomachaches or backaches or pains in their joints. The young mothers said their kids had coughs, toothaches, and fevers. No matter what the ailment, the medic's remedy was always the same: a packet of twelve aspirin, with instructions to take two every four hours. It was a very hot day. At first, he listened carefully to the people describing their symptoms, but as the line grew longer and the day hotter, he began to pass out the aspirin before the people got a chance to say what was bothering them or their kids.

The first lieutenant, who sat in the front passenger seat, asked the medic why he did not make more thorough diagnoses and prescribe something other than aspirin. The officer was new to the country and the medic looked at him as if he had just asked why two and two equaled four.

"Orientals," he answered.

"I don't think I understand."

"Most of these people got nothin' wrong with 'em, el-tee. They just like it when we come here and give 'em aspirins."

"What about the ones who really are sick?"

"Nothin' we can do for 'em."

"Except make 'em think there's somethin' we can do," added the driver.

When the last person had been treated, the driver glanced at the medic, raised his eyebrows, and inclined his head.

"Yup," the medic said. "It's part of our rounds."

"Shit."

"You don't hafta come in this time. The el-tee can give me a hand."

They drove through the village. Gangs of children ran out of the huts yelling, "Hey, you you you souvenir me you." The driver dipped into his pockets and tossed fistfuls of hard candy at the kids, who scrabbled for them in the dust.

At the edge of the village, he stopped in front of a thatch-roofed shack that perched atop a knoll, under the shade of a pineapple palm.

The medic looked at the first lieutenant. "Okay, el-tee? It ain't a pretty sight."

"Guess I'd better get used to unpretty sights."

"It's the smell mostly," the medic said.

Inside, an old couple sat on a bench while a young woman, holding a wicker fan, stood beside a man who lay on a bamboo bed, staring at the ceiling. Despite the heat, two heavy blankets covered him to the neck. He was so still that, at first, the officer thought he was dead; then he saw the man blink.

"That's mamasan and papasan," the medic said, pointing at the couple. "The young one's his wife. She has the blankets on him to keep the flies offa him." He gestured at the man's wife. "Take covers off. Okay, take off."

The woman pulled the blankets back. As soon as she did, flies swarmed all over the man and the smell struck the first lieutenant like a blow.

"Warned you, el-tee."

Now the woman took off her husband's shirt and tugged his trousers down past his buttocks. He did not so much as twitch. He looked dead, except for the blinking eyes. His mother and father were almost as still as they watched from the bench.

"Okay, el-tee, if you'll take his ankles, me and his old lady'll get his shoulders and arms."

Holding his breath, the first lieutenant gripped the man's ankles, which felt as thin as a child's wrists.

Okay, real easy now, roll him over onta his side," the medic said.

After they did and the woman peeled off the sticky, blackened dressings from her husband's back, the first lieutenant knew there were some sights he would never get used to.

"What in God's name did this?" he asked, staring, almost fascinated, at the man's back.

"Could be some kinda gangrene, could be some kinda real bad impetigo, could be leprosy, but it's probly somethin' nobody on God's green earth gotta name for yet. Yup, el-tee, I just might be makin' medical hist'ry out here and not know it."

The woman was waving the fan to keep the flies off the slick red levees of rotting flesh that humped alongside the white canal of her husband's exposed spinal cord. The medic took a tube from his kit, slipped on a pair of rubber gloves, and began to apply a clear ointment to the sores.

"Doc, we've got to call a chopper, get this guy to a hospital," said the first lieutenant, feeling a need to assert his authority and to take action.

"She doesn't want him to go to a hospital." The medic waved a hand at the old people, motionless as stuffed birds. "And neither does mamasan and papasan."

"Why not?"

"Who knows? Orientals. Who knows about them?"

"Listen. It doesn't make any difference what they want. You're a medic, you've got a responsibility."

"Right, el-tee. A medic. I ain't no real doctor, didn't take no hypocritical oath so the only gotta I gotta do is to go with the flow, ease with breeze and get back home. These folks want him here, fine with me. Anyways, he can't be moved. Couldn't get him to a hospital. It's gone too far. Too far for anyone to do a damn thing."

The first lieutenant had a hard time believing that; there was always something that could be done, always some remedy.

"If it's all so hopeless, then what's that stuff you're putting on him?"

"Antifungicide. Pretty much the same thing you use for athlete's foot, only it's stronger."

"How in the hell is that going to help him?"

The medic ripped off the gloves.

"God-damn, el-tee, you just don't get it, do you? It's for them, not him. It's for us, too, so's these people'll think we done all we could when he ups and dies and he's gonna in a couple weeks. That rot's gonna eat right through his nervous system and kill him, and one day I'll come in here and he'll be dead."

The medic pulled a roll of gauze from his kit and redressed the strips of decayed flesh; then he, the first lieutenant, and the man's wife turned the man onto his back again. He was staring at the ceiling.

"Must be something we can do," the officer said, though he said it, now, only because he thought it was the kind of thing an officer should say.

The medic packed his kit.

"Cam ong, bac-si," the wife said as the two men started to leave.

The medic gave the old people an awkward bow. They did not move.

Outside, walking down the knoll to the jeep, the first lieutenant drew in breath after breath of fresh air. He hadn't realized how bad the smell was until he stopped smelling it.

"How did that guy get like that?"

"Oh, he got wounded and sent back home," the medic explained. "Shrapnel or somethin'. He come back here and laid himself down on that bamboo bed and said he wasn't gonna move no more. He wasn't hit that bad, el-tee, from what his old lady told me. I guess she tried to get him some help, but he just refused to move or even let anybody touch him. Then this rot set in about three months ago."

The first lieutenant looked back. He could not see inside the hut. The door was a black rectangle in the bamboo wall and the shadows of the pineapple palm, stirring in a breeze, moved back and forth across the thatch roof.

"Well, I can't figure that one."

The medic opened his mouth. The officer raised his hand, palm outward.

"I know, doc. Orientals."

"There it is."

They climbed in the jeep. Six or seven kids gathered around, touching the men, tugging at their sleeves. "Hey you you you souvenir me you gimme cigret gimme candy you." The driver went into his pocket and tossed a handful of candy high into the air. It came down like sweet little pieces of fruit falling from an invisible tree. The driver threw the jeep in gear and popped the clutch, throwing up a cloud of red dust. When the officer looked back, he saw the kids, fighting in the dust for the candy.

FIVE

First Casualties

Foreign correspondents do not work five-day weeks. In Rome, I made it a point to check in at Reuters' office at least once every weekend to make sure I wasn't missing anything on my immense beat. October 6, 1973, was a Saturday, Yom Kippur for the Jews, the Tenth of Ramadan for Moslems, that is, a slow news day in the Middle East. After a look at the wires, I picked up a *cafelatte* from the coffee bar downstairs and shot the breeze with Barry Moody, the weekend deskman. Teletypes clattered in the background like a steno pool. From outside came the clop of a horse-drawn cab wheeling Fred and Ethel from Des Moines toward the Trevi Fountain. The warning bells on the world wire—the machine that carried Reuters dispatches from around the globe—clanged like alarms in a fire station. Moody went to the Teletype, ripped a story, and passed it to me.

"Think this might interest you."

There were the usual transmission codes, the time group—10061235 GMT (or something like that)—and then this (or something like this):

TEL AVIV—URGENT-URGENT-URGENT—
EGYPT AND SYRIA LAUNCHED A MASSIVE, COORDINATED
ATTACK TODAY AGAINST ISRAELI TROOPS DEFENDING THE
SUEZ CANAL AND THE OCCUPIED GOLAN HEIGHTS, ACCORD-

ING TO AN ANNOUNCEMENT BY A SPOKESMAN FOR THE
ISRAELI DEFENCE FORCES.
MORE-MORE-MORE.
THE ATTACK, INVOLVING ARMOUR AND INFANTRY FORCES
SUPPORTED BY ARTILLERY, PLANES AND ANTIAIRCRAFT MIS-
SILES, CAME AT APPROXIMATELY 1400 LOCAL TIME. ALL MILI-
TARY LEAVES FOR THE JEWISH YOM KIPPUR HOLIDAY HAVE
BEEN CANCELLED AND A GENERAL CALL-UP OF RESERVISTS
IS UNDERWAY, THE SPOKESMAN SAID.
MORE-MORE-MORE.

Moody gave me a grin and a wave.
"Ta-ta, Phil."

Sunday evening, after camping out beside the El Al desk at Fiumicino
airport, I and a squad of other Rome-based correspondents were
allowed onto a flight into Tel Aviv. We were the only civilians aboard.
The rest of the passengers, a hundred and fifty or more, were Israeli
reservists recalled to duty from jobs and schools abroad.

By now, the fall of the Bar Lev Line had been confirmed; the
Egyptians were digging in on the east bank of the canal. Knowing I
probably would have to file something as soon as I found a hotel
room, I started interviewing the passengers. One young idiot boasted,
"So they're on the east bank? What are they going to do there? Starve
or die of thirst? It's no problem. We've got them where we want
them." From across the aisle, a tall, rugged paratroop officer looked at
the fool and snickered. "Listen here, it is a very hard war we are fighting this time. We are facing two huge armies. This is a full-scale
onslaught. The Egyptians and the Syrians have come to conquer
Israel."

About then, the pilot announced that we were leaving cruising
altitude and beginning our descent into Lod airport. He blacked out
the plane; even the navigation lights went off. I looked out the window and saw an Israeli Phantom, so close to our wing tip I probably
could have made out the pilot's face if it had been daylight. A second
Phantom hugged the other wing. A tough fight. If we needed a fighter escort just to get into Tel Aviv, I guessed it was going to be that and
more.

❂   ❂   ❂

Taking a cab from Lod to the Hilton, I did not see a light on anywhere in the city. Diezengoff Street, Tel Aviv's Via Veneto, was dark and deserted except for a few military vehicles and taxis, all with their headlights off or covered by blue filters. At the front desk, a cheerful, business-as-usual reservations clerk took imprints of our credit cards and held a flashlight while we signed the registration forms. The line at the bottom asked, "Length of Stay." We wrote "indefinitely." The clerk gave us a wry and cocky grin.

"Oh, why don't you put down until October seventeenth?" he asked, pulling a date out of the air. "That will give you plenty of time to write about the war and you will also have time to write about it afterwards."

A bellgirl showed me to my room (the bellboys were in other uniforms now) and, in the manner of a concerned Jewish mother, instructed me to never never never withdraw the blackout curtain while my light was on.

After she left, I set my Olivetti on the desk and started to write up the interviews. It was to be what's known in the news business as a mood piece. The mood of the Israelis the day after the Arab attack. No boasting but no panic either—a calm confidence. I ought to have waited—what the hell did I know about Israel's mood beyond what a few reservists and a desk clerk had told me—but it was all I had, and I knew the paper wanted to establish straightaway that their man was among the first in.

I might have been a page into the piece when I heard a sound I had heard before only in make-believe: the dismal, this-is-how-the-world-ends moan of air-raid sirens. I flicked off the light and opened the door. The bellgirl was in the corridor, rousing the guests—correspondents mostly, but also a few tourists who had not been able to find flights out of Israel.

"This way, this way," the bellgirl called, directing us to the elevator with her flashlight.

I got in with a dozen people, one an elderly woman who slumped in a corner sobbing.

"Mama, Mama, please, it will be all right," said the younger woman with her.

She muttered something in Yiddish.

"Stop crying, Mama, it will be all right."

The elevator landed in the basement. The bellgirl ushered us into a hall and told us to sit down and wait for the all-clear.

The elderly lady folded her knees to her head and sobbed and mumbled.

"It will be all right, Mama."

Early cold war memories came to me: of watching civil defense films in the recreation hall at Divine Infant Jesus school, the narrator lecturing in a voice overflowing with assurance, "When the alert sounds, proceed quickly and calmly to the nearest shelter" ... Shots of calm kids quickly filing to the nearest shelter ... Shots of cute calm kids ducking under their desks, as if an inch of oak or maple could save them from the power of the universe.

"Mama, please, please ..."

The young woman glanced at me with exasperation, anger, and sadness mingled in her eyes. She volunteered that her name was Cohen, that she came from Toronto, that she had brought her mother to Israel just three days ago. It was the old woman's first visit to the Jewish homeland.

"And now this, *this*. Mama escaped from Poland in thirty-nine. She was in London all through the Blitz. And she comes to Israel for this, *this*. Goddamn the Arabs."

"All clear, all clear," announced the bellgirl about ten minutes later. "Please go back to your rooms."

Miss Cohen's mother did not move.

"Mama, it's all right now! All clear."

She pulled at the old woman's arms, trying to lift her to her feet. I gave Miss Cohen a hand. Her mother stood but was still sobbing and mumbling in Yiddish.

"Stop crying now, Mama! It's all clear, I'm telling you."

In the elevator, Miss Cohen shot me a look full of pain and exhausted patience, a look that asked for understanding. I understood. The only air raid sirens I'd ever heard had been in instructional films. The old woman had heard the ones that wail and wail in the memory and never sound the all-clear.

Back in my room, I tried to think of a way to work her into the piece, but she did not exactly fit into the mood of calm confidence, did she? It was past one in the morning, my brain and body cried for sleep. I wrapped up my first war dispatch in under five hundred words, ran it over to the censor at the press center in Beit Sokoloff, a stark government building not far from the Hilton. The censor, a youngish captain, approved it and gave it to the telex operator, and Arabs who accused the western media of a pro-Israeli bias would have had plenty of fodder with my piece. I had described the Arab assault as an invasion of Israel. The fact was, the Egyptians had invaded Egypt and the Syrians Syria because the Sinai and the Golan, like the West Bank, were territories occupied by Israel; but most Israelis had come to think of them as part of their country. Apparently I did, too. I didn't realize my mistake until the next morning. When I did, I put in an overseas call to the foreign desk, told them to change the lead, and told myself to start paying attention. The first casualty in war is the truth, went the axiom, and, without intending to, I had given the truth a flesh wound.

In the next few days, an anonymous squad of Israeli reserve officers, known only as "military spokesmen," almost nuked it.

Israel, in the first few days of the war, was a land of literal and figurative darkness. The blackout remained in effect every night and, day or night, almost everyone was in the dark about the situation at the fronts. Israel's mood of calm confidence was the confidence of ignorance. No one except the fighting men had a clear idea of how bad things were, though Israelis and foreigners alike sensed that something had gone terribly, terribly wrong. How had the Egyptians and Syrians been able to mass thousands of tanks and hundreds of thousands of troops and attack without a word of warning? Why had the supposedly impregnable Bar Lev Line—a string of formidable bunkers and tank traps stretching the length of the Suez Canal—fallen in less than a day? How had the Syrians seized half the Golan Heights? And hidden within those questions like a bomb inside a shoebox was *the* big question: Were the Arabs winning?

Israeli civilians wanted answers, the press wanted answers, but all anybody got from official sources was a gumbo of half truths and falsehoods seasoned with a light sprinkling of fact and drenched in a sauce of wishful thinking.

The chefs were the anonymous Spokesmen, although Famous Names like Defense Minister Moshe Dayan sometimes added morale-enhancing morsels to the pot. The main kitchen was the pressroom in Beit Sokoloff, where the Spokesmen spoke at nightly briefings to an ever-growing audience of foreign and native correspondents. Old Vietnam hands said the briefings had some of the Alice in Wonderland atmosphere of those in Saigon—the infamous "Five O'Clock Follies."

At first, all eyes were on the northern front, and for a couple of reasons. The Egyptian army's crossing of the canal had been the greater military achievement, but a hundred and fifty miles of very hostile desert lay between the Egyptians and Israel's border. Also, the Israelis were not as afraid of the Egyptians as they were of the Syrians, of whom they felt primal dread. In their eyes, the Egyptians belonged to the Mediterranean world. They were reasonable, civilized, they could be talked to. The Israeli image of the Syrian was different: a better fighting man than the Egyptian, but dour, truculent, barbaric, bad to the bone. It was, like most propagandist pictures, a cartoon; but the important thing was that the Israelis believed it to be accurate. And a horde of those nasties was up on the Golan Heights, *the strategic* Golan Heights, strategic being shorthand for the military importance of that lava ridge frowning above the Jordan River valley, Lake Tiberias, and the hills of northern Israel. Less than twenty miles wide at its widest point, the Golan was a huge, natural platform for artillery, a launch pad for missiles. As for tanks and mechanized infantry, well, once they got up there, it was all downhill to the Mediterranean.

By all the unofficial accounts we heard in Tel Aviv, the attack had been awesome. Some of the people who'd seen it searched for metaphors to describe it. *Like ... like rivers of steel ... like ... a tide, a tide of tanks.*

All right, call it a tide: fourteen hundred tanks backed by missile-toting motorized infantry swept over Israel's first line of defense—a line of bunkers and paramilitary settlements called *nahals*—like a typhoon's storm surge over a flimsy breakwater. And they had hardly fired a shot—the Syrian tank commanders had their turret hatches open and rode into battle, for Christ's sake, standing at attention! That inspired a UN observer on the old cease-fire line to come up with a nonaquatic metaphor: "It was like a parade-ground demonstration."

Two Israeli armored brigades—the mobile second line of defense—put a stop to the parade-ground stuff, but not to the advance. Line abreast, the tanks and APCs rolled on. It could have been an image out of Byron's poetry—*The Assyrian came down like the wolf on the fold, And his cohorts were gleaming in purple and gold*—except those cohorts wore mottled khaki and brown and their chariots were Soviet T-54s and T-55s and new T-62s, so new that, later, some were found with only thirty miles on their odometers.

They came up the road through Kuneitra, the biggest city on the Heights. They came up another road through a town called Rafid and headed south, toward Lake Tiberias. They scattered and destroyed one of the defending brigades, bloodied the other, shot down something like thirty of Israel's Skyhawk fighter-bombers, overran an Israeli headquarters, and got to within five miles of the Daughters of Jacob Bridge, a beautiful name for an ugly iron-girder structure that spanned the Jordan. On the other side was Israel. One last push and the Syrian armor would be chopping through Israel itself, bringing to life the apocalyptic horror that lurked in the Israelis' collective subconscious—a figurative sea of Arabs pushing them into the geographical sea at their backs. But the Syrians stopped. Some of the tanks ran out of gas, having advanced too rapidly for their fuel and supply trucks to catch up. That gave the Israelis enough time to launch a counterattack, about which stories floated into Tel Aviv.

In the Hilton bar, I talked to a gunner, a big Samson of a guy with thick curly black hair, whose Centurion tank had been disabled by a Sagger missile. Still dressed in his filthy, sweaty jumpsuit, he was awaiting reassignment, getting astonishingly drunk, and groping at every woman who got within arm's reach. He could hardly talk, an incoherence brought on by more than the Scotches he downed like ginger ale, but he made enough sense to paint an appalling portrait. Point-blank armor duels, Israeli tank crews (among the best in the world, as accurate with their cannon as American frontiersmen were with Kentucky long rifles) knocking out three, four, even five T-54s before running out of ammunition or getting knocked out themselves, of hand-to-hand combat, and no figure of speech either, actually hand-to-hand, they were having *fistfights* up there amidst the Golan's black rocks. He inhaled another Scotch and went on in his accented English. "Tunks. Tunks and tunks. I never saw so many ... all around ... tunks and tunks ... hit ours, a good hit ... treads ... another hit ... burning ... we ran out ... ran and ran ... all we had were pistols ... an

Uzi maybe ... nothing, booby, against all those tunks ..."

Israelis running from Arabs! Had I heard right?

"Oh, yes, and we weren't the only ones."

I wrote up what he told me, went to file it at the press center, and watched the censor, with an apologetic smile, turn it into confetti. "Sorry, we can't let them know what they did, not yet," he said.

And the Spokesmen weren't about to let anyone know.

This was what we, and the Israeli public, were told had happened: On Monday, October 8, the Spokesmen reported that the Syrians, having achieved some shallow penetrations of the Israeli defenses, had been driven from the Golan and were retreating in disarray.

Not quite, the newspapers reported the next day. The retreat had been an orderly, fighting withdrawal and some "pockets of resistance" remained. General Chaim Herzog, the army's chief public commentator, that is, the Commander of the Spokesmen, apparently did not like that situation; he donned the robes of military augur and foretold the imminent disintegration of the Syrian army.

It didn't happen. The afternoon of Herzog's prophecy, the Jerusalem *Post* reported that the Syrians, instead of retreating and disintegrating, were counterattacking the Israeli counterattack and "fiercely contesting each inch of ground."

The Spokesmen were compelled to call in another Famous Name to contradict the *Post:* General David Elazar, the chief of staff. He said the tide of battle had turned. The Israeli army had driven the Syrians ten miles beyond the 1967 cease-fire line. But Elazar was not quite famous enough to overcome the grim, alarming tales that kept flowing back into Tel Aviv, so Defense Minister Dayan was drafted into informational service. *Dayan.* The architect of the '67 victories, a legend who looked like one, black eyepatch slanting piratically across his forehead. He predicted that the fighting on the northern front would be finished in a day or two (it didn't end until the cease-fire on October 24 and then started again and went on for another eight months). According to Dayan, the Syrians were again retreating in disarray; they were practically broken, a rabble. But facts intruded once more, and within twenty-four hours even the Spokesmen were forced to confess that the Syrians were "fighting tenaciously for every position."

If they were throwing out a chaff of misinformation about the northern front, they had nothing at all to say about the Sinai. There, the disastrous fall of the Bar Lev Line had been followed by a catastrophe. Israel's 190th Armored Battalion, thrown into a desperate counterattack against the Egyptian bridgeheads across the canal, was wiped out. Fifty or sixty tanks and scores of men had been lost in a matter of minutes. The Israeli command said nothing about the defeat. No one in Israel knew a thing about it until the battalion commander, a Colonel Yagouri, became a media star—in Cairo. Captured by the Egyptians, he was packed off to the city by the Nile, where he agreed to describe the battle on a TV news show.

His humiliation notwithstanding, Dayan, Elazar, and company made upbeat pronouncements about turning tides and enemies retreating in disarray. They were not deliberately lying to con everyone into thinking the situation was under control. They probably believed what they said. Israel's lightning victory in 1967 had created two myths: the Arabs were incompetent cowards, too backward to handle modern weapons, and the Israeli army was invincible. The myths were in time enshrined as immutable truths. General Ariel Sharon, another Famous Name, once proclaimed that Israel could conquer everything from Baghdad to Algeria in a week. One of my sources told me, even as the Egyptians were setting up housekeeping in the Bar Lev Line bunkers, "The Egyptians are like the Italians— they don't like to fight in wars." For them to have done what they had done, for the Syrians to be conducting an orderly, fighting withdrawal—*the* most difficult battlefield maneuver—was like a winged horse: conceivable but highly improbable. When the Egyptians and Syrians failed to obey what the Israelis saw as laws of nature, the Spokesmen and Famous Names were at a loss to explain the phenomenon. So they did not try to explain. They went on predicting the disintegration of the Arab armies, apparently in the belief that if they made the prophecy often enough it would in time fulfill itself.

"The Arabs learned to fight from us," editorialized the English-language Jerusalem *Post*. "And we learned how to handle information from them."

The only sure way to find out what was going on was to see for yourself. But the information system had suffered another sort of breakdown, for physical rather than psychological reasons. The Israeli Defense Forces could not possibly supply an escort for each of the six hundred correspondents covering the war. Requests for escorts and the special passes that allowed a reporter to go to the front were handled by a harassed little band of public affairs officers in Beit Sokoloff. They functioned as a kind of travel agency. Correspondents lined up and begged, filled out forms, and then waited for word of where and when they could go, if they could go. Although the Harassed Little Band never said so, they practiced a certain necessary discrimination: American reporters got priority, for it was America that sent the Phantom jets, the bombs, the missiles, along with monetary contributions from Jewish-American organizations. Among U.S. reporters, those from the three TV networks, the *New York Times,* the Washington *Post, Time,* and *Newsweek* got first dibs; then came the second string—the smaller broadcast systems like Mutual, the big regional papers like the *Tribune* and the Miami *Herald.*

Aware that I was at a disadvantage, I tapped all the sources and connections I had made in my trips to Israel but had to wait my turn.

I waited three days and on the fourth, having learned nothing from my experience in Beirut, decided to make a dash for the front without official permission. Go as far as you can as fast as you can. With a radio reporter from Mutual Broadcasting, I rented a car, got hold of a map, and headed for Sinai. The military police caught us when we were halfway across the desert and sent us back to Tel Aviv, with the warning that we'd lose our press credentials if we tried again.

Early the next day, when I checked in to see if I had yet been assigned an escort officer, the Harassed Little Band gave me a tongue-lashing for breaking the rules. They punished me. I had been assigned an escort, they said, but they had decided to reassign him to another correspondent. I postured in submission. I offered contrition, but they would hear none of it. The best they could do was to send me with a press pool leaving soon for the northern front. I told them I hated press pools and pack journalism.

"You should be happy we're letting you go at all," scolded one of the Little Band. "It's a good story up there. Did you hear the radio this morning? We've given those Syrians a good beating. They're ..."

"I heard. Retreating in disarray."

"And now you have a chance to watch them."

It wasn't a press pool, it was a lake: forty-five reporters and photographers and cameramen crammed into a yellow school bus. I recognized no one, understood no one—they all seemed to be from Scandinavian countries. Shouldering through the blond, babbling crowd to find a seat, I finally saw a familiar face: Nick Proffitt. I had not seen him since Beirut. Sitting next to him, I reintroduced myself.

"I know who you are," he growled. "You're the dumb fuck who got himself captured."

I did not say anything. He knit his eyebrows and puckered his lips.

"I don't know if I want you sitting next to me. That was just about the dumbest fucking thing anyone could do."

I said I couldn't argue with that.

"Do me a favor. Do everybody a favor. Don't do any dumb-fuck things on this trip. From what we hear, the sand-suckers are still taking names up there."

"They're supposed to be retreating in disarray."

"If you believe that, you are the dumbest of dumb fucks."

It was an odd beginning to what would become a lasting friendship.

Five hours later, the bus dropped us off in a pleasant eucalyptus grove. Above, the Golan Heights glowered like a giant's brow. We were herded to a hastily set up briefing area, where an officer waited with the tools of his trade: a pointer, a big map tacked to a plywood board, and facts. Out of the fourteen hundred tanks Syria had thrown into the battle, over half had been destroyed. One thousand prisoners taken. The IDF was now deep in Syria, driving on Damascus. The officer's confident voice was underlined by the shriek of low-flying jets, by the great waves of sound made by bombs and artillery. The bombs were Israeli, but the guns were Syrian, as we were soon to learn.

Back to the bus, cameras dangling from our necks so that we must have looked like a package tour. We crawled up a narrow, winding asphalt road, crossed the Daughters of Jacob Bridge, and climbed some more, past ruined Ottoman forts, past old mine fields and the rusting hulks of Syrian tanks left over from the Six-day War, past antitank guns ready for use in this war. Far below was the calm blue eye of Lake Tiberias.

Although the day was warm and bright, the Golan looked just as somber as it did when I first saw it, on a cold, misty afternoon the previous December. It was a broad, gently rolling expanse crisscrossed by crumbled stone fences and dotted with Druze villages, all smashed to bits and hardly distinguishable from the basalt rocks and boulders that covered the plain like Druidic ruins. A friend of mine had said the Heights reminded him of a British moor, but there was something mysterious about a moor. The Golan was desolate without mystery. It looked like a vast gravel pit.

Garbage pit would have been more accurate on that day. It was strewn with live shells and spent shells and shell casings, with ammunition crates, jerry cans, tin cans, ration boxes, tires, and trucks transformed by shellfire into piles of blackened steel linguine, with burnt-out tanks, tank barrels, tank treads, and tank turrets knocked off the chassis like hats off a haberdasher's counter.

Off to the north rose Mount Hermon, an extinct volcano ten thousand feet high. Israeli soldiers skied there in winter, but the lifts would be closed this season: Syrian commandos had captured it in a helicopter assault and still held it. From up there, artillery spotters could drop shells anywhere they wanted on the Golan.

Farther up the road, our bright-yellow school bus passed tanks and half-tracks clattering toward the front. We came over a rise and stopped. Below was a shallow bowl filled with the wreckage of what looked like every tank in the world.

"That place is called Khushniye," explained our battlefield guide, turning in his seat to face us. "The heaviest fighting was there. What you see is all that is left of a Syrian tank division. Nothing. We will go now to have a look."

A puff of wind came up, carrying the stench of who knew how many corpses. Oh, that stink—it ought to be bottled and sold to every president, prime minister, king, dictator, and general for use when he gets an idea in his head to go to war. It is a fusion of odors, for which the recipe would be the following: five pounds of rotten ground beef, a pile of garbage that's ripened in a heat wave, the crotch of a pair of underwear that hasn't been changed in a week, the inside of a gym locker in which sweaty socks have hung for a season, then equal parts of dog shit, ammonia, marsh muck, and untreated sewage, with a dash of road-kill skunk.

A quarter of a mile down the road, the bus stopped again and our young captain said we could get out to take photographs, have a look around. The photographers and TV crews were busy, but it wasn't any kind of story for the pencil press. I walked off a short distance to a Syrian tank, its hatches sprung open. It didn't look damaged, so I climbed up and got a mild shock when my face almost bumped into the face of the commander, slumped in the turret. He had a military mustache and brown hair that was ruffled slightly by the breeze. He would have made a good-looking corpse if one side of his head had not been shredded. Ropes of dried blood stuck to his neck like tallow to a candle, but it was the hair that got to me. Not mussed at all, so lifelike, the way it rippled in the breeze. Below, the driver stared at me through his hatch, his colorless eyes set in a yellow-green face. I jumped off, almost landing atop a mound of human intestine, napalm fried to the whiteness of a dead fish's eye. It sat in the middle of the ashen outline of a man. That was all, just a silhouette of ashes. I practically ran back to the bus, thinking, *This isn't journalism, this is voyeurism.*

Shells started bursting on the ridge eastward. The escort officer thought it would be best if we got back aboard and moved to a safer spot. We thought so, too: a spotter with cataracts could have seen that yellow bus. The shells kept hitting as we drove back, the escort explaining that they were one hundred-thirty millimeters and that the Syrians were trying to interdict the supply convoys headed for the Israelis who were supposed to have routed the Syrians in disarray. We stopped again to let an ambulance pass. In the distance, the convoys kept crawling down the road into a spreading pall of smoke that seemed to swallow them all.

The Syrians started to walk the shells along the road, each burst a little closer to us than the last.

"Ah, we must go back a little more," said our captain.

"This proves it," Proffitt grumbled. "The final indignity is that there is no final indignity."

"Oh, yes there is," I said, remembering that little pile of fried gut, like an obscene white bouquet in the center of the ashes. Siren wailing, another ambulance sped by, then another. I saw a young nurse in the front seat, saw her for only an instant, yet I can see her still, leaning forward in the seat, face blanched, eyes fixed straight ahead with an expression that told me she now knew what one-thir-ties could do. The lesson was in the back of the ambulance, and it was too bad she had had to learn it so young. Behind her was a sight almost as incongruous as our school bus: a lumbering convoy of Tel Aviv city buses, dragooned into service as ambulances. Each one was jammed to capacity. Men wearing turbans of battle dressings, men with arms in slings, with white, bloodstained patches over their eyes.

A truck rolled behind the buses, its bed piled past the rails with body bags. They weren't empty.

The shells kept coming up the road, and we moved farther back, and then farther still, and in half an hour we had been driven back down to the eucalyptus grove, where a field hospital was being set up. Stretchers were stacked against the tent walls, plasma bottles hung from metal rods, the long clear worms of intravenous tubes waiting to crawl into the arms of the men who kept coming and coming in the ambulances.

The map was gone and so was the briefing officer and his rub-ber-tipped pointer.

First casualties ...

The Spokesman stood at the podium and gave the figures for the first week of fighting. Israeli tanks lost: six hundred out of seventeen hundred; Israeli planes shot down, seventy out of three hundred and fifty; Israeli dead, about six hundred. The Egyptians and Syrians had each lost two or three times that, but they had more people to lose.

He was a middle-aged lawyer and he bought us all drinks in the bar at the Tel Aviv Hilton, he was so happy.

"He is alive! We heard that a tank in his unit had been hit with a rocket and I was desperate to find out if he was all right. We hadn't heard from him. The rocket was a shaped charge and when it explod-ed it splattered the crew all over. They got the battalion chaplain to put the pieces of them together so they could identify the men. That night my boy phoned and I almost cried."

We were all happy for him, but we wondered what nights were going to be like for that battalion chaplain.

❋   ❋   ❋

Late in the week, a new menace appeared: the Iraqis sent an armored division to fight alongside the Syrians. Within hours, the Spokesmen were forecasting its imminent destruction. Any moment now and the Iraqis would be retreating in disarray. This time, I was going to see for myself, and in accordance with the rules of the game. I had my pass and my escort officer, a fifty-two-year-old import-export man named Zvi.

We drove to the war in a rented red Fiat. That's the kind of war it had become for the press corps. It was the Yom Kippur War to the Israelis, the War of Ten Ramadan to the Arabs, the October War to the rest of the world, the Hertz rent-a-war to us.

It was a five-hour drive to the northern front, first through the flat, sandy strip of Israel between the West Bank and the sea, and then through Galilee, where Deborah defeated the Canaanites and the Maccabees fought the Assyrians and Saladin routed the Crusaders. Holy Land, bloody land. The chariots and spears from those long-ago conflicts were buried deep beneath the stony hills, and there were few signs of the present one. Orange and olive groves greened the valleys, cotton waved brown and white in the wind, irrigation sprinklers flung mists over tomato fields.

"Do you think it would look like this if we didn't have the Golan?" Zvi asked rhetorically. "You can imagine what would have happened if the Syrians didn't have to take the Golan. These fields would be battlefields now."

Like most Israelis, he did not buy the theory, then passing around the diplomatic circuit, that Arab objectives did not extend beyond retaking the Heights and the Sinai; no, the Arabs had come to annihilate Israel. I did not argue with him because he was a veteran of Israel's three previous wars and both his sons were fighting in this one. He would not have taken kindly to a suggestion that the Arabs were fighting only to regain what was theirs. Anyhow, you don't argue politics in the Middle East, not if you want to keep your sources and friends. You just agree. So I agreed, yes, the farm fields would be battlefields now. But I wasn't sure.

Late in the morning, we reached Rosh Pinna, a village at the foot of the Golan. It wasn't much of a town—a few red-roofed cottages, a shop or two, a gas station—the Israeli equivalent of a Georgia crossroads. The war had touched it: the Syrians had shelled part of it with long-range guns, and one of their new Russian surface-to-surface missiles had exploded in a field outside town. Now its streets were solid with half-tracks, tank carriers, and dusty soldiers. Zvi stopped to top off our fuel—no sense in going up to the front without every drop the Fiat could hold. Four or five cars idled in front of us, along with a couple of troop trucks and a few jeeps.

Zvi seemed oblivious to all the racket. He had been born in Rosh Pinna. Looking toward an olive grove where he had played as a boy, he told me about the old days in Palestine, how his grandfather had migrated from Russia in the 1880s to pioneer in Galilee, how the family had prospered until it became one of the richest in Israel. He talked about working the fields in his youth, the blistering summer suns, the chill winds of winter, the mosquitoes and flies, and about growing up with Arab boys, teaching them Hebrew while they taught him Arabic. A tone of regret ran through his reminiscences, as if that had been a better time for all its hardships. Probably it had been. No shells or nuclear age missiles screamed down on Rosh Pinna then.

Up on the Heights, a one-five-five battery was firing, the guns leaping back on the recoil, then lunging forward. A tank column clanked down a bulldozed trail alongside the road in rooster tails of thick, mustard-colored dust. We rolled up the windows and weaved around a line of half-tracks, each one flying a blue-and-white-striped guidon from its radio antenna. There were the guidons snapping in the wind, the swaying antennae, the troopers with dust-coated faces flashing V-for-victory signs when they saw us, and the guns and the tanks and the dust billowing across the road and over the rocky fields.

"Look at this!" Zvi shouted. "Tiny little Israel! See what tiny little Israel can do!"

He was a prosperous, middle-aged businessman and he looked it, with his horn-rimmed glasses, his paunch, his ill-fitting too new uniform. He had a sensualist's love of life—all he talked about on the drive up from Tel Aviv were the trips he'd made to Europe, the cities he'd seen, the girls he'd slept with, the wine he'd drunk—but the sound of the guns did something to him. He let out a whoop and went racing down the road, running through the gears like a stock-car jockey at Daytona, the Fiat rattling and groaning over shell craters that should have burst the tires but didn't. Like its driver, the Fiat was a shade too old for war, but it was doing its best.

Half a mile from Kuneitra, a traffic jam brought an end to Zvi's one-man drag race. He pulled off the road to let a few half-tracks pass. Now, in between the sharp cracks of the outgoing one-five-fives, came the dull, sobering thud of incoming. Neither of us did any talking. In a few minutes we would be embraced by the arms of the front. Twenty or thirty feet away were the charred hulks of three Syrian tanks. We could hardly distinguish the bodies from the noncorporeal debris strewn around them. One corpse had no face; it had been burned off. The soldier's jaw was shoved to one side, like the photograph of a boxer taking a shot on the chin, and one of his legs was blown off at the knee, and his swollen belly had popped his shirt buttons. The flies found him delightful. On that day—or maybe it was on another day—President Sadat announced on Radio Cairo that the war had restored Arab pride.

The shelling stopped and the convoy bumped forward. We tagged behind, keeping the windows open so we could hear the hiss of incoming.

After driving perhaps a mile, we came to a junction, where a group of engineers hunkered in a ditch beside a bulldozer. One, in a helmet and flak jacket, flagged us down.

"You had better wait here with us. They're shelling this road. They've got this road zeroed in very nicely."

I told Zvi to go on—if they had the crossroad zeroed, why the hell stick around? Zvi thought it best to wait.

The engineers moved us into their shelter—a culvert in whose protective powers I was not confident. I squatted beside a shabby phenomenon, a civilian in his late thirties or early forties, with narrow shoulders and a pale face that wore the perpetually benevolent smile of a harmless idiot. He was dressed in a faded sport shirt, worn shoes, and a baggy suit that looked like a donation from a charitable organization.

"What the hell is he?" I asked. "A POW?"

The engineers laughed. One, an officer, said something to the man in a language I did not recognize, and then the civilian laughed. The officer turned to me.

"I just told him what you said. He's a Russian immigrant. He came to Israel only a few weeks ago. He hardly speaks Hebrew, but he volunteered to help out and one day he just showed up here."

"He *fights?*"

"No. After a shelling, he goes out with the medics and picks up the wounded and carries them back to the aid station. Sometimes he doesn't wait until the shelling's over."

I looked at the immigrant, who didn't seem capable of helping an old lady cross the street.

"Well, you tell him I think he's one helluva guy."

The officer translated and the Russian acknowledged the compliment with a nod and his sweet smile. If he was the stuff the Israelis were made of, then maybe the Spokesmen's confident forecasts weren't so off the mark.

The shelling started again, and in the intervals between the explosions, I heard machine-gun and rifle fire. The fighting seemed to be taking place somewhere between us and Kuneitra.

"What, exactly, is going on here?" I asked the officer.

He looked at me as if I'd lost my mind.

"A war."

I explained my question: in Tel Aviv, the Spokesmen had said the Syrians had been driven *twelve* miles back from the cease-fire line. The officer gave me a primer. The small-arms fire was probably a skirmish with one of the Syrian commando teams operating behind Israeli lines. As for the shelling, only *some* of the Syrians had been driven back twelve miles, those on the Kuneitra-Damascus highway. The others were dug into the hills south of the highway, with some positions literally a stone's throw from the '67 cease-fire line.

I turned to Zvi, who confirmed everything the officer said. The Israelis had attacked on a narrow front. Their southern, that is their right, flank was exposed, hanging in midair. That's what the day's fighting was all about: an Israeli column, hooking up from the south to widen the front and guard the flank of the main advance, had run into the Iraqi division.

I felt the journalist's satisfaction of discovery. The Syrian retreat had not been anything near a rout. Routed armies don't send commando teams into the enemy's rear, they don't pause in their flight to shell the enemy's routes of advance. I told Zvi that we should get on to Rafid, near the old cease-fire line. I wanted to see what was happening to the Iraqi division. And this as well: I wanted to file a war dispatch that would impress the editors the way Don Kirk's had from Vietnam. So far, nothing I'd sent measured up to his work.

With the engineers politely expressing doubts about our sanity, Zvi and I took off.

The Fiat suffered more torments, the Rafid road having been pummeled into something between pavement and gravel. The engineer-officer's talk about commando teams had got my imagination going. The Golan's landscape, brooding and spooky in the best of times, became downright sinister. I could almost see Syrians, hiding in ambush behind the rocky ridges. Up ahead, a hill rose from the brown plain. It looked like a big slag heap. The Israeli observation post was supposed to be on top. We parked and hiked up, Zvi slapping a magazine into his Uzi and muttering something about not being sure who held the hill.

"Christ," I said, "I thought you *knew.*"

He squatted behind a boulder and hollered hello in English. The answer of *"Shalom!"* was gratifying.

We climbed the rest of the way, trudging past lunarlike shell craters. In the car, racing wildly down the roads, it had been easy to pretend I was the daring war correspondent, dashing to the front. The illusion wasn't so easy to maintain on foot, not with those yawning craters and that ominous, not-so-distant growling of the monster, war, devouring its victims.

A tube of heavy-gauge steel tunneled through the hill and led up into a deep zigzag trench, where six artillery forward observers were peering through binoculars and plotting registration points on their maps with an air of scientific detachment. They might have been astronomers tracking the course of some newly discovered comet. Zvi made the introductions. A blue-eyed corporal with a freckled face greeted us: "Welcome. Welcome to our position."

He gave his name as Shlomo and brought us at a crawl to the forward-most point of the trench. He loaned me his field glasses. I stood and, for the first time since it started, got a good look at the war. From the foot of Mount Hermon, bleak and bare against the clear sky, to the foot of Jebel Harrah eight miles south, shells and bombs raised a cloud of smoke and yellow and rust-red dust as solid as a line squall. At first glance, the scene looked epic, like something out of Tolstoy or like one of those battle panoramas that hang in art galleries, but something was missing from the picture: men. There were no columns of grim-faced infantry at fixed bayonets, no commanders raising their swords, no shakoed guardsmen falling in balletic death. Tanks scurried over the fields and into the cloud. Two Skyhawks, painted in green-and-brown camouflage, came in from nowhere, contour flying, hugging the ridges. They dropped their bombs, then streaked up in high, graceful barrel rolls. A Syrian SAM missile battery thumped. A fiery ball trailing vapor rose from behind a ridge line, rose toward a Phantom fighter bomber that was just a silver speck in the sky. A puff appeared in midair, followed by a dull boom. The SAM had missed, and the Phantom kept flying, north and east, toward Damascus. It was one of the strangest sights I had seen in combat—one package of applied physics and circuitry against another—but there were no men. I knew men were there, driving the tanks, flying the planes, firing the missiles, but I could not see them, and their invisibility made the war look more like Buck Rogers than Tolstoy.

Two more Skyhawks came in, flying so low they seemed to be skipping over the ground the way a flat stone skips across a pond. The Syrians opened up with antiaircraft guns, batteries of them thumping away, flak and tracers flashing in the sky. The planes dropped their bombs—napalm. Billows of flame, oily smoke, the planes barrel rolling again as they climbed away. One tumbled as suddenly as a head-shot mallard and struck the earth with a roar. His wingman circled, made a pass over the flaming wreckage, then streaked home alone.

"Damnit," Zvi cursed. "Goddamnit."

His son-in-law was a fighter pilot.

Shlomo said nothing and showed no sign of emotion. He must have felt something, but how much destruction had he seen in the past six days?

We watched the battle for about half an hour more, with only a little more discomfort than a movie audience. Sometimes the wind shifted, carrying the death stink as a reminder that this was no MGM fantasy. More convincing reminders arrived shortly. A shell hissed in and exploded near a party of engineers clearing a road below and in front of the observation post (OP). The Syrians had it in for engineers that day. A second and a third burst, and the engineers leapt from their bulldozers and scattered, running almost on all fours, throwing themselves down when they heard the *sssssssuuuuuuu* of the next shell, then springing up to run again in that stumbling, apelike crouch. *Sssssssuuuuu-whomp, sssssssuuuuu-whomp.* A hail of shrapnel whipped over our heads, and Zvi and I went down in an undignified heap.

"My, oh, my," he said. "My goodness, that was close."

Shlomo and the others merely squatted, as if they were waiting out a rainstorm. For all their volubility in peacetime, Israelis were master stoics on the battlefield.

The shelling lifted and we peered cautiously over the parapet. Below, the engineers were crawling out of their hidey-holes.

Shlomo checked his watch and tuned a transistor radio to Col-Israel, the state-run broadcast service. He wanted to hear the hourly news so he could find out what was going on, proving that the front was not the best place to learn what was happening at the front. He and Zvi, smoking cigarettes, huddled beside the radio while the guns, bombs, and tanks boomed in the distance.

"There's good news," Zvi said, smiling at me. "Very good news."

"What?"

"Wait till it's over and I'll tell you."

The announcer rattled on in Hebrew for another few minutes. Zvi clenched a fist, punched the air, and said with relish, "Ah-hah!" He turned toward me, squinting in the bright afternoon sun, and told the good news. I could have guessed it: the Iraqis had been routed.

"One of their brigades was completely destroyed. That's what we have seen today. They lost over a hundred tanks. The poor bastards didn't even know where they were. They were lost!"

I looked eastward, into Syria.

"If they've been routed, what the hell is all that out there?"

"A battle," said Shlomo, another master of the obvious.

I borrowed his field glasses, but it was impossible to tell what was happening. The fog of war. I therefore deferred to Col-Israel and wrote in my notebook that the Iraqis had been routed.

A one-thirty banged into a ruined mosque about seventy-five yards from the trench. My shirt flattened against my skin, as from a sudden, violent gust of wind, and a chunk of shrapnel twanged past my ear. We were again flat on our bellies, and this time Shlomo and his fellow observers were flat with us. Two more shells, much closer than the first, the ground vibrating. The guns were firing from some-where in front of the OP, that is, from the positions held by the Iraqi division supposedly routed.

"Hey, Zvi," I shouted. "They must not have been listening to the radio."

"No time for jokes."

"I thought you routed them."

"I said this wasn't going to be easy," Shlomo reminded me as another shell tore overhead to explode on the reverse slope.

Bracketed. The next shipment would be delivered right to our doorstep. An amiable grin broke on Shlomo's Norman Rockwell face.

"We are in for it now. Would you please get inside the bunker? We don't want an American killed on our position."

Because I was the only American on their position, I didn't either. I slithered inside, Zvi and Shlomo behind me.

The Syrians or the Iraqis—somebody—gave the hill a nice going over.

"Do they hit you like this every day?"

Shlomo dragged on his cigarette like a joint.

"Several times a day."

"Were you up here on the sixth?"

"No. I was working in South Africa. Diamonds. As soon as I heard, I flew up to rejoin my unit. It's funny, I could not wait to get into the war. I was afraid it would be over before I got here." He smiled a gentle, regretful smile, such as a wise veteran might give to a foolish boy hot for glory. "Now it looks like I could have taken a ship and still not been late."

The fire stopped. Zvi glanced at me with a worried What-am-I-doing-here look.

"I should not have brought you here. I'm responsible for you." He sounded like an errant uncle who had dragged his nephew into a strip joint. "We should go now."

"You should stay here," Shlomo cautioned. "They haven't stopped yet."

I agreed; the quarter mile of open ground between us and the Fiat afforded as much cover as a waffle iron. Zvi insisted, saying we could be trapped for hours.

"That's better than being killed," said Shlomo. He was talking my kind of language, but Zvi continued to insist, so with Shlomo's wishes of shalom and good luck we ran out.

We hadn't gone twenty yards before we heard that now familiar wind-rushing sound, growing louder and louder.

"INCOMING!" I screamed, and we flung ourselves down on the sharp volcanic rock. The shell thundered into the slope above. A black rain of dirt and pulverized basalt.

"There!" Zvi pointed at a broken stone fence. "We'll take cover there!"

We crouched behind the fence, but it gave no more protection than an umbrella. We broke for the bunker, sliding into it belly-first. The fence disappeared, the blast that made it disappear hammering a piece of shrapnel as big as a railroad spike into a timber at the bunker's entrance. The OP was taking direct hits from the routed Syrians and Iraqis. Shlomo, in the trench above, was yelling something in Hebrew.

"Hey, Shlomo!" I hollered. "We're back inside. We're all right!"

"Good! Stay here, please!"

"No worries about that."

"See how the bunker is shaking now," Zvi said, nervous eyes turned upward. "It's shaking. The bunker is shaking now."

"They say you have a better than eighty percent chance of surviving a shelling if you're under cover."

"It's the twenty percent I'm worried about. I shouldn't have brought you here. They told me in Tel Aviv it was dangerous around Rafid. I shouldn't have brought you here. I'm responsible for you."

"I can take care of myself," I snapped, a little peeved at all the parental protectiveness. Why had he brought himself there? He could have had a cushy staff job. Why had he volunteered to be an escort officer, him with his fiftyish belly? The circumstances didn't seem right to ask him; then again, why not? He gave a vague answer— something about not being able to live with himself if he played it safe while others took risks—and then he went back to moaning about how we would be trapped for hours.

But the barrage lasted only twenty minutes.

Whatever had happened to the Iraqis, we were certainly routed. Time for the rent-a-car warriors to bug out. Once more we said good-bye to Shlomo, once more we ran toward the car. It had survived without a scratch. We jumped in. Of course it wouldn't start. I looked at the fresh excavations all around. The old soldier's axiom that shells, like lightning, never hit the same place twice was no comfort at all.

"Goddamnit damnit damnit." Zvi wrenched the ignition key.

The engine turned over, he put the pedal to the floor, and we were gone. One of the distinctions between a war correspondent and a soldier is that a correspondent can run away without fear of a court-martial or a firing squad. But there was no such privilege for Shlomo and his buddies up there on the hill near Rafid, or the engineers and the Russian immigrant huddled in the ditch, or for all the thousands of Arab and Israeli youth killing each other out on the stony plains of Syria.

The next day, I picked up the Jerusalem *Post* in the Hilton news and tobacco shop. The headline read:

IRAQIS ROUTED! TANK TOLL: 130.

The following day, though routed in the press, the Iraqis reappeared. This time they suffered a worse fate:

IRAQI FORCE SMASHED!

The paper proclaimed that the Iraqi division had ceased "to exist as a fighting unit," that a "good few dozen Iraqi tanks were knocked out," that the surviving troops had been "scattered in retreat."

But that afternoon, the nonexistent Iraqis joined the Syrians in a major counterattack. The Spokesmen, somewhat at a loss to explain the miraculous resurrection, described the counterattacking Iraqis as "remnants of the division which was virtually wiped out on Monday."

IRAQIS MAULED!

Indeed they seemed to have been because nothing was heard of them for another two weeks. Then, on October 24, when the Syrians and Egyptians agreed to a cease-fire, the *Post* reported that the resilient Iraqis were withdrawing their division to protest Syria's signing of the armistice. The paper did not explain how Iraq could with-

draw a division that had been routed, smashed, and mauled several
times.

First casualties ...
The Spokesman stood at the podium. Israeli losses for the first
two weeks of fighting. Tanks: seven hundred and fifty. Planes: one
hundred. Killed: about two thousand.

He was somewhere in his early twenties, a gunner on a Centurion,
and he was sitting on the turret, holding his crash helmet under his
arm like a football player waiting to be called back into a game. The
tank's long gun pointed at the tail end of an Egyptian supply convoy
less than fifty yards down the road. Some of the trucks lay on their
sides in a ditch and some sat crossways on the road and one was
upside down, its upended tires burning in a neat square. Some of the
bodies were still burning, too, but you had to look hard to know they
were bodies.
"They didn't have any tanks with them," the gunner was saying.
"No infantry with missiles either. Just the trucks. We caught them
where you see them. We used the cannon first, but we did not want to
waste the ammunition, so we opened up with this"—he slapped the
swivel-mounted machine gun—"and we got the last of them with it."
He wiped the sweatband of his helmet. "You know, it wasn't war, it
was murder."

Scoop.
From the sleaziest tabloid celebrity chaser to the tweediest gentleman of the press, from the greenest cub on a backwoods county
weekly to the most elegantly coiffed network anchor, there isn't a
reporter who doesn't dream about one, who won't risk almost anything to get a story ahead of his opposition.

Midway into the second week of the war, Israel's public-information
machine, like its military machine, had recovered from the shock of
October 6. It continued to inflict casualties on the truth, but its shots
were now aimed and deliberate and not the random firing of panic
and confusion. The Spokesmen were fostering military secrecy by
withholding information or passing out disinformation, which made

perfect sense to the press corps but did not stop us from trying to find out what the Spokesmen did not want us to find out. They maintained an impenetrable silence about the situation in Sinai, the military police an impenetrable barrier of checkpoints against any correspondents trying to get within earshot of the front. Israeli reporters were there, but scanning the Jerusalem *Post* and translations of the Hebrew-language press was next to useless; their stuff had been censored and recensored into informational mush. No word at all emerged until Tuesday, October 16, when Golda Meir, the ex-Milwaukee schoolteacher turned prime minister, addressed the Knesset.

I drove up to Jerusalem to cover her speech and to take a holiday from the military briefings, from the dangerous trips to the Golan (Zvi and I had made three more), the long, irritating hours of telexing or phoning in my stories, the arguments with the censors, the battles with my editors for more space and better play. I was exhausted; in ten days, I had not slept more than four or five hours a night, mostly because I was the only staff correspondent covering the Israeli side for the *Tribune*. The lordly *New York Times* had four staffers and two stringers. Eventually, the *Tribune* sent reinforcements, in the form of twenty-six-year-old Rick Soll, who wrote columns for the paper in the manner of the New York *Post*'s Pete Hamill and the *Sun Times*'s Bob Greene. Rick was a terrific writer, but he had had no experience in foreign assignments, much less in war correspondence. He made up for those deficiencies in enterprise and daring, but in the end, the two of us were no match for the competition.

And so, leaving Rick to hold the fort in Tel Aviv, I went to Jerusalem for Mrs. Meir's speech. I listened to it on the radio in Charlie Weiss's house. He provided a simultaneous translation. The only real news in it—and it was big news—came at the very end, when Meir announced that an IDF "task force" had broken through Egyptian lines and was operating on the western bank of the Suez Canal. She said no more. We heard the Knesset members applaud and cheer. I turned to Weiss. What did he know about this task force?

"It's the first I heard about it."

I raced back to Tel Aviv, where I learned that it was the first anyone had heard of it. There were rumors that the task force was being led by the unorthodox but brilliant General Sharon. At the briefing that night, the Spokesmen would neither confirm nor deny that

Sharon was in charge; they would not give the size of the task force, or its mission, except to say that it was a commando raiding party knocking out enemy artillery and missile batteries. But how had this band broken through the Egyptians, who had two armies deployed on the west bank of the canal, a total of forty thousand men? The Spokesmen would not say.

The next day, they described an odd metamorphosis in the task force: it had become something called an "armored wedge" rammed through the Egyptian lines. Rumors made the rounds, reporters interviewed each other, and the rumors became facts that were later contradicted by new rumors. Sharon had been killed crossing the canal under fire ... The task force had been wiped out ... No, it was intact and wreaking havoc on the Egyptian missile and gun emplacements ... Israeli units were being redeployed from the northern to the Sinai front ... Big push in the works to destroy the two Egyptian armies ... No, Henry Kissinger had got the Israelis to agree to a cease-fire in place ... No, the Israelis had not agreed and intended to destroy the Second and Third Egyptian armies first, then agree to a cease-fire ...

Rumors of another kind reached me through, I think, Nick Proffitt. All right, for the sake of the story, let's say it was he. We would have been drinking in the noisy, smoky, supermacho atmosphere of the Hilton bar, long since cleared of everyone except war correspondents and an absolutely bizarre convention of self-styled mercenaries, mostly Jewish-American Vietnam veterans whose offers to employ their jungle-fighting skills had been politely declined by the desert-fighting Israelis, forcing the mercs to fight the war from poolside. Nick and I would have been complaining about the mute Spokesmen and our desks pressing us for more and more bang-bang. Nick, puckering his lips and knitting his eyebrows in the way he did, would have mentioned in passing that he'd heard the operation in Sinai, whatever it was, was going well, that any day now the Israelis were going to send in another pool, but selected correspondents would be allowed to go in ahead of the pool, probably on Sunday, the twenty-first.

I was not one of the elect, possibly because of my earlier sin, possibly because the provincial *Tribune* did not wield the influence of the *Times* or the Washington *Post*. Winning a piece of a Pulitzer had not exorcised the devils of my ambition or quieted the insecurities that were the wellsprings of that ambition. I still required validation of my professional worth and my worth as a man from other people. Prizes and awards and congratulatory messages from my editors (herograms we called them), the applause of my peers. You're okay, a great correspondent and a worthwhile human being. Somehow I had to get to the Sinai front ahead of the pool, ahead of everyone.

Zvi agreed to meet me at an outdoor café on Diezengoff Street. He was in civilian clothes, and we sat under an umbrella sipping demitasses of dense bitter Turkish coffee. Chain-smoking Marlboros, he pondered my request: could he help me get into Sinai on Saturday?

"Phil, that's tomorrow. It's impossible."

I appealed to the bond knit between us on those trips to the Golan. I cajoled, I whined, I demanded, I was a real pain in the ass. He said he would see what he could do.

We made an arrangement that had the trappings of an espionage operation. Because the censors monitored all correspondents' phones, Zvi would call me and ask for someone else. I would say he had the wrong number. If he replied, "Oh, I am very sorry," it would mean he had been unsuccessful, but if he said, "Oh, excuse me," it would mean good news and that I was to meet him at the same café to hear the details.

"Oh, excuse me."

I hung up and, with a tingling in my toes and fingertips, walked to the café. Zvi was at a table, appraising a couple of girls young enough to be his daughters. With a grin, he showed me a pass, dated for Saturday. That was the good news; the bad news was, I would not have the story all to myself but would have to share it with a West German correspondent who had been given permission to go in ahead of the pack. In fact, I would be hitching a ride with the West German (whom I'll call Axel). The privileged Axel was a reporter for a big chain of West German papers owned by his father, an ardent champion of Israel.

"We like to take care of our friends in the press, especially the German press," Zvi said. "I've been assigned to escort him and his photographer. He said it would be all right if you went along. It was the best I could do."

There was one other hitch: the pass specifically prohibited us from going beyond the forward headquarters at Bîr Gifǧafa.

"But the Sinai is a big place." Zvi's eyes twinkled behind the black, horn-rimmed glasses. "Easy to get lost."

Covering a war with a press baron's son had some advantages. Axel, a tall man in his early thirties with an ursine chest and a porcine stomach, led us across the Hertz parking lot to a new Volvo sedan with leather seats and air conditioning (no beat-up budget Fiat for Axel). He opened the trunk and flipped the lid of a picnic cooler crammed with sandwiches, apples, and several six-packs of Heineken (no box lunch slapped together from surplus army rations, no canteen filled with warm water, not for Axel).

"What trouble I had getting these!" He grabbed a sandwich, opened its plastic wrapper, and put it to my nose. "Ham! Ya! Do you know how hard it is to find a ham sandwich in Israel?"

But Israel took care of its friends in the press. That included looking out for their safety as well as their driving comfort and dietary preferences. Zvi opened the trunk and issued each of us a flak jacket and a steel helmet, the shallow, brimmed kind worn by Montgomery's Desert Rats.

So we set off in style in the early-morning dark, Zvi driving, Axel beside him. I sat in the backseat with Horst, the six-foot-five-inch photographer, the flak vests and collector-item helmets piled between us.

The pass got us through the rear area checkpoints with ease. Three or four hours later, we came to a junction. One road led east, past Bîr Gifǧafa, the other south, toward the Gidi Pass. Zvi turned down the south road.

"Now we are getting lost."

Traffic was light, we reached the Gidi in forty-five minutes, Axel guzzling a Heineken and joking about something or other. He was so full of Oktoberfest friendliness that I felt guilty about my secret thoughts, which were: How do I ditch this guy and get the story alone? And if I ditch him, how do I get back to Tel Aviv on time to meet my deadline?

Air conditioner blowing on us, radio blaring an exotic mix of war news, rock, and Hebrew DJ patter, we climbed through the Gidi, then headed across the plateau that rises some twenty miles east of the canal. We bumped into a convoy. It was moving only a little faster than a walk, but moving steadily, inexorably. Zvi fell in behind the last vehicle, a lumbering water truck.

"So, we will see where this takes us," he said.

"It's not taking us far," Axel said fifteen minutes later. We hadn't covered more than a kilometer. "See if you can get round this thing."

Zvi turned out and gave the Volvo gas. I watched the odometer click off the distance. Three kilometers, five, ten, twelve. The vehicles were solid: troop trucks and supply trucks and jeeps, civilian delivery vans, eighteen-wheel tractor trailers, buses from Egged, the Israeli tourist agency, and even a few Tel Aviv taxicabs. Thirteen kilometers, fourteen, fifteen. All war machines now—tanks on carriers, half-tracks full of helmeted troopers flashing victory signs, huge self-propelled howitzers with CAIRO EXPRESS crudely painted on the barrels. We went over the edge of the plateau and saw no end to the convoy. A river of olive drab flowing through the desert's tan, it vanished in a haze at the horizon.

"Zvi, all this isn't for some half-assed task force on a commando raid," I said. "This looks like D day."

He braked to a slow stop; a couple of hundred yards ahead, a squad of military police manned a checkpoint.

"Put on the helmets, so they'll think we're soldiers," Zvi said gleefully. He was now more newsman than escort officer, getting into the spirit of going as far as you can as fast as you can and the hell with regulations.

Helmets and flak vests on, we waved and shouted "*Shalom!*" to the MPs without slowing down, leaving them no time to wonder what four soldiers were doing, rushing to the front in a rented Volvo.

The front wasn't far away now. Its sound was distinct—not like thunder because it was too constant. If it resembled anything, it was the noise a thousand empty oil drums would make rolling through an endless tunnel.

The road curved and ran north, within a couple of miles of the Great Bitter Lake, a brackish inland sea through which the canal passes before it empties into the Gulf of Suez. Once, I thought I saw the lake, but it might have been a mirage. The convoys never thinned and the roar of the front grew louder, an eventful rumbling.

We came to another junction. A tank retriever with a crane like a brontosaurus's neck was hauling a disabled Centurion out of the road. The tank had not been hit by enemy fire—there was none—but had run off its treads somehow. Trucks and armored personnel carriers detoured around the wreck in a whine of low gears, tires and tracks spinning in the deep sand. Zvi pulled over onto a patch of gravel.

"We must stop now. We'll get stuck if we try to go around."

A short distance away, tanks were being driven onto mobile barges. Bridge pontoons sat across a carrier.

"How far is the canal?" I asked.

"Three or four kilometers."

"How about a little lunch before we go on?" Axel suggested.

We climbed out into the scorch of a Sinai noon. Axel opened the cooler and asked Zvi if he were kosher.

"Not always."

"I brought kosher salami just for you."

Four Phantoms screamed so low we almost ducked. Munching our sandwiches and gulping beer, we saw them lay their bombs into a palm and eucalyptus forest west of the canal. High explosives threw up immense pillars of smoke, napalm burst like miniature solar flares. Horst dropped his lunch and picked up his cameras. A half-track driver, urging his hybrid vehicle around the crippled tank, shouted at him. "Hey, take our picture!"

Horst turned the lens on him. He grinned through the dust caking his face, and the troops in the back yelled and gave us thumbs up.

"It will be good!" the driver hollered. "We'll show them now! We'll be in Cairo!"

I was taking notes, making marks on my maps, asking Zvi where we were exactly. Over there, he said, pointing toward the smoke, was the canal-side town of Ismailia. The Egyptian Second Army was dug in there, on both banks of the canal. South and west, near the Great Bitter Lake and Suez City, was the Third Army. Directly in front of us was the bridgehead Sharon's troops had thrown between the two. That was the geography and a little bit of history; as for current events, he had no idea what was going on. I glanced at Axel, slugging down another beer. So far, his notebook and pens had not left his pockets. Either he had a photographic memory or, being a press baron's son, he did not feel he had to take notes. Whatever, it looked as though I didn't have to worry about protecting a scoop: Axel didn't seem to know we were just three or four kilometers away from getting one. Maybe he didn't care—another privilege of baronial progeny.

We saw our first Egyptian soldiers: a truckload of prisoners came up from the direction of the canal. They were very young, most of them, their dark skin making their pale-buff uniforms look white. Horst raised his camera and the POWs stared into it with the sad, dumb look of captured animals.

"They came out dying of thirst!" an Israeli guard shouted down from the truck. "No food, no water, they just walked up to us with their hands in the air!"

"When?"

"This morning."

Enough of our desert picnic. Far as you can fast as you can.

"Can we drive to the canal?" I asked Zvi.

"I don't want to risk it."

I put on my old-timey helmet, slipped my field glasses over my neck. Zvi slung his Uzi. We started hiking. Huffing and puffing, Axel hauled his bulk down the road, the helmet riding high on his big head. The land dipped, then rose up a low, gravelly ridge. We stopped there. Below, rutted with tread marks, sand flats angled down for a mile or a mile and a half to a line of high sand ridges too regular to be dunes. I raised the field glasses and there it was, thin, straight, and blue between the embankments: the Suez Canal. We were the first correspondents to see it since the Egyptians stormed it fourteen days before.

A fifteen-minute walk off the road brought us to a shallow ravine. A scorched Egyptian tank lay in it, beside a mobile field kitchen. The urns and vats were holed by bullets, likewise a water tanker and its driver, still behind the wheel and grown far too big for his clothes. Fifty yards further along, near where the ravine rose back to the desert floor, an Israeli brigadier huddled with four or five staff officers around an armored personnel carrier and a jeep, its hood blanketed by maps, its rear seat taken up by a huge radio.

Zvi called out a hello. The officers looked up and stared at us as if they were seeing things: one portly Israeli armed only with an Uzi, two giant Germans, and one short American, all costumed like extras for *The Rats of Tobruk*.

Zvi made the introductions. I was sure we would be ordered out of there, but the brigadier and his staff seemed to welcome the diversion, to be a little flattered by the attention. The general had dark, penetrating eyes set deep under black brows, a well-barbered mustache, a field cap with Desert Fox goggles pulled over the brim, field glasses hanging from a tanned, muscular neck. He struck me as the kind of Jew the early Zionists had hoped an Israel would create: no ghetto dweller with bowed back, no fussy scholar splitting Talmudic hairs, but a man who knew what had to be done and how to do it and then did it: a warrior Jew, a Gideon.

He was happy to take a break from his war council and give me a long, detailed account of how his mechanized infantry brigade had rolled across the bridgehead three nights ago and smashed several Egyptian SAM batteries. It did not sound like it had been a modern, well-planned military operation; a free-for-all rather, a kind of Apache raid, with maximum initiative given to small unit commanders to hit targets of opportunity.

"One of my battalions just drove up the road, fast as they could go in the middle of night," he said, pointing toward Ismailia. "Up that way somewhere. They saw the Egyptian battery out on the desert and drove right into it. The Egyptians thought our troop carriers were their own. We caught them napping! Before they knew it, my boys were shooting up the place. Killed most of them, captured the rest, set charges under the missiles, and blew them to bits. That was our mission—open up a hole in those missile defenses and artillery positions so our planes could cover our boys. Did you see the way we're crossing now? Not a shot from the other side! I don't think they know what's happening."

I scribbled in my notebook. Axel stood around, hands in his pockets, smiling amiably. Amazing.

I thanked the brigadier for the recent history and told him we didn't know what was happening either. Could he bring us up to date? What about the so-called armored wedge? How large was it? Where was it?

He paused and seemed to exchange glances with one of his officers, a rangy lieutenant colonel with long gray hair streaming in the wind.

"I can't say, but I can tell you, it's not really a wedge anymore.

We're moving in all directions on the other side, to the left and right ..."

The colonel coughed and the brigadier interrupted himself.

"It's this way—we've split their army in two, that's what. The Second Army is cut off from the Third. Because of what we did to their missiles, they have no defense now against our air force." He turned, squinting westward at the towering cloud, anvil-shaped, black, and angry, like a gigantic tornado. "Look at that sky! Those aren't rain clouds. That's smoke from our bombs. They had a crazy idea, and now we're making them pay for it. If they had taken all the money this cost them and put it to better use they could have built for every Arab a villa."

Another good quote, long on color, short on hard information. I asked the brigadier for specifics. What did he mean, the Israelis were moving in *all* directions on the west side of the Canal? Where to and for what reason? How many troops were involved in the operation? Was this a full-scale counteroffensive, and what were its objectives? To march on Cairo, to drive the Second and Third armies back across Suez?

"I can tell you we've got some boys less than a hundred kilometers from Cairo right now."

He started to elaborate, but the tall, thin colonel gave him a censoring look.

"I can't tell you any more now. You should ask them in Tel Aviv."

I gestured at the smoke and tried from another angle.

"That's the Second Army over there, right? You're pounding hell out of them. Are they giving you more resistance than you thought they would?"

It was the colonel who answered.

"We've been pounding them for two days, and I must say they haven't broken yet. But we're hitting them now."

"I can see that, what I want to know ..."

The brigadier crossed and uncrossed his wrists, like an umpire calling a runner safe.

"Now the press conference is over, yes? Please excuse us."

And he bowed over the maps spread flat on the hood of the jeep. I took a peek—a lot of arrows and symbols—but it would have taken a man of Horst's height to see clearly over the wall of shoulders and backs.

The colonel turned around and said something to Zvi.

"Phil, he's asking us to go now."

Zvi started back to the car. That goddamned staff colonel. If I could have gotten the general alone ...

I scrambled up the ravine, sat down with maps and notebooks in my lap, and swept my binoculars over the canal. I recalled a few old lessons from Quantico and what the guard had said about the Egyptian prisoners. I thought about the length of the convoy and the brigadier's comment that the Israelis were within sixty miles of Cairo. I studied the map as if it were a puzzle.

"Phil," said an anxious Zvi, "it could take us eight hours to get back with all this traffic. What are you doing?"

"Playing armchair general."

The real general, meanwhile, was driving off in his jeep. His staff officers stayed by the APC, pointing and looking through field glasses. Things were clicking in my head, falling into place, like the tumblers in a lock. I drew a rough sketch in my notebook, refined it, then penciled in a final version on the map. I felt the elation of the mathematician who finally solves the stubborn equation, of the poet who at last hears the elusive stanza sing. I knew I had it right, but I would need confirmation, an authoritative source to credit.

I was about to go to the conclave of staff officers, but they saved me the trouble by walking toward me. The gray-haired colonel paused, gave my sketch work a long look, and, telling the others he'd be along in a moment, sat companionably beside me. He asked for the map. I handed it to him.

"Interesting," he said with an ironic half smile. "May I ask what this is?"

"What I would do if I were in charge."

"Interesting, interesting. You've had some military experience?"

"Some."

"Unusual. Most of the correspondents I've met don't know shit about tactics. We show them a little shellfire, a few tanks, a few dead bodies, they're happy. So where did you acquire your military experience?"

"Vietnam."

"That wasn't a war."

"It seemed like one to me."

"It was stupid, senseless butchery."

"That, too."

Zvi, Horst, and Axel stood off to the side, watching. Across the canal, Phantoms soared through the smoke cloud like hawks through a forest fire.

"So what *would* you do if you were in charge? What does this arrow mean?"

"That's the force you're sending up the middle, toward Cairo."

He nodded.

"And these other two arrows, the ones hooking off to the right and left?"

"They're what you're sending around the rear of the Second and Third armies. Kind of a double envelopment, a pincers movement, except instead of hitting their flanks, you're going round behind them. Trying to, anyway. My guess is that you've just about done it in the south, with the Third Army. But it looks like the Second might have figured out what you're up to and counterattacked. They're holding you up."

"This really is interesting. Who gave you this information?"

"The general."

"I don't recall that he said anything of this nature."

"Before you cut him off, he made it a point to tell me that these guys"—I pointed to the center arrow—"are less than a hundred kilometers from Cairo. He wanted me to think the same thing all you people want the Egyptians to think—that you're advancing on Cairo."

"And what do you think we're doing?"

"Threatening Cairo, to keep the Egyptian reserves pinned down to defend their capital. You wouldn't want them to come barreling down the pike and hit those pincers movements in the flanks."

"Certainly not. And what of those pincers?"

"Basically, you had only two ways to knock the Egyptians off the east bank. Frontal assault, which would have cost you more people than you can afford, or the way you're doing it now. It's a little like what Von Runstedt did when he broke through the Maginot Line."

"A student of military history, too," he said with barely concealed mockery. "Interesting and unusual. But you still haven't explained *what* we are doing."

"Putting the Egyptians in a trap, with only two ways out ..."

His half smile turned into a malign grin.

"Feet first or with their tongues hanging out."

"And your big problem now is that the Second Army is holding you up and you want to close the trap quickly, before all the politicians and diplomats get into the act and order a cease-fire in place."

"We are going to see those bastards, all forty thousand of them, come walking out with their tongues down to their chins."

"How the hell did Sharon get his men across in the first place? Let's start there."

"You should for that information ask Arik himself," he answered, using Sharon's nickname.

"If I can get to him, I will. How about we not play any games? My editors won't buy it if I give them all this and say it's just my own thinking. I need confirmation, you know, a high-ranking military source."

"Do you consider a lieutenant colonel to be a high rank?"

"If he's on a brigadier's staff, sure, high enough."

"You wish me to confirm the accuracy of your speculations? Very well, I confirm them. With a few minor exceptions, you guessed right."

My heart did a somersault. At the same time, I knew it was too good, too easy to be true.

"Of course, if you're up to something else, that's what you'd want me to believe."

"No, I mean it. You guessed right. Really, it's a pleasure to meet a journalist who knows a little something about military affairs."

"What are the minor exceptions?"

He shook his head.

"How about how many men you've got in this? That convoy back there is fifteen miles long. Can't imagine you'd even try with less than fifty thousand."

"Another good guess."

"Thanks, Colonel."

"No trouble. A pleasure, really." He stood on his long bony legs and looked down on me like a towering heron on the minnow it's about to snap up. "Of course, you're not going to get one single word of your story out of Israel. Not until we have got all forty thousand of those bastards with their hands up and their tongues out."

"What are you going to do, phone Tel Aviv and tell them to head me off at the pass?"

"Don't be ridiculous. I'll lose my respect for you. No, young man, there is not in all of Israel a censor dumb enough to let one word of this story pass."

"We'll see," I said with a false confidence. "Thanks anyway."

"No trouble."

I shook his hand, and he walked away.

I was proud of myself, puffed up like a pouter pigeon. Axel, who had caught only snatches of the conversation, asked me to fill in the blanks. I folded the map so he could not see it and mumbled some vagaries about a counterattack, a hole in the Egyptian lines. He actually broke out his virgin notebook and made a jotting or two.

Lockup for the *Tribune*'s final edition was 10:00 P.M. Chicago time, 6:00 A.M. Israeli time. Even if the return to Tel Aviv took till midnight, I had a wealth of hours. Still, I wasn't going to squander a minute. I curled up in the backseat and roughed out a piece in longhand, revised it, and revised it again:

> With Israeli Forces at the Suez Canal, Oct. 20—The Israeli army, overwhelmed by the surprise Arab attack in Sinai two weeks ago, has retaken the initiative and mounted a major counteroffensive that has split Egyptian forces in two and will, if successful, trap 40,000 enemy soldiers on the east bank of the Suez Canal, senior Israeli field officers told the *Tribune* today.
>
> They described a three-pronged attack that has sent one armored column across the Canal toward Cairo, to pin down Egyptian reserves while two other columns sweep north and south in a pincers movement behind the Second and Third Egyptian armies, which overran Israel's Bar Lev Line on October 6th ...

The more I wrote, the more excited I got. Intoxicated. I could see the story splashed across page one, under a boldface EXCLUSIVE. I could hear the rockets the *Times*'s and the *Post*'s foreign desks would fire at their correspondents. *Scoop!* My self-inflated balloon would have risen into the ionosphere of fantasy if it hadn't been tethered by worry about the censors. The one sure way to get past them would be to fly out of the country and file the story from Cyprus or Rome. Two problems there—correspondents would be at the canal by tomorrow noon at the latest; a plane delay, a problem in transmission, and my exclusive could be lost. Also, the Israelis were very prickly about violations of military censorship; if I smuggled the story out, I would not be able to get myself back in, leaving Rick Soll to cover the rest of the war on his own. Why not give the story to Rick? But that tack had its own problems. I had sent him to cover the northern front; if he got back too late, there might not be any flights anywhere. Lod had been reopened to civilian traffic, but, with a shooting war still going on, it was not exactly a hub of air travel. Still, Rick seemed my best bet.

As soon as we were back at the Hilton, I ran up to my room and called the airport. There was a midnight flight to London. Fully booked, lots of people still clamoring to get out of Israel, sorry. The next one wasn't until six-thirty in the morning—half an hour past the Final deadline—but in plenty of time for the replate. I called Rick's room to see if he could make the flight. He wasn't there, or in the lobby, or the bar. The hell with it, my only real option was to risk the censor. After phoning the desk to tell them I had a beat coming, I typed the story and ran it to the telex room at Beit Sokoloff.

"This is a very good story," the censor, an enlisted man, said when he was done reading.

"Thank you."

"How did you get it?"

"Oh, my usual enterprise and daring."

"A good sense of humor. That's good. Excuse me, but I think I better show this to the lieutenant."

He went into an inner office and came out in ten or fifteen minutes with the lieutenant, dark-haired and sallow, old-looking for his rank.

"Could you step in for a moment, Mister Caputo?" he asked, sounding like a professor displeased with a student term paper.

In his bleak office, I saw my story on the desk. It was covered with red pencil marks.

"You don't have to tell me," said the lieutenant, sitting down. "But I'd like to know how you got to the bridgehead."

"Just drove. Nothing fancy."

He picked up the copy and said it was very good, and I thanked him for the A-plus.

"But it is not a news story."

I looked at it. Virtually everything of news value had been censored out of it. What remained was a feature, a color story. *Bang-bang.*

"You're right, with what you've done to it."

"No. *Now* it is a newspaper story. Before it was an intelligence report to General Ismail," he said, referring to the Egyptian commander in chief.

"Oh, *come on* ..."

"Believe me. If we didn't know who you were and we saw this, we would have said, 'This fellow is an Egyptian agent.'"

"Lieutenant, your troops have been across the canal for four days. Ismail has got to have a picture of what's going on. I'm not saying a damn thing he doesn't know already."

"He doesn't know. None of them do. They don't have the slightest idea that we've got the Third Army trapped and that we're closing in on the Second."

"How the hell do you know they don't know?"

"I can't tell you, but I know. Please write another version."

Defeated and deflated, I slouched back to the Hilton. The telex waiting for me at the front desk brought on a mild nausea. A rocket from Chicago. Where was the Sinai piece? Watergate was going to take up the entire front page if I didn't file soon. Nixon had fired Cox and Ruckelshaus, chief investigators ... Elliot Richardson had quit the Justice Department in protest ... The Saturday Night Massacre.

In my room, I typed a new draft, leaving in some of the stuff the lieutenant had taken out, and tried to phone the story in. The moment I gave the dateline—with Israeli forces at the Suez Canal—I heard a beep and then a voice: "Hello, Mister Caputo? This is the censor's office. Please read your story to me before you transmit."

"You son-of-a-bitch."

"Please, sir. Go ahead."

I did, and he instructed that, no, I could not say the convoy was fifteen miles long, and no, I could not quote the brigadier as saying that the armored wedge was more than a wedge, and no, I could not say the operation was a trap.

Reconnected to Chicago, I told the desk I was having censorship problems, and would they call me back in half an hour? It was almost two in the morning. Whoozy with exhaustion, I refueled on my emergency bottle of duty-free Scotch but could not think of a thing to say. There was a knock at the door. I opened it and saw a dust-floured Rick Soll staring at me with eyes as big and white as porcelain quarters.

"Where the hell have you been, for Christ's sake? Damascus?"

Damn near, Rick said. Actually, where he had been wasn't so much geographical as psychological. His eyes should have told me— his first time under fire. A helluva story, he said, but an awful, awful time. Evaded the escort officer route ... Hooked up with an Israeli reconnaissance platoon exploring a pocket of resistance ... Went too far ... Cut off by Syrians and Iraqis for a while ... Raced back to the Golan Heights in half-tracks through artillery fire ... Had to abandon the vehicles, run to friendly lines, chased by Arab fire the whole way ... Israeli trooper behind him hit by shrapnel, screaming, clutching a gold Star of David hung from his neck ... Rick helped the platoon commander pull the man to safety ...

I told him to have a drink and then phone his story in asap. If I couldn't steal a chunk of page one, maybe he could.

He turned his eyes to my red-marked copy and asked me what had gone on. I told him.

"Don't know what the hell to say now," I whined. "They haven't left me with a damn thing."

Rick's brush with Dr. Doom had given him clarity of mind.

"You were the first one there, right? Then make that the lead. That'll have to be the news. The censors can't tell you that's a military secret."

"Guess you're right."

I batted out a shameful, I-was-there lead and showed it to Rick.

"That'll do it. That's the stuff. Can I have some more Scotch?"

I said he was welcome to the whole bottle, and he said he could use it. Just before he left, he turned to me and promised that what he had done that day was something he would never never do again.

I finished up, following the lead with whatever hard news I could infiltrate into long paragraphs full of whining jets, bursting bombs, and rolling tanks. *Bang-bang.* Before I left to file, I looked at the original version, all marked in red. An appropriate color: it was the truth and it had been massacred.

*   *   *

First casualties, last casualties ...

The Spokesman stood at the podium. Israeli losses as of the October 24 cease-fire: Tanks: eight hundred. Planes: one hundred and fifteen. Killed: 2,523.

It was called in Hebrew "Kiryat Shaul," which meant "Village of Saul." He was the Jewish warrior-king who died fighting the Philistines, and the village named for him was founded soon after the Israeli war of independence. It had grown considerably since then. It was overcrowded. That was why a subdivision had been built, just outside the village's stone walls, for the ninety citizens who would be added to its census that day. Like all new subdivisions, it was raw and dusty and had no trees or grass or flowers or walkways. Those would come later, but for now there was just a leveled field printed by the treads of a bulldozer and a backhoe, which had finished their work that morning. The machines would have more work to do soon. They were parked beside the wall, under a big spreading tree. In the field, almost a thousand people waited to welcome the new citizens to their new home.

The people came from everywhere: Russian and East European immigrants in baggy suits and dresses too dark and heavy for the climate; Jews from Iraq and Kurdistan and Yemen in biblical costumes, the women decorated with heavy, tribal bracelets and necklaces; native Israelis in loose cotton clothes and jeans and shirts open at the neck. The sun was very hot and the people were wiping their faces with handkerchiefs and fanning themselves with their hats or hands.

It was cooler in the old, established neighborhoods of Saul's Village. Rows of cypress trees shaded expanses of grass and the narrow, well-swept lanes between ranks of gold-white stones carved with the names of the residents and the dates of their births and deaths. The names meant nothing to anyone who could not read Hebrew. Anyone who could would notice that all were the names of men. The dates needed no translation. There was seldom a great span between them; most of Kiryat Shaul's citizens were young.

A few visitors, mostly women, walked among the stones or sat beside them, lips moving silently. Some carried wreaths with an air of mournful dignity, of a grief dulled by time to a sad acceptance that allowed politicians, on the days set aside for memorials, to make speeches about honor, valor, and duty without being interrupted by loud, disturbing displays of emotion from their listeners. There would not be any speeches today in the hot, dusty field outside the walls. Like the trees and the grass, those would come later.

A small truck convoy moved slowly up the road leading to the village gate, then turned and parked beside the field. Several women in the crowd started to cry, and one fainted and had to be carried into the shade, although she had not fainted from heat. A squad of paratroopers, green trousers bloused over their black jump boots, climbed off the first truck and with shouldered rifles marched stiffly to the middle of the field. They halted and formed a rank behind an army chaplain, a bearded rabbi in olive drab standing alongside a torch planted in the earth. The big crowd broke up into smaller crowds that gathered around the ninety holes dug by the backhoe. The people knew which grave they were supposed to go to because each one had a wooden marker painted with a name and an army service number. There were no gold-white headstones. Those would come later, with the trees and the grass and the speeches.

Another detachment of paratroopers began to unload the coffins from the trucks, and the women from Iraq, Kurdistan, and Yemen, heavy jewelry clattering, sat down in the dust and started ululating. It was plain, from the expressions on their faces, that many of the people from Russia and Europe had never heard that sound before and that it bothered them. It was a chorus of short, sharp shrieks and high-pitched warbling, a primitive cry that rose out of the ages when the Hebrews were a wandering desert tribe.

The paratroopers were carrying the coffins to the graves. There weren't enough of them to carry all the coffins at once. They took five or six at a time, lifted them to their shoulders, leaning their heads out and away so their red berets did not fall off, then lowered the coffins. There was some embarrassment when a stout woman threw herself into a grave. Two paratroopers pulled her out. The Kurdish and Iraqi and Yemenite women kept shrieking. It was so loud almost no one could hear the rabbi's eulogies. It drowned out the Russians and Europeans, who were murmuring the prayer for the dead. Some of them fell silent and listened to that howling, a sound of pain as raw and new as the graves. The women did not try to subdue it, and their ululations seemed to free everyone from restraint. Fathers called out the names of their sons, children started to wail for their fathers, and a woman in a shabby dress turned her face toward the clear sky and screamed, *"Lama? Lama?"*—"Why? Why?"

No one noticed that the rabbi had concluded his eulogies and that the honor guard behind him had come to attention.

"AIM!" commanded their sergeant.

The paratroopers pointed their rifles at the sky. A young man was embracing one of the wooden markers. His mother sat next to him, bowing up and down and groaning.

"FIRE!"

The rifles made a ragged popping.

"AIM ..."

"Lama? Lama?"

"FIRE!"

The rifles popped again. Several women fainted and were being carried away on stretchers.

"AIM ..."

A heavyset woman in a sweat-spotted blue dress stumbled around in a circle and then turned and faced the honor guard and screamed: "I want only one thing! I want my son back! Give me my son! I want my son!"

"FIRE!"

The rifles popped a third and final time and the paratroopers lowered them smartly and a bugler raised a silver bugle to his lips and began blowing taps. Still, the ululating did not stop. A young girl called out to the keening women, "Quiet, please! Grandfather is reciting the Kaddish," but the women kept shrieking above the old man reading the Kaddish and the high, clear notes of the silver bugle.

Then the ceremony ended. The paratroopers marched back to the trucks. The rabbi went with them. The people stayed by the graves, except one—the stout woman in the blue dress. She climbed a low set of stairs and passed through a gate in the wall and walked down one of the cool, quiet lanes and stopped at the grave of another man, who had died in another war at another time. The howling from the field grew quieter, then stopped all at once. The bulldozer's engine coughed. The woman paid no attention to it. She was not crying or screaming anymore but whispering something to the man buried under the handsome gold-white headstone. One day, she would speak like that to the boy who lay in the dusty field, but that would come later, when the grass and the trees had been planted and the parliamentarians made speeches and the bulldozers leveled fresh ground for whoever would then be the new citizens of the Village of Saul.

DISASTERS OF WAR

Saleh Suaweid sat with his wife in front of their stone-walled hut, sorting tobacco leaves to dry in the sun. We got out of the car. Palmer told his cameraman to ask Suaweid if it would be all right to interview him on camera. Suaweid, who was short and dark, with a deeply lined face that made him look older than thirty-three, said he did not mind at all.

Palmer's crew set up, taking light readings and testing sound levels. Suaweid's wife looked at them while her hands pulled and tugged at the tobacco leaves to make them lie flat. Her youngest child, a boy of less than two, sat beside her, staring. His two older brothers were atop the cistern, and they were staring in the same way as he—with the glassiness you see in the eyes of drug addicts or soldiers after a battle. The eldest child, a daughter who might have been ten, was pacing back and forth, her head twitching as from a series of small electric shocks.

The camera rolling, Palmer asked Suaweid to describe what it was like, trying to farm with shells falling in his fields almost every day.

"You want to know, I'll show you," he said, and got up and led us behind the house to his fields, which fell gently into a shallow valley. A rocky ridge rose on the other side of the valley, and the olive groves on the slopes of the ridge had been flattened and burned.

"Look at this." Suaweid's arm made a sweep of the fields, where the tobacco plants had been uprooted and shell craters made it difficult to walk. "How do you expect us to farm with this?"

He bent down, picked up a piece of shrapnel, and handed it to me. It was still warm. I threw it away and saw shrapnel everywhere, like fragments of clay pigeons at a trap range.

"We're going to have to leave our land if this keeps up. Why are the Israelis doing this?"

It wasn't a rhetorical question, so I answered that it was in retaliation for fedayeen massacres of Israeli civilians.

"There aren't any fedayeen here. Did you see any fedayeen?"

This time I did not answer. The terrorists had cleared out of their camps with the first Israeli shell. Suaweid could not clear out. It was the old story.

We walked back to the house and a shell exploded in the field where we had been not two minutes before. We went flat, all except Suaweid's wife, who hunched over the little boy. The daughter, lying on the ground, twitched and flinched. The woman shouted at us. A second shell whistled in. We could hear the shrapnel hissing through the air above the house. Palmer asked his cameraman to translate what Suaweid's wife had said.

"That they have nowhere to hide except the cistern and it is full with water."

A third shell struck. It was the last one. We got up. The two boys returned to their perch on the cistern, staring with eyes that hardly blinked, and their sister was pacing again, her head making that odd, jerking movement.

Suaweid's wife started to cry, and she shouted a second time.

"Now she says," translated the cameraman, "'Look at them! Why are the Israelis doing this? They're making my kids crazy!'"

The cameraman trained the lens on her. She put the baby down and stood and tore open her blouse. Her breasts fell out. She cupped them in her hands and held them up to the camera and cried and yelled.

Saleh Suaweid spoke quietly to his wife, but she kept holding her breasts in front of the camera. She did not know the cameraman had switched it off; there was no way he could get bare breasts on prime-time news.

"What the hell is she doing?" Palmer asked, sounding a little alarmed.

"She says she wants the world to look at her breasts. She wants the Lebanese government to look at her breasts so they will send her half a liter of milk each day."

The woman let one breast fall as she pointed at the small boy sitting beside a stack of tobacco leaves.

"I don't get it," Palmer said.

"The shelling," the cameraman explained. "It's made her so frightened her breasts have dried up so she cannot feed the baby. It's starving."

SIX

The Old Country

A memory took me south of Rome to the land of my ancestors, a memory that had, by the spring of 1974, taken on the sepia-tone charm of an old photograph. The time was the late forties and I was a boy of eight or nine in my grandparents' Berwyn bungalow. I was handing a bundle of cast-off clothes to my grandmother Enrichetta, who set them on the kitchen table and, with my mother's help, boxed and wrapped them, writing the addresses in a strange language. When I asked where she was sending my old blue jeans, T-shirts, and gym shoes, she replied in her broken English: "To my relatives in the Old Country." That answer prompted another question: Why couldn't her relatives buy jeans and T-shirts and gym shoes for their kids? They had no money, Enrichetta said matter-of-factly, as though it were a natural condition. Poor to begin with, the war had made them very poor.

It was the first time I'd learned that I had cousins in the far, mysterious land of my grandparents' birth and that their lives were less blessed than mine. I also became aware of another, sharper distinction between them and me: Enrichetta had said "my," not "our" relatives. I didn't know if her use of the singular possessive had been intentional, but it gave me the clear impression that I possessed a unique identity: I was an American, a sprig of the family tree growing apart from the foreign roots to which my grandparents remained connected.

"*Il vecchio paese*"—the old country—was how they had always referred to the homeland they'd left, bound for the New World in an immigrant ship. *Il vecchio paese,* in the way they used the phrase, did not refer to the nation of Italy; Italians of their generation, born soon after the country had been reunified out of what had been, ever since the fall of the Roman Empire, a hodgepodge of dukedoms, Arab or Norman colonies, and Papal States, seldom thought in nationalistic terms. *Paese* meant your region or province and, more narrowly still, your village and its surrounding countryside.

My family's *paese* was in the rugged hills rising between the Tyrrhenian Sea and Cosenza, a provincial city in Calabria. Caputos, Napolitanos, Marcheses, Micelis, Blasis, all the families whose blood ran in my veins, came from three neighboring towns—San Fili, Rende, and Parantoro. They emigrated between 1884 and 1912, staying in New York just long enough to buy train tickets for sprawling, brawling Chicago. It must have seemed utterly alien to them, a raw gray place compared with the sunny vineyards and olive groves they had left behind. Yet I had never heard them speak nostalgically or affectionately of the old country the way some other immigrants did. I grew up thinking of it as a place of incurable poverty and limited opportunities, the place where my old clothes were sent.

Whatever emotional ties Fiore and Enrichetta had to it, they made sure their children and grandchildren became thoroughly American. They never made me feel anything but proud of my origins but did not expect me to wear them on my sleeve. In my grandparents' eyes, that was sentimentality and nostalgia. This was *America* and who needed reminders here of the old country with its poverty and stifling customs?

Chicago, where the melting pot was more reality than myth, must have had a lot to do with their total embrace of the New World. Immigrants who stayed in the big northeastern cities seemed to keep one eye cocked back across the Atlantic. They did not want to plunge too far into the immense continent west of the Hudson and the Alleghenies, as if they feared cutting themselves from a line of retreat in case America's promise proved false. They took their cue, I guess, from the old blue-blood families of New York, Boston, and Philadelphia, who hadn't gone west with the pioneer wagons but stayed put and looked as much toward Europe as to their own country for lessons on how to behave, what to wear, to read, to think, and forever scampered like busy squirrels through the branches of their family trees, seeking evidence of royal descent. Easterners, whether they'd come to America on the *Mayflower* in the early seventeenth century or in steerage in the early twentieth, had an Old World sense of history. But the essence of being an American was—is—to be historyless, to look ever to the future and not the past. Chicagoans turned their eyes and backs away from the Atlantic. They looked north, toward the Michigan and Minnesota woods, where the iron ranges were plundered to feed the fiery guts of the steel mills blasting along Lake Michigan's shore, and west, toward the farm and range lands whose grain crammed the boxcars lined up for miles in the switchyards, whose hogs and cattle bawled and squealed up stockyard chutes into skull-bashing mauls swung by greenhorn Poles or by blacks just off an Illinois Central freight hopped in flight from the Jim Crow bottomlands of Mississippi. Sandburg's city of the big shoulders, honest yet crooked, cultured yet brutal, home to one of the best symphony orchestras in the world as well as the most corrupt political machine, Chicago was the most American of America's big cities in its appetites, its boundless optimism, its rough virtues and gargantuan vices.

My grandparents left it in the mid-1920s. As they had fled the old country, so they fled the old neighborhood, to live among Czechs, Irish, and Dutch in Berwyn. My parents furthered the process with their migration to Westchester, where I acquired friends and classmates with really exotic names like Appleby, Hastings, and Nelson.

Our family had been melted down in the melting pot but had suffered in that social forge a loss of historical and cultural heritage. If my grandparents' decision to emigrate had given me the chance to grow up in freedom and prosperity, it had also severed me from a rich and ancient tradition. I spoke English but knew hardly a word of Italian, I had read Whitman but not Dante, I had learned about Washington, Jefferson, and Lincoln but nothing about Garibaldi, Mazzini, and Cavour.

I don't recall when I became conscious of the shallowness of my American roots and of the depths of my roots in Italy, which reached down to the very origins of western civilization. I only know that I grew more and more curious about *il vecchio paese*. I wanted to see it, to walk where my forebears had walked for centuries, to restore my ties to the past.

Heading south on the *autostrada* on a fine April morning in 1974, I wondered why I had waited so long to make the trip. Too busy, I supposed. I was going to be busier in the near future: the *Tribune* was closing its Rome bureau and was sending me to Beirut to open a new Middle East bureau. Things there had settled down in the year since my misadventure. The nomad in me was looking forward to pulling up stakes once again, but the paterfamilias in me yearned for a rootedness impossible in my vagabond trade. I seemed to spend most of my life in hotels, train stations, and airports, mostly airports, which merged in my brain into a metaport, the Platonic *idea* of an airport, crawling with metacops, submachine guns slung for quick use in case the Children of the Beast showed up on a group terror tour. I was beginning to suffer from chronic jet lag and becoming a stranger to my family. After the October War, I was sent on a long reporting trip to Egypt, Saudi Arabia, and the Persian Gulf to gauge the new confidence early successes in the war and the oil embargo had instilled in the Arabs. Quite suddenly, they had become a potent factor in world affairs. The hotels of remote emirates were booked to capacity with Western and Japanese businessmen, modern-day Marco Polos in suits and ties, seeking contracts, the riches of Arabia. I was gone six weeks. When I returned home, three-year-old Geoff stared at me for what must have been a full minute, as if trying to recall who I was. I glanced in the mirror and almost could not recall myself. Who *is* this puffy-faced globetrotter with constantly bloodshot eyes who spends half his life in goofy places? Where did he come from? That was when the memory flickered in my mind—the kitchen table and my grandmother and the brown packages bound for the old country.

I stopped for a lunch of piquant pasta arrabbiata in Positano, the most enchanting town on the Amalfi coast. I could have stayed there forever, but I was back on the coast road after lunch, and, south of Salerno, back on the *autostrada,* my Alfa hitting eighty through Campania and Basilicata. An hour or so later, I was in the mountains of Calabria— dry, rock-strewn, cut up by twisting, covert valleys. It had been bandit country in the old days, then a hideout for the Italian partisans fighting Mussolini and the Germans. It retained a certain sullen, dangerous look. Not that I was expecting trouble. I didn't know what to expect. How would I be greeted—as a long-lost native son or as a stranger? In the glove compartment I had copies of my paternal great-grandfather's 1848 birth certificate, his wife, Theresa's, passport, issued in 1892, and the address of two of my grandmother's cousins in San Fili, Alfredo and Arafina DeLeo. My father—the only child of an only child—had written that there was no one left in Italy from either side of his family; emigration had claimed them all. But on my mother's side, one branch of the Napolitanos remained, a clan headed by her first cousin, Gisberto. He and his wife, Ada, had three children—two sons, Angelo and Attilio, and a daughter, Francesca. For some odd reason, my mother did not have their address, but, she'd said, the DeLeos could put me in touch with them.

In midafternoon, I caught sight of the Grande Sila Mountains, still a wild and lonely range where shepherds carried ten-gauge luparas against marauding wolves. The highway dipped into the valley of the Crati and Busento rivers. Cosenza stood at the rivers' junction. It was a provincial city of modest population and ordinary appearance, but it had experienced all the triumphs and catastrophes of Italy's long history, going back to pre-Roman times. Driving past its outskirts, I reflected on my native city's callow age. Chicago celebrated its one hundred and forty-first birthday that year; Cosenza had been that old at least two centuries before Julius Caesar was born.

I saw the sign for Rende and San Fili and turned off the *autostrada* onto a side road winding up out of Cosenza's valley like the coils of a spring. It climbed into a range of forested hills that peaked at about two thousand feet before they fell westward into the Tyrrhenian. The old town of Rende, where my father's father—the rags-to-riches-to-rags hero of my boyhood—had been born in 1888. I came to a fork, the sign for San Fili pointing to the right. The land fell away, steeper and steeper; a fast river whispered in a wooded gorge way below. Then the road wrung itself around a sheer hillside, the oak and chestnut woods opened up, and I could see San Fili, clinging precariously to a mountaintop across the gorge: red, clay-tile roofs, stone walls that seemed to grow out of the mountain, the bell tower of Santissima Annunziata, the thousand-year-old church where my grandmother had been baptized. Dark-green hills rose and tumbled beyond the town. The cries of herdsmen, the bleating of sheep, the barks of dogs came out of the gorge with the rushing sound of the river. *Il vecchio paese*—it was beautiful. I could not imagine why my grandparents had left it.

I drove slowly up the town's narrow main street, the Via Venti Settèmbre, named for the day the great Garibaldi drove the French and the Papal forces out of Italy. The street was empty, except for a handful of old men in front of a coffee shop, raising cups of espressi to their lips with wrinkled, quivering hands. I parked in the Piazza San Giovanni, the town square. In the middle stood a statue of a fallen man, a hand raised toward the skies, a tormented expression on his face. I thought it was a monument to some martyred saint until I saw the list of names on the base and the legend: "TO THE FALLEN OF SAN FILI. 1915–1918." A war memorial. The Italians had been on the winning side in World War I, but the statue reflected their view of war. No hero on horseback, no noble general pointing with his sword, no one raising a flag on a conquered hill—just a fallen man, facing death in pain. Looking at the statue, I felt a connection, tenuous as a strand of spider's silk: one of my grandfather's younger brothers, Julio, had been killed at Caporetto in 1918. I searched the roll for his name, but couldn't find it; then I remembered that he'd come from Parantoro, which was about ten miles away.

"Che bella machina!"

And again, another voice: *"Che bella machina!"*—"What a beautiful car!"

I turned. A few kids and a couple of adults were admiring the Alfa, touching its silver steel reverently, as if it were a wheeled altar. One of the kids, a scruffy-looking boy in his early teens, wanted to know if it were mine. I said it was and, taking the DeLeos' address from the glove compartment, asked if he could lead me to their house. A look of southern Italian suspicion closed over the kid's face like a goalie's mask. And who wanted to know? Their cousin from America. The mask flipped up.

"Un cugino Americano—Lei?" he asked in his Calabrian accent, a rough, lazy drawl filled with dropped and aspirated endings. *Un goojeeen Ameddigan?*

I nodded. He led me back down the Via Venti Settèmbre to a terraced street between gray-and-beige houses with small wrought-iron balconies. In a doorway at the top of the street, a silver-haired woman in fateful black sat knitting—a tableau that could have been a hundred years old.

The kid pointed. The DeLeos' house was the third one up on the right.

A little nervous, I knocked on the thick wooden door. The man who opened it had gray hair and sharp blue eyes and was slightly bent by age or illness. I asked if he were Alfredo DeLeo. He nodded.

I was about to tell him that I was the grandson of his wife's cousin, Enrichetta, when I was struck by a sudden linguistic amnesia, forgetting every word of Italian I knew. I broke out in a mild sweat. Alfredo must have thought I was suffering from the midday heat. He waved me inside, into a cool, dim entry hall.

"Excuse me," he said (I could understand the language that had mysteriously deserted my tongue). "But who are you?"

At that moment, I saw a montage of photographs, pasted like Christmas cards around a large mirror on the wall. Photographs of my grandparents celebrating their fiftieth wedding anniversary, of my uncle Fred in his navy uniform, a color photograph of me on the day I was commissioned, standing on the front lawn of the buff-brick trilevel in Marine Corps dress blues. There were fading black-and-whites of my cousins, my sister, and I as toddlers. Another black-and-white showed a trim, handsome young man in a double-breasted suit and two-toned shoes; beside him was a glamourous woman with long wavy hair and wearing a dress with a pinched waist and padded shoulders. It took me a moment to recognize the youthful couple as my parents. There must have been three dozen pictures altogether, images of the New World family sent over the years across five thousand miles of land and ocean to the Old. Each one had the charm of the photograph in my memory, each one, fastened to the ancient stone wall of that house, was a visual conjunctive joining my divided heritages.

The language returned to me. I pointed to the snapshot of me in the dress blues.

"That's me. I am the grandson of Arafina's cousin Enrichetta."

Alfredo thumped his forehead with the heel of his hand.

"*Madonna mia!*"

He gave me a warm *abbraccio* and kissed both cheeks and practically dragged me up a dark staircase, calling, "Arafin'! Arafin'! See who's come!"

She was a stout woman in her midsixties, and her face, as is not uncommon in some elderly southern Italian women, wore a look of suffering patiently but resentfully endured. She, too, embraced and kissed me, and there was nothing ritualistic or pro forma about the greeting. For a Calabrian, as for a Sicilian, blood was a sacred bond. Immediately, she began to slice salami, cheese, and bread, apologizing for not cooking me a proper meal.

"I would have been prepared if I had known you were coming. But I can fry some eels."

While she lit her stove, Alfredo ushered me to the kitchen table. He broke out a bottle of his homemade wine and filled two glasses.

"Salud," he said, raising his.

"Salud."

I told him it was very good.

"Sure. It's my seventy-one, my best year. I save it only for important guests and family." A broad grin plowed new furrows into his face. "And you are family."

He clutched my forearm; a stranger no longer, I was a native son who had returned home.

Arafina laid out the salamis, cheeses, and eels, deep fried in the purest, greenest olive oil.

"I wish I had known you were coming. This is a disgrace," she said.

I slapped a mound of provolone and salami and eel between two slices of the bread she had baked that morning, chomped into the sandwich, and told her it was the best-tasting disgrace I had ever eaten.

She smiled weakly in thanks.

"You have a good appetite, God bless you. Your grandmother and I write to each other about once a month. She's told us all about you. But when you see her, please apologize to her for me. I haven't written in a long time. I've been sick."

"Ah, Arafin', you're always sick," Alfredo scolded with the affectionate exasperation of a husband who knows his wife too well. "You were sick when you were a girl. You were sick when we were married. In heaven, you'll be sick."

"But it's true," Arafina protested, scraping her frying pan, plump arms quivering. "Today finds me sick."

"*Senta*, Arafin'. Today finds our cousin here all the way from America. And what have you to say? 'I'm sick.' There is the disgrace." Alfredo took a sip of wine and turned to me. "*Allora, Filippo.* What brings you to San Fili? *Mi dica.*"

I explained.

"So, you wanted to see where you came from? That's a good thing to know. Well, what do you think of what you've seen so far?"

I said that San Fili was so beautiful that I couldn't understand why my ancestors had left.

"It's simple. They left because there were too many people and not enough work. There were no *possibilities*. In America, if you worked hard, you or your children could study and become a scientist or an engineer. Look at you, a journalist for a big American newspaper. Do you think you would have been a journalist if your ancestors stayed here?" He shook his head. "In Italy, if you worked hard—*è fatto niente*—it made no difference."

Some things had changed since then, but a lot had not, Alfredo said with another shake of his head: the old country's main export continued to be immigrants.

"Ten years ago, San Fili had fifty-eight hundred people. Know what it is today? Three thousand. If that keeps up, in another ten years Arafin' and I will be the only ones left."

"If we are still on this earth," Arafina interrupted dolefully.

"*I* will be," Alfredo said.

"*Anche io*"—"Me, too"—she said, sounding not altogether pleased by the prospect. She threw a glance at my half-eaten sandwich. "Hey, Filippo, *mangia, mangia.* You'll need your strength to listen to this old man's speeches."

"Arafin', *piacere.* He wants to know why his ancestors left. I am telling him." He turned in his chair to gaze out the window at the puzzle of tile roofs. "Yes, a beautiful town, but we have no industries and no money. Take me. I'm retired. I used to be municipal treasurer of this town, but my pension is only forty-two thousand lire a month (sixty dollars at the exchange rate then). "The air is clean in Calabria, the wine is good, and the fruit and the bread, but there's no money and no *possibilities*. So the young people keep going away. They've all gone to America, to Australia, to Canada, to Germany. And to Milano, Torino, and Genoa, the only cities in all Italy with big industries."

"But it's not so bad as it used to be," Arafina cut in. "After the war ..."

Alfredo's hand again went to his forehead.

"*Madonna mia!* Yes, it was bad here then. One man got one slice of bread a day. But with the Marshall Plan, a miracle was made. Listen to me. A miracle! Now life is much better, but ..."

A sinewy young man with jet-black hair came up the kitchen stairs: Tommaso, youngest of the DeLeos' seven children. He sat down, turning the chair backward, and poured a glass of wine.

"Guess who this is, Tommaso," Alfredo said, jerking his head at me.

Tommaso shrugged.

"Our American cousin! You know Enrichet', your mother's cousin? Well, this is her grandson, Filippo."

He gave me a firm handshake and welcomed me to San Fili.

"I was just telling him why his ancestors left here, why all the young people are leaving. No money, no industries, no *possibilities.*"

Tommaso, who later told me he was an engineer on the state railroad, nodded. But he had a different take on things than his father. Possibly because of television and modern communications, he knew that the bright promise of far countries and cities was often a mirage. Working hard in some factory didn't always open up all those possibilities.

"A lot of friends of mine have gone up to Torino and Milano. Made a lot of money they could never make here. But you know what those northerners think of us southerners, don't you?"

"They call you Africans."

"Exactly! We're Arabs to them. They think we all carry knives in our boots and they discriminate against us. Who wants that? And those miserable little apartments we have to live in up there? And all that bad air? You can hardly breathe. This is a beautiful country down here. I love Calabria. I love to hunt and fish. That's all I do when I'm off work. I hunt rabbit and wild boar and fish for trout. We have trout because in Calabria the waters are pure."

I told him that I also loved to fish and hunt (though in my pursuit of success and possibilities, I had little time for either). The conversation turned to rods and guns and how, no matter how many times you'd experienced it, your heart always grew big at the strike of a trout, at the whir of a game bird's wings when it flushed.

An hour later, as the sky darkened toward twilight, the DeLeos' kitchen was crowded with children and grandchildren, brothers and brothers-in-law, to all of whom I was introduced as the American cousin. These gatherings were a daily event, the family members stopping by to gossip over coffee and anisette. The clannish atmosphere took me back twenty-five years, to the holiday feasts in my grandparents' basement, where the strong old cavalry sergeant (now crippled by Parkinson's disease) would strop his carving knife. If I had been able to get in a word amidst all the DeLeos' conversation, I would have told Alfredo about the downside of the Land of Possibilities: the extended families fragmented into nuclear families living in suburban isolation, the rising divorce rate that was, like a social cyclotron, smashing the nuclear families into subatomic particles. I would have told him that *il vecchio paese* had other advantages besides the clean air, the good wine and fruit, the pure streams flashing with trout: families lived within walking distance of each other, they had time for each other, so there were few psychiatrists in Calabria, and of those few, fewer still earned a good living.

The road to Parantoro, potholed and hardly wide enough for Francesca's Fiat, wound through a hilly, beige-and-green landscape speckled by stone farmhouses. The bronzed farmers riding donkeys at the roadside did not look like anachronisms in that preindustrial countryside; *we* were the anachronism.

"Let's surprise him," Francesca said, a little smile on her broad, strong face. "He'll never guess who you are."

A twenty-eight-year-old schoolteacher, she was married to Francesco Gambaro, the secretary of the local Christian Democratic party organization. They and their three-year-old son, Giovanni, lived in a renovated eighteenth-century house with modern appliances, owned two cars, and had enough leisure to devote themselves to hobbies like oil painting and watercolors. She was doing well by anyone's standards, wonderfully well by the standards of the Mezzogiorno. The way she described it, all the Napolitanos who had remained in Italy were living the good life. Her father was a local *patrone;* he owned a grain mill that employed fifty or sixty people, a construction company that specialized in restoring old houses, and a grocery store. His middle child, Attilio, managed the store; his youngest, Angelo, was studying law in Bari.

I quipped that possibly my grandfather made a mistake by emigrating. I could now be the son of a big *padrone.*

"Oh, no. There are still few opportunities. Francesco and I want to send our son to university. When he graduates, what will there be for him to do in Calabria? Very little. He'll have to go north, like everybody else. Ah, here we are."

She parked at the roadside. The mill nestled in a shallow valley below. We walked into a yard where grain lay like sawdust on the floor of an old-fashioned butcher shop. A man, giving orders to a few workers stacking huge white sacks, stood with his back to us. He wasn't more than five-eight, but so massively built he looked as if he could have hefted one of those sacks in each strong hand. When, hearing Francesca's call of "Papa, Papa," he turned around, I almost stopped dead in my tracks. The face in front of me was a photocopy of the old cavalry sergeant as he looked when I was a small boy: the stern set of the mouth, the strong jaw, the thin hedge of hair encircling a bald head, the head held so proud and erect you were surprised, standing next to him, that he wasn't six feet tall.

"Papa," Francesca said. "Do you recognize this man?"

Gisberto studied me for a moment.

"Am I supposed to?"

When she told him, his *abbraccio* threatened to break my ribs. Of course he recognized me. His Uncle Fiore's grandson! Sure, now he could see the resemblance. He whacked me on the back and clamped his hands around my upper arms, almost numbing them below the elbow.

"Why didn't you tell us you were coming? Why this surprise?"

I tried to explain that I was often a creature of impulse, but my Italian was not up to it. I apologized, both for failing to announce my visit and for my lousy ability with the language. Gisberto said I spoke it very well. Did my grandparents teach me? No, I had been living and working in Rome the past two years as a journalist.

"A journalist? *Un dottore!*" He gave me another slap on the back. "We have a doctor in the family!"

(In Italy, the honorific *dottore* is bestowed on anyone who claims to have a profession instead of a job.)

After Francesca left for school, Gisberto took me on a tour of his mill, pointing enthusiastically at the machinery, explaining the functions of the steel grinding rolls, the sieves and purifiers.

"All very modern, electronic, the latest stuff. And I'll bet you thought Calabria was like the Middle East. Well, see for yourself, the latest stuff!" Gisberto bellowed, as if I were a potential investor.

He dipped his hands into a sack with a vigorous sensuality and scooped out the raw grain and brought it up to his nose.

"By the end of the shift this will be flour, pure flour, and by the end of the week? Who knows? Lasagna. Penne. Linguine. Come on, cousin, I want you to meet some of my workers."

He nudged me toward a bespectacled man in his fifties, the operator of a sifter. Or maybe it was a purifier. Anyway, it resembled a gigantic funnel.

"Hey, Frederico, meet my cousin from America. Filippo, meet Frederico Napolitano."

I shook hands with him, and then, in a storage bin, with Michele Napolitano, and then, on a loading dock, with a burly Giancarlo Napolitano.

"Must be a very common name around here," I said.

A great laugh shook Gisberto's monumental torso. He said it sure as hell was and that he would explain why later, after he showed me his farm.

"You own a farm, too?"

"*Certo!* It's been in the family over a hundred years."

It was set in the gentle hills outside Parantoro: fig orchards and olive groves. Gisberto's small Fiat seemed to sigh with relief when he got out. Clamping my arm again, he pulled me through a tumbledown fence, tore off a handful of figs from a low branch, and commanded me to *mangia, mangia.*

"Good, eh? Life in Calabria is good now." He drew in a deep breath, hauling his belly into his chest, which ballooned to the size of a heavyweight wrestler's. "Smell that? Smell that air. The air is clean in Calabria. Life is good here now, but it was very very poor when your grandfather left. No electricity, no toilets, no running water, no nothing. I'll bet you thought it was still like that, eh? Like the Middle East, very, very poor."

No, not exactly ...

"But you can see for yourself." His hand described a rough half circle in the air. "Life goes well here now. We've got a lot of problems, but life goes well."

He walked me through the orchards, explaining that they were a small part of what once had been a large farm owned by his grandfather and my maternal great-grandfather, Angelo Napolitano. It had the hauntingly beautiful name of "La Donna Rosanna" and had produced grain and sheep besides olives and figs. The sheep's wool was spun into bolts of fabric at a textile mill near Parantoro and sold to wholesalers by Angelo's eldest son, Attilio.

"And not just in Calabria," Gisberto said proudly. "Not only in Italy, but throughout Europe. It's true, my Uncle Attilio traveled through all Europe, selling our fabrics. Listen, the Napolitanos were a big family back then. We weren't nobility, but we weren't peasants either."

Then what about my grandfather? What was he doing while his oldest brother journeyed on sales trips through Europe? Why, if the Napolitanos were such big shots, did he emigrate for an uncertain future in America?

Gisberto's answer, with its frequent lapses into the strange Calabrian dialect, was difficult to follow. It went something like this: my grandfather helped worked the farm and was one of eight children, six of whom were boys. Divided among that many sons, La Donna Rosanna would not have been much of an estate. The second eldest son, Giuseppe, emigrated to America shortly after my grandfather was discharged from the army; then the third left, going to Argentina (a branch of the family with whom all contact had been lost). My grandfather was next, twenty-four years old when he sailed to join Giuseppe in Chicago. The two remaining sons, one of whom was Gisberto's father, remained in the old country.

"So there you have it, the story of your family. C'mon and I'll show you the house where they were born, all of them."

I asked him to wait a moment, then walked off a short distance by myself. The breezes moved quietly through the trees, the very same trees beneath which my grandfather must have walked as a boy and a young man. I pressed my feet into the earth, the same earth his feet must have trod. I bent down and scooped up a handful of dirt, wanting to *feel* the soil that had nourished my roots.

Gisberto's talk about a grand farm with a grand name had led me to expect the farmhouse to resemble Tara. On the outskirts of Parantoro, which was more a hamlet than a town, the house was big enough, big as a barn. Part of it, in fact, had been a barn; before refrigeration, chickens and livestock destined for the table were kept in a stable under the kitchen. The thick stone and stucco walls now enclosed, on the second floor, a commodious apartment, renovated by Gisberto's construction company for the daughter and son-in-law of my grandfather's youngest sister, Virgilia. The first floor had been left in its original state, except for a room Gisberto had converted into an office for himself. We had a cup of coffee there, after which Gisberto picked up the phone, excusing himself to attend to some business.

I got up to have a look around. As I wandered through the rooms, bare of furniture but otherwise unchanged from the day in 1887 when Fiore Napolitano first set eyes on them, I sensed yesterday filtering into today. The past seemed alive in the kitchen. I stood by its one window, paneless and shuttered against the sun, and saw my great-grandmother, bent over a smoky hearth under the crude beams, cooking for her eight children. I saw the kids, who now were dead or white with age, sitting at a rustic table, their father, upon whose face my imagination painted a martial mustache, sitting at the head.

Pushing open the shutters, I gazed outside and, watching the distant olive leaves flutter green then not green, I tried to cast myself into the world as it had been when those people were not mere ghosts of the imagination. What was the world like before it had been shrunk by radio, television, and telephones, when it turned under skies no plane or satellite had ever crossed? It must have seemed vast to a farm boy from a tiny Calabrian village. When you left home in those days for a distant land, you were *gone*. No swift 747s to wing you back in half a day or less, no international dialing system to put you in touch with Mama and Papa at the speed of light. A letter home might take a month or more to arrive, the reply another month, and Mama and Papa could be in their graves for weeks before you knew they'd died. What could have prodded my grandfather to turn his back on all that was familiar and safe to try his luck in a place where he could not speak a word of the language and knew hardly a soul? Gisberto's explanation did not satisfy me. That my grandfather would have gotten only a fourth or a fifth of the family holdings instead of a third or half didn't seem sufficient motive. Hopeless poverty, yes, a diminished inheritance, no.

I stood by the window and, looking at the ancient trees, thought of the awed, reverential way Alfredo DeLeo had spoken the word *possibilities*. The wind blew in, wrapped its warm arms around me, and carried me on a brief, fanciful flight backward in time. I *became* my grandfather, as he had been more than sixty years ago; I knew, through the logic of blood, not of the mind, that he had not wanted La Donna Rosanna, not a fifth, not a half, not all. He had wanted what I had those days on the suburban prairies, listening to train whistles blow: escape. Escape from what? I wasn't sure, but sensed that he had not felt rooted to *il vecchio paese;* chained to it, rather, by three kinds of history: the history of tired Europe, whose class laws had legislated, from the instant he'd drawn his first breath, what he could do, who he could be, how far he could go in life; the history of his family, each generation a link in an iron tether binding him to the land; and the history of the land itself, that old Italian earth, walked on and plowed under and fought over for three thousand years.

But America was void of history and full of promise. My grandfather left because he'd had the vision to see new possibilities for himself in the new land calling from beyond the western horizon, possibilities more alluring than the mere chance to get rich. In America, he would not have to be or do what his father demanded, or the citizens of Parantoro expected, or the village priest, sermonizing from a narrow pulpit, dictated. Nor would he feel the cold, dead grip of his ancestors, reaching up from their graves to hold him fast. In America, he would be free to reinvent himself. But what, I wondered, had put that vision in his young head? Something he'd read? Heard? Some incident in his life? More than imagination was needed to answer that.

That night, the family gathered in Gisberto's and Ada's dining room for a dinner in my honor. Francesca and Francesco were there

248 / PHILIP CAPUTO

with son Giovanni, Attilio with his wife, Theresa. There was enough food for another eight people (Southern Italy is one of the few places left in the world where obesity is considered a sign of health). Afterward, over espresso and several varieties of ices and sweets, Ada echoed her daughter's lament about Calabria: "The young people here get out of school, cannot find work, so they go to Milano or Torino and do menial labor and live in slums." I had heard that refrain once too often and to change the subject reminded Gisberto of his promise to reveal why there were so many Napolitanos around San Fili. All eyes turned to Gisberto, who shrugged and raised his eyebrows.

"He met some of the men at the mill," he said, as if justifying himself against some unspoken accusation.

"Are you going to tell him, Papa?"

"I said I would, so I will."

Francesca turned to me.

"*È un scandalo.*"

It was more than a scandal. It was a feat of excess. It seemed that Great-grandfather Angelo had incredible sexual appetites combined with what must have been a record-breaking sperm count. His wife was pregnant eleven times during their marriage before she, not surprisingly, died in her midforties. Apparently dissatisfied with the eight legitimate children she bore him, the fifty-year-old Angelo took up with a twenty-year-old mistress and had so many children by her that I wasn't sure I'd heard the number correctly.

"*Quattordici?*" I asked. *Fourteen?*

"*Sì. Quattordici.*"

"After he was fifty years old?"

"*Sì.* Right up to the end. He died at seventy-seven."

"My God."

"God had nothing to do with it," Francesca said flatly.

"And those men at the mill?"

Gisberto nodded.

"Descendants of the mistress. All very poor, you understand. Their grandparents were not entitled to anything from my grandfather, they were bastards. So that's what they got. Nothing. And their children—again nothing. And their children, the ones who work for me—again nothing. I feel responsible for them, so I give them work."

❖   ❖   ❖

I spent the night in the Gambaros' guest room. I was awakened long before dawn by the clop-clop of hooves on the cobblestone street. Looking out the window, I saw an old farmer leading a donkey toward the fields in the valley below the town. A floppy hat covered his head, his shoulders were stooped, by more weight than the burden of his years. No wonder the young people left for Torino and Milano.

Getting back to sleep was difficult. I thought about the farmer, lashed to the land and a way of life that hadn't changed much in centuries; I thought about Great-grandfather Angelo. Everyone who traces his genealogical roots hopes to find either a nobleman or a horse thief among his ancestors. I'd known my chances of finding even a trace of blue in my blood were nil but had hoped for an outlaw. I'd never expected to discover the sire of fourteen bastards. Not entitled to anything, Gisberto had said. Disenfranchised because of an old man with no restraint and even less common sense. And the curse of their illicit birth had not stopped with them but had been passed on, like some ugly genetic trait, into the next generation, and the one after that. I rather admired Gisberto's sense of responsibility, even if it was a little feudal and paternalistic; in a way he was atoning for his grandfather's sins. History. They were all caught by it, the son of the legitimate son as much as the sons of the bastards' sons.

I wonder now if Angelo's excesses put the New World visions in my grandfather's head. While writing Gisberto's account of family scandal, I heard in memory's ear a remark my mother made years ago: her father, she believed, had not gotten along with his father. Fiore was a man of the strictest morals, and—here I'm conjecturing—living in a small village that was yearly being populated with his father's illicit offspring must have filled him with shame, revulsion, and anger. La Donna Rosanna must have seemed tainted by Angelo's sins, so my grandfather rejected his inheritance, turned his back on his past, and decided to put an ocean between him and it, between him and his father.

In the morning, Francesco Gambaro, something of an expert on local history, lore and legend, took me inside the parish church, Santissima Annunziata. Pointing to the late baroque decorations, he said it had been built and designed by local artisans on the foundations of a Gothic basilica that dated back to the Normans. The ruins of a Roman temple were supposed to lie beneath the basilica. No one had excavated them, or was likely to, but I was intrigued by the notion that my ancestors might have been worshipping on that mountaintop since the ages when togaed priests burnt offerings to pagan gods.

That afternoon, Gisberto organized a family picnic in the Grande Sila. A two-hour drive took us up into a landscape that belonged to Austria or northern Italy: vast pine forests, alpine lakes, the clear streams where Tommaso DeLeo fished for trout. The altitude, combined with a wretched excess of food and Gisberto's relentless commands to *mangia, mangia,* made me sick. I left the table and went into the woods and threw up. My relatives were amused rather than insulted.

We were back in San Fili before dusk. Francesco suggested I work off the effects of altitude and gastronomic illness with a walk to a place he called "The Romans' Bridge."

He, Attilio, and I reached it by way of an old road that wound out of town and past an enormous chestnut tree that was six hundred years old. Along the way, we passed the same farmer I had seen that morning. Plodding with the same stoop to his shoulders, he was leading his donkey back from the fields. *"Una vita dura,"* Attilio said, glancing at him: a hard life. Oh, yes.

The road dipped through a woods to the Emoli, a small stream spanned by an arch of stone and earth—the Romans' Bridge. Francesco told me it dated back to before the eighth century. Its top so overgrown that I could hardly tell what had been made by man and what by nature, the bridge struck my imagination. It had survived over twelve centuries of wars, floods, and quakes, rather like Calabria itself. I climbed up to it and walked to the middle, wondering if, perhaps, I was following in the sandaled steps of some distant ancestor. I liked to think so. I liked to think that my life was part of the long succession of lives that had sprung from that same tragic, beautiful, enduring Italian earth. The river slid beneath me and past Francesco and Attilio, waiting on the bank. The people my grandmother had called her relatives I now had made mine. Attilio, almost the same height and build as I, with the same dark-brown hair, was the man I might have been. I looked away from him and toward the oak and chestnuts moving in the wind, turning light then dark in the wind, rippling as if the wind were blowing beneath as well as over them. It touched me, the past touched me, and I touched the past. I did not try to embrace it and make it mine because I was an American. I only touched it, to acknowledge that it was a part of me, and then I let it go.

DISASTERS OF WAR

The two old men were sitting on a bench in the town square, under the Civil War memorial—a tall statue of a Confederate soldier with a musket and a plaster cape billowing in an eternal wind. The statue's shadow slanted across the square and over the two men, who sat very still except to fan themselves now and then with folded newspapers.

The man on the left was missing an ear. As soon as I walked up, he volunteered that he also had been in the marines, but a long time ago, in World War I. That was where he'd lost the ear, at Belleau Wood.

I asked if he could direct me to Lotus Street. I had driven over half the town looking for it. The other man, who was wearing a baseball cap that advertised a farm implement manufacturer, raised his head and stared at me with hard, violent eyes.

"Plannin' to split you a black oak?"

"Excuse me?"

"Never mind him," said the man without the ear. "He's got a trashy mind and a trashy mouth. You got business over by Lotus Street?"

"Yes."

"I can just about guess what hit 'tis, too."

"Sure you can, Charles. Gonna go split him some black oak."

"What the hell are you talking about?" I said, irritated. It had been a long, hot drive up from the base, first down the interstate, then onto a state highway, then a county road, and off that onto another, smaller road, all through a land of leached-out tobacco fields and pine barrens that didn't look as if it had changed since one-eared Charles had marched off to Belleau Wood.

"Harley, why don't you just shut up now," he said to his friend. "Just shut up your trashy mouth." He looked back at me. "'Bout all I can tell you is that hit's over by nigra town."

That was what he said. Not Negro town, not nigger town, but nigra town. He told me how to find it, and I thanked him and got back in the olive-drab staff car with the white lettering on the door: UNITED STATES MARINE CORPS. As I drove away, I caught a glimpse of Charles and Harley in the side-view mirror. They were fanning themselves again with the folded newspapers but were otherwise motionless. There was a suggestion of the territorial in their rigid postures, as if the bench was theirs alone, the place where the old men of the town had always come to pass hot summer afternoons and always would, as long as there was a town and old men in it.

Nigra town sprawled away from a muddy river that divided it from the white neighborhoods. Shacks and shanties with sprung porch planks and sagging walls. Cinder streets and broken-down automobiles and yards full of kids playing amidst heaps of rusted washing machines, plowshares, bedsprings, and junk decayed beyond recognition as anything that had ever been useful. Where was the New South I had been hearing so much about? Like the interstate, it seemed to have bypassed that place.

There weren't any street signs or numbers on the houses. I had to ask several people for directions, feeling self-conscious about my uniform, with its bright rank insignia, about my white skin above all. The base adjutant hadn't told me that Sergeant Harris was black. That wasn't supposed to make a difference, but it did.

The Harrises' house was two stories and might have been painted white once. It stood at the T of a junction, backed up against a woods whose cool darkness I could almost feel, whose piny scent I could smell as I climbed four or five creaky steps to the door. I knocked. There was no answer. I knocked again, sweating through my uniform, and it wasn't just the heat.

I knocked a third time. The door had a small, rectangular window about a third of the way from the top. Suddenly, a face appeared in it, a face with the sharply cut features of an African mask. Lillian Harris stared at me for half a second, perplexed; then her eyes widened in horrified recognition, as if I were some awful thing she had seen before. I guess she had. She must have awakened every morning with fears that she would see a man in a military uniform at her front door.

"Mrs. Harris?"

She yelled, or screamed, or half yelled and half screamed. I'm not sure how to describe that sound.

"Mrs. Harris, I'm … I mean, I've been sent from Camp Lejeune."

"Go way from here!" she hollered. "Go way now!"

I saw my reflection superimposed on her face and noticed that I was wearing an idiotic, nervous smile. I was trying to assure her I meant no harm, which didn't mean I wasn't going to cause her any.

"Please, Mrs. Harris? Could you let me in for a minute? I've been sent here from Camp Lejeune to …"

"I know why you here! I ain't 'lowin' you in my house!"

She turned and disappeared into the darkness inside. A sticky substance was sliding down the window. She had spit at me.

I walked down the steps, back up again, back down, totally at a loss what to do. On the drive up, I had rehearsed my speech. The adjutant had even given me written instructions on what to say and how to conduct myself. It was just like the military to devise a procedure for compassion.

I went to the car for the pack of cigarettes I had left on the front seat. It was Lillian Harris's immediate recognition of why I was there that confused me most; I'd thought there would be an interval between my arrival and the moment I broke the news, some brief moment for us both to compose ourselves. While I smoked, debating what to do next—this was a kind of mission and it had to be accomplished—Lillian Harris opened the door. She was a woman of average height but with thick legs and a stout body suggesting masculine strength. She motioned me inside.

A photograph of Sergeant Roy Harris in dress blues stood in an easel frame on a lamp stand. Now I knew what he looked like. Lillian Harris did not ask me to sit down, so I stayed on my feet, sweating in stifling air barely stirred by the small fan on the table in front of the couch on which she sat. She was looking at me with so much rage and so much grief the two had cancelled each other out, leaving an expression that would have been taken for indifference by someone ignorant of what had happened.

"Say what you gotta say, then get out," she said.

I tried to summon the words I had rehearsed.

"Mrs. Harris, Sergeant ... Roy, I mean ... Your son, Roy? I regret to inform you that he died in Vietnam two days ago. He was wounded by a mortar shell. It ... after he was wounded, he died in the hospital. I'd like to express my personal regrets and on behalf of the commandant of the Marine Corps ... I mean, he wishes to express his regrets ..."

I fell silent, shocked by my inarticulateness, by the counterfeit sorrow in my voice. Fifteen of my friends had been killed the year I was in the war. I had bled and bled inside for them, until I could not bleed for anyone anymore, least of all for a stranger.

"So you said what you gotta say. Now get out. Y'all just get on out of here."

I was supposed to ask if she wanted a military ceremony but decided to leave that to someone else. Some missions had to be aborted. Lillian Harris saw me to the door, then slammed it behind me. Looking over my shoulder, I saw the dark mask of her face in the window; then she turned into the house.

Driving out of nigra town, I saw the same kids playing amidst the same heaps of rusted junk. Across the river, the two old men still sat under the statue of the Confederate soldier. Its shadow had hardly moved.

SEVEN

Bye-bye, Everybody

The tear sheets in my scrapbook already have the patina of historical documents. Their headlines would look to today's generation as those from World War II looked to me.

SAIGON DEFENSES WEAKEN;
U.S. MOVING OUT ALL YANKS

RESCUE LAST YANKS

LONGEST U.S. WAR ENDS

Yes, it was the longest in our history, but because it was also the weirdest, no one could say how long, no one could fix the date of its beginning. There had been no Pearl Harbor, no crossing of a 38th Parallel, so when did it start? Historians argued about it like cosmologists debating the moment of the Big Bang. If you wanted to take the broad, epic view, you could say that our involvement in Vietnam really began in December 1675, when the New England colonists trapped a thousand of King Philip's Indians in a Rhode Island swamp and did God's work by killing them all. Or, at the other end of Manifest Destiny, you could say it started in 1890, when the U.S. Census Bureau proclaimed the frontier closed, the last Sioux brave fell to the Winchesters at Wounded Knee, and we found ourselves in undisputed possession of everything from sea to shining sea and, in need of new frontiers as well as new Devils to conquer or convert, gazed across the Pacific toward Asia. Eight years later, we took the Philippines from the Spanish, and then spent nearly three years battling Moro guerrillas in a nasty foreshadowing of what we would do in Indochina.

But maybe that view is a little *too* broad.

Then there's the view of the men who fought in the war. For them, it started the day they landed in-country, though it did not necessarily end when they left at the end of their tours. Wars never end for the warriors, unless, of course, they're killed.

But that view is a little *too* narrow.

Look for a date, at least a year, for Christ's sake. Trying to pin one down is like trying to hold a droplet of mercury between your fingertips. Was it in 1954, when, with a handful of bush spooks and military advisers, we filled the vacuum left by the departing, defeated French? When the first adviser was killed in 1961? When U.S. helicopter pilots began ferrying South Vietnamese troops into battle in 1963? When Lyndon Johnson bamboozled Congress into passing the Tonkin Gulf Resolution in August 1964? When U.S. planes began bombing North Vietnam in February 1965? When the first brigade of marines landed at Da Nang four weeks later? When?

The Vietnamese had no problems with their historical calendars. The war had a clear beginning for them: November 23, 1946, when the French fleet shelled Haiphong, killing six thousand civilians. The Vietnamese didn't make any but the most cursory distinctions between the French war and the American one. They didn't care what language was spoken by the men who fired the shells and dropped the bombs, didn't care if the soldier stomping through their rice paddies came from Lyon or Philadelphia, so perhaps it was fitting that the Vietnamese, in the spring of 1975, were bringing the war to a conclusion whose date would not be subject to doubt or discussion.

We had been in Beirut for nine or ten months when news of renewed fighting in Vietnam clattered from the wire service telexes; Beirut as it was before the Lebanese Civil War, a glittering city. The vast apartment Jill and I rented near the American University overlooked the Mediterranean from the front, its rear terrace faced the mountains.

Almost every expatriate we knew had a place like ours, everyone had a live-in maid and nanny, dined out several times a week, and threw parties catered by squads of Arab waiters in white jackets. For roving correspondents, the city was a base of operations as well as a refuge. It had a lot wrong with it—trash piled in stinking mounds in the best neighborhoods ("worse than New York," the bankers grumbled), you had to baksheesh the phone man and the electric company if you wanted to talk to your friends and not live in the dark, the water supply was contaminated with typhus and other microbes—but after a time in dour Damascus, or in teeming Cairo, or in dry Riyadh, the sight of Beirut, shining like a tiara along her crescent shore, made your heart rise into your throat.

"This is as good as it gets," Nick Proffitt said to me often. "I come back from one of those bongo-land shitholes, I hit this town on the run."

Not that we spent much time in town. In early seventy-five, I was on the road more than I was at home, spending the first half of January in Algiers, to cover an OPEC Conference, half of February in Cairo, for a visit to Egypt by then Soviet foreign minister Andrei Gromyko, and then two or three days in Paris, to cover an arms-buying trip by Egypt's President Sadat.

I had been back less than two weeks when Oneway knocked at my front door. He had temporarily inhabited the body of Charlie Glass, who is today a well-known ABC television correspondent but who was then a young, obscure stringer. Half Lebanese (the other half was Irish), Glass had been in the Middle East for a few years and had a lot of contacts. Among them was a man named Omar, an agent for guerrillas fighting the Ethiopians for the independence of the former Italian colony of Eritrea. First against the American-backed emperor, Haile Selassie, and now against the Soviet-backed Marxist government that dethroned him, the Eritrean Liberation Front had been at war for almost fifteen years, but no foreign correspondents had covered the rebellion. Conditions were very harsh. Much of Eritrea was desert, with summer temperatures of a hundred and thirty degrees; the rebels, lacking motor transport, traveled on foot and horseback, sometimes by camel caravan, and the Ethiopians had warned that any correspondent caught with them would be executed.

Omar was in Beirut lobbying for the Front. Its leaders, deciding they needed publicity as well, had authorized him to invite western journalists to cover the rebellion. He went to Charlie, and Charlie had come to me.

If I was game, he said, we would leave for Khartoum, where the ELF underground would help us get to Kassala, near the Sudanese-Eritrean frontier. From there, guerrillas would have to smuggle us over the border at night because the Sudan wished to maintain good relations with Ethiopia and didn't want it publicized that the rebels were operating from its territory.

My blood was up, and if I did not already know that Glass was really Oneway, weaving another spell, his parting words convinced me: "We really oughta go, Phil. You know there's parts of Eritrea no white man has ever seen."

Three days later, I was in Khartoum. I had gone more or less against orders. At first, the foreign desk had given me the green light; a while later, foreign editor Yuenger phoned to say he was having second thoughts. Wasn't there too much going on in the Middle East for me to vanish into the wastes to cover some bush rebellion? *No, no!* He wanted a day or two to think it over. While he did, I booked passage on Air Sudan and went AWOL, banking on recent successes to avoid being fired: I had won an Overseas Press Club Award for the series on my capture, and the *Tribune* had given me its in-house prize, the Edward Scott Beck Award, for my coverage of the October War. I was also counting on getting a story of sufficient drama to overcome objections to my going over the hill.

As things turned out, I had to rely on the stature vouchsafed by the prizes: there was no story. Glass and I, accompanied by three other journalists—Don McCullin, who was taking photographs for the London *Sunday Times*, Colin Smith from the London *Observer*, and Stefan Haimersson, a Swedish correspondent—spent almost two weeks walking across the desert with a rebel band escorting an arms caravan to a provincial town where the ELF had besieged a small Ethiopian garrison. We trekked over two hundred miles, suffering bouts of dysentery from the stinking water drawn from muddy wells but never heard so much as a single rifle shot. Besides heat, sand, thirst, and loose bowels, we had to endure our guide and translator, a miserable, buck-toothed ideologue who seemed incapable of speaking except in Marxist slogans and who took every opportunity to tell

Glass and me that America was the cause of all Third World suffering. It was useless to remind him that the Russians were the Ethiopians' new sponsor.

Eritrea did turn out to be something of a terra incognita. Resting in a wadi through the blaze of one afternoon, a young tribal boy came up to us and started rubbing our skin because he thought the white had been painted on. Occasionally we came across wandering bands of Hadendowa and Beni-Amer warriors, wild-looking men wearing bushel baskets of wiry hair, armed with ancient Mausers, even with swords and spears. Once, a group of Baggara horsemen, magnificent anachronisms in streaming white robes, galloped past us on their Arabian ponies. I was thrilled to see all that, and it would have been great stuff if I had been on assignment for *National Geographic*.

When we straggled back into Khartoum, we scared up a few spooks and political officers in the American and British embassies to give us off-the-record background on the rebellion, so we would have something to say. With that and generous padding, I managed to write two dispatches. They helped save me from the unemployment office. Still, when I returned to Beirut, I got a long-distance chewing out from Yuenger, who suggested that I send out my résumé the next time I got an idea to disappear.

On the other side of Asia, the cease-fire in Vietnam had collapsed, after holding, more or less, for two years. The North Vietnamese had seized a few districts and towns in border provinces, but it did not look like a general offensive. I went through the motions of family life for the next three weeks, then I was on a plane for Saudi Arabia with Proffitt and John Palmer, then NBC's Middle East correspondent. King Faisal had been assassinated, not, as was first thought, by a revolutionary, but by a mad nephew.

Nick and I returned to Beirut five days later. On the flight back, all we talked about was Vietnam, for Hue and Da Nang had fallen by then. All that stood between the North Vietnamese and Saigon were one or two government divisions that, Nick said, "couldn't lick the California National Guard."

Hue and Da Nang, now Vietcong property. Da Nang, where I had landed with that first marine brigade ten years before, almost to the day. I was distracted and restless, unable to even go through the motions of husbanding and fathering, unable to concentrate in the office. I shared it with Palmer and drove him and our secretary, Lillian Siman, half crazy, asking if they had heard anything new about the situation in Vietnam. The office was on a small street three blocks from Reuters, so when I wasn't pestering Palmer and Lillian, I plagued Reuters with requests for copies of their Saigon correspondent's stories. Qui Nhon, Quang Ngai, Kontum, Pleiku, Phan Rang, Loc Ninh, An Loc—all had fallen, all those places with the eerie, menacing names that had been in American living rooms for a decade.

Proffitt phoned me in the office. Had I seen the latest? There was fighting in the Delta now; the VC and North Vietnamese army were closing on Saigon from three directions.

"Looks like it's the bottom of the ninth and Charlie's got his best pitcher on the mound."

I said what I had been afraid to say, even to myself.

"Nick, it's crazy, but I've got to be there. I don't know why, I've just got to."

"Know what you mean, el-tee. There's an Air France leaving for Saigon tomorrow. I'm on it. Fucking *volunteered*."

I hung up, more distracted than ever. I couldn't do it to Jill and the kids. To go off on something like this ... What would happen if I got stuck in Saigon when the boys with the red stars on their pith helmets marched in? While I wrestled with my moral quandary, Lillian came in with a telex that absolved me of responsibility.

CAPUTO: YATES NEEDS HELP IN SAIGON. WHEN CAN U LEAVE? CHEERS/YUENGER.

I phoned Air France. Of course there were plenty of seats available. Sitting in front of the telex, I tapped out a message that gave me a weird feeling, some alloy of excitement and terror.

YUENGER: SAIGONWARDS AIR FRANCE TOMORROW FOUR PYEM. RGDS/CAPUTO/BEIRUT.

Nick and I settled back in the ample seats as the stewardess spread a linen cloth on our trays. She set down champagne glasses while another stewardess wheeled up a cart with the bubbly chilling in an ice bucket. *Newsweek* and the *Tribune* allowed their correspondents to travel first-class on flights of over eight hours, and we'd taken advantage of that policy. Why not?

Nick raised his glass in toast.

"This is as good as it's gonna get, el-tee."

I was glad we were together. Somehow Nick's presence made the venture seem less crazy. With him beside me, I could look upon leaving wife and children for a surrounded capital as a reasonable thing to do. The son of a career army sergeant out of Harlan County, Kentucky, Nick had been raised at Fort Huachuca, Arizona. After leaving high school, he enlisted and got his sergeant's stripes during the early part of the Vietnam War. He had not fought in it; he'd buried its dead as a member of the Third Infantry, "The Old Guard." They're the blue-clad soldiers who carry the coffins to Arlington, who fire the salutes and play taps and fold the flags and hand them to the widows. After his discharge, Nick took a journalism degree from the University of Arizona, did a spell with AP, then joined *Newsweek*, which sent him to Saigon when he was twenty-eight, the youngest bureau chief in the magazine's history.

He had his romantic side—he had bought a small ranch in northern Montana and vowed to go there someday to write a novel—but, as befitted an army brat and an ex–news agency man, he was generally tough-minded and clearheaded, not given to the morbid introspectiveness that often made me brood about things for hours. I needn't feel guilty about going back to Vietnam, in his view, needn't dig into my psyche for deep motives and justifications. We were newsmen, and the North Vietnamese offensive was a big story. If Saigon fell, it would be one of the biggest stories of the decade.

But I wasn't sure that's why I was going and, despite Nick's injunctions against it, plunged into self-examination. I had plenty of time for it during that sixteen-hour flight. We touched down in Tehran for refueling when I confessed to myself that my job was only an excuse to get myself into Vietnam. My motives had little to do with journalism; they were literary and personal. I had been working again on *A Rumor of War* after a long hiatus and had decided to make it a memoir rather a novel. The book seemed to be working better as nonfiction, but it still went into frequent narrative stalls because I had not gotten over the war; it remained an open emotional circuit. Vietnam, both as historical event and as personal experience, lacked closure. Now the event was moving toward completion, and if I were there to witness it, perhaps the circle would be closed within myself.

But that was only half the answer. We were thirty thousand feet over India as I focused my temporal telescope on a balmy night in 1959, when two friends and I sat at a suburban bus stop dreaming aloud about lions and Africa. Mike Pope and Larry Downey were my classmates at Fenwick, a stern Catholic school for boys in Oak Park. Its three stories of fieldstone walls looked down on Washington Boulevard with the severe, unshakable serenity of its Dominican priests' convictions; its classrooms, somber in the light admitted by narrow Gothic windows, enclosed boys in sweaters and ties, droning Algebraic formulas, Latin declensions, the precepts of Thomas Aquinas. It was a great prep school for the sons of working stiffs, but we three were romantic dreamers united by a yearning to flee it, its discipline, and our middle-class homes for lives of adventure. We were going to be test pilots and scuba-diving heroes like Lloyd Bridges' Mike Nelson on the TV series "Sea Hunt." Charmed by another show, "Route 66," we talked about buying a Corvette and taking off down the fabled highway. Hemingway, Oak Park's most famous native son, was the inspiration for another scheme. After reading *The Green Hills of Africa*, Mike persuaded Larry and me to forget the Corvette, forget the scuba diving, and go on safari to Africa.

Now he and Larry both had a flair for stirring phrases. Once in our armchair adventuring, Larry had declared, "Boys, we are going to dedicate our lives to the conquest of human limitations!" Mike's rhetorical gifts were the greater, and he had a penchant for the threatrical probably inherited from the amateur actors in his family. He gave his finest performance one fine spring night during our safari planning. Mike, who lived in Oak Park, had come out to Westchester after school to discuss the guns we would need and whether we should go to Uganda, Kenya, or Tanganyika. We settled on Tanganyika because we liked the sound of it and because it was the home of the Serengeti Plain. Mike had read about the Serengeti in *The Green Hills of Africa*.

It was dark when we finished talking. The warm winds and earthy smells made us more restless than ever as Larry and I walked Mike to the stop where he would catch a bus back to Oak Park.

Under a dome of stars, we sat on the bench to wait with him. Looking past the glare of the street lamp beside the phone booth, Mike began to talk about the skies over the Serengeti. His soliloquy was spellbinding. He described those African heavens so vividly I could see them, as I could see the gun bearer M'cola's face in the firelight, as I could hear the roar of lions and Masai drums. It was a remarkable performance for a seventeen-year-old who had never been closer to Africa than a geography book. When he was through, I felt I could not stand another second of my life if we did not leave immediately, but Mike was not yet finished with his sorcery. Somehow, he segued into reading from Eugene O'Neill. He had a copy of O'Neill's plays, one of which, *Beyond the Horizon,* we were supposed to read for our American Lit class. Larry and I had been too busy researching elephant guns to begin it. Mike had, and he begged us to listen. First, he set up the scene—a country road, plowed fields, Robert Mayo, a farm boy with itchy feet, sitting on a fence, talking to his pragmatic brother, Andrew, who has asked him why he's leaving home to go to sea.

"Here's Robert's answer," Mike said. "You guys have got to listen to this." He cleared his throat and, holding the book up to the street lamp, began to read. "'Supposing I was to tell you that it's just Beauty that's calling me. The beauty of the far off and unknown, the mystery and spell of the East which lures me in the books I've read, the need of the freedom of great wide spaces, the joy of wandering on and on—in quest of the secret which is hidden over there, beyond the horizon? Suppose I told you that was the one and only reason for my going?'"

"Holy shit! That's great!" said Larry as Mike closed the book.

I asked to look at it, as if I didn't believe such words could exist. I read silently … *beauty of the far off and unknown … spell of the East … in quest of the secret which is hidden over there, beyond the horizon …* Those phrases could have been our trio's anthem and battle cry, our challenge hurled at the mundane tyranny of the split-levels across the street, at the dreary bus stop and its cracked bench painted with advertisements for E-Z credit and hemorrhoid remedies. Each word was a goblet of fat dripping into my smoldering imagination, raising it to a bright and blinding flame. In its glare I saw, or thought I did, my purpose in my life: to go in quest of a hidden secret. If some hardhead pragmatist like Andrew Mayo—my father, say—had asked,

"What secret?" I would not have known the answer. Probably, I did not want to know. To have identified the secret would have been to limit the limitless possibilities promised by a quest with no definite goal.

But why, I wondered as the skies over Burma brightened, had I ended up in so many ugly places, on battlefields and the terrorist's killing fields, if all I'd wanted in my youth was to find the secret and beauty beyond the horizon? The temporal telescope extended farther back, to when I was in eighth grade, studying for a parish scholarship to Fenwick, although I dreaded going to the school. My parents and my eighth-grade teacher, one Sister Joan Clare, however, had more or less sworn I would attend whatever my feelings about it. Sister saw in me signs of delinquency which Fenwick's boot-camp regimen would curb; my family hoped its strong academics would help me get into college, for they believed in the American metaphor of the generational ladder. My immigrant great-grandfather had been a total illiterate, his daughter, my grandmother Rose, had finished grammar school, her son high school ... so, you, Philip, ARE GOING TO GET A DEGREE. I studied for the scholarship with a zeal, studied to the point that I suffered from monster migraines that knocked me flat. A sense of filial duty was only one of the reasons I worked so hard; fear was the other. Reluctant as I was to subject myself to Fenwick's rigors, I was frightened that if I did not get in, I would never go to college and become a disappointment, a leather-jacketed loser in a ducktail haircut, a broken rung on the generational ladder. Yet I realized, in a way I could not articulate, that my mother and father had lived with that same fear of failure ever since the Great Depression. It was a kind of social vertigo: you could stick to the straight and narrow and play by the rules and still fall from the ladder, toward poverty's abyss. To take chances, do the unusual, play by your own rules instead of life's would be to *invite* a disastrous plummet.

So I studied deep into the nights, and the image of my thirteen-year-old self, squinting under a desk lamp with my head pounding, showed me the source of my attraction to dangerous and violent situations. My parents' caution had become my own caution, and I hated it, even as an eighth-grade kid. It was dragging me against my will to a strict school I dreaded attending; in the future, if I did not overcome it, it would drag me into a life I dreaded leading, a narrow life of restricted horizons. I would marry, settle down, do what was expected of me, but would never discover the undiscovered country. Because childhood, like a chronic disease, is something we never get over, that *fear of risk* never left me. I could no more get rid of it than I could change the color of my eyes, and its despotism had to be defied by periodically throwing myself into harm's way. I couldn't wage that struggle by taking up hang gliding or skydiving because stunts did not interest me, because the battlefield was the kingdom of the great mother fear of the great mother death. To vanquish it, I thought, was to vanquish all its children.

The needle-nose F-5s were roaring off the military runway at Tan Son Nhut airport. They had South Vietnamese markings now; so did the helicopters parked near the terminal, like huge home appliances awaiting shipment. A couple of American technicians were crawling over them as the Air France plane taxied to a stop. Small men wearing earphones towed the boarding stairs across the tarmac, the door opened, and Nick and I stepped into that familiar heat—like warm, wet plastic food wrapper clamping over your face. A medevac chopper twirled out of the monsoon clouds toward a landing zone marked by a big red cross.

"Home sweet home," Proffitt said.

Tony Clifton, one of *Newsweek*'s team, met us at the terminal and led us to a jeep driven by an unusually chipper Vietnamese named Hoang.

"Okay, I'm here," said Nick, tossing his luggage in back, "you can rotate back to Hong Kong."

"Yeah, don't I bloody wish," Clifton answered in his Australian accent. "Yeahr donaye blahdy wish."

"Only reason Rome wasn't built in a day ..."

"I know, I know, Proffitt. 'Cuz you weren't in charge of that detail."

"There it is."

First the rice paddies and the villages peeking from behind bamboo and palm, like guerrillas in ambush. Then the endless acres of refugee slums, shacks nailed together out of America's trash, walls made of flattened beer cans. The hordes of kids with inflamed skin ulcers, as if they'd been hugged by an octopus whose suckers ripped off circles of skin when it let them go. The women in conical hats jouncing under shoulder poles. The stilt huts alongside canals black as tar, plague and malaria in the air. Then the city, its streets even in those final days a chaos of bikes and scooters and old Dodges with proud tail fins. Near the center of town you could walk on the traffic if you were very nimble. The currency hucksters stood by their stalls, offering rolls of piasters with big denominations on top and wads of worthless paper underneath, the gangs of cyclo drivers lurked at the corners on their pedal-driven rickshaws, each hissing to every foreigner that he knew a girl numbah one virgin no VD no shit very cheap. A man with twisted arms and legs crawled on his belly. No one paid the least attention to him, inching along like a crippled crab. Saigon was the same as ever, an old harlot of a city, disgusting and sad.

Clifton brought us up-to-date. The North Vietnamese, after seizing half the country and destroying the South's best divisions, had stopped their advance. They were probably digesting, but the pause had inspired the Great American Delusion machine, still functioning smoothly after all these years, to create a new Wishful Thought: the Communists did not want to conquer the South, just enough of it to put themselves in a strong position for a negotiated settlement.

"That's what *your* embassy is saying. The Charlies want to bargain for a coalition government."

Nick shook his head.

"They've been fighting for this for thirty years, and now they've almost got it and we think they want to *talk?*"

"As you say, 'There it is.'"

Near the intersection of Tu Do Street and Le Loi Boulevard, Hoang almost ran over a legless man whose trunk sat on a board to which furniture casters had been attached. In an amazing display of survival, he wheeled himself across the boulevard and through the traffic, propelling himself with his arms.

We pulled up in front of the Continental Palace, oozing mildewed colonial splendor. The ground floor, an expansive terrace with arches opened to the street, was known as the Continental Shelf. It had always been the social center for Saigon's community of journalists, diplomats, and double, triple, and quadruple agents, but the journalists claimed it exclusively on that day. There appeared to be hundreds of them, boisterously slaking their thirsts with tart citron pressés, keeping off the malaria with gin and tonics, and creating, as journalists always do en masse, an atmosphere of cheap excitement. As Nick and I climbed out of the jeep, I heard a familiar British voice call out, "Hey, Caputo! ... Phil! ... What the hell are you doing here? Last time I saw you, a camel was farting in your face."

I looked toward the Shelf and saw Colin Smith's boyish face. Had it been only six weeks since we trekked together across Eritrea? I reached up to shake his hand, and a small horde of urchins leapt past me and onto the Shelf. One snatched the sandwich off Colin's plate and ran off, the others chasing him, like gulls after the one bird that caught the fish.

"Bloody little bastard," Smith huffed. "Stealing everything from me. Some tart nicked my passport right off the bar the other night. Tried to use it to get out of the country."

"Any resemblance?"

"None that I know of," he said, grinning through his sunburn. "Anyway, I got it back. Good to see you. We must have dinner after you've checked in."

Meanwhile, Proffitt, the old Saigon bureau chief, was being greeted by half the press corps. It was like a class reunion. Every newsman who had spent more than a week in Vietnam had returned.

"All come for end," Hoang said to me with his cheerful smile.

The desk clerk gave me a third-floor room. A wizened old man in white cotton pajamas led me to it, his sandaled feet whispering on the tiles of the stifling corridor. The room was already occupied—sitting on the dresser like a stuffed animal in a child's room was a rat about the size of a house cat. The old man whisked him out with a broom. Gecko lizards clung to the walls, but we did not evict them because they were supposed to bring good luck. Also, they ate mosquitoes. The old man turned on the overhead fan and the air conditioner—neither worked very well—and asked with gestures if I wanted opium. I shook my head. With more gestures, he asked if I desired a girl. I shook my head again and with gestures of my own told him all I wanted was sleep. I tipped him for all services rendered as well as those offered and refused.

After he left, I stood in front of the air conditioner—the only way to feel its effect—and looked down at the neoclassical opera house that had become the National Assembly Building. Across the square was the Caravelle, an ugly hotel with a great rooftop bar. I had gotten very drunk there one night on R and R and watched flares hanging over the Delta like sparkling candelabra. It wasn't those lights I remembered, though, but the sight of the evil green hills around Da Nang falling away from me the day I left Vietnam, July 12, 1966. I had never felt so relieved to see anything in my life; those awful hills with their snipers and ambushes and booby traps, their dripping forests and sawtoothed elephant grass, falling away. I had promised myself never to return, but now I had and wondered how I felt about it. Not about how I was supposed to feel, not about the manufactured, boilerplate emotions that were the journalist's stock-in-trade when he or she wrote mood pieces or tearjerkers, but how I truly felt. That was when a ghost sergeant began to call a ghostly roll in my head. Fernandez. Gauthier. Guzman. Levy. Lockhart. Manning. Page. Reasoner. Simpson. Sissler. Snow. Sullivan. Warner. West. All present and accounted for, *sir.* All dead, and, if the North Vietnamese won, dead for nothing. I guessed I felt angry about that, sold out, betrayed, though by whom I could not say. The Congress? General Westmoreland? Jane Fonda? All of the above? Then I thought about those orphans downstairs, forced to steal food off plates, and about the legless man wheeling himself on his homemade cart, and about the day, long ago, when I'd flown with a colonel to a valley that was being cleared by our battalion. Three companies had been dropped on the north side of the Vu Gia River, one on the south side. I had been an assistant operations officer then, and I had practically begged my boss and the colonel not to leave that one company isolated, with a wide river between them and reinforcements. Whatchyew talking about lootenant? They're gonna have a forward air controller with them, gonna have an artillery forward observer with them, any trouble, they'll call the wrath of God down on Charlie. *Firepower,* lootenant. So they went and walked into a battalion of NVA regulars, who taught a lesson about firepower by opening up all at once with machine guns, mortars, and recoilless cannon. In less than half an hour, one hundred and seventy-two officers and men became sixty-four. Now the battalion was taking revenge. As the colonel and I flew over the valley, a dozen or more villages were burning and a Skyhawk was torching a few more with napalm. The colonel said: "My, it certainly is a lovely valley, isn't it?"

I guessed I felt angry about all that, too. Maybe the other side did not deserve to win, but ours sure as hell deserved to lose.

Ron Yates, then the *Tribune's* man in Southeast Asia, was a genial young giant, six-four in his stocking feet, to which the cowboy boots he sometimes wore added another inch and a half. With his soft prairie drawl and his brushy brown mustache, he might have been the reincarnation of his great-grandfather, a frontier Kansas sheriff shot to death while leading a posse against a gang of bank robbers. For the past month, Yates had been covering both the North Vietnamese onslaught and the Khmer Rouge offensive in Cambodia. Out to the Central Highlands, up to Da Nang, back to Saigon, off to Phnom Penh. When I knocked at his door, on the Continental's second floor, he was as glad to see me as I had been to see Rick Soll in Israel. He opened an ice chest, crammed with beer purchased from the U.S. Commissary at Tan Son Nhut, and popped a can for each of us. He had been under a lot of competitive pressure from the Chicago *Daily News,* which had two correspondents in Vietnam: a young one named Bob Tamarkin and an old one, Keyes Beech, one of the deans of the Far East press corps. Beech had been covering Asia over thirty years. From Japan to Thailand, there was hardly a politician, general, spook, or ambassador who didn't know him, and those who didn't had at least heard of him. So far, Yates said with some pride, he had been more than holding his own—youth counted for something—but he was delighted I'd showed up to lend a hand.

It was a very hot afternoon and we opened two more beers, Yates echoing Clifton about the Great American Delusion Machine. The embassy was floating a story that a negotiated settlement was still possible, if the army held and if President Thieu resigned. That was the current party line, although, with a single exception, no one believed it, not even the embassy political officers who were feeding it to the press. The exception was Ambassador Graham Martin. He had convinced himself there was still a chance, possibly because he had a personal, emotional stake in seeing that South Vietnam remained on the map: his son, a platoon commander, had been killed in action in 1966. The facts, though, made it impossible for Martin to convince anyone else.

The feudal army of a feudal society, officered by corrupt warlords, the Arvin's (Army of the Republic of Vietnam) inherent flaws ripped wide open once the American prop was pulled out from under it and it had to face its first real test in battle on its own. It had not just retreated in the Central Highlands and at Hue and Da Nang, it had dissolved, whole regiments at a time. Yates's guess was that the North Vietnamese had paused not to figure *what* to do but how to take Saigon as quickly and cleanly as possible. Once they formulated their plan, their big green machine (they had sixteen divisions in the South) would roll toward the capital. It would be my job to cover the military story while Yates handled the political and diplomatic angles. Once again, I was to be the paper's *bang-bang* correspondent.

So it was odd that my first story had nothing to do with bombardments, battalions, attacks, and repulses but with a far more commonplace horror—a plane crash. A C5-A cargo plane carrying 319 people, 243 of them Vietnamese war orphans, had a pressurization failure minutes after takeoff from Tan Son Nhut. Its rear cargo doors blew out, and it went down in the rice paddies north of the city, killing 199, most of them kids. It was the worst air disaster in American aviation history.

Impossible to look at all those small bodies, burnt and dismembered in the paddy mud, and not go numb. The only thing I felt was a dull anger. The U.S. Defense Attaché's Office, which was organizing the evacuation of the orphans, had more flights planned. The operation had been dubbed a "mission of mercy" and the aircraft were called "mercy planes," but the real purpose of the flights was to provide a cover for evacuating Americans. Forty-three of DAO's female employees had been aboard the C5-A that had unmercifully crashed, and half of them had been killed. After touring the crash site, I went to the DAO compound to gather the necessary statistics. It was in "Pentagon East," the big brick building—it reminded me of an enormous high school—that had been Westmoreland's headquarters. I got the numbers and then began to ask a few impertinent questions of a woman with the prickly, defensive manner of a midlevel bureaucrat, a

GS-10, say. Where were these kids being flown to? To a processing center in the United States, to wait there for American families to adopt them. Why had we waited until now to evacuate them? She looked at me as if I were mad. The *Communists* were overrunning the country, orphanages had been abandoned. But, Madame, do we suppose the Communists are incapable of caring for orphans? The fact is, aren't we using these kids as a way of getting our nonessential personnel out of the country without alarming the South Vietnamese? The woman glared at me. I softened the question. These kids were Vietnamese, so what right did we have to pluck them out of their country and spirit them to ours? Every right in the world, the woman said with her gray eyes boring into mine, and I saw it then—the righteous glimmer of the American missionary off to save the world. One could argue that if we had left well enough alone, one hundred and forty-three children would not have been spewed across a rice paddy—a literal case of better Red than dead—but the habit of rescuing Vietnamese from themselves was too ingrained. The spirit of Graham Greene's quiet American, Pyle, lived on: a destructive innocence.

I filed a hard-news piece: no anger, no horror, just the straight stuff: SAIGON—*At least 199 persons, most of them orphans between eight months and 12 years old, died Friday when ...*

Proffitt had the right take on the mercy mission.

"It's a goddamned government-sponsored kidnapping."

My memories of the next week to ten days are fragmentary. The yellowing clips in my scrapbooks are of little help. There are none between the plane crash, at the beginning of April, and the renewal of the offensive, two weeks later, because nothing happened. As a military correspondent, I was temporarily unemployed; so was Nick, who had the same assignment as I. We covered the briefings the Arvin command held at five o'clock every afternoon. Officers standing on a stage in crisp, starched uniforms and speaking nonsense while they pointed at a big lighted map covered in military symbols—the sessions were the Five o'clock Follies all over again, minstrel shows in yellow face. The North Vietnamese had been stopped, said the briefers, who had been Through the Looking Glass so long they couldn't remember what it looked like on the other side. The Arvin were pulling themselves together ... If need be, they would turn Saigon into another Stalingrad ...

But when it came to creativity, the North Vietnamese proved themselves as superior to the Southerners as they had on the battle-field. Yes, it was our weirdest war, and the press conferences held at the North Vietnamese army compound were among its weirdest moments. The 1973 truce permitted the NVA to keep a detachment of "cease-fire observers" in Saigon. Their compound, a few quonset huts surrounded by barbed wire and guarded by *bo-doi* (the NVA equivalent of GIs), was near Tan Son Nhut.

The first briefing I attended was fascinating, though not for any-thing they said. It was fascinating to meet, without fear of death or capture, the invisible enemy I had fought for sixteen months. When the press bus parked in front of the compound, I was almost hypno-tized by the sight of the young *bo-doi* sentry with his green pith hel-met and AK-47. I wanted to touch him to assure myself he was not a deadly phantom but a creature of flesh and blood. I wanted to ask him a thousand questions. Were you guys as scared of us as we were of you? How did you always know where we were and what we were doing? What was it like to be under a B-52 strike? What did you eat? Did you get R and R, letters from home, packages from Mom? What about your officers? Were they assholes? Your buddies? Did you lose a lot of them? How did you learn to move so well at night? Do you miss your girlfriend? Ever feel like throwing your rifle down and say-ing Fuck this war and going home and getting laid? What are you going to do when it's over?

We filed into a Quonset hut and sat at a long table. There, in front of me, at a table perpendicular to ours, sat a dozen phantoms. Officer phantoms, wearing light-green shirts, olive-green trousers, red shoulder tabs with their rank insignia in gold. I gawked. They were smoking cigarettes. Smoke came out of their mouths and nos-trils, so they must have been real people. Proffitt saw me staring and understood why.

"Beaucoup VC, right, el-tee?" he said with a laugh.

They were led by a colonel with sunken eyes, sunken cheeks, a pointy chin, and crooked teeth. He resembled a death's head in need of a dental appointment. He began to read from a prepared text, its prose, overburdened by the clichés of the Third World canon, lumbering like a truck with bad shocks. In brief, it was this: there were no North Vietnamese divisions in the South, and what we in the bourgeois press called an offensive was in reality a People's Uprising against the the corrupt puppet regime and the U.S. imperialist aggressors.

It took the colonel some twenty minutes to say that. Most of the correspondents were shaking their heads; what they had just heard made the Follies sound as true as mathematics. The colonel called for questions. No one raised his hand except me. I knew I was being a little naive, knew I should have thanked the colonel for telling us the North's side of the story and gone back to the bus, but I was angry again. I was angry that the colonel took us for such fools, angry because I had seen, just two days before, a small horror no amount of lies and propaganda could sanitize.

Colin Smith and I had gone to the Delta to cover the aftermath of a minor skirmish. It had been the only action in several days and an unusual event: the Arvins had won, repelling a Vietcong assault on an airfield. Smith and I got there for the mop-up, joining a South Vietnamese battalion as it swept across a plain of reeds toward some villages that were being strafed by gunships. The reeds, chest high, made it difficult to see what lay ahead. That was how I stepped into the brains of a North Vietnamese soldier. Lying on his back, his AK just beyond the grasp of his curled fingers, he had been shot between the eyes *bangyerdead.* The back of his skull had been blown out. What had been the hair on the back of his head was now one with what had been on top, the piece extending from his forehead like a pelt. Flattened by the bullet, his brains lay a few inches beyond. I thought they resembled a blob of gray pudding as, tottering to avoid tripping over the soldier's body, I stepped into them. I let out a panicked half yell, half laugh, leapt aside, and scraped my boot in the dirt as if I were trying to remove a wad of chewing gum. I made some sort of awful joke about giving the dead man a headache, which shocked Colin. He must have thought me extremely callous when all I really was was hysterical. The brain, after all, is what distinguishes us from beasts, isn't it? The repository of each human being's thoughts, memories, dreads, hopes, and longings, isn't it? Now the dead soldier's thoughts, memories, dreads, hopes, and longings were on the sole of my boot. It seemed as if they, to punish me for such a desecration, would seep through rubber and leather and into my bloodstream to haunt my own brain for the rest of my life. So I laughed like a looney and tried to joke my horror away.

The colonel's nonsense not only cheapened that horror but mocked the sacrifice of that young soldier. What the hell do you mean, a *people's uprising?* I asked. Tanks rolled through Hue and Da Nang, there was at least one armored division in the South, and Arvin soldiers were being shelled by long-range heavy guns. Where the hell did *the people* get all that hardware? Did they make it in backyard machine shops?

The colonel lit a cigarette and said that The People were using weapons and equipment captured from the puppet army. Excuse me, sir, but the tanks were Russian T-54s, the guns Russian-made one-thirties. Ah, he answered, The People also had weapons and equipment supplied by fraternal socialist nations. And which nations were those?

My colleagues were coughing, telling me with looks, Come off it, Caputo. The colonel knows it's bullshit, he knows that we know it's bullshit, it's a game. So shut up and let's get the hell out of here and have a beer. The colonel sensed their restlessness and made good use of it to avoid further questions. With an uneven grin, he called an end to the press conference and invited us to tea.

Triangulated by disinformation from Saigon, Hanoi, and the U.S. Embassy, Proffitt and I found refuge in one of his old sources: Frank Snepp, the CIA's military analyst in Saigon. Snepp would later become a cause célèbre when, in defiance of the Agency's secrecy codes, he published *Decent Interval,* his outraged exposé of American bungling in the final weeks of the war. He was in his thirties when I met him, a wirly built man with curly, light-brown hair and a clean-cut face that seemed to belong in a Yale or Princeton yearbook. His office was on the embassy's sixth floor, the Agency's floor, and it was an air-conditioned sanctuary from the heat and from the propaganda of both sides. Snepp had been six years in Vietnam. Though about the same age as Nick and I, he belonged to an earlier generation, to the romantic days of the spooks' war, when young agents were the Leatherstockings of the New Frontier and drove into the bush in sports cars, grenades in the glove compartment, Swedish submachine guns in gun racks beneath the dash. Snepp was deskbound now, piecing together shreds of information from radio intercepts, satellites, and what the Agency called HUMINT resources, that is, people, that is, spies. Most of his networks had been rolled up and scattered, but he still had enough from them to assemble a picture of what was happening and probably would happen.

It was painted on his map, which displayed a score of rectangles, symbolizing enemy divisions and independent regiments, in a rough semicircle around Saigon. That map could have been a martial pinup feeding the unfulfilled fantasies of General Westmoreland: no scattered guerrilla battalions, no phantoms of the bush, but massed enemy divisions that could be inundated by tsunamis of napalm and high explosive. But that was not to be.

To oppose Hanoi's legions, Thieu's government had only three divisions, an airborne brigade, a handful of Ranger battalions, and a few thousand cadets from the military academy. They were outnumbered three to one. There would be no negotiated settlement, yet Washington and Ambassador Martin continued to hold out that hope and were pressuring Thieu to resign, as if that empty gesture would induce the North to sit down at a bargaining table. Martin, in the meantime, refused to go ahead with plans to evacuate the six thousand Americans still in Vietnam. The Agency, along with a few embassy staffers, had urged him to cut down a tall tamarind tree in the embassy compound to clear the way for a helicopter landing zone. Marine embassy guards had been standing ready with chain saws, but Martin called them off. His reasoning, if that's what it could be called, went like this: when the South Vietnamese saw Americans drop the tree, they would know why, lose heart, and panic, and the fall of Saigon would be assured. Nick and I wanted to shake our heads in disbelief, but we knew too much about the war to disbelieve anything. The episode contained the whole of the American folly in Vietnam: the morale of an army and the fate of a nation rested upon a single tamarind tree remaining upright.

Since we were on the subject of fantasies, I mentioned, more or less as a passing joke, the North Vietnamese colonel's fable about a people's uprising. Snepp laughed.

"It's about as much a people's uprising as Sherman's march to the sea," he said.

It was a straight-out, straight-ahead conventional campaign. The Ho Chi Minh Trail was paved now, so crowded with convoys that parts of it looked like the Ventura Freeway at rush hour. Pipelines carrying fuel for the North's tanks, trucks, and self-propelled guns ran alongside its many branches and side roads. Stripped of Marxist and New Left mythology, the North Vietnamese campaign was going successfully for one reason: they got there first with the most men.

Snepp made a forecast: the next round of fighting would be at Xuan Loc, a provincial capital forty miles northeast of Saigon. The North's aim would be to destroy the Arvin 18th Division, which held the city, and to draw Saigon's airborne reserves into the battle and chop them up. Afterward, Communist divisions would attack from the northwest, moving against the South's remaining units. The object of the campaign came out of Clausewitz, not Mao Tse-tung: destroy the enemy's forces and his will to resist. Hanoi did not want to seize Saigon by storm, didn't want a lot of messy, destructive house-to-house fighting. It wanted to smash up what was left of the South Vietnamese army and walk in.

And that was what it did.

Memories like shell fragments. I cannot arrange them into a coherent narrative. The yellowed clippings help a little, as do barely legible notes, scrawled at times under fire, at other times in a bouncing jeep, my shaky handwriting expressing more than the words the fear or panic or haste I felt at the time. What I see with memory's eye are glimpses of things long past, and to each I assign a dateline.

HUNG LOC, April 13—It was a village about ten miles west of Xuan Loc, on Highway One, the road the French called "the street without joy." The enemy attack on Xuan Loc had begun; some North Vietnamese—A company? A battalion? We didn't know—set up a blocking position in Hung Loc to stop supplies from getting through to the 18th Division. Over a period of days, a battalion of Rangers tried to dislodge the roadblock but were thrown back every time. Colin Smith and I stood watching them make another attempt. I looked down at my feet for a moment—I don't know why—and saw something white showing through the dirt: a stone tablet. I brushed the dirt away and read the inscription chiseled onto it long ago in French: "Here are buried Lieutenant [it gave a name I've forgotten] and four Montagnards, 1st Company, 11th Colonial Infantry, killed in action at this place, May 23rd, 1948." Things crawled up and down my neck and I leapt off the marker as if it were an armed land mine.

XUAN LOC, April 24—The 18th surprised everyone, themselves most of all, by holding the city against an assault by two North Vietnamese divisions. The 18th's defense refilled the draining fuel tank of the Great American Delusion Machine: the South could hold Saigon and force the North into a negotiated settlement. Thieu's government, proud of its only victory in the campaign, flew a press pool out to the city for a firsthand look at triumph. There, the division's commanding general told us he would hold Xuan Loc at all costs; no matter how many divisions the North threw at him, he would "knock them down." He then boarded a helicopter and flew back to his Saigon villa.

One of his regimental commanders took us on a tour of the city. It had been hit by six thousand shells in four days, so there wasn't much of it to see. Xuan Loc looked like a burning landfill. There were bodies everywhere—a North Vietnamese soldier with all his face blown off except for one piece of flesh twisting across it like a bloody rag, another with wide-open eyes and blood trickling out of his nostrils so that he did not look dead so much as like a stunned boxer whose nose had been broken. Shells were still falling as the colonel took us on his walking tour. "No sweat," he kept saying in his American slang while we reporters cringed and crouched at each blast. "This morning, Communists attacked with twelve tanks but we drove them off ... no sweat."

When the visit ended, we hiked back to the landing zone to wait for a helicopter to Saigon. There was a maddened rush of people as the chopper landed. Hundreds of civilians and Arvin deserters poured out of the surrounding rubber plantations, trampling each other to get on. Two young soldiers were trying to medevac a wounded buddy. They did not have a stretcher; one held the casualty by the ankles, the other under the arms. Fighting their way through the crowds, they dropped the wounded man twice. I went to help, sliding my hands under one of his arms. Sliced by shrapnel, it started to come apart, the meat pulling from the bone like an overdone sparerib. I clamped both hands over the wound to hold the arm together. Blood pumped through my fingers and splashed over my hands and watch. We lifted him on board. Two deserters tried to pull him off to make room for themselves. I punched them both in the face and leapt on as the helicopter lifted off, my legs dangling in midair before Bruce Wilson, an Australian correspondent, grabbed my collar and yanked me inside. A medic wrapped a tourniquet and splint around the casualty's half-severed arm. I squatted beside him, fanning him. The medic fanned him, too; it was so crowded inside even the healthy had a hard time breathing. The man's breath came in short, shallow gasps, faster and faster; then his eyes opened and grew still, his chest ceased heaving. "Checked out," Wilson said. I nodded and recited to myself the grunt's Vietnam mantra, "Don't mean nothin', don't mean a thing." But it must have meant something because I did not wash my hands or clean my watch for two days. I smelled the man's blood whenever I raised a hand near my face, I read the time through a film of red.

LONG BINH, April 27—I sat in a thatch hut and watched. That was my job, to watch. There was nothing else I could do anyway. A hundred yards away, North Vietnamese mortars and rockets slammed into Arvin bunkers guarding the bridge over the Dong Hai River, serene brown waters flowing through rice fields and swamps. A monsoon rain dimpled the river. Pouring over the bridge were thousands upon thousands of refugees and beaten soldiers fleeing Xuan Loc, which had finally fallen, and Long Thanh, Trang Bom, and Vung Tau. The column reached forward and backward as far as the eye could see, dense as a crowd coming out of a football stadium and more than twenty miles long. The refugees filed past the hut on foot, heads bowed and shoulders hunched against the rain. They rode past on motor scooters, in cars, in trucks and buses, on bullock carts piled high with crates, suitcases, and bundles of clothes. Sometimes the noise of the vehicles was deafening, but not so loud as to drown out the wind-rushing sound of an incoming rocket that would whip over their heads to burst in the paddies beyond the river. At other times, all I could hear was the shuffling of sandaled feet, solemn and processional. That and choirs of crying children. A boy of three or four, face and hands covered with sores and insect bites, toylike sun helmet on his head, toddled down the road, whimpering for his lost parents. I was there to watch, but sometimes you had to do more than just look. I picked him up and carried him along, asking people in sign language, Is he yours? Is he yours? Finally I found his father and mother. The kid stopped whimpering as they propped him on the back of their motor scooter. Walking back to the hut, I came across the naked leg (of a man? a woman?) lying in the middle of the road, bent at the knee, as if it had been blown off in the middle of a run. The rain fell on it as it fell on the crowds that parted around it like a river around a rock. There were a lot of Arvins mixed in with the refugees, some with their rifles, most without. A truck loaded with wounded soldiers idled on the bridge, waiting for a chance to move through the jam. The rain kept falling. The men were from the 18th, and one of them said that as far as he knew they were all that was left of their battalion. Their eyes looked at me from sockets deep as thumbprints pressed into soft clay, but I knew they did not see me.

The truck bumped forward. Behind it, an old woman with teeth lacquered dark red from betel nut screamed at the soldiers to pick her up. The driver stopped. The woman tried to lift her bundle of clothes, but it was probably as heavy as she and broke open. Shirts and trousers started to fly everywhere in the wind and rain. The truck jerked forward again and rolled on down the road. The woman sat on what was left of her bundle and screamed, the rain falling on her no differently than it fell on the soldiers, on the wounded and the whole, on the sick and the young and the old. I ran back into the hut to get out of the rain and go on with my watching and recording. Fighters flashed overhead. Towers of smoke rose toward the clouds and leaned in the wind like the pillars of a falling temple. A teenage boy, behind the wheel of a rickety truck, his parents, grandparents, brothers, and sisters sitting in the back atop a mound of belongings, looked at me and said: "We come from Long Thanh. Many shells fall on us last night. Many VC in Long Thanh. Many die." The rain never stopped.

SAIGON, April 28—Our weirdest war, and the weirdnesses kept coming at you, like pop-up skeletons and monsters in a carnival spook house. They kept coming right up to the fifty-ninth minute of the eleventh hour. The war had become so Americanized, even long after

it was supposed to have been Vietnamized, that Saigon had a functioning American Legion post, Post 34. I had heard about it from
someone but didn't believe it. An American Legion post belonged in
some rural Iowa or Minnesota town, where potbellied veterans wearing hats ornamented with patriotic buttons marched in Fourth of July
parades, served up hot dogs and brats at Memorial Day picnics. What
the hell were American Legionnaires doing in Saigon, especially at
that moment? At night, eating dinner in the Continental's courtyard,
we heard NVA shells falling on the airfield at Bien Hoa, just a few
miles away. The *bo-doi* would be marching down Tu Do Street in a
matter of days, hours for all we knew, so I decided to pay a call on the
Legionnaires to learn what plans they had made for the immediate
future. I guess it was fitting that I went to the interview with America's chronicler of the weird, the self-proclaimed gonzo journalist,
Hunter S. Thompson. He had appeared in the city about a week after
Nick and I got there, on assignment for *Rolling Stone.* We figured he
was going to do *Fear and Loathing in Saigon.* There were certainly
plenty of both. Somehow Thompson heard where I was going and
asked if he could come along; the story was made-to-order gonzo. I
said his company would be welcome, but I had to issue some uptight,
establishment-press instructions: Thompson, who had come to Vietnam well supplied with his usual pharmaceuticals and hallucinogens,
would have to stay straight because I didn't want the interview ruined
with Merry Prankster antics.

Hunter promised to behave himself, would even, if that suited
me, not ask a single question. That suited me.

My notes tell me the post was on Cach Mang Street, but I can't
recall where that was and can't find a street by that name on my faded
Saigon map. The building, a whitewashed colonial-era villa, stood
behind a wall covered in bougainvillea. We would have missed it but
for the small sign over the gate—the Legion's starlike symbol and the
words POST 34. We passed through the courtyard into a big, dim room
where, under spinning fans, a couple of bar girls in *ao-dais* were
shooting pool and about a dozen more sat at a bar. There had not
been much action for them since the GIs left, so they descended on
Hunter and me like dust-bowl crows on a road kill. Hey you you come
buy me one drink you you drink come sit by me oh you sooo handsome ooooh you such big man (to the six-foot-three-inch Thompson,

squeezing his bicep) sooo big strong you sit by me buy one drink you. We swatted them off, ordered a couple of beers, and asked the bartender, a wan-looking Vietnamese, where the Legionnaires were. He told us to wait.

We killed time by having a look around. The post was a little chunk of Rotarian America set down in Southeast Asia. There was a barbershop in an adjoining room, a vintage piano, a library of mildewed paperbacks, with a heavy emphasis on westerns and war novels (I did not see *The Quiet American*), a jukebox with a heavy emphasis on country and western, a snack bar with a row of shabby booths covered in torn black vinyl. The menu was on the wall:

BILL OF FARE
SANDWICHES
HAM N' CHEESE
POLISH SAUSAGE
HOT DOG
HAMBURGER
BLT

The most haunting decorations were the battle paintings that hung in long rows on almost every wall. In the tones and style of Frederic Remington, they portrayed U.S. Army victories over a span of nearly two centuries. The Wagon Box Fight—blue-coated troopers of the Ninth Infantry fighting off a Sioux attack in 1867. A picture of the Second Dragoons charging the Mexicans at Resaca de la Palma in Texas. Soldiers in wide-brimmed campaign hats whipping the Moros at Bagsok Mountain in the Philippines. The Ninth Armored blasting across the Remagen bridgehead in 1945. The 23rd Infantry breaking the Chinese encirclement at Chipyong-Ni in 1951. Trenton. Ticonderoga. New Orleans. Chapultepec. Antietam. San Juan Hill. Manila Bay. Château-Thierry. The Bulge. It gave me chills to read those names because their long, unbroken record of triumph was about to be broken.

The bartender came out with a man who stood about five-nine and had sandy blond hair and light eyes. He did not fit the image of the overweight legionnaire serving up brats in Iowa but was lean and hard-muscled, face and arms tanned to the color of a well-broken baseball glove. Yet there was something unhealthy about him, a ravaged look that spoke of too much sun and too many nights fighting off the malaria with gin. His name was Roger Matuszak, he said, squinting at Hunter and me in a way that told us he didn't think much of reporters. He was forty-three years old and came from Green Bay, Wisconsin.

He sat at a table. A pregnant Vietnamese woman in black blouse and trousers came out from the kitchen and perched on his lap. It was Roger's wife, Han. He ordered beers all around and asked what we wanted to know. I told him.

American Legion Post 34, he answered, had been inaugurated in 1965 and, at the height of its membership, had forty-eight hundred members. It was the largest post in the whole damned legion, made up of men who worked in Vietnam as civilians. Electricians. Foremen and heavy-equipment operators and highway engineers for big construction outfits like RMK. The one requirement was American citizenship and proof that you had served in any American war.

"Hell," Matuszak said, all the while rubbing Han's back, "once we had guys who fought in World War One right alongside guys who'd fought here."

He had served in Vietnam with the First Division, the Big Red One, and in Korea before that. Career army man, temporary promotion to warrant officer, but got out of the army in seventy two, when it riffed him back to the enlisted ranks. Met Han in Vietnam, had one kid and now—the hand on her back moving to her belly—"got another one in the oven."

And what did American Legionnaires do in Vietnam? March in July 4th parades, dish out the brats and dogs on Memorial Day? Hell, no. The Post was a place for civilian Yanks to get together, eat American chow, drink good American beer instead of that Vietnamese brew, which, for its taste and tiger's head logo, was known as "panther piss." The legion also did good works, in the best tradition of the American Rotarian abroad. He pointed at a wall, where achievement awards for aiding Vietnamese orphans and refugees hung alongside the portraits of long-ago battles.

Another man came out. Like Matuszak, he was tanned, whipcord lean, and ravaged-looking: Don Chad, a fifty-one-year-old engineer who hailed from Lincoln, Nebraska. He had been in the Far

East for thirty-three years, first with the navy in 1942. Transferred over to the army at the end of the war, served with Vinegar Joe Stilwell, and in 1947 did a spell with Chennault's Flying Tigers. He'd been in China when it fell to the Communists in 1949, then in the Philippines, then in Korea and Japan. Been in Nam since sixty-seven, and did we know that his wife was a name actress in Japan?

Matuszak's wife slipped off his lap and brought us another round of beers. The two men started to talk about why they'd been out east so long—Chad had not been back home in twenty-three years.

"Where else but here," Chad said, "can you live like a king on three hundred fifty a month? Everything taken care of for you. Only thing you've got to do by yourself is get up in the morning. Meals, laundry, drinks, always some little honeywa to take care of everything for you. My idea of staying out here is to make a lotta dough and then go back. Take the money and build some apartment buildings on some property I own in Lincoln, right near the University of Nebraska. Cornhuskers, yeah. Hell, I do that, I won't have to worry about working the rest of my life."

He finished his beer in two or three long pumps of his Adam's apple and waved the bottle at a bar girl. She brought him another. Always some little honeywa ... I mentioned that the Vietcong were going to cut short his Vietnam stay. What would happen to his proposed apartment project then?

"I'm in no hurry to get out of this town, 'cause I don't think the VC are comin' in."

I thought of introducing him to Ambassador Martin.

"They're awful close," I said. "They started shelling Bien Hoa last night."

"If they do, they'll welcome us. Hell, I got a buddy who was in Phnom Penh, and the Khmer Rouge already asked him to come back. They wanted his know-how."

"Damn right," Matuszak said. "They'll welcome back Americans. They want dollars and our know-how."

More beers came. I asked Chad what his plans were if the VC decided they didn't need his dollars or know-how. He grinned, multiplying by three the wrinkles in his sun-creased skin.

"Got two airplanes in country. One of 'em all gassed up and ready to go. Manila or Singapore. Can make either one, 'cause I gota spare tank sittin' in the back, just full o' fuel. So let the Commies come. They didn't shoot me in China in forty-nine. Anyhow, you only die once, gotta die someday." He frowned and shook his head, as if he had just remembered something unpleasant. "Gotta get back to the States one way or the other, see my mother before she dies. Gotta bury my oldest son."

What happened to him?

"He was killed in an auto accident a few months ago," Chad said, slurring his words now.

But hadn't he been buried by this time? Chad was looking off toward the wall where portraits of triumph hung. He seemed not to have heard me.

"Still gotta figure out how to get that second plane out of here," he mumbled.

When Matuszak and Chad started to sing elegies to the American presence and to curse the hippies and pinkos and the Congress for selling Vietnam down the river, Hunter and I decided to leave. They would turn on the press next and things could get messy.

Thompson had been true to his word; he hadn't said a thing and he'd stayed straight. The interview had been hallucinogenic enough, in no need of assistance. Christ, he said, could you imagine Don and Roger standing at the gates of Saigon with their résumés in hand? Here you are, Mr. Charles. A summary of my qualifications and know-how. What do you guys pay an hour?

At six that evening, two attack planes captured from the South Vietnamese air force came in about a hundred feet over Saigon's rooftops. Every soldier in the city seemed to fire at them, an eruption of gunshots that became one prolonged roar. The planes didn't take a single bullet and dropped five-hundred- and seven-hundred-and-fifty-pound bombs on Tan Son Nhut. We watched the air strike, the North's first and only of the war, from the top-floor bar at the Caravelle. Then the airport came under rocket and artillery fire. I thought about Chad's planes. No matter how much fuel they carried, they weren't taking him anywhere.

SAIGON, April 29—It was ten-thirty in the morning. Yates, Proffitt, and I, in company with two dozen other correspondents, huddled in the first-floor corridor of the Continental, its old walls dancing the shimmy-shake from the one-thirties falling all around the city. The barrage had begun at four, knocking us all out of bed. We had been waiting it out ever since, waiting, too, for word of where to go and what to do when the evacuation came. *If* it came. Had I been any-where but Vietnam, I would not have believed it possible, but the Great American Delusion Machine continued to hum, running on its own momentum. Less than twenty-fours ago, we had received our instructions and our assignments to evacuation teams, each of which was issued a CB radio to monitor coded traffic. We had been given the secret signal to move to our assigned assembly points; then Ambassador Martin cabled Washington with cheery news: the situa-tion was well in hand, cancel all evacuation plans. The CIA and a band of embassy young Turks staged a palace coup and gave Wash-ington the bleak facts. The White House cabled a reply in fifteen minutes: the evacuation was back on. Yet as far as we knew, the tamarind tree still stood. And we had not heard the code for evacua-tion: "The temperature in Saigon is one hundred and five degrees and rising," followed by a few bars of "White Christmas."

Every now and then, Yates or I would make the block-and-a-half walk to UPI's offices to file a retop to the running story or to check on developments. It was my turn to make the trip. I felt a little reluctant; it was dangerous outside, not so much from the shellfire, which was some distance off, as from the South Vietnamese. They felt aban-doned by the Americans, as they had every right to. There were rumors they might fire on the evacuation buses and the helicopters that were now on carriers offshore. A twenty-four-hour curfew was on, the streets empty except for the Home Defense militia, which was made up of gangs of Saigon cowboys—dope pushers, pimps, and pickpockets given carbines and a license to do what they had been doing unlicensed most of their young lives.

The morning was overcast and windless, so humid you sweated like a jogger just standing still. The red-and-yellow Vietnamese flag over the National Assembly Building clung to its pole like a wet bed sheet. A TV crew lumbered across Lam Son Square with their cam-eras and sound equipment. Across the square, and several stories up, more cameras were ranked on the terrace of the Caravelle bar, film-ing the smoke and flames rising high above Tan Son Nhut. The Great

American Delusion Machine had been Vietnamized: from loudspeakers on every street corner patriotic music and slogans blared to inspire the Saigonese to resist. Meanwhile, ex-President Thieu (he'd resigned on April 21, which hadn't impressed Hanoi one bit) and Madame Thieu were making plans to evacuate themselves and all their belongings.

I was about halfway to UPI when I heard, above the inspiring anthems, the drumming of heavy machine guns and the sharp, distinctive cracks of tank cannon.

Alan Dawson, the UPI bureau chief, was hammering away on his typewriter. Any word? I asked. No, not yet. Two marine guards were killed by rocket fire at Tan Son Nhut, maybe the last Americans to die in the war. Dawson showed me their names and ages—nineteen and twenty. Christ, they'd been nine and ten years old when I landed at Da Nang. Long, long war, I said and asked if those were the tanks I'd heard. Sure were, Dawson answered. NVA armor's attacking the Newport Bridge. Newport! The bridge, the main link between Saigon and Bien Hoa, was less than three miles away. They've got armor as close as Newport? Fuckin' A right. I put that in the new lead, then ran back to the Continental, where I was besieged by so many questions I felt like a celebrity at a news conference. *What's goin' on what's goin' on what in the hell is goin' on?*

"From the sounds of it, a serious disagreement."

"That's not funny, el-tee," Proffitt said, puckering his lips and eyebrows.

"The bad guys have armor at Newport Bridge."

Nick gritted his teeth and grimaced as if someone were running fingernails across a blackboard.

"Tanks! Oooooooooh sheeeeee-it."

"That's really not funny," said Yates. He stretched his long legs halfway across the corridor. "Know how I feel? The way you do at a football game when it's the last two minutes of the fourth quarter and the score's fifty-six to zip and your side's the one with zip."

Essential supplies of beer and dope were running low. We sipped the last warm cans from the now iceless coolers. Someone produced a Thai stick and passed it around. I did not like grass, but took a hit anyway, inhaling enough to keep my nerves from running amok but not so much as to lose judgment or important motor skills like running. The bomber came back to me as a roach and I took another, deeper hit. Because Vietnam had always been a wonderful land in which to make self-discoveries. Something in the air, I guessed. A climate that could strip the bluing off a rifle barrel in no time peeled away your self-flattering illusions even quicker. I had discovered a truth that, possibly, I had been trying to escape a good part of my life: I was yellow. The lesson had begun some five days earlier, when Nick and I, returning from another happy road trip to the front, came under shellfire out near gloomy, glowering Black Virgin Mountain. The shells kept coming down the road, seeming to chase our jeep, an experience I can only liken to driving through a terrible thunderstorm with aimed lightning bolts striking all around you. We left the highway and sped toward an Arvin fire base off on a dirt side road, two shells banging into the crossroad not three seconds later. We dove into a bunker, whose Arvin occupants made room for us. I pulled out a cigarette but could not hold it or my lighter steady. No slight trembling either, but a palsy. The Arvins were amused. Nick took pity and lit the smoke for me, but I had to slink off to a dark corner and turn my back on everyone because the shaking wouldn't stop no matter what I did. My nerves were in rebellion against my will. It was odd because I'd been under far worse fire without flinching, which led me to conclude that courage, like coal or oil, was a finite resource. Draw down your reserves often enough, and you'd probably end up too scared to walk out your front door.

Now, in the corridor, the trembling in the floors and walls were passing into my hands and limbs. I made fists just in case the quaking became obvious. A picture kept flashing in my mind: breakfast time in the dining room of our Beirut apartment, sunlight flooding onto the table, where scrambled eggs simmered in a silver chafing dish beside a bowl of oranges and a polished coffee pot. Marc and Geoff's blond heads shone in the light, and Jill's long fair hair looked golden as butter as she poured the coffee. I wanted to get back to them with such intensity it seemed I could think myself there. I took a third hit. People in past wars had spoken of whiskey courage. This was dope courage. When the tank started to run dry, you refilled it any way you could.

Voices came through the static on the CB, speaking their bizarre lingo ... Leatherneck six, this is Dragon ... Diamond two four niner ... I'm running out of fuel ... One niner one Diamond Control give zero one four status report every two minutes ... Roger roger ... Are you taking hostile fire? Negative ... But they sure were close that time, if that's what you mean ..."

The reporter appointed as our CB warden hollered for everyone to keep quiet.

"Sounds like choppers on the way," he shouted, and everyone cheered. The warden turned the volume to max, and we heard this: "All Diamond substations except one niner one and one one four, unless you have emergency traffic, clear this circuit, I say again. ..."

A litany of "rogers" ... then:

"Whiskey Six, Whiskey Six, this is Diamond Control, over ..."

The warden held up his hand in a plea for silence, though no one was speaking a word. Whiskey Six was the embassy's radio call sign.

"Diamond Control this is Whiskey Six. Have you crossed India Papa, over?"

"Roger, over."

"Diamond Control, this is Whiskey Six. Temperature in Saigon is one zero five degrees and rising, over."

"Roger, roger. All Diamond stations, did you roger that? Temperature in Saigon is one zero five and rising ..."

The warden jumped up and yelled down the hall in both directions. "That's it! One hundred percent evacuation! We're outta here!"

"Hey," said someone near the radio, "they're supposed to play 'White Christmas' next. They didn't play 'White Christmas.'"

"Fuck Bing Crosby!" the warden hollered. "It's bye-bye everybody!"

We grabbed our bags and shambled into the smothering heat. There were one hundred and fifty in our team, more than half Americans, the rest French, Germans, Australians, Swedes. At our assembly point, an apartment building on Pham Van Tan Street, we packed into the lobby, where we waited and sweated for someone to tell us what to do. A fat U.S. security guard in khaki showed up, waving his M-16 like a wand. He had wonderful manners.

"You buncha idiots, whatchya doin here? This ain't your assembly point. It's over by Gia Dinh Street, number thirty-five. The hospital. Get your asses in gear."

The warden showed him our instructions: Pham Van Tan Street.

"Get the fuck over to Gia Dinh, you don't want the Veeet Cong beatin' on your idiot heads."

It was a four-block walk, past sullen Vietnamese, some cursing us, some asking, "You di di now? War finish?" Yates called over his shoulder, yes, war finish, we were leaving, bye-bye, everybody. You could say our intervention had been a colossal mistake at best, a crime at worst, and you'd be right. You could say it had always been the Vietnamese's war to win or lose, and you'd be right again. But by their gods and our gods, I felt ashamed of myself and my country, I felt like a deserter.

At the hospital on Gia Dinh, we waited while wounded Arvin looked down on us from the balconies. Armed Arvins cruised by in jeeps, and it wasn't difficult to see in which direction they wanted to point their rifles. The monsoon had cleared and the sun fell in blows and from all around came the ceaseless rumble of incoming. Confusion was one hundred percent. We were told nothing, given no instructions, provided no security. We stood waiting for an Arvin trooper to hose us down with a machine gun, for a North Vietnamese rocket that would drop us like bowling pins. Someone claimed he heard a tank. It was someone with an overactive imagination: a staff car with flashing blue light pulled up, trailed by two olive-drab buses, windows covered with stout wire mesh against grenades. Three or four marines in camouflage uniforms and full combat gear stepped out. We were all happy to see them; they were the only ones around with at least a vague idea of what they were doing. They quickly divided us into two groups and herded us onto the buses. We drove around, aimlessly it seemed. Past Lam Son Square. Past the spired Protestant church, then past the embassy, a huge white fortress of a building with narrow windows like firing slits and an eight- or ten-foot wall around it, topped by coiled wire. I would never forget the scene there. It looked like a soccer riot: thousands of Vietnamese almost trampling each other, trying to climb the walls, to smash through the iron gates. Marines atop the walls bashed knuckles with rifle butts, marines and embassy guards at the gates allowed Vietnamese with proper evacuation papers through, clubbed and punched the rest.

"The final indignity ..." Proffitt mumbled.

He did not have to finish. At least the French had gone out with a little class, their generals marching solemnly across a bridge to surrender to the Viet Minh. Our great Indochina enterprise ended with marines clubbing the very people they had once been sent to save so a few crooked Vietnamese politicians, American diplomats, and foreign news hacks could abandon the American Embassy in safety.

The buses moved on. At the curbside, a gang of Home Defense lads were stripping an automobile with the speed of a pit crew. Nearby, two white mice, as Saigon's traffic cops were called for the color of their uniforms, guarded treasures pillaged earlier: carburetors, batteries, headlights, spark plugs, bumpers. I had to admire the citizens of the sad old harlot, stealing, hustling to the end. The buses moved on. An Arvin lieutenant on the street called to the marine captain in the staff car, Could we please take him and his family? *Sin loi,* said the captain. Couldn't do it. Already, the U.S. had taken out twenty-five thousand Vietnamese. *Sin loi.* Sorry about that. The buses moved on. Near the ruined Majestic, the limbless man I'd seen a month ago perched on his cart, parked where cyclo drivers used to lure GIs with promises of no VD no VC. He looked up at us, we at him, our silence giving answer to his silent question. *Sin loi.* And the buses moved on.

Around half-past two, they rolled through the main gate of the airport's military side. The shelling was louder now, small arms rattled not far away. A firefight? Arvins shooting at fleeing Americans? We came to a double-barbed-wire barricade, guarded by security police in dull gray uniforms. Their sergeant started talking to our captain. We waited again. The bus stank of sweat; physical sweat and nervous sweat, fear's musk. A French photographer got out to snap pictures. A cop shouted at him, "You shoot photo, I shoot you." He kept snapping, and an American yelled, "Yo, Froggie! Put—the—fuckin'—camera—*down!*" The cop raised his carbine, aiming it at the Frenchman's head, and that solved the language problem. He jumped back on the bus.

The sergeant waved us through. We drove a few minutes and parked in front of Pentagon East. Again we waited. One runway was still in use, despite all the shellfire: a South Vietnamse C-119 cargo plane rose steeply, making for the low monsoon clouds that had once again closed in.

"Wonder how close the Cong have moved their SAM-sevens," Yates said. The Cong satisfied his curiosity about ten seconds later. A bright-red ball shot up from the rice paddies and slammed into one of the plane's wings, blowing it off, wing and smoking fuselage tumbling separately. They hit the ground in a balloon of orange flame. A collective groan went up in the bus, a chorus of "Oooohh shits." The door opened. The marines gestured for us to get off. One at a time, now, make it fast but make it orderly. I was standing in the aisle, waiting my turn, when I heard it. *Sssssssssuuuuuuuu.* A terrific bang on the runway, less than a hundred yards away. There was a wild rush down the aisle, bodies jamming themselves into the door. Ssssssssssssuuuuuuuuu-whomp! Ssssssssuuuuuuu-whomp! "Steady, people! Steadeee, goddamnit!" I yelled. "One at a time, or nobody'll get off." Everyone settled down. Walking toward the building, Proffitt clapped my shoulder.

"Nice going, el-tee." He turned with a sneer at our fellow newsmen, then to me with a grin. "Fuckin' civilians."

I confessed that I shouted to check my own panic more than anyone else's, the "Steady, people" echoing in my head as "Steady, Phil!"

We filed into the basement corridor, a perfect asylum of Vietnamese refugees, Vietnamese officers of exalted rank, and civilians of many nations, but mostly white male Americans. An air force sergeant moved along the hallway, collecting guns. Weapons, weapons, you gotta weapon give it to me. We were lined up against a wall and given tags, which looked ominously like casualty tags, and told to fill them out and tie them to our shirts. People milled around, squatting here and there to write on suitcases or on each other's backs, an air force colonel yelling, "Please stay in line against the wall, in line against the goddamned wall!" Nick, Yates, and I sat down, lighting up our smokes. A Vietnamese three-star general, trailed by wife, children, and enough relatives to populate a hamlet, walked by, escorted with utmost deference by a marine captain. The general looked intensely happy. If he'd stayed, the best he could have hoped for was a lifetime of stern lectures in a reeducation camp. A shell burst outside. The building rocked. I lit another cigarette off the butt of the old. A bowl of oranges beside a silver chafing dish, aroma of coffee from a gleaming silver pot, sunlight on fair hair. I made a vow and sealed it by speaking it aloud.

"Old Sarge," I said. "This is the last one of these things I'm going to cover."

"You'll have company. Last one for me, no more bongo wars."

I started to talk too much. The last one. I was sick of it, sick of the noise and the stink of it, sick of feeling afraid all the time, sick of looking at bodies, sick of unusual experiences like stepping into a man's brains. Nick spoke of the ranch in the Yak River valley, near the British Columbia line. Elk grazing in the front yard of his cabin like sheep in a meadow, bugling in the mountains during the rut, trout half the size of salmon in the river, the morning sun on the hay meadow. No more bongo wars, good-bye to all that, bye-bye, everybody. We made a pact. When the time seemed ripe, I would quit to finish *A Rumor of War* and he would go off to the ranch to write a novel of his days burying the war dead. He was going to call it *Gardens of Stone*.

An army major, full of false jollity, handed each of us a manifest card.

"This is a first-class flight, gentlemen, but without stewardesses."

Ho, ho, Major. What humor in the face of death!

"Just put your names on the top and bottom, and don't worry about your final destination."

Trenchant wit, Major!

"We're just going to get you out of Vietnam."

Much better, Major.

We were divided into helicopter teams of fifty people each, told to move down the corridor. We did. Told to sit down. We did. Move again. We did. A marine colonel, resembling an NFL lineman in his helmet and flak vest, stomped by, snarling into a radio.

"I've got the GSF [ground security force] due in here at fifteen hundred and I'm gonna need some air for flak suppression."

Flak? We all saw the choppers going down like the cargo plane.

Move. We did, rounding a corner into another hallway. At its far end was a double door, guarded by a squad of marines.

"Gentleman!" Nick announced. "We have turned the corner in Vietnam!"

"Yeah," an Australian newsman answered, "and if you look down this hall, you'll see ..."

In unison, a dozen voices finished for him:

"THE LIGHT AT THE END OF THE TUNNEL!"

We heard now the industrial throbbing of helicopter rotors. The doors swung open, the throbbing grew louder and so did the blast of shells on the runway.

"Move out!" a marine bellowed. "Move in your heli teams! Move move move!"

The first fifty people ran out and the marine hollered to drop luggage, no luggage on board. Quickly I opened my big suitcase, and pulled out my passport wallet, but I didn't have enough time to save anything else except my notebooks, field glasses, maps, and the faithful Olivetti portable. Everything else was left behind in the corridor, including photographs of Jill and the kids, a picture taken of me in dress blues the day I was commissioned. Why in God's name I'd brought *that* to the fall of Saigon was one of the Great Mysteries.

Now we crouched at the door, through which we saw a squadron of giant Marine Sea Stallions—each capable of carrying as many people as an old DC-3. They squatted on the tennis courts where Westmoreland used to work on his backhand. *Sssssssssssuuu*, then a truly stunning WHOMP! as the shell crashed into the oil-storage depot across the airfield, tanks rupturing like all the napalm Dow Chemical ever made. A marine put his hand on my shoulder and told me to stand by. I will not panic, I said to myself. I will behave with courage and dignity. If any women and children must board before me, I will let them. I will be brave and honorable.

"GO!"

Most of the women could not run very fast because they were carrying bags filled with gold ingots, and, forgetting my instructions to myself, I nearly trampled them as I made for the chopper. Marines crouched in foxholes around the tennis court–LZ, rifles and machine guns pointed. In the middle of all the noise and desperation, confident as a Presbyterian holding a royal flush, sat the company gunnery sergeant, one of those grand Old Breed marines. He was smoking a cigarette and winked at me as I made for the rear hatch of my team's chopper.

"So long," he said. "We'll hold 'em off at the pass."

So many people stuffed the chopper I wondered if it could get off the ground. Forward, two door gunners wearing visored helmets and thick canvas gauntlets stood behind fifty-caliber machine guns, brass snakes of belted ammunition coiled on the deck. The crew chief closed the hatch. I could see nothing outside. The chopper gathered itself, like a standing broad jumper, then leapt into the air. I worked my way forward, trying not to step on anyone. A woman nursing an infant at her breast stared up at me, as if she expected me to say or do something, but there was nothing to be said and no more to be done. By the time I got to the door, the squadron was at seven or eight thousand feet. Below, columns of smoke rolled up from everywhere, from the rubber plantations, the Delta marshes, the paddy lands slashed by brown canals and slow khaki rivers.

It was quite suddenly *there*, rising toward the choppers, twirling like a ruby disco ball. I had my field glasses on it for an instant; it was bearing for the lead helicopter. A dozen gigantic flash bulbs popped in the air. The missile angled off sharply, drawn toward the decoy flares, then blew up in space. I don't recall that I'd felt afraid; fascinated, rather. But I must have been afraid because Yates snapped a picture of me the moment after the missile blew up. I still have it. My eyes are shut, my mouth a little ajar, my head thrown back. I look like a man who's just been reprieved from the electric chair.

I state for the historical record that we crossed the coast at 4:17 P.M. (the time is in my notes). No danger of SAM now. The door gunners let go of their fifty calibers, flipped up their visors, and raised their thumbs to mark the happy event. A familiar electricity circuited through me; I had made another escape. Good night, Saigon, bye-bye, Arvins, bye-bye, Charlie, bye-bye, everybody. Beneath us now was a lot of lovely blue water and many gray ships—half the Seventh Fleet, all its might perfectly useless against Uncle Ho's peasant army. Scattered among the warships were freighters pressed into military service, decks so crowded with refugees they looked like Hong Kong ferries at 5:00 P.M.

We circled a helicopter carrier, like a passenger plane in a holding pattern. We had to wait for the decks to be cleared of the two Vietnamese Huey gunships. We found out later that the pilots had flown them out of the Delta town of Cam Lo, evacuating themselves and their families on their own authority. The carrier's skipper had had no choice but to give them permission to land. Now the choppers had to be swept off the decks. That made another sight I would not forget. The Huey was the symbol of the war and the embodiment of all its paradoxes. Gunship, ambulance, transport truck, supply truck, mail truck and hearse, it was good and evil wrapped up in a million dollars worth of turboprop engine, steel plate, and electronics, and now two of those ugly gorgeous savior killers were wrestled toward the edge of the flight deck by a horde of antlike sailors, who shoved them overboard. I watched them hit with a splash. They floated briefly before sinking out of sight. It was as if the war had been given a burial at sea, and that's when I knew it was over.

Levy ... Sullivan ... West ... Bye-bye to you, too.

Our helicopter touched down. The hatch opened, letting in the smells of salt air, hot grease, and aviation fuel. I walked out, behind a woman leaning sideways at a forty-five-degree angle from the weight of the smuggled gold in her flight bag. A sailor slapped me on the back as I stepped onto the flight deck.

"Welcome to the U.S.S. Denver," he said. "Welcome home, buddy."

IN THE SOUTH CHINA SEA, April 30 (last dispatch)—We were transferred to the U.S.S. *Blue Ridge,* the flagship. That afternoon, as we watched a movie in the wardroom, the skipper announced over the intercom that the Saigon government had formally surrendered. The war with an uncertain beginning had come to a quite certain end. There were no cheers, moans, or curses. We went back to the movie. The only one who seemed affected, who said anything at all, was Frank Snepp. I saw him later on, when I went out on deck for a breath of fresh air. He was sitting in a hatchway, hands folded between his knees, looking down at his feet. I said hello. He glanced up, but I don't think he saw me. His eyes seemed to be looking back toward the country whose hot green coast was still visible across the metallic brilliance of sea, the land where he had given not just six years of his youth but all of it. My heart went out to him; good men can serve bad causes well.

"It's the end of an era," he said, more to himself than to me, and I said, yeah, it was, and went out on deck. About five miles off, a flotilla of fishing junks was sailing toward the fleet: the first boat people. Beyond the junks, the coast shimmered, a strand of white fringed in green. I guessed my youth was there, too, and always would be.

Kipling said it long ago: We have but one virginity to lose, and where we lost it, there our hearts will always be.

But it was the end of an era, in Vietnamese history and our own. History is the record of the crimes and follies of mankind, Gibbon said, and what a record had been written in Vietnam, in the red ink of over four million wounded and dead, three hundred and sixty-five thousand of them our own. What a terrible chronicle we had inscribed on the page of that land with napalm and defoliants and bomb tonnages almost beyond measure. Chemical sprays had embrowned rain forests that had never known a natural autumn, and the wild elephant that once trumpeted there had starved or fled. In the places we knew as War Zone C and the Iron Triangle, now cratered and devoid of life, some of the world's last Javan rhino had wallowed in the riverbanks and by the waterholes. Carpet bombing had moonscaped the high Annamese Cordillera, where Bengal tigers once crouched in thickets, waiting to pounce on deer that had roamed the jungles in thousands. And on more hilltops than you could count, daisy-cutter bombs weighing seven and a half tons each had been dropped to clear helicopter landing zones, felling in an instant teak and mahogany trees that had been saplings when the pilgrims landed at Plymouth Rock. Only shrubs and grasses grew in their place, and the sun, which used to fall to the songs and shrieks of parrots and crested mynahs, now set in silence. We had not gone to war only with the Vietcong; we had made war against Nature herself, much as we had done in our westward march across our own continent. Vietnam had been the first war of the New Frontier and the last, lurid battle of the old one. The wagon ruts of the Oregon Trail led across water and time to the tracks our tanks and APCs dug into the Asian rice paddies. An evolutionary line could be traced from the pioneer's ax to those daisy-cutter bombs, from the Winchesters at Wounded Knee to the M-16s at My Lai. Yes, it was the end of an era, and maybe that was just as well. Maybe we had to lose the war because we had to lose the myth that our destiny was manifest.

DISASTERS OF WAR

"Goddamnit, sir, he had a grenade!"

The marine's eyes were bloodshot. He'd probably been up all night, guarding this worthless bridge, the captain thought.

"Gook's walkin' at me with a freakin' grenade, what'm I sup-posed to do?"

The whole village seemed to be there. All were staring at him and the two marine sentries with silent, unreadable expressions, except for an old man whom the captain took for the village elder. He wore a long, white goatee and was gesturing and talking nonstop. The captain couldn't understand a word. Nearby, a woman, whom the captain took to be the boy's mother, sat in the dust beside the corpse (it wasn't even that, the captain thought, it was just a mess). She sat silently, looking off into space. Someone had covered what was left of the body with a couple of reed mats, but the captain could see enough of it to feel a little queasy. He could not understand how the woman could sit so near it without getting sick or hysterical. She just stared at nothing and chewed her betel nut. A man in a dark shirt and cork sun helmet, holding a pair of sticks, walked along the riverbank, looking at the ground and into the bushes.

"So help me God," the red-eyed marine was saying, "I didn't

throw no grenade at him. I shot him. He musta had the pin pulled, because the thing went off in his hand. Boom."

The old man kept talking, standing on tiptoe so he could shout into the captain's ear.

"Did you see anything?" the captain asked the second marine.

"No, sir. I was makin' a head call. But I heard the shot. First the shot, then the grenade." He grabbed the first marine's rifle, which was propped against the sandbagged bunker where the two had sat up all night, guarding the bridge. "Here, sir, take a look at the barrel."

The captain jacked the bolt back and held the muzzle to his eye. He could see the powder grains inside the barrel. That did not prove anything; the marine could have thrown the grenade, then fired his rifle, and persuaded his buddy to back up his story.

"Son, this is a friendly ville. They're solid here. Hasn't been an incident here since nobody can remember when. Solid friendlies. Why would that kid be coming at you with a grenade?"

"How the freakin' hell do I know, sir? Why would I kill a kid for no good reason?"

Up all night, thought the captain. Waiting, listening, looking into the darkness, scared and fed up, that's why.

"Please, sir, you can't run me up. I didn't do nothin'."

The man by the riverbank picked up something long and thin and pink with the sticks, carried it delicately up to the village, then placed it under the reed mats. The captain was sure he was going to be sick. The woman looked off into space and spat a stream of betel nut. The elder talked and talked. The captain held a hand in front of his face to stop him from talking.

"I ... don't ... understand," he said. "Do ... you ... speak ... any English? Eng-lish? Eeeeeng-leeesh?"

The old man looked a little baffled and pulled at his goatee.

"Pas de l'Anglais," he said. "Mais, je parle français. Parlez-vous français?"

"Eeeeng-leesh," said the captain.

The old man started talking again, this time in French. The captain could not understand a thing, but he heard the old man repeating one word over and over. Pishee or pashay or peshee, something like that.

"Skipper, I don't know what this old dude's tellin' you, but the kid had a grenade. I didn't do nothin'. You gotta believe me."

"Anybody in your company speak French?" he asked.

"Yes, sir," the second marine said after thinking a moment. "Doucette. He's a French Canadian, I think."

"Get him here chop-chop."

The elder kept pointing at the river and saying pishee pashay peshee while the man with the sticks picked up every shred of the boy he could find and brought each one back, placing it under the mats. The woman's eyes stayed on the point in space. How could she be so impassive? Was she in shock? Maybe these people just don't have normal human feelings, the captain thought. Finally, the marine returned with Doucette, who began speaking to the village elder in French. The captain heard that word again. Pishee pashay peshee.

Doucette turned to the captain.

"Sir, the old guy, he says the kid was goin' to go fishin'. Just goin' down to the river to fish, then he gets shot."

The red-eyed marine raised his hand as if he were going to swat the old man.

"He wasn't fishin'! He had a freakin' grenade!"

The captain understood now and told Doucette to ask the elder if the boy was going to fish with a hand grenade. Doucette translated the question. The old man answered, "Oui, oui, oui." The captain understood that, but nothing else of what the old man said.

"What he's saying, Skipper," explained Doucette, "is that the kid's family lost their sampan and their nets a few days ago. So the kid got a grenade from somebody and was goin' to toss it in the river and pick up the dead fish, but then he got shot."

The marine with the bloodshot eyes seemed to be trying to smile.

"Told you, Skipper. What was I supposed to do?"

The captain did not say anything.

"How'm I supposed to know the kid's goin' fishin'? You go fishin' with a fishin' rod, not a freakin' grenade. I see a gook comin' toward me with a grenade, I grease him. What would you have done, sir?"

Still, the captain said nothing. The man with the sticks brought the last piece of the boy and tucked it under the mats. He said something to the woman, who suddenly started howling, throwing her hands up and down and howling. Why had she waited so long? What had the man said to her? the captain wondered. Damned people made no sense. He turned to the marine.

"Okay, carry on," he said.

The marine blew out his cheeks in relief.

"Told you I didn't do nothin'."

EIGHT

States of Extremes

We had no lawns to mow, no leaves to rake, or walks to shovel in the wintertime. We did not chat with neighbors across backyard fences, ride to offices on a train, or attend meetings at the PTA. We did not golf or go fishing with the boys. We spoke to our bosses through international phone lines six or seven or ten thousand miles long and got our assignments via telex signals shot down from manmade stars. Our children attended odd expatriate schools. We hardly knew our children. What we did know was: the broadcast times of the BBC World Service and the Voice of America, how to say, "Don't shoot, I am a foreign journalist" in several languages, the schedules of at least a dozen foreign airlines, which airports were safe from terrorists and which were not. We spent almost as much time away from our wives as sailors. We kept overnight bags always packed in our bedrooms, in case we got the midnight call to catch the next flight to (fill in the blank). We smoked too much, drank too much, caught gastroenteritis, cranked up on amphetamines and worked fourteen hours a day for days at a stretch, then did next to nothing for days on end. We dramatized ourselves as history's assault troops, writing history's first rough draft, because self drama is necessary when you risk your neck and your health for something so evanescent as a news story. Yet we were not without our own brand of passionate intensity, fired with a conviction that we were messengers who brought the light of truth out of places where thugs and dictators tried to extinguish it. We lived at the extremities of experience. We did not have ordinary lives because, each for his own reason, we did not want them.

I had read an old book, *Adventures in Journalism*, by a man named Philip Gibbs. This is what he said about the trade:

"It was, after all, a great game! It is still one of the best games in the world for a young man with quick eyes, a sense of humor, some touch of quality in his use of words, and curiosity in his soul for the truth and pageant of our human drama, provided he keeps his soul unsullied from the dirt."

Not bad, pretty good as a matter of fact. To bring it up to date, you would only have to include young women. Male or female, the tricky part was keeping your soul unsullied. Too much time in certain places, seeing certain things, could make it as tricky as keeping mud off your shoes crossing a swamp. Not that I know much about souls. I've never seen one. I guess it's that small light, that fragile flame of divinity that burns in our breathing, eating, excreting, copulating selves and makes us human. Snuff it out, with ideology, religious zealotry, bigotry, greed, hate, fear, and all you have is a cunning, bipedal predator with a tendency to overpopulate.

To keep the soul unsullied from the dirt—sometimes the dirt got on you merely by watching the pageant of our human drama.

TERRORISTS KILL 18 IN ATTACK ON ISRAELI TOWN

JERUSALEM, April 11—Arab terrorists massacred 16 civilians in an Israeli town near the Lebanese border today, overshadowing the deepening political crisis that brought calls for Prime Minister Golda Meir's resignation ...

Thirteen of the victims in the attack on Qiryat Shemona were women and children ...

The raid, conducted by a three-man squad from the Popular Front for the Liberation of Palestine–General Command, stunned this troubled nation on the usually joyous Passover holiday ...

DAYAN WARNS LEBANON:
STOP TERRORISTS OR BE DESTROYED

TEL AVIV, April 13—Israeli Defense Minister Moshe Dayan has threatened to turn southern Lebanon into a wasteland if the Lebanese government fails to curb Arab terrorists operating within its borders.

Last night's Israeli raid on six Lebanese border towns, carried out in reprisal for 18 Israelis massacred by Arab guerrillas on Thursday, is understood to be the first application of this new antiterrorist policy ...

Lebanese officials said 24 homes were destroyed and 13 people taken captive in the raid. They said two Arab women were killed ...

TERRORISTS KILL 21 ISRAELI TEENS SEIZED AS HOSTAGES

MAALOT, ISRAEL, May 15—Palestinian terrorists struck again in Israel today, killing 21 of 86 Israeli students held hostage in a high school here. The three terrorists, members of the Popular Democratic Front for the Liberation of Palestine, opened up on the hostages with rifles and grenades as Israeli commandos stormed the school in an attempted rescue ...

ISRAELI JETS, GUNS POUND S. LEBANON
RETALIATION FOR MASSACRE OF STUDENTS

ARAB ROCKETS STRIKE ISRAELI BORDER SETTLEMENT

ISRAEL MOURNS MAALOT'S SLAIN TEENS

I was there for the funeral.

It was a pageant of sorts. Heads bowed, feet raising a thin veil of dust, the people tramped through the dry scrub grass toward the cluster of white headstones clustered on the hillside above. There were sixteen headstones and probably ten mourners for each one. I walked alongside them, with my notebook. When I looked back, the long, shuffling column resembled a broken army in retreat.

The sun was hot; spring in the Middle East is just a figure of speech. One old man, too weak to climb any farther, sat down on a rock and wept quietly, and the rest of the people walked past, raising ocher dust radiant in the afternoon light. Wreaths had been laid on some of the graves, freshly dug. The gravediggers' shovels and pickaxes hadn't been cleared away yet. The mourners gathered around and waited for the rabbi to begin the service. The women howled their laments. I had heard that sound so often in Israel I sometimes imagined that it dwelled permanently in the air, like windsong, although it did not sound like windsong. A man who looked like an ancient Hebrew patriarch in his skullcap and long white beard saw me taking notes. He walked over and said, gesturing at the white tablets with the names of dead children chiseled on them, "This is not a wound of today. This is a scar that will remain for all eternity."

The rabbi opened his prayer book. A band of students, friends of the dead, unfurled a banner. On it was a drawing of an Arab with a noose around his neck and the words: DEATH TO THE ARABS! EXECUTE THE ARABS!

That is what the kids chanted as the rabbi began to recite the Kaddish. "Death to the Arabs! Execute the Arabs!"

Spring is just a figure of speech, but there is winter in parts of the Middle East, and it can be bitter. A cold wind whipped down from the spare Judean hills and through the streets of Kalandia refugee camp, on the West Bank. Schoolboys, hair shorn to prevent ringworm, laughing the ignorant laughter of children, ran alongside me and the man from the UN Relief Agency. Goats, chickens, and cows fed in the yards of the mud huts; rain and sewage had dug gullies a foot deep in the streets. The old men sitting around the mosque blew into their hands as they waited for the muezzin to call them to prayer. There wasn't much else for them to do except sit and wait and pray. The young men playing at cards in a fly-blown coffee shop warmed their hands at a brazier. There wasn't much else for them to do except play cards.

Muhammad Ahmad Abdulkarder wasn't playing cards, he wasn't waiting for the muezzin. An old man at fifty-five, face as creased and dried as the hills from which the cold wind blew, he was sitting in front of his hut, holding his cane like a shepherd holds a staff. Once he owned thirty-five acres, half of them planted with olives that, he said, had been there from the time of the Romans. His head was full of memories of the farm he'd been driven from twenty-five years ago, full of dreams of returning. Memory and dreams had become one, the future had become that time when he could reclaim his lost past.

"In nineteen forty-eight, we fled our village because of the fighting then. We fled when we saw a nearby village surrounded by the Israeli soldiers. Everyone fled—men, women, children. We fled eastward. It was in the middle of the summer and a few of the very old died of thirst, for we were all on foot then, walking through the valleys and the rocky passes of the mountains. We were scattered in the valleys and the mountains. Each family did it in its own way, but when we reached Ramallah, we gathered together and some went to Gaza and some to the cities and some came here. We came here, to Kalandia. We lost everything. Everything was left behind—money, property—but we thought we would return home in a week. We have been here now almost twenty-five years because our return was only a dream. The Arab leaders sold us away."

He paused to glance at the coffee shop where the young men shuffled the cards and held their hands over the coal brazier.

"I shall never forget my land. I feel a strain from being away from my land. Here, I feel a strain." He pressed his palm to his chest. "My return is in the hands of Allah, but if I were younger and stronger, I would join the guerrillas. They're not terrorists. They are fighting for their homeland. If they weren't fighting for a usurped right, then they would be terrorists."

The rabbi told the students to be still. He read the Prayer for the Dead. A dark-haired man started shouting in the middle of it.

"Where's it going to happen next? First Qiryat Shemona. Now here. Where are these security forces who are supposed to protect us? Where are they? I have no heart left."

The rabbi went on reading, and the women, sitting in the dust, went on ululating. A man with a thick neck and crew cut, wearing a leather jacket, gave the rabbi a disgusted wave.

"You are praying to God? Where is God? Where is He? If we are His chosen people, why has He done this to us in our land?"

"Nasser is dead, but Arafat is here!" chanted the students from Bir Zeit University. "National Front! National Power!"

It was a small, pretty campus: cypress trees, buildings of a yellowish stone that turned copper-colored when the sunlight was at the right angle. The students were coming down in a solid mass, marching toward the road under green-and-black Palestinian flags. Israeli soldiers were marching up from the other direction, the Uzis slung from their necks swinging across their belts like pendants.

"National Front! National Power! Nasser is dead, but Arafat is here! National Front! National Power!"

The students marched toward the soldiers, the soldiers toward them. Some of the soldiers were loading tear-gas grenades in grenade launchers. An Arab woman ran out of her house and planted herself in the road between the students and the soldiers.

"Get out of here!" she hollered at the rank of men with the Uzis.

There was a series of ragged clicks as the men behind them closed the breaches of the grenade launchers.

"Get out of here! What are you doing in our country?"

"What do you mean, *your* country?" a soldier shouted back. "It's our country!"

There it was, summed up in a few seconds—four thousand years of history, going back to the Hebrews and the Canaanites. The launchers made popping noises and the gas grenades arched overhead, trailing corkscrews of smoke.

"Will you please be quiet?" the rabbi asked softly. "You should remember Rabbi Akiva."

"Who is that?" I whispered to a man beside me.

"A rabbi who preached here two thousand years ago," he answered.

"Remember," this rabbi was saying, "and compare the children who lie here to his flowers who also suffered death from sickness and war and yet the Jewish race went on."

The men stopped shouting, but the women sitting in the dust kept up their eerie hooting. I wished they would stop. I think everyone wanted them to stop.

"I don't want a penny in repayment. I don't want compensation."

Alisha Aquil, dressed in the red-and-black gown of an Arab peasant woman, sat on a sofa beside her husband, Jamil, in the drafty living room of their house.

It was a rude stone place, one of five or six atop French Hill, outside Jerusalem. Below, the Wadi el Joz cut a ditch in the land, dividing the hill from the walls of the Old City.

"We had to leave our old village in forty-eight. Deir Yassin was a neighboring town, and when we heard about the Irgun massacre there, we left with babies in arms and hardly pennies to spend."

They moved to French Hill, farming five acres, building their new house, first out of scrap lumber, then out of stone. After the sixty-seven war, when East Jerusalem was incorporated into the Israeli cap-

ital, the five acres were confiscated. Where the Aquils had grown figs
and olives, apartment buildings stood now, big rectangular things, like
giant obelisks. The same had happened to the other Arab families.
Only their houses and yards were left, and now those were going, too.
They were to be razed to clear the way for a housing complex for students from the Hebrew University. The proper notices had been sent,
the proper offers made. New houses would be built for the families in
the same neighborhood; if they didn't accept, they would be evicted
by force.

The Aquils had not accepted, and they were waiting for the
police and the bulldozers.

"I'll stay here and I'll die here," Alisha said. "Dying in my own
house is better than anything else."

The rabbi, adjusting his glasses, returned to reading the Kaddish. He was interrupted again, this time by a motorcade that had
parked below the graveyard. Yigal Allon, the deputy prime minister,
and Ephraim Katzir, the president, stepped out of a car. Surrounded
by security men with flat alert eyes, they passed through a line of border police guarding the cemetery and started up the hill to pay their
respects, to soothe fears, to do whatever politicians do at such
moments. Seven or eight men—one was the guy with the crew cut
who wondered where God had gone—rushed down from the cemetery, shouting curses and shaking their fists. The rabbi sighed and
folded his book, marking his place with a finger. Screaming, "Where's
our security forces, why can't you protect us?" the men rushed Allon
and Katzir. The border guards raised their truncheons and, holding
them at the horizontal, made a barricade. The angry men stood outside it, shouting for a few minutes before they quieted down. The
rabbi resumed his prayers, but he did not get very far. The students
with the banner started their chant again.

"Execute the Arabs, Allon! Death to the Arabs!"

The men standing in front of the border guards picked up a
chant of their own.

"Allon, revenge! Allon, revenge! Revenge! Revenge! Revenge!"

Allon looked a little frightened. He did not say anything. He did
not have to. The air force did his talking for him. Four Phantoms
screeched overhead. They drowned out the chants, the prayers, the
calls for vengeance, the howls of lament. They flew right through the

air currents that carried the women's cries from one end of the country to the other. All anyone could hear was the technohowl of the jets.
In ten minutes, they would be bombing and strafing the Palestinian
refugee camps in southern Lebanon.

After the funerals, the Israeli press and the country's ever contentious
politicians began conducting the usual autopsies. Why had security
failed? How had the three terrorists slipped through the cordon sanitaire at the border and eluded the police and border patrols for two
days before they took the kids hostage? Who was to blame for the
breach? How could things be fixed so it did not happen again? I
reported the debates dutifully, but I wasn't interested in the tactics of
counterterrorism. I wanted to know what had given those three young
men the power to slaughter twenty-one school kids. They'd done
more than that, by the way: the night before seizing the students, in a
kind of warming-up exercise, they ambushed a truckload of Arab
women returning home from a factory night shift, killing one. Later,
they crept into Maalot, broke into the home of a Jewish settler named
Yosef Cohen, and murdered him, his wife, and his four-year-old son.
The only one of the family to escape was an eighteen-month-old baby
sleeping in another room. The baby was a deaf mute and did not hear
the gunshots and so did not start crying; otherwise, because little
Zionists grow up to be big Zionists, it probably would have been
killed, too.

In ancient Hebrew myth, there was a place called the Kingdom
of Azazel, a wilderness exempt from the Ten Commandments, where
people committed whatever evil came into their heads. I thought
those early Jews had it *almost* right—God's reign was not universal on
earth—but I didn't think the province of evil should have only geographical boundaries. Azazel's wilderness was temporal as well. There
were periods in history when the tablets were shattered, people
behaved abysmally, and the devil was given his due. We seemed to be
living through such a period, the Age of Terrorism. I thought I might
understand it better if I could understand what had made Ali Hassan,
Ziad Rahim, and Abdel Saleh commit mass murder. What had
snuffed the frail flame of divinity in those three men? I wondered.
How coldly analytical, you say. Perhaps, but I was a journalist, curious
about finding the truth in the pageant of our modern human drama.

I would need a little imagination, but the facts had to come first.

The students had gone on a two-day nature hike. Kids were hiking all over Israel in mid-May, the anniversary of Israel's founding. It was a tradition, part of the Zionist effort to rusticate the Jew, make him strong and self-reliant. On the hike were a hundred students from the Netiv Meir school in Maalot and eight adult chaperones, two armed with rifles. I pictured them, strung out along a trail in the wooded hills and valleys of Galilee, narrow-brimmed kibbutz hats on their heads. Maybe they sang patriotic songs to keep their spirits up. Only a month had passed since the massacre at Quiryat Shemona, and there were reports of terrorist operations to be timed for Israel's twenty-sixth anniversary. Some of the students' parents had asked the Ministry of Education to cancel the hike, but the ministry went ahead with it to prove that threats could not disturb the normality of life in Galilee.

Galilee is rugged, wooded country, cut up by valleys and draws. It is good country for guerrillas. Two nights before the students began their nature hike, Hassan, Rahim, and Saleh slipped across the Lebanese border and set off on a hike of their own. They would not have done any singing. They would have moved silently by night and hid in tree-dimmed ravines by day, playing cat and mouse with the Israeli border patrol that had spotted their tracks in the no-man's-land along the border.

I pictured them. Because they belonged to the Popular Democratic Front for the Liberation of Palestine—the same faction that had captured me—I gave them the faces of three of my captors. Hassan, the eldest at twenty-seven, became the stony-eyed Erebia; twenty-two-year-old Rahim the strutting sniper I called The Happy Warrior; Saleh, nineteen, took the appearance of Mahmoud the Mad.

I saw them darting and dodging through the trees, well trained in infiltration. They carried Kalashnikovs, hand grenades, and packs. In each pack were ten pounds of plastic explosive, fuse cord, and detonators. Hassan would have been the leader. There was not a suggestion the fragile spark had ever glowed in the eyes I had imaginatively transplanted into his head. He was a killer, a technician of terror, but also a professional who did not want any unnecessary bloodshed. All he thought about was the mission: capture the students, hold them hostage, demanding in exchange for their lives the release of twenty

Palestinian commandos held in Israeli jails. No prisoners, no live kids. Simple.

Rahim and Saleh would have been more volatile because they were younger and less experienced, on their first mission. They had never been in Palestine before, which was what they would have called Israel. They had been born in the refugee camps of Lebanon. All their lives they had heard about Palestine from their fathers and uncles: the orange and olive groves, the pastures, the villages, the Mosque of Omar in old Jerusalem, the whole intoxicating blend of old men's memories transformed into myths the young men would kill and die for. *The orange groves, the olive groves, that's what you would now have, my son, if not for the Zionists.* The Jews had stolen the mythic land, in collusion with the imperial powers. Every Jew on the soil of Palestine was an occupier, yes, every Jew, man, woman, child, was a soldier in an army of occupation. Fair game. *You are not a terrorist but a freedom fighter. If you were not going on this mission to reclaim a usurped right, my son, then you would be a terrorist.*

At the end of the day, the students marched into the Netiv Meir school to spend the night. A stark concrete building, it was on a hill overlooking Maalot. The kids, dusty from the hike, filed in and spread out their bedrolls on the first floor while the guards locked their weapons in a van to prevent firearms accidents. Then they went inside and lay down in their sleeping bags. The school had a regular watchman, a middle-aged man who also worked as its janitor. He fell asleep in the entry hall.

Fact: the truck carrying the Arab women from the factory came down the road leading into Maalot about two-thirty in the morning. There was a short burst of gunfire, and the woman was killed.

It made no sense. Why would the terrorists compromise the secrecy of the mission by shooting at a truckload of workers? *Arab* women, no less. Of course, they might not have known they were Arab women in the darkness. Possibly they thought it was a truck of Israeli soldiers and fired in a panic. A short burst of gunfire, the reports had said. Maybe one of the guerrillas, the teenage Saleh, I speculated, had opened fire and then was stopped by the others. That made some sense, and that was the trouble with it. It didn't explain the murders of Yosef Cohen, his wife, and son fifteen minutes later. Why did Hassan, Rahim, and Saleh decide to break into a house instead of going straight to the school? Why Cohen's house? What unique property did it have over the hundred-odd other houses they could have picked? Was it its color, its size, its shape, its location? And why shoot a four-year-old kid in cold blood? Because little Zionists grow into big ones? Because he was there to be killed?

My imaginative construct was already breaking down. The ambush of the truck could have been explained as an accident, but the slaughter of the Cohen family had been too deliberate. If Hassan had been the leader, the cold professional, he would not have allowed it to happen, unless ... A lot of possibilities suggested themselves. Cohen might have awakened in the middle of night because he heard a strange noise, or because he had to go to the bathroom, or because he was an insomniac—who could say? He spotted the terrorists as they moved through town, called out a warning. But there had been no mention in the reports of a warning cry, no empirical evidence to support that flight of fancy.

It occurred to me that the attempts to imagine my way into the minds and hearts of the terrorists were not imaginative enough. I was trying to make logical deductions. I had to let go of logic, to forget about rational connections, cause and effect. When I did, I had a vision. I saw sparks—not the sparks of divinity but those of misfiring synapses, the same lunatic flickers Mahmoud the Mad's eyes had given off when he'd tied me up, shoved the rifle in my face. Suppose, then, it was Abdel Saleh who had fired the first shots in the Cohens' house. His thoughts might have run like this: dark ... my hand ... gun ... Jews inside ... shoot ... fun ... *You are not a terrorist, my son, you're just crazy.* And Rahim? Maybe he was crazy, too. And Hassan? Maybe he wasn't in charge. Maybe no one was. Maybe all three had felt the thrill of license and had not been able to resist the temptation to wreak some mayhem on their own authority. And why had they chosen the Cohens' house? For no more reason than a tornado chooses to obliterate one house while leaving its neighbor untouched.

It was after the slaughter of the Cohens that the guerrillas' acts reentered the domain of logic. It was a brutal logic, but you could link one act to the next, at least up until the end.

The whole incident assumed a logic, inevitable as Greek drama.

It happened this way:

3:45 A.M. Hassan, Rahim, and Saleh broke into the school, woke up the watchman, and asked him in Hebrew if the kids were inside. He said yes. The terrorists said *"to-dah"*—Hebrew for thank you—then overpowered the man, tied him up, and broke into the building. They woke the students (imagine that scene, the lights flicking on, the kids and their escorts opening their eyes to the sight of three men with assault rifles and grenades) and herded them upstairs, into two classrooms on the top floor, the third. In the confusion, about twenty students and most of the escorts escaped by leaping out of windows.

4 A.M. Hassan, Rahim, and Saleh methodically planted explosive charges around the rooms, locked the remaining eighty-six students inside, and dispatched one of the adult escorts, a female soldier, with their demands: the release of twenty guerrillas held in Israeli jails in exchange for the lives of the hostages. One of the guerrillas was Kozo Okamoto, a Japanese terrorist-for-hire who had masterminded the massacre of Christian pilgrims at Tel Aviv's Lod Airport in 1972.

5 A.M. Prime Minister Meir, Defense Minister Dayan, and the minister of police were informed of the incident and of the terrorists' demands.

6:30 A.M. Dayan arrived in Maalot with a unit of Israeli snipers and antiterrorist commandos. The soldiers surrounded the school. The guerrillas opened fire on them from the third-floor windows.

9 A.M. The Israeli cabinet began to debate whether to negotiate with the terrorists. It had been Israeli policy never to give in to terrorism. Precious time was lost in argument.

10 A.M. The terrorists announced that they would negotiate the prisoner-hostage exchange through the French and Romanian ambassadors.

11 A.M. Meir and the cabinet decided to agree to the demands, but the three men complicated matters with a new requirement: the French and Romanian envoys could not act as mediators until they obtained a secret code word from the guerrillas' headquarters in Beirut.

12 P.M.–2:55 P.M. The Israelis, French, and Romanians launched a major effort to obtain the code word, but the tangled line of communication—Jerusalem—Tel Aviv—Paris—Bucharest—Beirut —made it impossible.

2:55 P.M. The French foreign ministry informed the Israeli Embassy in Paris of new guerrilla conditions, which the ministry obtained in its conversations with Beirut: the jailed terrorists were to be flown to Damascus; when they landed safely, PDFLP headquarters would issue the code word. Afterward, the three terrorists would release only half the students; the other half, along with the French and Romanian ambassadors, a Red Cross official, and the terrorists themselves were to fly to Damascus. If the new demand was not met by 6.00 P.M., the guerrillas would blow up the school. The Israelis were in a new quandary—they could not permit forty-odd of their children to be flown to an Arab capital.

4 P.M. The government asked for the deadline to be extended. The terrorists refused. The Israeli commandos were ordered to assault the school if there was no movement in negotiations by half-past five.

5:10 P.M. Jean Herly, the French ambassador to Israel, arrived at Maalot. An Israeli officer asked if he had the code word. Herly said, "No."

5:30 P.M. Israeli Chief of Staff Mordechai Gur gave the go-ahead for an assault. The plan was to try to pick off the terrorists with sniper fire while the commandos rushed the school.

5:45 P.M. The assault began, but the snipers missed their targets, only wounding Hassan, Rahim, and Saleh. One of the terrorists (which one?) turned his AK on a fifteen-year-old boy and blew his head off. Another (which one?) shot to death a sixteen-year-old girl, then all three tossed hand grenades and sprayed the hostages with gunfire before the commandos killed them.

Eighteen kids were dead, three more later died in the hospital. All the others had been wounded. The only military casualty was an Israeli army photographer, sniped by one of the guerrillas (which one?) sometime during the siege.

None of us who were there to observe and record history in the making had been allowed near Maalot during the stand-off. Afterward, we were brought to the schoolhouse and given an escorted walk-through, although we could not walk on the third floor because it was still sticky with blood. The escort officer, who had been there for the assault, said he had never seen so much blood, though he had been in four wars.

"It was a ghastly scene. I have seen enough dead in my life, but when you see kids on the floor screaming and wounded, it's a vicious, vicious thing."

The sixteen-year-old girl, he told us, had written a farewell note to her parents while the negotiations were going on. It was found in her hand, bloodstained but legible: "I am sorry for not listening to you. I should not have gone on this hike."

That was the vignette that sent me on my imaginative expedition to map the terrorists' interiors. I had seen enough dead, too, enough viciousness in men driven past the last extremities, but God almighty, what happened in that little Galilean town belonged to an order of savagery that defied categorization. How had he (which one?) pulled the trigger on that sixteen-year-old girl clutching her last note? How had they all rampaged through those rooms crowded with young life, shooting and throwing grenades when they had known (they must have known) it would not free the men whose freedom they'd demanded, would not do themselves or their cause any good whatso-ever? I rejected insanity; madmen don't carry code words, make demands for asylum, negotiate with ambassadors.

In the end, science, not imagination, gave me a kind of answer: the theory of black holes—stars which implode, molecules into molecules, atoms into atoms, until their density becomes infinite and their gravitational force so powerful not even light cannot escape its grasp. Black holes are surrounded by something called an event hori-zon, which the textbooks define as "a boundary across which observa-tion of events becomes impossible because of inherent differences in space-time between the two sides of the boundary." If you are inside a black hole, you can't see out; if you're outside, you can't see in. Imagi-nation's light was not strong enough to show me what I wanted to know. No light was, because Hassan, Rahim, and Saleh had flown beyond a moral event horizon into some impenetrable night of the soul. If I wanted to know what made them pull the triggers, I would have to go there myself, but that would be one horizon too far.

We were supposed to be objective, to keep our own emotions out of the stories we filed. It wasn't easy at first. You saw things that made your heart ache and swell—sometimes it felt as if you had a basketball pumping in your chest—and you went back to your hotel room and sat in front of your portable and wrestled with the pity or the anger or the disgust that barged into your copy. It could be a real struggle, but after a while, it got easier; after a while longer, there was no trick to it at all. You could look upon the most terrible sights, report them in prose as clean, smooth, and cool as a refrigerated egg, and then head to the bar no more troubled than a drill-press operator at the end of his shift.

It could wound your heart and dirty your soul, but sometimes, in the world's States of Extremes, the drama of the human pageant could kill you outright.

LEBANESE JUNTA RESIGNS TO END THREAT OF CIVIL WAR

BEIRUT, May 26—The first military government in Lebanon's history resigned today, a move that pulled the country back from the brink of a sectarian civil war between its Moslem and Christian communities ...

KARAMI USED AS ROPE IN LEBANESE TUG-OF-WAR

BEIRUT, June 3—Lebanese premier-designate Rashid Karami, a powerful Moslem leader appointed to his new post after a military government resigned last week, struggled today to form a coalition government to end the country's fratricidal strife ...

Thursday night, four more people were killed in clashes between Phalangist militiamen and Palestinian guerrillas, bringing the number killed in the past 10 days to 100 ...

SALVATION GOVERNMENT INSTALLED
BY LEBANON AS BATTLE TOLL HITS 700

BEIRUT, July 1—A "salvation government" aimed at averting civil war was installed in Lebanon today as gunfire and rocket exchanges began to die down ...

The city was ablaze early Tuesday with dozens of fires from more than 100 explosions during the night ... The casualty toll for a week of fighting between Right- and Left-wing militias rose to 215 dead and more than 1,000 wounded ... The factional warfare has taken more than 700 lives in the past three months.

DEAD IN LEBANON STRIFE REACHES 1,000
2,500 DEAD IN LEBANON WAR

SEVEN-MONTH TOLL IN LEBANON IS 7,000
COP SAYS: NO ONE COUNTING ANYMORE

From the old quarter, a maze of tight, crooked streets and covered bazaars crowded around the port, to the glassy high-rise ramparts fronting the Mediterranean, Beirut wasn't a city so much as a crazy quilt of ghettoes—Christians in East Beirut, Moslems in West, Jews in a tiny quarter somewhere in between, Palestinians in the stinking camps of Sabra and Chatilla, colonies of Armenians, Circassians, and Syrians scattered here and there. The one thing that had held the whole thing together, until religious passions and class hatreds tore it to pieces, was the pursuit of money. The Lebanese were descendants of the Phoenicians, bartering and bargaining written into their genetic code. You could sell anything in Beirut, including yourself, and you could buy anything if you had the money, from prime hash to the finest Isfahans to rocket-propelled grenades.

Petro princes flocked to the city on holiday from the boozeless sands of their ascetic emirates. They drank freely and openly and gambled their millions at the Casino du Liban, a place that combined the best and worst features of Las Vegas, Monte Carlo, and the Folies-Bergère. In the winter, they spent their mornings skiing in the mountains and their afternoons on the beach, chatting up girls in string bikinis. A modified version of the white-slave trade operated in the bars and nightclubs near the harbor front: European girls down on their luck signed two- and three-year contracts to work as bartenders and cocktail waitresses and whatever else the Lebanese owners wanted them to do. The contracts had no escape clauses, the owners had the right to hold the girls' passports. They were stuck for the duration, but if they played their hands right and avoided serious venereal diseases, they could go back to England or Holland with a nice stake in their purses.

The city was best known as the financial hub of the Middle East. The world's biggest banks had branches in Beirut; so did a lot of smaller institutions with questionable depositors like gunrunners and

Palestinian guerrillas. The presence of so much money made the city a natural headquarters for middlemen brokering deals between foreign businessmen and Arab clients. Adnan Kashoggi was the king of them all. Some were legitimate, some had the ethics of three-card monte shufflers and could swindle you and your company out of every dime so fast you wouldn't know anything had happened until your checks started to bounce.

The biggest sales item was not material. Beirut was a bazaar of information—good information, bad information, disinformation, insinuations, innuendo, and propaganda. That had turned it into a mecca for journalists and spooks of all nations, as well as for political assassins and free-lance killers using the information to carry out covert government missions or to settle personal scores. The Mossad was active in the city. The KGB and CIA fielded strong teams; so did the French SDECE, for old times' sake if nothing else.

The city pretended to a certain French sophistication. Its Christian population, some of whom claimed descent from Frankish Crusaders, spoke French as a second language, named their kids Pierre and Michelle, and referred to Moslems as "the Arabs." Half a dozen restaurants served dishes as good as any you'd find in Paris or New York, and the sommeliers in the St. Georges, the Vendome, or the Phoenicia could tell you with the hautiest Gallic sniff that the sixty-four Latour you had just ordered was much inferior to the sixty-two.

The rube was likely to mistake this appearance of civilization for civilization itself and to think he was in a place governed by familiar rules and standards. It was a common misimpression, and it could be fatal because all those banks and fancy restaurants, all those ski resorts and flesh-dappled beaches, all those waiters suggesting you select the sixty-two over the sixty-four were sets and actors in an elaborate show, a gorgeous costuming of a fractious, violent, tribal society smoldering with hatreds that went back so far into history no one could date when they had begun.

The country, which liked to think of itself as a multi-confessional, multiethnic enclave à la Switzerland, was a kind of box-within-a-box trick of religious and political antagonisms (and in Lebanon, as in Northern Ireland, one's politics was largely determined by one's religion). You opened the first box and found Christians and Moslems, the second showed you Christians divided among Maronite Catholics

—the dominant sect—Roman Catholics, and Eastern Orthodox. The third revealed Moslems split among Sunnis, Shiites and Druze, to name the three major sects (the minor ones would require half a page). An array of political parties more or less corresponded to the religious faiths: the Christians had the Phalangist and Chamounist parties, the Moslems had Arab socialists, Arab fascists, Arab Communists, and Arab monarchists, along with pro-Syrian Baathists, pro-Iraqi Baathists, and pan-Arab Nasserites with visions of establishing a grand Moslem-socialist caliphate from Morocco to the Persian Gulf. The leader of each party was part politician, part Mafia don, and part warlord because each party maintained an armed militia. Yet with all that, a Lebanese's first allegiance was to his clan, and even within families there was a pyramid of loyalties and enmities. An old Levantine proverb put it this way: *I against my brother, my brother and I against our cousin, my brother, my cousin and I against the stranger.* No holds were barred. Once, in a village north of Beirut, a clash between two Christian clans led gunmen from one to machine-gun members of the other in a *Maronite church during Sunday Mass.*

The blood feud and civil strife were a way of life in Lebanon long before the war began. Vicious battles between Christians and Moslems were fought in the 1860s. After independence from the French, a complicated but precarious system of power sharing was set up, with various government ministries and military positions apportioned according to religious affiliation—the presidency to one, the prime ministership to another, the ministry of defense to a third, and so forth—but the Christians, better educated and more numerous, held the lion's share of political and economic power. The Moslems rose up in 1958, when their population grew numerically closer to the Christians', but that conflict was a finger exercise compared to the one that started in the spring of 1975.

It wasn't a war when Proffitt and I returned to Beirut from Saigon in mid-May; it was *fighting.* The Christian Phalange had fired the first shots the previous month, when a gang of its militia ambushed a busload of Palestinians, killing and wounding some thirty people. At first, the *fighting* was confined to the Phalange and a couple of factions of the PLO. It was likewise geographically restricted to the suburbs and the Palestinian camps. In the heart of the city, the Lebanese went on

320 / PHILIP CAPUTO

trading and bargaining, the ladies shopped in the exclusive stores on the Rue Hamra, the bankers continued to swing deals, sunbathers lay on the beaches or at the poolside decks of the seaside hotels.

Gradually, though, the *fighting* spread. By the end of June, at least ten identifiable militias were mixed up in it. Untrained, undisciplined, but very well armed, they waged it with a cruelty that made Vietnam look like Agincourt and turned Beirut into a bloody laboratory for anyone interested in what happens when the social contract goes into the shredder. Everyone got into the act: taxi drivers, grocery clerks, antique dealers, carpet merchants, mechanics, and schoolteachers became gunmen. Fourteen-year-old boys fired RPGs from behind barricades with sixty-year-old men shooting assault rifles. Hashish smugglers and extortionists coalesced into a militia of their own, the Mourabitoun, which means "ambushers," though we called them "The Looney Tunes" because they were psychopaths, the worst of the Beast's children. The army tried to keep order for a while, but soldiers began deserting to join whatever militia their faith and politics called them to. The red-bereted security police from Squad-16 signed on, too, and so did women. Christian females took up sniper rifles, Moslem women, more repressed, stayed at home as a kind of ladies' auxiliary, keeping the hate fires burning by encouraging their sons, brothers, and husbands to take up arms for Allah and vengeance.

No, it was not a war. There were no advances and retreats, no frontal assaults or flanking movements, above all, no purpose. One neighborhood would start shooting at another, which would shoot back, and the shooting would keep on until the gunmen ran out of ammunition or got tired of pulling triggers. Any one block of Beirut could be totally at peace at noon, totally at war by one o'clock, and return to peace by two. Anything could happen anywhere at any moment. Or nothing. There was no way to predict events or read people. The jovial cabdriver who took you home could, in an hour, stick twenty pounds of *plastique* in the basement of your building and light the fuse without giving you a second thought, unless you'd shorted him on the tip. Once, when the *fighting* was still sporadic, a visiting French businessman was lunching in the home of a Lebanese colleague in the Christian quarter of Ashrafiyah. The Lebanese looked the image of Levantine style in his fine imported suit, silk shirt, and pearl cuff links. The best white wine was served—the Frenchman would later recall it was a Montrachet. They discussed affairs of commerce over coffee, after which the guest was invited to have a look at the rooftop garden. The Lebanese had not brought him there to show off his begonias or bonsai plants. He pulled at a tarp, unveiling an 82 millimeter mortar, then picked up a shell, set the proper charges in the tail fin—the Frenchman would later recall that the man knew what to do—and, instructing his guest to plug his ears, dropped the shell into the tube. The Frenchman thought it was a dummy, part of a nasty practical joke, but, ten or fifteen seconds later, the shell exploded on a house a couple of blocks off. As the Lebanese picked up another projectile, the astonished Frenchman grabbed his arm and asked him what in the name of God was he doing: there were *people* over there. The Lebanese made a dismissive gesture. "No, just Moslems."

Governments were formed to stop the violence, governments collapsed, and new governments were formed, but there was no government or law of any kind except the government and law of the big warlords: Pierre Gemayel, chief of the Phalangists, and Walid Jumblatt, chief of the Socialists (whose great-grandfather had been a Moslem leader in the 1860s civil war; among the Jumblatts, killing Christians was a family tradition). Sometimes the Phalangists battled with their rival Christian party, the Chamounists, named after their leader, Camille Chamoun; sometimes one PLO faction would willynilly make alliance with the Christians to fight another PLO faction. Sometimes half a dozen wars raged at once.

So far as I know, Lebanon is the only country in modern history to have committed suicide. Christian *plastiquers* ranged through the souks in the old quarter one night, setting off a hundred bombs, obliterating marketplaces, entombing you-count-how-many people in sepulchers of rubble. Mortar fire shut down the port; every warehouse in it was destroyed, though only after gunmen raided them of refrigerators, foodstuffs, construction steel, liquor, TV sets, automobiles, and on and on and on. The stolen goods were peddled on the black market, proceeds going toward arms and ammunition, also purchased on the black market. Free-lance thugs and warring factions looted collections of art and Oriental carpets, antiques, silver, and rare books from stores, homes, and museums. A band of Phalangists and Chamounists broke into the British Bank, discovered nearly twenty million dollars in cash and negotiable traveler's checks, got into a gunfight over the treasure, each side losing three men before they declared a truce, made off with the take, and cashed the traveler's checks in Switzerland. After that, the international banks began to close their doors and pull their staffs out to Athens and Cairo. The big multinational corporations did the same. By the fall, Bechtel, IBM, and International Harvester were gone or on their way. When the followers of Jesus and the faithful of Muhammad began battling for control of the hotel district (because it had the highest buildings in town), tourists decided the sun was just as warm in Cyprus and Greece. The Holiday Inn was blasted to shambles, the St. Georges and the Vendome sacked and burned. Some neighborhoods, like the one we lived in near the university, were untouched, others resembled Berlin in 1945. The awesome demolition had not been the work of an invading army, no, the Lebanese had done it to themselves. Beirut was what Hobbes must have had in mind when he described the state of nature in *Leviathan:* "In such a condition, there are no arts; no letters; no society; and which is worst of all, continual fear and danger of violent death; and the life of man, solitary, poor, nasty, brutish and short."

Nick and I made good on our pact not to cover another war. We wrote about the *fighting,* but we did not cover it. We phoned our sources from our offices and pirated from the local press, but we stayed away from the *fighting.* Because there was no point to it, there was no point in risking our lives to cover it. The October War had been a classical narrative, with beginning, middle, and end, and some sort of moral. Even Vietnam had a facsimile of structure and meaning. But in war as story, the *fighting* in Lebanon was pure postmodernism: random, chaotic, and senseless. Because journalists are required to make sense of the senseless, we filed occasional thumbsuckers that said it was not just a religious war but also a class war between the Christian haves and the Moslem have-nots, though we knew there were plenty of Christian poor and Moslem rich, though we knew the bloodshed would have gone on even if all the wealth had been redistributed in perfectly equal shares. We called the Christians "rightists" and the Moslems "leftists," though we knew the Moslems had monarchist and fascist factions and that one faction, The Looney Tunes, had no politics at all except those of robbery and murder. We wrote in off-the-rack prose, using ready-made phrases like "Moslem and Christian communities," though we knew there was no community left anywhere. We wrote that stuff to keep our editors' and readers' needs for coherence satisfied. Also, it made us look smart to offer thoughtful commentaries on the facts behind the facts, to reveal the real, hidden meaning behind the *fighting*. But of course there was none. It had become something quite distinct from those doing it, a whole greater than the sum of its parts, an entity with its own personality, a psychotic killer wandering the city with capricious vagrancy.

I wasn't surprised when I started to get bombarded by rockets from the foreign desk. Why all the agency-style copy? Where was the strong, front-line reporting, the *bang-bang*, with which I had distinguished myself in Israel, Cyprus, and Vietnam? The paper wasn't paying me to duplicate the wire services. Another correspondent had filed an eyewitness story from behind a Moslem barricade *at night*. Why couldn't I? I telexed my reply: TRAVELING BEIRUT IN DAYTIME EXTREMELY DANGEROUS, SUICIDE AT NIGHT. WILL NOT RPT NOT DO IT. RGDS/CAPUTO/BEIRUT.

But the rockets continued. They were preferable to the exploding kind, but were almost as dangerous in their way. After a while, I knew I was going to have to do something to stop them from coming. It so happened that John Palmer, my office mate, had been on the receiving end of similar missiles from NBC. He had arranged to spend a night at a Christian position with his French cameraman, who was going to experiment with then innovative fast film for shooting in darkness. I was welcome to come along. When a cease-fire was declared, we decided to try it, though we knew, as a saying among correspondents put it, that a cease-fire in Lebanon was as useful as a screen door on a submarine. Still, we might have an hour or two to reach Ashrafiyah before the shooting resumed.

We left late in the afternoon, with John's Lebanese driver at the wheel. The most dangerous moment came when we had to cross the Green Line, which was the only feature that gave any coherence to the Beirut battlefield. It divided the Christian East from the Moslem West and was covered by snipers from both denominations. We were vastly thankful when the driver sped across it without a shot being fired. The narrow, winding streets in Ashrafiyah were empty, glittering with pools of shattered glass from blown-out shop and apartment windows, gouged by mortar and rocket craters. Mangled scroll iron railings hung like electrical cord from ruined balconies. We drove up a hill, an urban bluff actually, and stopped at a new apartment building overlooking Shiyah, a Moslem and Palestinian neighborhood. I kept a diary of the night's work, and because it gives a good picture of just how stupid and pointless the *fighting* was, I offer it now with only some editing.

July 1, 6:30 P.M.: Sandbagged firing positions are set up at the four corners of the building's walled parking lot, giving the militiamen a sniper's-eye view of what might be called enemy territory.

The Phalangist militia are called *Kataeb* in Arabic. There are about a dozen of them here, dressed in motley uniforms, wearing armbands with the cedar-tree symbol of their party. Some are wearing black berets, some olive-drab ski masks to hide their identities. Their weapons are a gun collector's dream, but the most prevalent are the Russian Kalashnikovs, which, one militiaman tells us, were bought from the Palestinian guerrillas whom he is now fighting.

"Very funny, don't you think? They're getting shot with their own weapons."

Brass litters the pavement, but for the moment the Phalangists are holding to the cease-fire. The other side is not, and an occasional bullet whips overhead.

7:30 P.M.: A phone rings. It is answered by the leader of this band, a tall heavyset man with an ugly scar on his face. His name is George, and he is outfitted in green army pants, a white undershirt, and a hunting vest. George is a graduate in agriculture from the American University, but he seems to have other skills besides knowing what fertilizers to use. The call is from headquarters and instructs him to extend the cease-fire. He passes the order to the *Kataeb*. Exasperated by the incoming gunshots (I think that's the reason, but maybe it's not), the militiamen ignore it, crouch behind the sandbags, and loose several bursts.

"I guess we don't agree with the order," says one of the men, a gold crucifix hanging prominently around his neck. "It's those extremist fedayeen. They have no discipline. What a mentality." The man, a fifty-three-year-old father of eight, explains that he was in the French army in World War II, then gestures in a way to emphasize his disgust with warfare.

7:45 P.M. Looks like the cease-fire is another casualty of the "crisis," as this fratricide is euphemistically known. The younger *Kataeb* shout excitedly when a target is spotted and seem to regard all this as healthy outdoor fun. One, armed with an M-16 that cost $1,000 on the black market and a huge, chrome-plated .44 magnum revolver, grins as he sends a fusillade into the buildings half a mile away. In contrast to his gaiety is the professional seriousness of a middle-aged fellow whose nickname is "Steve McQueen." Stubble-bearded and bleary-eyed, he stays up all night and day shooting Moslems. We watch him move around like a cat, ducking behind walls, eyes roving over the houses opposite, raising his Russian rifle when he spots something, aiming carefully, and then cracking off a round with businesslike coolness. A bullet whacks over his head. He looks up scornfully and says: "Hoo-hoo."

8:15 P.M.: We have been joined by a famed sportsman, a gray-haired ironic gent who used to be national rifle champion of Lebanon. He was wounded, literally at his front door, two months ago by a shell, but he carries no weapon. "I don't like killing people," he says, though he shows a lively and expert interest in the various merits of the rifles carried by the *Kataeb*. He takes us on a brief tour of the neighborhood. A block down the street used to be a border between the Moslems and Christians, but the Phalange seized it by storm five days ago, he says. A lot of dead on both sides, but mostly Moslem. Blood running in the streets, and no figure of speech either, he says. The brother of George, the local leader, was hit by an antiaircraft gun, and his guts were blown out, the sportsman continues, shaking his head at the "mentality" that would use such a weapon against people. He shows us a gutted building—charred baby dolls lying around, smashed crockery and glass, chandeliers hanging forlornly over an ashen living room. A loudspeaker is playing "The Colonel Bogey March" from somewhere. The sportsman, who tells us he trains the militia in marksmanship, shakes his head. "This damn business has made me miss my fishing and shooting season."

8:30 P.M.: Back at the apartment building. A man, his wife, and two small children are huddled in the hallway. The kids, about three and five, carry toy pistols and a toy M-16 that looks too much like the real thing. Hero worship in their eyes, the two little boys gaze at the militia's real guns and run around shouting what I guess is the Arabic equivalent of bang-bang.

The ex-rifle champ asks me rhetorically: "What will all this accomplish? Who knows? These people are mad and this is a mad country. Today they are killing each other. A week from now, they'll be hugging and kissing."

11:30 P.M.: We have been taken to Phalange party headquarters to get permission from Sheikh Beshir Gemayel (Phalange party leader Pierre Gemayel's eldest son) to remain the night. Inside, it is crowded with secretaries and party workers answering phones and, except for all the machine guns and the guards with AK-47s (some with pictures of Our Lady of Mount Lebanon painted on the stocks), reminds me of a Chicago ward headquarters on election night. An elderly man named Alexander lectures us on the reason for the fighting—it is a fight against communism, he says—and tells what life in Ashrafiya has been like: "You call this a life? Some sleep in their basements. To be able to sleep is a matter of having good nerves. They shelled us last night until six-thirty this morning."

Sheikh Beshir grants us permission. We ask him if this is a religious fight—the Christian cross versus the Moslem crescent—or a political one.

"It is a fight against communism. Tell the people in America that if we don't fight, Lebanon today would be another Syria or Iraq."

July 2, 1:00 A.M.: Back at the firing line, George and his comrades invite us for an excellent dinner—lamb kebab, hommos, tabouli, pita, tea, and wine. There is that air of desperate cheeriness and masculine good fellowship: George tells us that the Phalange is fighting to keep Lebanon for the Lebanese. He and his friends lift their glasses and toast: "Long live Lebanon! Long live the blood of the cedars!" As if in disagreement, a hail of Moslem bullets whips past.

3:00 A.M.: Sometime tonight Premier Rashid Karami and Yasir Arafat agreed to yet another cease-fire. It's a cease-fire Lebanese-style. Machine guns, rifles, and mortars, for a few minutes silent, start again. A fire is burning in the Moslem area facing us, and on the southern horizon is a pale red flickering from a heavy bombardment. Unable to sleep, I get up to look, but an automatic rifle sends bullets singing viciously overhead, which sends me diving behind a wall.

6:00 A.M.: Fighting continues and an enormous pall of smoke rises over Shiyah. Steve McQueen is back on the job, cracking away as the early sun splashes gold light on the building and the hills beyond. We sip breakfast tea to the rattling of a Belgian FN rifle, fired by a youth wearing a mask that makes him resemble an Old West stage-coach robber.

8:00 A.M.: Weary but pleased to be alive, we leave "the front." There are more people on the street than yesterday. Some are sweep-ing up splintered glass. A car struck by a rocket looks like a cheese grater on wheels.

8:30 A.M.: Back at the office I hear that Radio Kuwait has announced that the emir of Kuwait, Sheikh Sabah, has decided not to spend his annual summer holiday in Lebanon this year.

It was always strange returning to our neighborhood. The *fighting* skirted it but never touched it. People relaxed on their terraces or around the pools, listening to gun and shellfire only two or three miles off. They watched the army's armored cars and half-tracks clanking down the Corniche as if on parade. Some expatriates, mostly bankers and businessmen, began to concoct fantasies that the factions had deliberately spared us because they did not want to drive foreign corporations and financial institutions out of the country. They know where their bread's buttered, they'll leave us alone to fight it out among themselves, and when they settle this thing, we'll be back to business. At dinners and other social gatherings I became Cassandra and Jeremiah all rolled into one, the resident prophet of doom. It's just a matter of time, I would say. This whole city, this whole country is finished.

Finally, sometime in late summer, we got a taste of it. Late one night, everybody in our building and in several buildings nearby were rocked out of their beds by an immense explosion. In our apartment, thick black smoke rolled through the windows. Jill and I ran into the boys' room, snatched them from their beds, and huddled in the hall, thinking the blast had been a shell and that others would soon follow. But it wasn't a mortar or artillery: Moslem *plastiquers*, retaliating for Christian bombings, had blown up Smith's, a Christian-owned super-market about three blocks away. Jill and other expat wives often shopped there. Leaving her and the boys in the hall, I took the elevator to the top floor, then climbed the stairs to the roof. A huge circle of fire glowed where Smith's had been, a devil's eye in the darkened face of the neighborhood. South and eastward, near the Palestinian camps, rifles and mortars flickered and tracers made continual, solid red lines across the night sky, like speeding taillights photographed on an expressway at a slow shutter speed. Counting by thousands between the shell bursts and their sound, I calculated that the *fighting* was within two miles of us. Yes, it would come and engulf us, too; there would be no exemptions, not in a place where a supermarket was considered a legitimate military target. I had a vision, almost a premonition, alone on the roof that noisy night alight with war's fires. I was watching a preview of coming attractions. If ever the day came when the social contract went into the shredder everywhere, then the whole of the civilized world would look like Beirut. The Beast had not slouched toward Bethlehem to be reborn; Beirut was its manger.

I think that's when my hatred and contempt of the Lebanese came squalling out of its womb. It was like the hatred and contempt a veteran beat cop feels for the citizens of a high-crime neighborhood, only it was deeper. I could not find a single redeeming quality in a people destroying themselves with such unflagging energy and enthusiasm. Now and then I thought of my journey through Sinai—which seemed so long ago—with Muhammad and Suleiman and of the codes of honor and behavior that governed the bedouin. City Arabs derided the nomads as primitives, but who were the real primitives? The tribesmen of Beirut wore suits instead of nomad's robes, rode in cars instead of on camels, lived in houses instead of goatskin tents, but in times of feud or war, they might as well have been Cro-Magnons, clubbing each other on some Mesolithic plain.

I broke my pact with Nick. I started to cover the *fighting* because its pointlessness was the point. It was war distilled to its essence, which was utterly senseless killing, war purified of the purposes and morals man gives to it to make it acceptable and coherent. All wars were ultimately meaningless, with the possible exception of the war against Hitler (and a thousand years from now, how much difference would it make that our side won?). Historians, as much as journalists, had an obsession with making sense of the senseless. Through the distorting lenses of hindsight and their own biases they would study some terrible battle, which must have seemed like a complete madhouse to the men in it, and find patterns and reasons for it, then conclude that its outcome could not have been otherwise and had had enduring consequences for humankind. But what if the view of the combatants was the right one? What if there had been no pattern but, rather, a swirl of events that happened to arrange themselves into a victory for one side? What if the outcome could have been otherwise and made no lasting difference to the course of human history? Would the world I'm living in, I thought, be significantly better or worse if Napoleon had *won* at Waterloo? If Julius Caesar had been defeated by Vercingetorix? Suppose it had been Washington who'd surrendered to Cornwallis at Yorktown, what then? The United States probably would have become another Canada or Australia, which wouldn't have been a catastrophe.

War showed its naked face in Beirut. I went out to paint it as I saw it.

A Christian militiaman, under fire for hours, crouches behind a barricade during a lull. A teenage boy comes up behind him and, playing a joke, sticks his rifle in the man's back and shouts, "Bangbangbang." *Bangyerdead.* The man spins around, cuts the boy almost in half with a burst, then falls to his knees and screams; he's killed his kid brother.

A Jesuit priest, walking on crutches from a month-old leg wound, crosses a street to say Mass in his church. A sniper hits him in the head. *Bangyerdead.*

On a street of shops shelled by heavy mortars, dismembered consumers and dismembered mannequins lie all over. You can't tell from a distance which legs and arms are flesh and which are plastic. A stiffened corpse sits in the doorway of a ladies' boutique, his palm out, and a laughing Moslem militiaman drops a few coins into the rigid hand.

I saw the humor in it, too. Lebanon's self-inflicted wound was funny, viewed askance, and askance was the only way you could look over there. You had to search for eccentric angles of vision because the Beast was loose and you could not stare him straight in the eye. So I looked at it all from the side and went home and had dinner and played with my boys and kissed my wife and never felt a thing. Not too surprising, is it? I was the guy who had stepped into a man's brains and scraped them from my boots as if they were dog shit. Even the hatred and contempt had gone. The *fighting* had become a gruesome amusement, the drama of the human pageant as dark comedy.

October brought the struggle for the hotel district. Men were killing and dying for possession of the Holiday Inn. That was less than a mile from our neighborhood, and you heard no more fantasies from the bankers and businessmen. They were packing up. Two who lived in our building, officers for Continental Illinois, had to ride to their branch in armored personnel carriers, loaned courtesy of the Lebanese army. I suggested they could become heroes in a comic book, possibly a TV series called "Fighting Financiers."

The foreign desk fired a new salvo of rockets. They had gotten enough bang-bang; now they wanted stories about the war's innocent victims, heart tuggers about what it was doing to the ordinary men and women of Beirut. It was no use reminding them that ordinary men and women were the ones doing the fighting. I went in search of innocent victims. I've described what I found: I was the correspondent who saw those Moslem women dead from a mortar attack, who thought the crumbs of bread lying in the pools of blood resembled croutons in dark-red bisque, who sat by his typewriter incapable of saying a thing because he was incapable of feeling a thing except scorn. The idiots, coming out on the street because there was a cease-fire, crowding together the way they did. They were asking for it. I telexed a message to Chicago: the Lebanese were not worth anyone's tears; there were no innocent victims in Beirut, all were agents of history—the men with the guns, the women who egged them on, the kids who played with toy guns, gazing with worshipful eyes at their murderous fathers and uncles. The fighting would end when the Lebanese annihilated themselves, which, I suggested, would be an excellent final solution. My emotional temperature had reached absolute zero.

October 25 was a Sunday, a day of cloudless sky and light that seemed to be falling through a topaz filter. A recoilless cannon cracked from the hotel district, as measured as a salute. Foreign embassies were making evacuation plans and had warned their citizens to stay inside. The streets were empty, traffic lights faithfully winking red yellow green to traffic that wasn't there. Jill and I were discussing how to get ourselves and our belongings out of Lebanon when the phone rang. It was the foreign desk: Joe Alex Morris, the Los Angeles *Times*'s Middle East correspondent, had filed a story about an attempt by Moslem militiamen to seize a Christian neighborhood by storm during the night. That represented a change in the war, which had been mostly static. Neither side had tried to take large pieces of territory from the other. The battle had taken place near the Rue Hamra, in the same area as my office. Did I know anything about it, and why hadn't I filed? Because the embassy had warned us to stay inside. Require six hundred words. I said it was too dangerous to go out. Of course it was dangerous, but damnit, that's your job.

I slammed the phone down and called Morris. What was this about a Moslem assault? Yes, one had taken place, but it had been thrown back. He was going to Reuters to file a retop and would be glad to give me a fill if I met him there in forty-five minutes. I got in my car, telling Jill I would be back in an hour or two, and drove to my office. It was less than three blocks from Reuters' Middle East headquarters. After checking the telex, I walked toward the building, passing the high walls of the Beirut College of Law (what law could they possibly have taught there?). I saw no one, not a sign of life anywhere. I cannot recall if I felt more apprehensive than usual, but when I look back through the temporal telescope and see myself walking down those deserted streets flooded in amber light, I feel the presence of a threat more metaphysical than physical, a sense not of danger but of evil. It is as if something invisible yet real is dogging my every step: the Beast, the everlasting Beast in man.

About a dozen of its Children were standing around the building's front entrance. They wore no armbands to distinguish which militia they belonged to. They did not have to; one look at them was enough to tell me they were Mourabitoun. I started to climb the steps. A man in his early twenties shoved his palm against my chest. Where are you going, who are you? He had shark's eyes (no spark of divinity there, no light at all) and a smile immediately recognizable as the one I'd seen in the mirror when I thought of those foolish women. It was the smile of someone incapable of perceiving another human being's pain. Flashing my card, I told him I was *sahafi*—press—and that I was going upstairs to Reuters. Another, older man told me to wait. He went inside and was gone for ten minutes or so. I waited in the middle of that pack of thugs, feeling the way I would in a cage full of pit bulls. I wished Morris were there. The older man came out and told me it was all right to go upstairs.

Reuters was usually crowded with correspondents, messengers, and telex operators, but only two Lebanese employees were there, packing up equipment. Several windows had been shot out; bullets had gouged the walls. I asked what had happened to everyone. The bureau, I was told, had moved to the Commodore Hotel. It was too dangerous to stay here. Early that morning, the building had been caught in the crossfire. Had anyone seen Mr. Morris from the Los Angeles *Times?* No. Perhaps he was at the Commodore (haunting to think of him now; five years later, during the Iranian Revolution, Joe Alex would be killed by a bullet in the heart). I tried to phone the hotel, but the lines were dead. I asked one of the Lebanese for copies of the stories about the night's action. He rummaged through a stack of papers, handed me some carbons, and told me to be quick. They were clearing out as soon as they could; fighting could break out again at any second. I made hurried notes and left, cursing Morris and the foreign desk, cursing myself for leaving my front door.

Outside, the same band of Looney Tunes lurked on the steps, their postures and sullen eyes suggesting a slum street gang looking for action. They had been joined by half a dozen men wearing the red-and-black patches of the Nasserite militia. The presence of the Nasserites wasn't the only difference. I was aware, as soon as I stepped out the door, of the change that used to come over Mahmoud the Mad when his synapses misfired. There were fifteen or sixteen Mahmouds now, and the molecules of their brains had rearranged themselves, for reasons I could never know, possibly for no reason at all, into a configuration of pure hate. The air itself felt different. There was murder in it. All the currents of evil in that city seemed to have converged at that one point, on the perfectly ordinary steps of that perfectly ordinary building. I was in Azazel's kingdom.

The same guy who'd stopped me from going in now stopped me from leaving. He wanted to see my press pass.

"I just showed it to ..." I looked around for the older man who had let me inside, but he wasn't there. "You just saw it."

He turned his palm up and fluttered his fingers, like a cop

demanding a driver's license. I pulled out the card. He drew a straight razor and started to slowly cut it down the middle. I have to explain that each militia issued its own press passes, and even God could not help the correspondent who accidentally showed a Christian pass to a Moslem faction. The one that could get you into any area, and, more important, out, was the laminated pass issued by the Ministry of Information. It could be the only thing between you and a bullet in the back of the head, which was why I snatched the card from the gunman's hand. With his predatory smile, he pressed the flat of the razor under my ear.

"*Sahafi Amerikai!*" he said, then spat at my shoe. "Maybe I cut your throat?"

I was not too scared because I was fairly sure he would do no such thing. Most of the militiamen were absolute cowards. They would plant a bomb, they would back-shoot you, but they weren't up to intimate killing. He was no exception to the rule. He jerked the razor back and slashed the air in a demented mimic of a musketeer flourishing a foil.

I turned to the left and started toward my office. The man grabbed my shoulder from behind and spun me around.

"Go that way."

He pointed down a side street that led past the Law School campus and toward the Rue Hamra.

"My car's that way," I said, gesturing in the other direction. He waved his rifle at the side street.

"That way."

The Rue Hamra, Beirut's main shopping and banking street, was one of the few thoroughfares still under the control of the dwindling Lebanese army. It was only a hundred yards away. If I could get there, I would be safe, or safer than I was now. I started walking, reigning in an urge to run. Running would only excite the Beast. I hadn't gone fifty feet when a sniper fired at me, the bullet chipping the top of the Law School wall. I knew it was a sniper because the gunshot came from a long way off. He would get me with the next one. I turned and headed back, but the man with the razor raised his Kalashnikov and fired a burst in the air. I turned, again making for the Rue Hamra at a fast walk. A second burst of automatic fire came from behind, the bullets chopping into the pavement and the wall. I broke into a dead run, tossing a fast glance over my shoulder. The guy was running after me, firing from the hip. That helped save me; even when well aimed, an assault rifle on full automatic is inaccurate. Still, it throws out a lot of lead. One round got me, a grazing shot that burned across my back; then something clubbed me in the head, like a well-thrown hook to the temple. I slumped to the sidewalk and blacked out. It's strange how the perceptions attain an incredible clarity in such moments, how time slows down. The blackout could not have lasted more than a second, yet I formed the clear thought that I had taken a round in the head, that in the next second blackness would be all I would see because *bangyerdead*. In the next instant I realized that a fragment from the wall had struck me and that I was a long way from dead.

I heard the clang of a rifle bolt striking an empty chamber. The gunman had run out of ammunition, yet he was still firing. My eyes saw again, and the nightmare continued. A second gunman was running up the street, firing wildly while the first knelt to load a fresh magazine. My mind took clear photographs of both: the first one, with a narrow face and a shock of thick black hair and that chill grin as he raised his rifle to shoot again, the second one middle-aged and fat, with a five o'clock shadow on his jowls. I screamed: "You filthy sons of bitches! Filthy cocksuckers!"

I was up and running again, at the ultimate extremity now, on the edge of the last yawning black maw. I could hear every round fired and tasted blood in my mouth—the blood trickling from my head. Blood oozed down my back, down my left arm, down my left calf. Running zigzag, the way they trained us in the marines, I looked back and saw both men, only forty, fifty feet away, kneeling to steady their aim, and then the guns bucking, muzzles and gunmen's faces blurred by the pale haze of the smokeless powder. I was knocked down. I rolled and was on my feet and running again, enough adrenaline in me to outrun a deer. Down again, up again, hobbling instead of running, still zigzagging. A fragment or ricochet had hit my right foot. Then I felt a terrific impact in my left ankle, like a blast from a compressed air hose. I was flying, lifted off my feet by the round that had hit me solid, fair and square. No fragment or ricochet that time. I landed on my belly and, not stopping to check how badly I'd been hit, scuttled on my elbows like a crab.

I was on the Rue Hamra. I had made it! Still, I was sure the gunmen would round the corner and finish me off. They never came, too scared, I figured, of being shot themselves by the army or by Christian snipers. Two blocks ahead, in front of the BANQUE CENTRALE DU LIBAN, a squad of soldiers manned a sandbagged barricade. Behind them an armored car threw off heat shimmers in the afternoon sun. I could see the big metal letters on the front of the building as if I were looking at them. BANQUE CENTRALE DU LIBAN. If I could get there, I would be all right. I knelt on my right knee and tried to stand, but my left leg folded like a pipe cleaner. I low-crawled again, and I do believe I was crawling as fast as I normally walked, yet the barricade never got any closer. I raised my hand and shouted for help, but my mouth was full of cotton and brass wool, my voice did not carry. BANQUE CENTRALE DU LIBAN. The soldiers were guarding the bank. Very Lebanese! Guard the money, to hell with everything and everyone else. I was growing weaker and rolled onto my back to see where I'd been hit the worst. Maybe I could tear my shirt to make a tourniquet.

I had taken a bullet though the left ankle. A hole the size of a man's fingernail pierced the outside of my boot; the hole in the other side was as big as a silver dollar, the leather shredded and black with blood. I clawed at my shirt—a red inkblot stained its left sleeve—and ripped a shred and tied it around my left calf. It wasn't tight enough. I pulled, and the strip tore in half. The hell with it. Get to the soldiers. BANQUE CENTRALE DU LIBAN. I yelled for help again. One of the soldiers saw me—he waved his rifle for me to come on. They were too scared to come out from behind the barricade. I had closed the distance to half a block when I knew I wasn't going to make it. I felt the same desertion of strength and will as a marathoner when he hits the wall at twenty miles.

"Help! Help me, goddamnit! I'm hit!"

"You are injured?"

I turned my head and saw a thin, frightened-looking man pressed against the wall of a cul-de-sac on the other side of the street.

"What the hell does it look like?"

"Please, come here. You will be safe."

"Give me a hand."

He didn't move. He wasn't going to risk a sniper or a random round. What the hell, if I made it I might live; if I didn't, a bullet in the head would be better than bleeding to death. I slithered across the street. When I got to the sidewalk, the man knelt down and extended his hand, like someone on a dock reaching out to an exhausted swimmer. I clutched it. He pulled me into the cul-de-sac, then got his hands under my arm and dragged me to the front steps of an apartment building. He looked at me, fear and confusion on his face. I had begun to feel cold; small tremors went rippling through me.

"Mister, is there anything I can bring you?"

"I'm going into shock. Put my feet up on the steps. Get a blanket."

He nodded. I had never been wounded but had seen enough people who were; the pain would come any minute now and it would be awful.

"Whiskey, too, if you have it. And a cigarette."

He elevated my legs and left, returning shortly with a blanket, a package of Marlboros, and a bottle of Remy Martin cognac.

"I had no whiskey. I hope this will do."

I said it would do very nicely, thanks. He went inside again. I tipped the bottle to my lips and drank about a fourth of it in one swallow. I had to get good and numb. Long ago, in a valley in Vietnam, I had heard the wounded from another company screaming because their corpsman had run out of morphine.

I lay drinking and smoking and wondering what to do next when my rescuer returned with a short, bald, slightly paunchy man in his early or midfifties. Strange, the details memory retains, the ones it erases. It has erased the short man's name, I'm ashamed to say, but kept what he was wearing: a pale-beige shirt worn outside his trousers, which were dark brown, and a pair of polished loafers. He was carrying what I mistook for a briefcase.

"How do you do?" he said, and I answered that I was doing as well as could be expected under the circumstances, that is, I was still breathing.

"I am Doctor Khouri. I live here in this building."

"A medical doctor, you mean."

"Yes, I am a vascular surgeon. I'll have a look at you."

I could not believe my luck and was not about to question what I'd done to deserve it.

Dr. Khouri opened the bag, took a scissors, and snipped off my shirt; then, with a larger scissors, he cut through my boots and pulled them off. I shut my eyes, but heard the blood splash when he turned the boots over. Opening my eyes again, I saw him removing my drenched socks. I did not feel a thing. My right foot was numb; so was my left leg from the knee down.

He took my blood pressure and knit his eyebrows.

"Just how bad am I?" I asked as he drenched my wounds in antiseptic and fashioned hasty dressings.

"You're going to live."

"Am I going to lose anything?"

"I don't think so. You're very lucky. It looks to me like that bullet in your left ankle just missed your Achilles tendon. No, I don't think you'll lose a thing if I can operate right away and stop any infection. We'll have to get you to the hospital."

The soldiers guarding the BANQUE CENTRALE DU LIBAN were summoned somehow or other. They pulled up in the armored car and carried me inside its iron guts, where I lay on a stretcher, Dr. Khouri crouched beneath the driver-gunner's feet. I thought I was being taken to the American University Hospital, which was in a fairly safe area near our apartment. But the good luck that had brought me to Khouri's doorstep was mixed with the bad: he practiced at Trad, a maternity hospital that had become a battlefield emergency station because it was in a Christian quarter in the eye of the storm.

I was on a gurney, rolling down a corridor with wooden floors and a high, dim ceiling, the lights above swaying from the shocks of shellfire. A male nurse cut off my jeans, a female nurse shoved plasma and antibiotic tubes into my veins. They rolled me down a ramp, toward double doors above which, in Arabic and French, were the words: SURGERY. Beside me was a nurses' station, with a telephone. I asked Dr. Khouri if I could phone my wife. Very well, he said, but I probably could not get through; most of the circuits were down. He was right. I tried three times and got only static. I dialed Proffitt's number, and it was weird, weird, to hear Martie, his wife, answer "Hello?" in the most normal voice. I attempted a similar tone and asked for Nick.

"One sec," she said.

"Hey, el-tee, what's goin' on?"

"Gotta make this fast. I've been shot. Looney Tunes did it. Nothing mortal, okay? Worst one's are in my left ankle and right foot. I'm in Trad, going into surgery."

"Jesus Christ, this just isn't your lucky town, is it?"

"Tell Jill. Don't alarm her. I'm all right. Nobody should try to see me. Trad's in the middle of the shit storm. Tell Jill I want her to get herself and the kids out of this country right away."

"She's not going to want to go with you wounded in a hospital."

"Then coldcock her and carry her out over your shoulder if you have to. I want her and the kids out of here."

"You got it."

"And telex the *Tribune*. Maybe they can send somebody over to help out."

"Okay. Got time to tell me what happened?"

"No."

Above, the operating-room lamp swung to and fro. From outside came the unnerving snarl and crash of rocket-propelled grenades, a kind of BRRRRRRRRRRROOOW ... WHOMP! Dr. Khouri and four or five assistants were gowned and masked. Instruments shone on a table. A little more of my luck ran out: the upper reading of my blood pressure had dipped to ninety, the lower hovered around sixty.

"I cannot risk putting you under a general anesthetic, Mister Caputo."

I looked at him.

"We have been cut off here for days, and you can see how many injured we have here. We have no block we can give you, just some local, and we are low on that, too."

I kept looking at him.

"I must take out the bullet fragments and debride the wounds. There is a lot of debris inside your ankle and your other foot. Leather from your shoes, cloth from your socks. Dirt. There has been damage to the metatarsals in your right foot, and I'm afraid the joint in your left between your ankle and heel has been destroyed."

I nodded and looked at him.

"The lower extremities are very sensitive," he went on. "A great complex nerve system ..."

"What are you trying to say?"

"The local will help a little, but I am afraid you are going to feel most of this. I ask you, if you can, not to move too much."

He filled a syringe or two with the local. I felt the needle's prick. A female nurse cradled my head between her hands while two men held me down by the shoulders. Dr. Khouri called for a probe. I watched the lamp, swinging back and forth, and tried to concentrate on its motion. Maybe I can hypnotize myself, I thought, and then it was as if someone had shoved a 220-volt wire into the hole in my ankle. My whole body jerked and went rigid, the way I'd seen people do in dramatizations of electroshock therapy.

"Oh my God, my God, my God ..."

"Yes, yes, my God," Dr. Khouri said soothingly.

Again the jolt of pain that gave new meaning to the word. I almost leapt off the table. The female nurse practically crushed my cheekbones to keep my head down, the two men leaned their weight on me.

Sweat poured out of me. It seemed important that I not scream or cry out, so I clamped my teeth as the probes dug into the wound, scraped bone, pricked nerves, scalding bolts of pain shooting all through me. Someone pried my jaws open and shoved a hard rubber bar between my teeth.

The body produces its own anesthetics when the artificial kind are not available. I blacked out. The last thing I recall was seeing the overhead lamp, swinging back and forth like a glowing pendulum.

And the next thing I remember was lying in a dark room, bandages on my head and arm and across my back (I had only superficial wounds there, a birdshot peppering of lead and concrete). Stained dressings encased my left leg to the knee, more wound around my right foot. Two other casualties were in with me, constantly talking to me in Arabic. Even if I had been able to understand, I could not have responded for the pain. I am in the business of describing things, but I don't have the vocabulary for that agony. I want to say that both legs, up to their thighs, felt as if they were being sprayed by a blowtorch or stabbed by countless scalding ice picks, but neither even comes close to what it felt like. It was the nearest thing to hell I was likely to suffer on earth—that's the best I can do.

I was thinking, *I'm not going to be able to endure this, I'm going to die from it,* when one of the male nurses came in, an Iraqi with a handsomely trimmed black mustache. He held a syringe.

"Do you have much pain, Mister Caputo?"

"Is that morphine?"

"Meperidine. Synthetic morphine."

"Please."

He shot me up, and within five or six minutes, I experienced the nearest thing to heaven I was likely to know on earth. The fighting was still going on, but I didn't hear it as I rose up out of myself. The blowtorch continued to burn, the ice picks kept jabbing, but I never felt them. *Oh, thank you, thank you, thank you. Thank you, Jesus!* My soul, my consciousness, give it whatever name you like, floated to the ceiling to look down on my wracked body with mixed pity and contempt. You wretched bag of bones, you miserable suffering assembly of mortal flesh and tender nerves, ah, I am so glad to be free of you, even for this little while.

The spiritual *I* levitated for a couple of hours, gradually losing altitude as the drug wore off, then slipped back into the physical *I*. The *I-I* spent another hour or two in hell, until that mustached angel returned with his needle and administered the blessed sacrament once again. And so, all night, I commuted between paradise and perdition, never making an intermediate stop. The Meperidine Express. I was sold on the stuff, I was a stone junkie before morning, whispering to the angel that great rewards would be his if he shot me up every two hours instead of four.

"I am sorry, Mister Caputo. This is highly addictive, and anyway we do not have enough."

The sky paled. I had survived my first night as a casualty of war. I began to wonder how much longer that would continue when an RPG hit a truck opposite the hospital. The window shattered. Black smoke stinking of burning gasoline poured into the room. Nurses and aides ran in and wheeled our beds into the corridor. I wasn't frightened because I was on the heaven-bound leg of my four-hourly journey.

Dr. Khouri returned me to hell a short while later. The dressings came off my feet, the hasty sutures were opened. He wanted to do another debridement. When that was done, the day-shift angel appeared and I was on the wing again.

That was how it went for the next four days. During that time, I found out later, I had become the topic of much speculation among my colleagues in the press corps. Why had the gunmen shot me? How had I managed to survive fifty or sixty bullets fired at close range? They were just doing their jobs, trying to make sense of the senseless.

I did not try, not at first. I was in too much pain, too terrified by the fighting around the hospital, and too happy for each moment of life to trouble myself with metaphysics. I would not have even if I had not been in peril and pain, having concluded that trying to make sense of the senseless was the most senseless thing anyone could do in Beirut. Certainly my narrow escape never struck me as part of God's wondrous design. God had abandoned the Beast's new Bethlehem, even though everyone there claimed to be fighting for Him. As to the gunmen's motives, I was satisfied that they had none. Beirut was quantum physics applied to human behavior and events. People just did things, and things just happened. I had been shot and had survived because events had arranged themselves that way. They could have as easily arranged themselves the other way. *Don't mean nothin', don't mean a thing.*

Later, during the ten months I spent recovering, I asked the Big Questions. Why had I been shot? Why had I survived? For a while, because I finished *A Rumor of War* during my convalescence, I thought I had been temporarily crippled so the book could live. Maybe so. But I had read somewhere that an estimated *half a billion* human beings have died or been injured in all the wars of this ghastly century. To think I'd become a casualty merely to complete a book smacked of the worst egocentricity.

As the weeks passed I came *almost* full circle to my original impression. What happened to me *was* senseless. In and of itself, it was as meaningless as a rock—if I wanted it to be. It was my choice to impart or not impart significance. Recalling how I'd laughed at those unfortunate Moslem women, I saw myself as a man who had become disconnected from human suffering. Scorning and blaming victims for their victimization, I was not too far from the altered moral state of the gunmen who'd shot me. Through my own suffering, I was plugged back into the current of human anguish that circuits this planet without end. I had been wounded to learn pain, and I had been made to know pain to learn pity once again.

Yet that old Vietnam mantra kept echoing in the back of my mind: *Don't mean nothin', don't mean a thing.*

The *fighting* went on day and night. Trad hospital remained cut off from the outside world. I heard nothing about Jill and the boys and was in continual anxiety, wondering if they had evacuated. Supplies ran low. The Angel of the Blessed Needle extended his visitations from every four, to every six, and, finally, to every eight hours. The anguish would have been unbearable, I would have begun to feel very sorry for myself if I had not heard the moans and screams of the freshly wounded, coming in with no letup. On one of those days, an exhausted Dr. Khouri, his surgeon's smock like a butcher's apron, told me I would need skin grafts to close the wounds in my ankle. He could not perform the operation under the circumstances and was trying to find somebody to evacuate me to the American University Hospital. The day before, he had managed to get through to the U.S. Embassy and explain the situation. He had not heard from them since; maybe the circuits were down again.

When, at last, the lull came, I was visited by John Andrews, NBC's radio correspondent. I was so glad to see a face from the out-side I would have hugged and kissed Andrews if I'd had the strength for it. He told me someone from the *Tribune*—couldn't recall who— was in Beirut and, with Proffitt's help, had put my family on a flight to Athens. They had even worked the miracle of loading all our belong-ings on a 747 cargo plane that was flying out with the household effects of embassy staffers. I felt an immense relief. My wife and kids were safe; for the moment, nothing else mattered.

"How the hell did you get here?" I asked Andrews.

"Got in the car and drove. Had to park several blocks away. Too dicey to drive, even with the cease-fire. You know what cease-fires are like here."

I certainly did, but, I said, I would appreciate it if he passed on to the embassy that reaching Trad was not impossible. The Angel of the Blessed Needle appeared, not, unfortunately, with his syringe but with a message that a call from the United States was waiting for me. He wheeled me to an orderly station.

It was Mike McGuire, recently promoted to foreign editor. His voice was so clear he sounded as if he were around the corner. The

Tribune took care of its own. On his end, Mike was doing all he could to get me evacuated; he was constantly on the phone with the State Department; arrangements were being made to have me treated by a specialist in traumatic foot injuries at Northwestern University Hospital in Chicago. Jim Yuenger was the man who had gotten my family out. He was still in Beirut, pressuring the embassy to rescue me from Trad. Yuenger had been on assignment in Morocco when he'd heard the news.

"He volunteered," McGuire said. "I'll never forget his telex: 'I willingly volunteer. I will move hellfire and high water. I'm going to get Caputo, goddamnit.' That's the kind of gutsy guy you've got looking after you. He knew he was flying into a real hell while other Americans were headed for safety in the other direction. That might embarrass you, but I can't call it a week until I get it off my chest."

More than embarrass me, it made me feel small and unworthy and stupid. I was putting a lot of people through a lot of grief, risk, and trouble.

That night, the *fighting* resumed and crashed on through the night into a dawn that reeked of burning rubber and cordite. The Beast's breath. I lay in the corridor, waiting for the Angel. A different sort of angel appeared, in the form of a tall, broad-shouldered American wearing a flak jacket over his sport coat. A Colt .38 was jammed into his waistband. He carried a second flak jacket. Two Lebanese security police walked beside him, and Dr. Khouri brought up the rear.

"Here is our famous patient," the doctor said.

"Caputo?" asked the tall man, holding out his hand. "Colonel Braun, U.S. Marines. I'm getting you out of here."

Orderlies rolled me off my bed into a wheelchair, extending the footrest so the blood did not rush into my feet, which caused extraordinary pain. To be sure I did not feel any, the Angel gave me, well, a parting shot. The colonel wrapped the spare flak jacket around my chest.

"Did the embassy send you?" I asked as the security cops wheeled me down the corridor.

"Yes and no," answered Colonel Braun, who was the security director for U.S. embassies in the Middle East. "I went to the ambassador myself, asked to borrow his driver and limo. It's bulletproof, armor-plated, and we'll need it. Lebanese security types were coming for you this morning, but their APC took a rocket. Had to turn back."

"Anybody killed? I don't want somebody getting killed on my account."

"I don't either." He gave me a faint grin. "Marines don't leave their wounded on the battlefield. You oughta know that, Lieutenant."

We came to the stairs. The policemen lifted me into a fireman's carry. An orderly folded the wheelchair while two more, flinching at the gunfire outside, swung the emergency entrance doors open.

I looked at Dr. Khouri and tried to think of the right thing to say. He gestured to say that he needed no thanks.

"I am a doctor, after all."

"And then some," I said.

Colonel Braun made sure my flak jacket was snapped.

"Let's go."

Bouncing in the cradle of the policemen's crossed arms, I saw only two things: the big black Chrysler limousine and a squad of *kataeb*, spraying rooftops with machine guns from behind a barricade on the other side of the street. I was tossed in the backseat—it wasn't the time for gentle handling—Colonel Braun jumping into the front, the policemen crowding in beside me. The driver (he and the ambassador would later be assassinated by Moslem gunmen) put the pedal to the floor, and we were gone in a squeal of tires. I shut my eyes, cringing against the blast of the RPG I was sure would hit us. The gunfire cracked and rumbled in diminuendo, the driver slowed down. In less than half an hour, I lay on another gurney, rolling down a quiet air-conditioned hall in the American University Hospital. I wanted to chalk up one more escape, though I had not escaped anything; I had been let go.

DISASTERS OF WAR

Madame Wadad Nasif stood on the porch of her old stone villa, the only house on the street left standing. She had pinned her gray hair in a bun, put on lipstick, face powder, and a plain black dress with a necklace of imitation pearls. She wanted to look presentable for the correspondents crowded below her, on the steps to her porch, asking questions and aiming still and TV cameras at her. She was seventy years old and a widow and had never thought to leave Kuneitra during all the months of shelling between the Syrians and the Israelis. Everyone else had fled, forty thousand people. The shelling was still going on, a long way off, but it was supposed to stop at noon, when an armistice was to be signed in Geneva. Madame Nasif smiled.

"So Kissinger has finally got something," she said in a high-pitched voice. She came from a wealthy Syrian family and spoke English and French fluently. "The world is topsy-turvy now, but there will be peace in my lifetime and things will be more beautiful than they were. We are on our way to a more beautiful world, and I'm going to see it in my lifetime."

She paused and gestured in the direction of the artillery fire.

"Now what is that? Boom, boom, bang, bang. Sometimes it's near, sometimes it's far, but there is good in everything." She pointed across the street, at a house with a collapsed roof and one wall leaning against the pile of bricks, beams, and stone block that had been the roof and the other walls. "Just the other day, a shell landed there and opened up a blocked well. It was wonderful. Now we have running water for the first time in months. And enough to water the plants."

One of the correspondents asked how she had found enough to eat. She answered that Israeli soldiers had brought her powdered milk, bread, and sugar, and her chickens laid eggs. A television reporter told his cameraman to get a shot of the chickens. The cameraman said he had not seen any chickens anywhere. He had not seen a single living thing in the city except Madame Nasif.

She smiled again, fingering her pearls, and said the Israeli soldiers had been very kind to her, as she was sure the Syrian soldiers would be when the armistice was signed and they moved back into Kuneitra.

"It's humanity. They're all basically good. Won't you please come inside? I want to show you where I watched the fighting."

It was dim inside because the windows had been boarded up. No one saw the plants Madame Nasif said she could water now that the well had been opened. There were, however, a great many cats. The house stank of them. Eight months of shellfire had made them a little crazy. They crouched and cringed and shrank back into dark corners or hissed and snarled and ran madly over the dusty furniture as the correspondents followed Madame Nasif up a staircase and out onto a widow's walk on her roof. From there, they could see all of Kuneitra, the dun fields beyond and the low, brown, ugly hills rising from the fields. Besides Madame Nasif's house, only the city's mosque remained upright. Everything else had been knocked to pieces. Even the cemetery, on the outskirts, had been hit. Bursting shells made shapes like huge, gray-black trees on a hill far off.

"Yes, Kuneitra is in ruins, but where is the old Jerusalem?" asked Madame Nasif rhetorically. "Torn down by the Romans. And where is ancient Rome? In ruins. All this will pass and things will go back to the way they were, only more beautiful than before. We are on our way to a more beautiful world."

It was past eleven now and the correspondents were anxious to leave. They wanted to be at the front to record the historic moment when the guns fell silent. Madame Nasif showed them to the door and made sure to say good-bye to each one. They got into their cars, leaving her on the porch in her black dress and pearls, and drove to the edge of the city and up a road toward an Israeli gun battery. Along the way, they passed the cemetery. It was pitted with deep, wide craters dug by heavy-caliber shells. Tombstones had been flattened and broken into bits. The ornate stone crosses of the Eastern Rite had been torn from the ground and hurled yards from the graves they had once marked. A number of coffins had been blown out of the graves and lay helter-skelter in the craters or on the piles of dirt thrown up by the explosions, which had also ripped a few coffins open. The correspondents could see the corpses inside. Two were men. They knew they were men by the dark suits rotting on the skeletons. A woman's coffin was nearest the road, leaning with one end atop a mound of earth. No eyes were left in the woman's head, and her nose was gone, but some brown, shriveled flesh still covered her face. Her hair sprouted out of her skull in an immense gray bush, like a fright wig in a novelty shop, and the bones of one hand lay in the lap of her maroon dress, while the other was flung over the edge of her coffin.

"Jesus," said a correspondent in one of the cars. The man next to him said he had heard that hair kept growing after death, but he had never seen it before. "Jesus, Jesus," the first correspondent said again. "It's like she died twice."

NINE

The Great Game

In the last month of my thirty-eighth year to heaven, I went into Afghanistan with my bad leg under me and a broken charm in my pocket. Afghanistan, of all places, dangerous in the best of times, an arena for tribal vendettas, rich in the opium poppies smugglers caravanned through the covert valleys of the Hindu Kush. Travelers who strayed off the few main roads—and they didn't have to stray far— were often held up by bandits and sometimes murdered. But the indigenous hazards of bandits and feuding tribesmen seemed quaintly Kiplingesque, suffused in the glow of an antique charm compared with the ones imported by the Russian army in the closing days of 1979: tanks, helicopter gunships, and a hundred thousand troops, bulling and burning their way through the country.

Five months after the invasion, *Esquire* magazine phoned me at home in Key West, offering me an assignment to cover the war. I took it, with hardly a second thought. Almost everyone I knew said it was a foolish thing to do, something you'd expect from a green correspondent eager to make his name or from a down-and-out free-lancer desperate for a chance to restore his fortunes and reputation. Nearing the head of the line for admission to middle age, I was a long way from green; a reasonably well-off and respected novelist, I wasn't desperate. There was also the liability of my left leg, grown stiff and unreliable from traumatic osteoarthritis. I could run only a few yards and walked with a limp. What on earth, asked some of my friends, made me think I could climb mountains with young guerrillas hot to die for Allah so they could go straight to Paradise?

Seeking support, I went to the length of phoning Proffitt in Nairobi, where he was serving his last tour of duty with *Newsweek*. In a year, he would be off to the Montana ranch to write his novel. I got no encouragement from him.

"If you're so anxious to get back into the shit, you oughta try plumbing. It's safer and the pay's better."

How could I argue with him? Lebanon should have finished my war correspondent's career. It did, for a while. After I'd recovered, the *Tribune* assigned me to its Moscow bureau. That was supposed to be the plum job for a foreign correspondent, but I hated every minute spent in Brezhnev's Russia, an enormous example of what happens when the revolutionary's passionate intensity congeals: an utterly dispassionate reign of bureaucratized terror. The assignment was to have lasted three years, but *A Rumor of War,* published seven months after I took over the bureau, opened an escape hatch. The book was a far greater success than I'd expected, the reviews almost embarrassingly favorable, the sales brisk enough to nudge it into best-sellerdom. When I got a generous advance to do a novel, *Horn of Africa,* I quit Moscow and journalism. Jill, the boys, and I moved to Key West, into a rambling, renovated house once owned by a wrecking captain. Three years later, the novel was done. In the meantime, the film version of *A Rumor of War* had been completed and was scheduled to be aired as a four-hour miniseries in September 1980, one month before *Horn of Africa's* publication date.

Big house, two cars, a boat, a measure of fame, money in the bank—I had most of the items on the laundry list of American success, and having them made the Afghan assignment seem all the more idiotic, a stunt, a caper. Worse, it seemed wrong. I had once almost made Jill a widow and the boys fatherless. I owed it to them not to risk my neck again unless it was for sound and sufficient reasons, so I conducted an autopsy of my motivational innards.

My forceps plucked out several reasons, though I could not swear to their soundness and sufficiency: my old taste for adventure and escape from the humdrum, an itch to flee the novelist's cloister and get back into the action, back into the pageant of history, a need to prove that I, bum leg and all, was still the man I'd been. The heart of it all, I thought then, was this: I was on a quest for The Good War, one I could report from as Hemingway and Dos Passos had from Spain. Vietnam and Lebanon, especially Lebanon, had left the temple of my faith in mankind looking like ground zero at Hiroshima. When I'd said yes to *Esquire* so quickly, it must have been because I saw in Afghanistan an armed struggle I might believe in unambiguously, a cause unclouded by moral murk, unsullied by moral horror. With the same Lee-Enfields they'd used against the troops of imperial Britain, the Afghans were now battling the Russian army and all its murderous technology. Native guts versus gunships, good versus evil, black hats versus white—I was practically writing my lead before I'd made plane reservations. My outlook was more suited to a propagandist than a journalist, though I was happy to discover that a small part of me had survived from the days when I went to the Ritz in Berwyn to cheer Lash LaRue as he triumphed over the guns of western badmen with only a whip.

Yet I wasn't entirely satisfied with all that. Some higher purpose was needed, but the only one to come to mind was that old horse: the Public's Right to Know. It failed to inspire. Did the Public truly have a *right* to know what was going on in Afghanistan? After all, it wasn't, like the right to vote, a necessary component of democratic citizenship. Furthermore, did the Public care? Inflation, interest rates, and unemployment were at or near double digits, and John Q. Public, struggling to make ends meet, wasn't burning to hear of events in the Hindu Kush.

Meanwhile, I worked hard to get into shape. The zeal with which I did was perhaps a sign that I was going through with the thing, whatever the soundness of my motives. I rapped out push-ups and did calf raises to strengthen my legs, banged punching bags, cycled the twelve miles around Key West twice a day in the dense South Florida heat. Throughout that period of sweaty preparation, Jill never spoke a word about the assignment, acting as if I were a sales manager who would soon be off to a conference. She had been a foreign correspondent's wife for five years, and that is like being an officer's wife. She had learned to forbear loneliness and fear without letting her anxieties show. It was not hard to tell, however, how apprehensive she was this time and, probably, angry as well. If she only knew how full of doubts I was, how I secretly wished she would put her foot down and tell me, "You are not going to do this. It's ridiculous. I need you. The boys need you." That would have given me an excuse to call *Esquire* and gracefully bow out, but a staleness had crept into our marriage and walls of silence had risen between us and we did not speak a word.

The closer I drew to departure, the jumpier I got.

The day before I flew to Miami (where I would catch a plane to London, then on to Rawalpindi and Peshawar) was the day the charm broke in half.

It was loaned to me by a Key West friend, Jean Geslin, a pale-eyed sailor with ginger hair. He had asked me to a bar for a farewell drink. After we'd downed them, Jean reached into his wallet, unfolded a tissue, and showed me a brass fish about an inch long, an eighth of an inch thick, and corroded by years at sea to a light green.

"Take this with you. It's got me through some tough spots, hah?"

"A good-luck piece?"

"It's more than that," he said, and then testified to its powers: it had floated him off a desolate Bahama bank where he'd run aground, kept him from capsizing in tropical gales, and pulled him through every other bad hand Mother Ocean had dealt him. Jean had been a design engineer for Xerox before he'd chucked his job and his first marriage to go a-roving in his sloop. Engineers are generally not prey to superstition, but Jean had spent the past ten years at sea, which, in its nastier moods, can make the most cold-headed logical positivist reach for a rabbit's foot and pray to gods whose existence he would deny in calm winds or on dry land. When I quipped that his talisman had performed more high-seas rescues than the U.S. Coast Guard, he said:

"This is no bullshit, Phil. I will not bullshit you. Hah? You know me, right? I don't believe the Blessed Virgin cured polio or whatever at Lourdes, but this"—he pointed to the corroded fish lying in his palm like a dead minnow—*"works."*

Feeling in need of all the help I could get, I extended my hand across the table. Jean dropped the talisman into my palm. It broke in half. Instantly, my internal organs took the express elevator to my ankles. An evil omen!

I looked away from the broken charm, my Reason battling my

Dread. Stop! it cried. Cease and desist! You are a citizen of the most developed nation on earth. You have a college degree, an honorable discharge, and most major credit cards. You are not some Carpathian peasant who wears garlic on his neck to keep the vampires off and bolts his door on nights when the wolfbane blooms.

Meanwhile, Jean was looking at me in the way people do at someone who has committed a terrible faux pas that must nevertheless be politely ignored.

"Hey, it wasn't your fault." He forced a smile. "Don't worry about it. The thing was old."

I shrugged, wrapped the halved fish tightly in a cocktail napkin, and put it in my wallet.

Jean stood and gave me a warm embrace. "You take care now, hah? You watch yourself, okay?" He paused for a beat. "About that thing, it was just a thing, just an old thing, a little brass fish, that's all."

"Sure. No problem," I lied, for despite Reason's commands, I felt as spooked as a Haitian who's found a voodoo doll on his doorstep.

With a look of rote suspicion in his hooded eyes, the border policeman checked my face against my photograph, stamped my passport, and waved me through. It was hot inside the terminal, the thick air redolent of sweat and strong tobacco. Several women shrouded head to toe in veils and black burqquas sat on a bench like nuns in a pew. Two representatives of Pakistan's new women, modeled on Benazir Bhutto, daughter of the prime minister hanged by the nation's current leader, glided toward a ticket counter in unveiled gorgeousness, diaphanous saris moving like curtains in a breeze. I committed adultery in my heart and shouldered through the crowds to baggage claim. After my luggage and portable Olivetti were inspected for contraband by a sleepy customs agent, I went to the currency exchange. A whiskered gentleman sidled up to me, gaining my attention with a viperous hiss. He said he could give me a far better rate than the bank. I declined, as I understood such transactions were punished with all the severity the sha'ira could muster; *id est*, the removal of a digit or appendage. With native currency in my pocket, I made for the front exit, above which hung a photograph of General Muhammad Zia, the president. He wore a slim mustache and a uniform spangled with medals, though Pakistan had fought only two brief, minor wars in its history, losing both to the visiting team, India.

Outside, a taxi driver agreed to take me to the Islamabad Holiday Inn for twenty-five rupees. We headed at hot-pursuit speed down a blacktop along which purple jacarandas bloomed and turbaned men cut roadside weeds with scythes. The driver zipped around a bullock cart, creaking on the pavement while an Air Pakistan 747 thundered down a runway not a quarter of a mile away. The scene made the sort of fatuous old versus new photograph favored by *National Geographic*. We entered Islamabad, its low, contemporary villas and stark government buildings clustered beneath green hills dotted with poplar and cypress. It would have looked like an architectural carbon of a Southern California suburb if it weren't for General Zia's national slogan, spelled out on the hillsides in huge letters of whitewashed rocks: UNITY FAITH DISCIPLINE. No way you would find *that* in Southern California. I lit a cigarette and closed my eyes, feeling every minute of the forty-eight hours I'd spent on planes and in airports. But now I was back in the world of alien creeds and black-market currencies, of Boeings and bullock carts, where prime ministers got hanged by generals decorated with medals for battles they never fought.

I had reentered history.

The desk clerk handed me a room key, his smile as practiced as the border policeman's suspicious scowl.

"Most welcome," he said. "Most welcome to our establishment. You are requiring assistance with your baggage?"

I shook my head and went to the elevator. The piped-in music system played Elvis Presley's "Burning Hunk of Love," and the lobby, from the looks of it, might have been the Holiday Inn in Dayton. The only object in my room that told me I was not in Dayton was the *qibli*—the arrow that points toward Mecca. It was decaled to the bureau so Moslem guests would know which way to face when the muezzin called the prayers. In the bathroom, a paper cordon sanitaire on the toilet seat informed me in English and Urdu that it had been placed there for my protection. Ditto for the plastic wrapping on the glasses. The time is fast approaching, I thought, when every place is going to be an imitation of every other place. People could rhapsodize all they wanted about the Global Village. I dreaded its coming because it would be the end of all variety in the world. There will be *no way out* for any of us.

I gazed out the window at white, flat-roofed houses climbing the hills in geometric patterns. The room was stuffy despite the air conditioner. I tried to open the window, but it was sealed—probably for my protection. It reminded me of why, in my foreign correspondent days, I'd avoided franchise hotels whenever possible. They made me feel isolated from whatever country I was in, sealed off from the smell and sense of the place in an air-conditioned bubble of multinational standardization. Worse, they fostered complacency. The predictable configurations of the rooms and corridors, the familiar placement of the furniture, the presence of modern conveniences bearing well-known brand names created the cozy impression that one was in a place where the people and events were also familiar and predictable, as easily understood as a room-service menu containing translations of strange native dishes. Why, this country isn't so different from home, Ethel, and these folks are *just like us*. That fallacy was safe enough in, say, Brussels, but it was dangerous in the world's States of Extremes, where no protection was offered against the variety of ways desperate men devised to harm or kill their fellow man to further some religious or political cause, or simply to relieve their frustrations. Who knows, in the Age of Terrorism, their atrocities may be promoted by the spread of the Global Village, with its ease of travel, its instant communications, its brutal, homogenized banality. As I looked out toward the hills and the square white roofs, I reminded myself that the longest, bloodiest battle in Beirut had been fought for possession of a Holiday Inn just like the one I was in, sanitary toilet seats and all. So keep your eye on the ball, I thought. You are not in Dayton, but in Pakistan, where elected prime ministers are strung up by juntas of religious zealots. Imagine what they might do to you if, wittingly or not, you step out of line.

Such morbid thoughts were a signal that my mental fan belt was loose, which in turn was a sign of other mechanical trouble: my body clock needed rewinding. I headed for the bar.

Photographs of dark-eyed women in traditional dress decorated the walls; otherwise, the bar, like the lobby, had been imported straight from Dayton. There was only one other customer, a sallow, gray-haired man sitting at a small round table under a toxic cloud of cigarette smoke. I ordered a Scotch. The bartender handed me two complicated-looking forms and asked me to fill them out.

"I don't think I understand," I said.

He pointed at a notice posted on the door. I swung off the stool to read it.

"Don't trouble yourself," the gray-haired man said in a British accent. "I'll tell you what it says: bar is closed to Moslems."

"Do I look Moslem?"

"A bit," he answered, stroking his sunken chin to indicate my beard. "Yank or Canadian?"

"Yank."

It sounded like dialogue from a World War II movie.

"Then so indicate on the forms. This chap is required to ask his customers to attest that they are Christian, Jew, Buddhist, Taoist, atheist—anything but bloody Moslem."

I completed the forms, which the bartender filed in a little metal box before he poured my Scotch. It was a short shot. The Englishman laughed, his laugh collapsing into an emphysemic cough.

"Even if you aren't bloody Moslem," he said when he recovered, "these Pakis make sure you don't overindulge. You're better off bringing your own and getting potted in your room."

"Why aren't you, then?"

"It isn't very sociable, is it? Not that it was terribly sociable in here until you dropped in." He lit a fresh cigarette off the butt of the old. "Care to join me?"

I passed through the toxic cloud and sat at his table. His name was David Martin, and he was the unhealthiest-looking human being I'd seen outside intensive care. Burst blood vessels branched across his clay-colored face like an infrared satellite photo of a river delta. His chest was hollow, but his belly was too big for his rumpled shirt and ovals of flesh pale as dead clams showed through the openings between the buttons. His eyes were puffy, as if he had not slept in a week, his hands trembled, and the mere act of speaking made him struggle heroically for each breath. One look at him made you vow never to take another drink or cigarette in your life.

He asked what had brought me to "Packers." He had that annoying British habit of referring to cities and countries by cute diminutives, as if they were charming children—a proprietariness held over from the days of Empire.

I told him I had come on business. The evasiveness was deliberate because I'd been warned that the country was full of spooks, double and triple agents working every end against several middles.

"May I ask what sort of business?"

"Journalism."

"Well, now, we've something in common. So am I. Been covering this part of the world since before, I would guess, you committed your first act of self-abuse."

"Who do you write for?"

"Oh, just a stringer, you know," he replied in a tone that discouraged further inquiry. "Just a stringer for a lot of breasts-and-bum rags. And you?

"*Esquire, Esquire,*" he mused aloud after I told him. "Oh, yes. Bit of tits and bum in that, isn't there?"

"Sometimes. But it's glossy."

Sputum rumbled in his collapsed chest as he laughed again.

"Glossy or newsprint, you're in the wrong place for bum and cleavage. They don't even let you see their *faces* over here. Here to cover the war, are you?"

I made a vague gesture.

"Of course you are. Beard gives you away. It's still coming in, and for what other reason would you be growing it except to make an unauthorized trip over the border? If you are willing to listen, I can give you a bit of advice and useful background."

"You've been?" I asked.

Once more, his laugh broke up into a hacking. He clutched for a breath, an effort that for one alarming moment seemed as futile as trying to snatch a mosquito in midair. At last he succeeded, but not before his face turned a color that suggested a diastolic pressure in the triple digits.

"My dear fellow," he gasped, "as you may well imagine, I cannot climb a set of stairs. Forget the Hindu Kush. No, I cover the war from Peshawar, but I am somewhat versed in mujahadin politics. You'll need to know about that if you're going to play this inning of the Great Game."

I listened carefully and took notes to fill in the sketchy research I had done at home. I had run into Englishmen like him before. Deracinés rather than expatriates, rootless wanderers of a postimperial earth who would rather breathe the air of lost colonies than the familiar air of home, they were always good sources of background information.

The "Great Game" was the name for the imperial rivalry between Russian and British intelligence services for control of Central Asia during the previous century. The term had been coined by a British officer who had played the Game and lost dreadfully: while on a mission of intrigue, an Uzbek emir took him prisoner, tossed him into a well full of rats and snakes for two months, then brought him up and beheaded him. The British suffered far greater losses later on, during the last year of the First Afghan War, 1842. Afghani tribesmen annihilated or scattered an army of forty-five hundred troops and twelve thousand camp followers as it retreated from Kabul through the Khyber Pass. The end came at a hill called Gondabek, where the rear guard, the 44th Foot, made a last stand as hopeless as Custer's.

"The Afghans still talk about that battle as if it happened yesterday," my tutor wheezed. "They sing about it and their bloody eyes light up when they do. How's that song go?" He paused and chased another elusive breath. "Ah, yes. *I am the Afghan, who made the British flee. My hand destroyed them at Gondabek. This is the land of the Afghan, and we won't be fooled.* It sounds better in Dari or Pashto than it does in English, but the Russians might do well to listen to it in any language. Gondabek. A whole regiment wiped out."

"They didn't have tanks or gunships."

"True. But tanks aren't much use in the Hindu Kush, and you can't hold a country with helicopters."

He resumed his history lesson. The debacle of 1842 did not discourage the British from fighting two more Afghan wars, one in 1878 and the last in 1919.

"Now, you may ask, why did we fight all those battles?" Martin asked rhetorically. "To counter a perceived threat from Russia. We thought they were trying to take Afghanistan as a steppingstone to seizing Persia and the Persian Gulf, and, of course, India. Sound familiar?"

I pointed out that the Russian threat today was considerably more than perceived.

"Oh, quite, quite. It was more than perceived back then as well.

The Russians really did want the Persian Gulf and India, as, I suspect, they do today. I am merely pointing out that the Great Game continues, but with different players."

Martin rewarded himself for his lecture by firing up another cigarette. He held out his squashed pack to me.

"Awfully sorry. Should have offered earlier."

"That's okay. You're smoking enough for the two of us."

His puffy eyes narrowed to slits that reminded me of an Eskimo's whalebone sunglasses.

"Another drink, then?"

I shook my head.

"Well, I shall have one."

He held up his empty glass, then turned back to me as the bartender refilled it.

"Do I detect in you a certain judgmentalism? A disapproval of my bad habits?"

I shook my head again, not wishing to offend the man who promised to give me helpful hints for playing the Great Game successfully. Because of what happened to me with the Palestinians, I was thinking about that officer, down in the well with rats and snakes.

"I should like to point out," the Englishman said, "that I am from East Anglia, of a family of Puritans who missed the boat to Plymouth Colony."

"Yes?"

"I was not always a drunk. It's this business we're in. Journalism lends itself to alcohol, tobacco, drugs, if you're young enough for narcotics. Believe it or not, I was once a teetotaler, a devout churchman, a reader of Scripture. Then, some years ago, back when I was a staffer and not a stringer, I was sent to East Pakistan—Bangladesh to you—to cover a disaster. Typhoon. Came in off the Bay of Bengal and drowned, oh, thousands of people. They'd been living in these flimsy shacks, you see, crowded on the coast cheek by jowl in these flimsy shacks God had not intended, or so I thought, for human habitation. The storm drowned them by the thousands. We found their bodies half a mile or more inland, half buried in the mud. Looked like a die-off of those fish you have over there in North America. What *are* those fish?"

"Alewives?"

"That's it! Alewives."

"And you're saying the sight horrified you so much you took to drinking."

"Not quite. A few years later is when that happened. I was sent back to East Pakistan to cover another damned typhoon. Of course, ten thousand people had been living on the same coast in the same sort of flimsy shacks. Hadn't learned a bloody thing. Another die-off of human alewives. That is when I ceased to believe, with any conviction, that a single sparrow does not fall without God's seeing it. And so I turned to this"—he pointed at his glass—"whiskey is much more reliable than the New Testament. The Old, too."

I asked what typhoons in East Pakistan had to do with the Great Game.

"Not a thing. But to return to that. You will be dealing mostly with Pathans in Peshawar. You're aware that they are the principal ethnic group in Afghanistan and the Northwest Frontier?"

"I am now."

"Splendid fellows. Absolutely splendid. The toughest, most ruthless practitioners of mountain warfare in the world, but splendid and honorable men. Don't be taken in by Russian propaganda about the way they treat prisoners of war."

"How do they treat them?"

"They shoot them."

"You mean the Russians *say* they shoot them?"

He waved his cigarette, drawing smoky designs in the air, like a skywriter.

"No. No. The Russians say, in effect, that when the muj get through with their prisoners they would be singing soprano if their mouths weren't full, but that isn't true. The Tadzhiks or Uzbeks may do things like that, but not the Pathans. They shoot them between the eyes or in the back of the head straight away. Quick and clean. They don't torture or commit atrocities on the bodies."

I took notes, feeling heartened. I did not approve of the summary execution of prisoners, but in the Age of Terrorism, one could not be morally fastidious.

"Atrocities don't fit in with *Pukhtunwali*," my teacher continued.

"That means 'The Code of the Pathan.' It has several principles, but the two most important for you to know are *tor* and *badal*. *Tor* means 'blackening.' It refers to dishonoring a woman. When you're up there, don't so much as look at a woman the wrong way. You could wind up very dead very quickly. *Badal* is revenge, which is what you take when someones mucks about with your missus or cheats you. It's one of the causes of most Pathan tribal feuds and those tribal differences are among the reasons why they have so many factions fighting the Russians. You are aware that they're rather balkanized."

"Six major factions."

"Yes. Some religious quibbling among them, but they're all Moslems of one stripe or other. Tribalism is the main cause of divisiveness. No different in that respect from other Third World liberation movements. If it weren't for their common enemy, they'd be at each other's throats tooth and claw."

I wrote that down, although it was not something I wanted to hear.

"In fact, they are often at each other's throats regardless. You heard about the bombing?"

"Just got here."

"Ah, well. A bomb went off near the headquarters of the Jamiyat Islami party—that's Professor Rabanni's mob. Killed a few people. Some say it was a rival faction, Younis Khalis's Hizbi Islami party. Others will tell you it was agents from the Khad—that's the Afghan secret police—trying to make it look like Khalis did it. And others will say it was Khalis after all, trying to make it look like the Khad." His eyes made whalebone sunglasses again as he smiled thinly. "The Great Game does get rather complicated."

I nodded.

"Then try this for further complication. There is a fourth theory that Gulbadin Hekmatayar committed the bombing. He's a young hothead, an absolute Moslem fundamentalist who broke away from Khalis and formed his own wing of the Hizbi Islami party. Supposedly, he wanted Khalis and Rabanni to start feuding so he could be in the driver's seat. I favor that theory. Hekmatayar is a bloody goon on a power trip."

I put my pen down, my eyes watering from the toxic nicotine

cloud, my head spinning from Scotch, jet lag, and informational over-load.

"Stay away from Hekmatayar's mob, that's more of my advice. If you can imagine what the Ayatollah Khomeini would have been like if he hadn't spent years in exile in Paris, you'll have a picture of Hek-matayar."

I asked who I should stick with.

"Younis Khalis. Splendid old fellow, an old-fashioned tribal chieftain. If not him, then Jamiyat-Islami. They've both got a lot of experience with the press, and they've also got a lot of men. They'll offer you the most protection if you go over."

"From the Russians or other Afghans?"

"Both," Martin said, and waved his empty whiskey glass at the bartender.

In the morning, I flew to Peshawar, provincial capital of the North-west Frontier and headquarters for the mujahadin leaders. I stepped off the plane into a heat that felt like second-degree sunburn, and asked a taxi driver to give me a quick tour before dropping me off at my hotel. I wanted to get a feel for the place, and he, of course, was grateful for the extra fare.

We hadn't gone far before we had to stop for a camel caravan, guarded by black-bearded men toting rifles and wearing crossed leather bandoliers jeweled with cartridges. I knew immediately that they were the Pathans; they carried themselves like royalty. A worm of excitement wriggled in my chest.

The driver followed a sequence of side roads into the Old City bazaars. Narrow lanes and alleyways, twilit even on that bright morn-ing, ran in all directions without pattern, like hidden passageways in the castle of a mad king. Looming over them was Fort Balahisar, built by a sixteenth-century Moghul emperor and now an army headquar-ters, its massive brick walls as red and frowning as the sides of a bad-lands mesa. We honked and inched our way through traffic com-pressed to a density that would have made a gridlocked Manhattan street look like a freeway. Bedford trucks painted up like gypsy wag-ons jousted for room with sputtering motor scooters, ox carts, and horse-drawn cabs called tongas.

The driver told me we were in Quissa Khawani, the Street of the Storytellers.

"In past times, sarr, travelers from the caravan roads are coming here to be amused by men who told them stories. To this day, there are such men here who will tell you a tale for a few rupees."

I wanted to believe him. The worm in my chest grew into a nest, wiggling and squiggling. The war had made Peshawar a headquarters for the international media, but it still had a street where professional storytellers spun their yarns. It was in its soul a city that predated the age of information and instant data, a city not yet incorporated into the Global Village.

The Railway Road led us out of the Old City and over a bridge into Peshawar Cantonment, a suburb the British had built for themselves in the days when Kipling worked in the city as a correspondent. He might have finished his day with a drink at Dean's, which was still *the* place to stay for most journalists. The white, stately hotel overlooked shrub-bordered lawns on which you could sip gin served by waiters in starched jackets and make believe you were waiting for Tyrone Power to report on how the Khyber Rifles had fared in the recent campaign. I had cabled Dean's from Islamabad but had been told they were full up. I had to settle for the Inter-Continental, which spread its glass wings on a rise above the Khyber Road. It was less aggressively modern than the Holiday Inn, but when I checked in, the muzak was playing Buddy Holly's "Peggy Sue."

I went straight to work, telephoning the guerrillas' various headquarters in the hopes that one of them would get me into Afghanistan, the quicker the better. Each faction had a kind of press liaison officer to handle such requests, for an unintended effect of the Soviet invasion had been to turn the glare of the world press onto the mujahadin. Warriors almost from birth, they were probably better prepared to meet the Russian invader than the onslaught of reporters, cameramen, and photographers, all demanding, in a babble of tongues, a trip to the front. Although their leaders were worldly, educated men, most of the guerrillas had had little contact with the press. A few had never heard of such marvels as radio and television much less seen them; they came from villages in roadless mountains where communications satellites circling midnight skies were likely to be mistaken for meteors or cosmic portents.

I called and called and concluded that the press officers were still learning the ropes; their telephones rang without an answer or were picked up by people who hung up as soon as they heard me speak English. I had no Urdu or Pashto, and my limited Arabic did not help either. After an hour, I succeeded in gaining only one audience. It was with Younis Khalis, who had come so highly recommended.

"Younis Khalis? Certainly I am knowing how to find his headquarters. Fifteen minutes, maximum, and you will be there."

Hussein, the driver I had hired for the day, was a classic Pathan with cinnamon skin, dark eyes, and a black beard trimmed to the width of a chin strap.

We got into his old but well-maintained Plymouth and sped down the Khyber Road. A quarter of an hour later—Hussein's timing was perfect, rare in a country where watches were more decorative than anything else—he parked in front of a low stone house surrounded by a mud-brick wall. It was somewhere on the city's outskirts, in a neighborhood of similar houses, their walls and the tight, dusty alleys between them creating a covert atmosphere, as if each enclosed compound were a repository of sinister secrets.

Inside the courtyard, an armed guard searched me and my camera bag, then led me through a double wooden door into a high-ceilinged room divided by a reed curtain. I was greeted by Sheikh Mazar, who was more or less the public relations director for Khalis's wing of Hizbi Islami.

He escorted me through the curtain. In bright light slanting through partly open casement windows, the chief leader, as Mazar called Khalis, sat on a sofa reading a blue-bound Koran. His face was long and angular, framed by a thick gray beard. He wore a white *pugri*, or turban, a gray vest over a white *kurta*, and a bullet-studded pistol belt that crossed his chest like an ambassadorial sash. Bodyguards sat at his feet on straw floor mats, Kalashnikovs resting on their laps. They all had hard dark eyes that looked at me with an expression made hostile by its very indifference, an attack dog sort of look. I had the immediate impression they would have shot me at a word from the chief leader.

Khalis did not at first acknowledge my presence. His eyes were fixed on the Koran. After several uncomfortable moments of silence, he looked up and exchanged a few words with Mazar.

"Our chief leader says he is ready now for your interviewing." Mazar smiled. "He wishes you to know he also was once a journalist before making jihad against the Russians."

"Oh? When? Where?"

The question prompted Khalis to offer his résumé. Sixty-one years old. Educated in British India. Taught mathematics and Islamic studies at an institute in Kabul. Later became a journalist and propagandist, writing broadsides against Mohammad Daoud Khan, who deposed Afghanistan's King Zahir Shah in 1973. Daoud sent Khalis into exile. He came to Peshawar, where he published political poems opposing Daoud, then Mohammad Taraki, who took power when Daoud was killed in an army coup, and finally, Hafizullah Amin, who seized the government and called for Soviet troops after Taraki was assassinated by agents of the Khad and the KGB (Afghan politics was a robust game). Khalis had fought them all with his pen, and now he was fighting with the sword as well.

"The other mujahadin leaders are jealous of me, they feud with me because I am always at the front," Khalis said, speaking with spare gestures and in a deep monotone, as if he were droning Koranic verses. "Sometimes I am here two or three days, but then I go back to the front. The others stay here all the time. They are bungalow mujahadin, but I am"—he patted his shoulder holster—"a field general. Now I will answer your questions."

I hadn't come prepared to interview him, only to enlist his help in getting to the front, but protocol required that I ask something. Delicately, I posed the question, How could the resistance hope to defeat the Russians if its leaders were feuding with one another?

Khalis must have been asked that many times; his answer was immediate, smooth, canned: "Our differences are only in Pakistan. There are no differences at the front. We fight as one."

"How's the fighting going?" I hoped the question would lead smoothly to my request.

"Nangarhar Province—that is where I was born—is three-fourths liberated." An excitement had entered his voice. "The Russians have guns, but we have these." He pointed a forefinger at one eye. "The villagers help us. When the Russian tanks come, the villagers crowd the roads, even the children, and at great risk to their lives because sometimes the Russians will run them over and crush them. But sometimes the Russians will stop and open the hatches to the tanks and stick out their heads to shout at the villagers to get out of the road. That is when we mujahadin, hiding in our sangars in the hills, shoot them with our Enfields. The Enfield is very good for that, better than the Kalash." Khalis allowed himself a chilly smile. "We are the best snipers, and we shoot them like partridges."

I saw my opening and said I would like to see his men in action, shooting Russians like partridges. Mazar translated, but Khalis did not seem to hear.

"Against the gunships, we have no defense. We don't fight when the planes come. Sometimes we will shoot at MiGs with the machine guns captured from the puppet army, but never at the gunships." A piercing light came into his eyes, hawk's eyes deeply set between a nose bent like a hawk's bill. He leaned forward, and now his voice crackled with passion. "We are fighting for Islam! We have launched jihad against the Communists and will fight to the last man! To the last bullet in the last rifle!"

Yes, yes, of course. And I very much wanted to see that jihad. That was why I had come so far. Could I accompany his men to the fighting? Again Mazar translated the request, but Khalis rolled on.

"The gunships bomb and destroy our villages. They drop napalm and burn our crops." Khalis was looking straight at me with his bird-of-prey eyes, and I saw in him the quality, for which "charisma" was too mild and shopworn a word, that had made him a leader of twenty thousand tough mountain guerrillas. "They drop *poison gas* and kill the people. Why don't the American people help us?"

It was a plea more than a question, and there was nothing rote about it; it was full of anger and grief. I had no idea what to say.

"We are persecuted by the Russians," he went on, his voice rising a fraction of an octave. "We are being killed by the Russians. Our Islamic women are raped by the Russians. I ask you again, why don't the Americans help us?"

I could only reply that I was a mere journalist, who did not set government policy.

Khalis waved a finger in a movement like a windshield wiper's. He said, in effect, that I should not underrate myself. Mere journalist indeed! He had been a journalist, against Daoud, Taraki, and Amin, and he knew there was the jihad of the rifle and the jihad of the pen. The mujahadin had that weapon on their side—public opinion.

Khalis's voice now sounded like the muezzin's, insistent and hypnotic. He was, after all, a holy man as well as a guerrilla chieftain, a warrior-priest, and his message came through in the very rhythms of his speech, making translation almost unnecessary. He considered me a volunteer in the "jihad of the pen"; if I wanted a trip to the front, the fare would be an understanding, tacit if not explicit, that my dispatches would be favorable to the cause and would, in their small way, influence the men who did make policy.

I asked what he wanted from America, as if I were a clerk taking an order.

"Not advisers. Not troops," he replied, wiping another invisible windshield with his finger. "We don't want the involvement of a foreign power because we wish to follow our destiny. It is *our* jihad."

"What *do* you want, then?"

"Stengah."

Sten guns? I turned to Mazar.

"The antiaircraft rocket that is fired from the shoulder," he explained.

"You mean the Stinger missile?"

"Yes. The Stengah. Our chief leader says the mujahadin want weapons like that to fight the helacoptayars. If we had them, then we would show all our power to the Russians."

Khalis exchanged a few more words with Mazar, ending with *"bas"*—Pashto for "enough." He sat back on the sofa and picked up the Koran with the dark-blue cover. The interview was over. Mazar ushered me through the reed curtain.

"The chief leader says you will go to the front very soon, *inshallah.*"

He walked me outside, into dust and harsh sun. Hussein was dozing behind the wheel of his Plymouth. Mazar instructed me on the dress code for sneaking over the border: shalwar, *kurta,* a *pakol* for my head, and the cloaklike blanket the Pathans call a *choga.*

"You should buy these things today." He took a step backward, looking me up and down. "Yes, you are dark and not too tall like most Americans. With proper kit, you will be looking like mujahid. At the front, you will be making photographs?"

"Yes."

"You will give them to us, please?"

It was a demand phrased as a request. I pointed out that it was my obligation to give the photographs to my magazine.

"Of course. But perhaps you can make photographs for us also? We need them for"—he smiled ironically—"the jihad of the pen."

A small crisis in professional ethics. If I agreed, it would probably grease the wheels, and anything that helped me get to the front, short of a felony, was to the good. *Esquire* had not hired me as a photographer—the pictures would be a bonus. What harm would there be in taking a few for Khalis? It's not a question of what you owe your employer but what you owe the profession, countered the voice of journalistic conscience. If you do what they're asking, your disguise won't be counterfeit, you'll *be* a mujahid, a kind of media mercenary.

I took the coward's way out: I stalled, telling Mazar I would give his proposition some thought.

Mazar nodded in the Pathan manner, inclining his head to one side, and repeated his promise that I would leave for the front very soon, *inshallah.*

I woke Hussein and asked if he knew where I could buy the clothes for my guerrilla costume.

"Oh my, yes. My uncles are owning shops. You will have proper kit in one jiffy, maximum."

I mulled things over on the way to the Old City. That I had not rejected Mazar's request out of hand testified to his chief leader's power to move emotions and sway minds. Of course, Younis Khalis had found in me emotions ready to be moved, a mind disposed to be swayed. With his talk about the jihad of the pen, he reminded me of Tom Smith, telling me that a newspaper is an instrument, a weapon. And once again, as I had when I worked for Smith, I saw myself as a soldier in the Forces of Light, with a special destiny that would offer more protection than a truckload of little brass fish. Khalis had shown me the higher purpose I sought. I would write an article that would move the men in Washington to take action, for the Afghans deserved all the support we could give. My power to fantasize jumped the corral and ran free. I heard congressmen and White House aides calling the Oval Office. *Did you see Caputo's piece in* Esquire, *Mister President? We have got to do something to help those people.* I pictured the president phoning the CIA director with orders to get those Stingers in the pipeline. *Yes, sir, Mister President.*

Hussein parked somewhere off Quissa Khawani, under the glower of Balahisar. We passed through a food market, the scents of onions and spices mingling with manure and sewage to create a single impression on the nostrils, at once savory and foul, then into an alleyway walled on both sides by tall houses with laundry-bannered poles sticking out from the balconies.

"Here we are. Scrap bazaar," said Hussein.

The shops and stalls were filled with army surplus. I bought a canteen for thirty rupees and, at Hussein's suggestion, a wool commando-style sweater for the cold in the mountains, even now in the spring it's cold in the mountains, saar. From there, we walked past the gleam and clatter of the coppersmiths' bazaar onto a street of tailors. Hussein guided me into a dry goods shop owned by a man with a black spade of a beard.

"He is mullah, holy man. Also my uncle."

While they talked, I rummaged among the shelves, picked out a dark-green *kurta* and a pair of shalwar the same color, and tried them on. The uncle gestured for me to have a look in a full-length mirror in need of resilvering. As I gazed at my reflection, he placed a beretlike *pakol* on my head and said something to his nephew.

"Uncle is saying you are looking like proper Pathan."

The older man moved behind me, tugging at the *kurta*'s sleeves to make a better fit. He muttered a few more words. Hussein laughed.

"He is saying you are looking so much like proper Pathan that soon you will be praying to Allah and having four wives."

"Tell him one's all I can handle."

A snapshot of Jill and the kids flashed in my mind, evoking a longing of unexpected power. At the same instant, the image of the fake Pathan in the mirror began to waver and blur, like a picture on a defective television screen. *What am I doing in this getup, twelve thousand miles from home?*

"You must have *choga* now," Hussein said. My reflection steadied itself.

I took one of the woolen cloaks from a shelf. It was cream-colored. Hussein snatched it from under my arm and put it back.

"Not that one." He chose another, grayish-brown. "This is the *choga* of the mujahadin."

I asked what made it so popular among the mujahadin.

"It's the same color like the rocks in Afghanistan." He raised and lowered his knees, like a soldier at mark time. "I am a mujahid, marching in the mountains. Then, *toptoptoptop*." His eyes widened theatrically, turning toward the cobwebbed ceiling. "Hearing Roosie helacoptayar! This is what I must do in one quick jiffy." He dropped to the floor suddenly and covered himself in the *choga*. "Roosie pilot is looking," came his muffled voice, "but is not seeing me." Hussein leapt up, giving the *choga* a flourish. "Thinking I am a rock, many thanks to this clever blanket."

The attempt to cross the border with Khalis's guerrillas collapsed into a comic adventure, *Gunga Din* played for laughs. Shortly after I got to the frontier, at Miram Shah, four Russian gunships violated Pakistani airspace and strafed the hills near an Afghan refugee camp. I took photographs, which gave my guerrilla disguise away. The Northwest Frontier police arrested me and sent me under guard to their Peshawar headquarters for questioning.

A plainclothesman grilled me in a room with a broken skylight, through which the rain dripped into a plastic bucket. My interrogator was a gaunt young man determined to prove he was one tough customer with no tolerance for alibis. When I showed him my passport and my *Esquire* press card, he gave both a brief, contemptuous glance before tossing them aside, with the disgust of a poker player discarding a worthless draw.

"Which state in the United States are you from?" he asked, affecting a slightly bored attitude.

"Florida."

"That is in the West, isn't it?"

"The South."

"How many states in the United States?"

"Fifty. Look, I really am an American. Just telephone Mister Archand," I said, mentioning the name of the American consul.

"Who is the president of the United States?"

"James Earl Carter. Why?"

"We suspect you of being a KGB agent, infiltrated into Pakistan with the Afghani refugees."

The Great Game redux! In my career as a foreign correspondent, I had often been branded a CIA agent, but this was the first time I had been accused of working for the opposition.

"If I were a KGB agent, do you suppose I would have gone around in broad daylight, taking pictures of Russian gunships bombing your country?"

"I will ask the questions. Which number president is President Carter?"

I thought for a moment. I could not remember. I began to take the proceedings more seriously. I had done just what I had warned myself not to do: taken my eyes off the ball.

"Listen," I said, stalling, "you can clear all this up by calling Mister Archand at the consulate."

"What number president is President Carter?"

"I'm pretty sure he's the thirty-ninth. I suppose next you're going to ask how many home runs Babe Ruth hit."

He gave me a hard stare.

"How many *did* he hit?"

"Single season or lifetime?"

"Both, please."

"Single season, sixty. Lifetime, seven hundred fourteen, a record that stood until Hank Aaron broke it in nineteen seventy-four."

"The KGB could have taught you such facts."

"Will you please call the consulate?"

The history and geography quiz went on. I think I was naming the capital of North Dakota when a balding man with bulging eyes and a jovial, urbane manner appeared. He said he was the secretary of Information for the Frontier Provinces, then apologized for the inconvenience I had undergone—procedure, you know—and told me I was free to go.

That night, showered and changed back into western dress, I went to the consulate to tell Doug Archand of my adventures. He empathized. Once a district adviser in Vietnam, he was often accused of being a spook instead of a consul, and I wondered if there was something to the charge when I noticed, on his table lamp, copies of *All the World's Artillery* and *Infantry Small Arms* stacked atop a collection of Flannery O'Connor's short stories.

"I have catholic reading tastes," he explained, "and I don't mean Flannery O'Connor's kind of Catholic."

He said the instrusion I witnessed was not the first time the Russians had violated Pakistani airspace, nor the first time they had dropped ordnance. It was the first time they had used gunships, but that was not much of a scoop, certainly nothing to rattle windows in Washington.

"Going to try again?"

"I'm going to see Jamiyat Islami tomorrow morning."

"Rabbani's boys. They aren't the biggest, but they're probably the best. Why are you so determined to go through with this?"

I mumbled some nonsense about my leg and the need to prove I could still run with the pack.

"If you want to prove your legs, *you,* are as good as you used to be, come trekking with me in Chitral next week, but don't go scrambling up mountains with gunships after you."

The headquarters of Jamiyat Islami were in a building cobwebbed with electrical wires. I was searched by a guard and then led through a hall and past a room filled with mujahadin who must have just come back from the front. Mud caked their feet, their clothes were tattered, and their eyes had that half-dreamy, half-crazed, far-away stare you can see in every war photograph from Don McCullin's shots of Hue to Mathew Brady's portraits of Gettysburg. They were not eyes a correspondent could look into without some embarrassment; they were compelled to see what the correspondent saw by choice.

I waited in a small room. One of its walls was almost covered by a map of Afghanistan, another by propaganda posters and photographs that showed triumphant mujahadin standing atop downed helicopters, swarming over ambushed convoys and gutted tanks. A banner hung above the photos. It must have been put up for the benefit of foreigners because its slogan was in English:

OUR MOTTO
ALLAH IS OUR FINAL GOAL
PROPHET MUHAMMAD OUR ULTIMATE LEADER
JIHAD OUR WAY
MARTYRDOM FOR THE FAITH OUR GREATEST DESIRE

Some of the posters were also in English. One showed a guerril-la downing a gunship by shouting the Koranic ejaculation *"Allahu Akhbar!"*—"God is great!"—into the heavens. I was tempted to laugh at such mystical nonsense—you needed a missile to drop a gunship—but when I considered that the Afghans were holding off the Soviets with little more than their faith and an Enfield rifle, which was the more laughable, their belief or my skepticism?

A young, clean-shaven man came in. He wore black-rimmed glasses and a pink *kurta* and introduced himself as Tamim, press liai-son for the political committee. Lighting up a Marlboro, he asked where I wanted to go and what I wished to see "inside." I mentioned Kahlis's report about chemical warfare.

"If you wish to confirm the reports of poison gas," Tamim said, moving to the map, "then you must go to here."

Starting at the border, his finger traced a network of river valleys northward, skipped over passes that stood at eighteen thousand feet, and finally stopped in Badakhshan, where one arm of the Hindu Kush reached out to touch the Soviet Pamirs and another embraced the Karakorams of far western China.

"You can see why the Russians use poison gas there. It is very far, more than six hundred kilometers, and it is on their borders. No cor-respondent has ever been there."

"How long would that one take?"

"Six weeks."

It looked like a killer of a trek, even on a map. Six weeks would put me well past my deadline, but if I could confirm that the Russians were using poison gas ...

"So I could be back here around the middle of July if I left soon?" I asked Tamim.

His thick, black eyebrows furrowed and his lips moved as he counted silently.

"Oh, no, dear saar. About the middle of September, and if you stayed much later than that, then you would not be back until the spring because of all the snows."

"Middle of September? You said six weeks."

"Six weeks just to get there."

If it had been ten years earlier and I had two reliable legs, I still might have gone for it, deadlines and blizzards be damned. But four months out there—a whole year if I got snowed in ... And if I were wounded, if I broke the bad leg on some mountainside, hundreds of miles from the nearest doctor or clinic ...

"I can't do it. Too far."

Then, suggested Tamim the battlefront travel agent, perhaps I would prefer something a little less rigorous and distant.

I looked at the map again, noticing that the word "Kafiristan" appeared in parentheses beneath "Nuristan." The former meant "Land of the Infidels," the latter "Land of Light." I asked Tamim why the region had two names.

Kafiristan, he explained, had been its old name. Its inhabitants, called the "Kafir-Kalash," or the Red Kafirs, for their gingery hair and light complexions, had been pagans until relatively recent times. I recalled that Kipling's short story "The Man Who Would Be King" was set in Kafiristan and was based on the myth that the Kafirs were descendants of legions Alexander left behind to garrison the Hindu Kush. It was a wonderful story, too wonderful to be true, yet there was the real Kafiristan right in front of my eyes, half known, remote, yet accessible, only a third as far as Badakhshan. I pressed my thumb into the center of all that glamour and mystery.

"When could I leave?"

"Very soon, *inshallah*."

That night, I went to Dean's to soak up the atmosphere of the vanished Raj. I had a couple of drinks with two young British free-lance photographers, Bob Wyckham and Steve Bent. Wyckham, a twenty-five-year-old ex-paratrooper who had done a tour in Belfast, had the bull-necked look of the military athlete, a suggestion, as he sat in the rattan chair sipping his beer, of speed and power in repose. Bent was nothing like his name, but thin and straight as a stick, a hundred and fifty pounds pulled over a six-foot frame as tautly as a hide over a tanner's rack. He was only twenty-one but did not look it; a scruffy blond beard added a few years to his face, which was shaped like a spade, and there was an oldness in his light-blue eyes and a toughness in his manner that must have come from growing up hard in the streets of Manchester. A century ago, he would have been in Peshawar in uniform, ready to risk a Khyberee bullet for Queen, country, and the few quid he sent home each month to the young missus.

Now he had come ready to risk a Russian bullet for a chance to launch himself out of journalistic obscurity onto the stage occupied by legendary British war photographers like McCullin, Phillip Jones Griffiths, and Tim Page.

Page was the one Bent and Wyckham admired most. Like them, he had been a free-lancer, and very young when he went to Vietnam. His work never matched McCullin's or Griffiths', but he turned his life into an art, and his irreverent behavior and outrageous daring were the models for every kid who wanted to make a name with a camera in dangerous places. Wyckham and Bent would not stop talking about him and asked if I knew him. I didn't, though I felt I did, having heard so much about him from correspondents who had worked with him.

"What did they say he was like?" Wyckham asked.

He embodied the paradoxes of his times, a psychedelic wild man who came out of the anarchic fringes of the sixties, that weird border region where opposites converged, the dope-smoking antiwarrior marching through Haight-Ashbury in army fatigues and love beads, not the mirror image but the obverse of the dope-smoking warrior who patrolled the bush wearing a peace symbol on his dog tags: dark romantics both, drawn to the extremes of emotion and experience. The two faces were joined in a man like Page, whose pictures screamed against the waste of war but who once said that you cannot take the glamour out of war. The last I had heard of him, he was working as a house painter and having a tough time on the scaffolds and ladders because his joints were held together by steel pins and his skull was a metal plate, a souvenir of a head wound that had upset his sense of balance.

"Yeahr, 'e can't do wars anymore," Wyckham said lugubriously, as if it were the worst fate that could befall anybody.

He had wrangled an assignment from *Soldier of Fortune,* the trade magazine for potbellied gun nuts with mercenary wet dreams, and said he wanted a picture of an exploding tank. "That's the kinda thing Piege woulda done, get a picshah of an explodin' tank."

Wyckham had found a faction willing to take him inside, but

Bent had not had any luck so far. He was the quieter and the more professional of the two—he had been a staff photographer for a provincial newspaper since he was sixteen. He had quit and, with no credentials or assignment whatever, cleaned out his savings and bought a one-way ticket to Karachi, where, to save money on air fare, he booked a third-class seat on a train for Peshawar. It was overflowing with Pathans, Punjabis, and Baluchis, the temperature near the top of the thermometer, but Bent loved it, riding with those tribesmen, wind and engine soot in his face, the train rattling over deserts and mountains and rivers Alexander had crossed, bound for the Northwest Frontier.

Our drinks finished, we went to Lala's Grille for dinner. It was in Green's Hotel, a shabby place that was, for some reason, *the* place to go for the spooks in Peshawar: spooks from the Khad, the KGB, the CIA, and the Pakistani secret service, all trying to listen in on each other's conversations while they wolfed down dripping kebabs and volcanic curries. If any of them had bugs planted under our table, they would have heard me delivering a boring monologue. Something had moved me to play the part of the salty veteran for the amusement and edification of my dinner companions. I inflicted on them tales about covering the fall of Saigon and told them more than they wanted to hear about the time McCullin and I crossed the desert with the rebels in Eritrea. I sounded like some garrulous ex-athlete, reliving past glories. I was embarrassed for myself, yet I went on. Possibly I had become jealous of the way Wyckham and Bent hero-worshipped Page and wanted them to know that I had done a thing or two in my day. Possibly it was something else: there they were, in the full power of their twenties, and there I was, flaps and landing gear down on final approach to middle age. Anyway, they were polite enough to act impressed, and, finally, I shut up.

We were walking back toward Dean's, beneath a sky that had the texture of a stage curtain, and Wyckham was talking about a new assault rifle the Russians were thought to be testing in Afghanistan. *Soldier of Fortune* wanted a picture of it, and he was going to get one, after he snapped a shot of the exploding tank. Bent was silent. He looked a little stricken. I was seized by one of my impulses.

"Listen," I said in an undertone. "How'd you like to work for a real magazine?"

He looked at me.

"I'm supposed to go inside with Jamiyat Islami any day now. I'll need a photographer."

"'ey, that'd be great."

"I can't promise anything, can't even pay your expenses, but if you get good stuff, I'll talk to *Esquire* and make sure they look at yours before they go to the files. That's the best I can do."

"It's good enough. I've got me kit, can go anytime."

We shook on it. I thought it might be a good idea to have someone else along who spoke English; besides, I liked him for coming out to the edge of the earth on a shoestring and a chance and without a return ticket. I felt he deserved a chance. Only later, after everything happened, did I see that I might have had other, less admirable motives.

Tamim phoned the next day; he wanted to see me at seven that night. He wouldn't say what for because he thought the phones were tapped.

I killed the afternoon in the worst way imaginable—by visiting the Red Cross hospital where the Afghan wounded were brought for treatment. Maybe it was the best way because a military hospital is the best place to see the horrors of war. There are too many distractions on the battlefield, where the wounded and the dying are mere details in a great and terrible drama. But in the quiet of a postsurgical ward the observer is better able to focus on the things modern weapons do to the human body and thus to see the casualties for what they are—small, frail fractions of the men they used to be, alone with their pain and missing parts.

The Red Cross hospital had been set up less than a month after the Soviet invasion. Since then, every kind of war injury had been treated by its small staff of two or three European doctors, assisted by a handful of Afghan aides.

An intern took me around. One young mujahid, his left arm paralyzed from a bullet wound, told me he wanted to go to the United States or Lebanon for restorative surgery. I suggested the States, Lebanese hospitals being filled with the victims of their own unending war.

"I'm afraid he won't be going anywhere," said the intern. "It's very expensive for us to send our wounded out of this country. Only the most serious are evacuated and then ..." His voice trailed off as he looked at the guerrilla fighter with his arm hanging uselessly at his side. "It's a pity. If only we could have gotten to him sooner, but he came out on a donkey. It took five days. They all come out on donkeys or camels. There is no other way."

I left and went to the bazaars, where I bought the most elaborate first-aid kit I could find.

Tamim showed up at seven-twenty. After giving me a brief salaam, he crossed the room in two or three quick strides and ran his fingers over the dresser, like a sergeant looking for dust at a barracks inspection. He made the same examination of the desk and the table. I figured he was searching for a hidden microphone.

"Where is the *qibli?*" he asked, nervously turning to me. "It is usually on the dresser."

That was the cause of his anxiety. It was time for the sunset prayer, and in the strange surroundings of the hotel, he did not know in which direction to face. Apparently, my room had been reserved for infidels; the *qibli* was absent. I walked out to the balcony, saw where the sun was setting, and showed Tamim which wall to face. He went to the bathroom, where he snatched a towel to use as a prayer rug, then knelt and bowed, murmuring praises to his God with a devoutness seldom seen in the secular west.

When he was done, he sat on the couch, lit a cigarette, and announced that I would be leaving for Afghanistan the next morning.

"Do you have everything?"

I showed him my gear: *kurta,* shalwar, *pakol,* and *choga;* canteen, hiking boots, camera bag, and a day pack containing a sweater, a change of socks and underwear, my notebooks and pens, a Swiss army knife, and the first-aid kit.

"Got this, too," I said, opening my wallet and carefully unfolding the South Florida cocktail napkin to show him the little brass fish.

"What's that?"

"A good-luck piece."

He gave it a nod of approval but said that the medical gear would be more useful.

"You might need it. We don't have any doctors, you know."

I told him I had seen the hospital.

*　　*　　*

Eleven of us climbed single file under a moon curved like a scythe. Above the town of Bejauer, northeast of Peshawar, the frontier meandered along the crest of a mountain range four or five thousand feet high. A tall mujahid, his white *kurta* bright in the moonlight, guided us toward it. Behind him came our nominal commander, Mahmud Hezrat, who was about fifty years old and bowed under a pack he had jury-rigged by wrapping a *choga* around his gear and supplies, then looping and knotting the tag ends into shoulder straps. It must have weighed thirty or forty pounds, but rib-thin Mahmud went up the mountainside as if he were on level ground with only a shirt on his back. I followed him, Bent followed me, his head and face swaddled in a *pugri* so the border guards would not notice his blond hair and beard. Trailing Bent were seven adolescent guerrillas, each carrying a burden heavier than Mahmud's. Not one looked past sixteen, not one was armed, which led me to guess that they were raw recruits pressed into service as porters until they got to wherever we were going. I had no idea where that was because not one of them spoke more English than I did Pashto; nor did Mahmud, beyond a few generic military terms and a short repertoire of monosyllabic commands: "Stand, sit, rest." Without a translator, I was going to have a hell of a time making sense of things or interviewing anyone, though I wasn't worried about interviews as we toiled up the mountain. I wanted someone to tell us our ultimate destination and why we were sailing off into Afghanistan with only one rifle—the guide's—among us. Bent and I felt a little like captives who were being led off to an unknown prison camp.

The walking had gone easily enough at first. I had taped my bad ankle to give it more support, but it began to ache and throb as the land pushed up and the trail rose in coils tight as a spring's. I swallowed a couple of Motrin tablets to dull the pain and offered a silent prayer of thanks when a gang of woodcutters and their mule train, moving downhill, forced us to stop at the side of the trail. Leaning against a boulder to catch my wind, I tried to appreciate the beauty of the valley below, its floor a geometry of yellow-and-brown grainfields. The mules, loaded down with logs, neck bells tinkling, wound around a bend until they were out of sight and there was only the sound of the bells in the high, cold air.

We started up once more. The border station lay just ahead—a low stone hut shadowed by the pines bristling on the mountain's crest. The guards, busy with a crowd of refugees, did not notice us. One by one, we ducked the border gate, which was nothing more than a pine log thrown across the trail, each end resting on an oil drum.

The guide led us through stands of cedar to a promontory, then shook hands with Mahmud and went back. Now we had no rifle. Wonderful.

After we filed through the woods to a treeless ridge line, Mahmud commanded, "Rest now." I could see a valley and part of a river, shoaled in the middle so that it looked like a gray-green python with a brown stripe down its back. Mahmud looked at me, his squint drawing cat's whiskers at the corners of his eyes. He patted the earth with his hand.

"Afghanistan," he said, then shouldered his pack and led us down the mountainside to a dirt track running beside the river. Terraced wheat fields rose in alternating bands of green and gold on both sides of the river, mud-walled villages stood atop the hills, the hills climbing toward the great blaze of white in the far distance: the Hindu Kush. It was magnificent country, but fresh tank tracks rutted the road and the field and villages were deserted. You did not need to be a military expert to figure out why: Kunar Province was a free-fire zone. Mahmud made the best use of his very limited English to describe the destruction to me and Steve Bent. Pointing at a huge hole blasted out of a mosque, he said: "Roosie tank"; at a house with its roof blown off, its timbers charred: "Roosie rocket." Two craters gaped in the middle of the road: "Roosie bomb"; a row of smashed houses stood forlornly on the far side of the river: "Roosie helacoptayar." Then, sweeping his arm back in the direction from which we'd come, Mahmud said: "*Majer, majer*—Pakistan," meaning, we guessed, that everyone had fled to the refugee camps across the border.

We walked all morning, the mujahadin mending their normally fast pace so Bent and I could stay with them. If there is one thing an Afghan can do better than anyone, it's walk. Turning away from the riverbed, we followed a narrow trail across the fields, the sun very hot in all that open country. The destruction seemed to get worse the farther we went. The Russians' MI-24s had so thoroughly worked over the villages that the rubble was indistinguishable from the piles left by rock slides and avalanches; it was as if man-made disaster had become the twin of natural.

At midmorning, after we had covered around ten miles and I was drenched in sweat, we stopped to rest by an abandoned grain mill. It was the only structure still standing in that devastated valley, its wheel, driven by water sluicing down irrigation pipes made of halved logs grooved in the middle and laid end to end, turning with ghostly squeaks. One of the teenage mujahid—he had a pitted face and close-cropped hair—filled a pan in the mill race and offered it to Bent and me. We drank until our bellies bulged.

The pockmarked guerrilla asked my name. He could not pronounce "Philip," so I told him to call me by my middle name, which was "Yusef" in Pashto.

"I," he said, patting his chest. "Saabjohn."

That's how his name struck my ear. I repeated it to make sure I'd gotten it right, but Saabjohn shook his head. I tried again. His name baffled my tongue as much as mine did his, so I said I would call him "Johnny."

He appeared to like the sound of it.

"Johnny? Amerikai?"

I nodded; yes, it was an American name.

"I ... visa ... U.S.A. I ... U.S.A. ... study medical ..."

"Where?"

"Harvardyale."

"Which one?"

"Harvardyale."

"No. Harvard is one school. Yale another school. Which one do you want to go to?"

Johnny smiled sheepishly and adjusted his cap, which wasn't a *pakol* but a little round hat that looked like a bellhop's.

"That one."

I was about to try to explain the difference once again but was interrupted by a loud crowing and bleating. Bent raised his camera and started shooting the column of refugees that came over a rise and passed us: old men and women, crooked into L's beneath rolled carpets, blankets, and mattresses, young women holding infants to their breasts, and a few children, some carrying kerosene lanterns, others with chickens cradled in their arms. A small herd of goats, so scrawny their ribs looked like X rays, straggled behind. Mahmud looked at the procession until it vanished around a hill.

"*Majer,* Pakistan." He faced me, jaw set and an expression in his eyes that made me feel sorry for any Russian soldier who ever fell into his hands. "*Majer,* Pakistan."

Why were the Russians laying waste to Afghanistan? Because they had the power to do it. If you have an unemployed army of four million men, it's no trouble to spare a hundred thousand to knock the hell out of a country of pastoral nomads. Give your lads a little combat experience, season your officer corps, test new weapons and equipment. Yet I could not think of the Russians as monstrous by nature. I remembered one of the young Muscovites I'd met, a graduate student named Kolya. He was specializing in Central Asian languages and could quote long passages of Persian poetry with great feeling. He loved to listen to jazz—forbidden at that time—and knew his Pushkin far better than I did my Whitman. I had heard he'd been drafted and sent to Afghanistan. Where was he now? Interrogating mujahadin prisoners? Flying gunships? It was hard to picture him, with his curly brown hair and lively blue eyes, doing either, but, then, it doesn't take long for a good drill sergeant to knock most of the poetry and music out of a young man.

"Yusef!" Mahmud commanded. "Stand! March now!"

After we had been on the move over eight hours, my leg began to hurt like hell. Sweat-soaked, parched, and hungry, Bent and I were led by Mahmud to a mud-brick hovel owned by a strongly built mujahid named Posli Akhbar. I dubbed him the "gay guerrilla" because, to abbreviate a story not worth telling at length, he exhibited extraordinary affection for Bent and me, stroking our arms with a lascivious look in his eye, holding our hands when we went out back to take a leak.

We were put up in Posli's guest house, a dark dirty shack abuzz with flies, fed a dinner of bread, goat's milk, and tea. In the evening, Posli made an ardent advance on Steve, who rebuffed him with a "get your bloody buggering hands offa me." One of the mujahid, a kid with a birthmark on his cheek, was more receptive, and the two went off for a hug and a kiss. Steve and I, meanwhile, made a determined effort to pry some information out of Mahmud. The conversation, if you could call it that, was conducted in pidgin English, pidgin Pashto, and much sign language, much drawing of pictures in the dirt. Johnny stopped by to help out. After more than an hour, we got some answers. Mahmud showed us an envelope with Pashto calligraphy written on it: a sealed message from Jamiyat Islami headquarters. His mission was to deliver it to a man named Sher Rahman, whom he described as a *turjoman,* which, we gathered, meant something like field commander. Sher Rahman's sangar was two days' march away, at a place called Kattar. We would spend a couple of days there with his men, see a bit of the war, and then hike back to Pakistan.

I felt better now that I knew what we were up to. I was also taken with the notion of delivering a secret message to a guerrilla chieftain. Sher Rahman. It was a wonderful name, something out of Kipling. We never found him.

The next morning started with the now familiar commands. "Stand! March now!"

We trekked three or four hours through more smashed villages and derelict fields, where flax and grain grew wild as weed and, a sight to make a junkie weep, swales of poppy went to rot. A tropical humidity thickened the air as storm clouds marshaled over the mountains to the north. We heard a rumbling, faint with distance, but too constant to be thunder or bombs.

"Konhara," said Mahmud, pointing in the direction of the noise.

The Konhara River. Once across it, getting back would not be an easy thing.

Rain clouds had turned the river from dark brown to milky gray as it hurtled between low, flinty cliffs. Far downstream, wide and calm in its maturity, the Konhara flowed quietly toward its end in the Kabul. Here, closer to its birthplace high in the Hindu Kush, suckled by melting snows and mountain storms, it was all roar and youthful belligerence, surging over boulders in ever moving curls of green and white, bellowing at the cliffs as if it meant to shout them down.

"Where's the bridge?" I yelled, but my voice was drowned by the river's, and Mahmud would not have understood me in any case.

The answer came in a few minutes, when we found a band of mujahadin squatting beside a lean-to of sewn goat hides. Moored in a small cove below them were two large rafts made of logs and planks lashed to truck inner tubes and inflated goatskins. Each was equipped with a tiller and rudder—a bent length of hardwood with one end resting in a notched sternpost—and a set of oars, which were poles fastened any old way to wooden paddles.

"Launch," said Mahmud.

Launch! I had never seen such sorry lash-ups.

"Do you mean we are going to cross *that*," I said, pointing at the river, "in one of *those?*"

My tone of voice needed no translation.

"*Inshallah,*" Mahmud answered.

The squall moved in. We crowded under a huge slab of rock resting on two others, like the roof of a half-fallen temple, and waited while one of the boatmen—actually he was a boy of no more than fifteen—blew up the goatskins of our raft with a bellows. When he was done, he signaled us to come aboard. We filed out from under the boulder, scanning the skies for helicopters, then climbed on. The scrap-lumber deck swayed like bog mat under our weight.

"*Bismillah, ar-rahman, ar-rahim!*" Mahmud prayed as we shoved off and spun into the current, the fast water splashing over the skins and inner tubes, the boatmen heaving on the oars, the pilot holding fast to the tiller. The Konhara flung itself at us, spewing like liquid cement out of a high-pressure hose. Thunder rolled and lightning flashed an image of a vascular system in the slaty sky. The raft, as if it were made of rubber, rose on one side while it dipped in the middle, then humped in the middle as the other side dipped. Water fountained through the chinks in the deck. The mujahadin were all chanting "*Bismillah, ar-rahman, ar-rahim!*"—"In the name of Allah, the all-merciful, the loving-kind!" We were sailing across at an angle, toward a cataract, the oarsmen hauling away against the current's weight and rush. They got the better of it and swung us on course for the far bank. When we bumped against it and stepped onto solid ground, the guerrillas spread their arms wide and cried, "*Allahu akhbar!*" If that's who got us safely across, then I thought he was pretty great, too.

We scrambled up a cliff to where a dirt road ran through a stretch of flat, open country broken by stone fences. Fresh tank tracks corrugated the road. There were old Russian foxholes ringed by rock and dirt parapets, a few burnt-out trucks, and scattered bits of flares and spent ammunition. I immediately started to hunt for gas masks and fragments of chemical bombs, but Mahmud signaled me to move quickly over the open ground. Move quickly we did, Steve loping on his long legs while I hippety-hopped on my gimpy one. Mahmud ran in short bursts, then dropped to look and listen, then ran again. I'd seen enough wars to know a real fighting man when I saw one, and he moved like a real fighting man. The younger guerillas, by contrast, sauntered behind, filled with that sense of invincibility that is the universal privilege of youth. When we stopped to catch our breath, I told Steve: "I'm sticking close to the old man from now on."

"Why's that?"

"Martyrdom for the faith is not his greatest desire. That gives me and him something in common."

We half ran, half walked into a gully, then climbed a trail to the outskirts of a village called Shinqaluq. Three mujahadin armed with ancient firearms sat near a cave they used as an air-raid shelter. It soon fulfilled its function. Two gunships appeared over a ridge line a quarter of a mile away. They flew straight at us, slowly and at an altitude of no more than five hundred feet, coming on not with the wap-wap-wap of American Hueys but with a throaty growl. We scrambled for cover. The cave could hold only two or three men; the rest of us lay flat, snuggled under the *chogas* that, we hoped, would make us look like rocks. No one dared look up as the rotors throbbed directly overhead. When the choppers passed on, I took a peek. Their slow speed suggested the leisurely confidence of predators with no natural enemies. It was clear that the pilots, crawling along almost within pistol range, weren't afraid of anything the mujahadin could shoot at them—and with good reason. The guerrilla beside me was aiming his rifle at the aircraft, and I silently prayed for him not to shoot and draw the gunships back. Stamped on the receiver were the intitials VR— Victoria Regina—and the date of the rifle's manufacture: 1878. It was a single-shot Martini-Henry, the standard infantry weapon of Kipling's British-Indian army.

Mahmud shouldered his pack and spoke the words I was already sick of hearing:

"Yusef! Stand! March now!"

*   *   *

Sometime before I left for Afghanistan, seeing the crepuscular glow of forty on the horizon, I began to think a lot about death. Given the life I'd led, that should come as no surprise, but I am not speaking of violent death, but natural death, everyday death, the long, slow closing of life's account, with annual payments of strength and vitality that lead to a final, flabby stop of a worn-out heart, a last breath indistinguishable from a sigh or yawn. The consciousness of that creeps into us about the time we're ready for our first pair of reading glasses and is the one distinction between youth and middle age that cannot be erased or overcome. We can create the illusion of youth with hair transplants, face-lifts, and tummy tucks; we can preserve some of its muscle tone and stamina with jogging and Nautilus machines; we can, by giving up the bad habits we enjoyed when we were young and indestructible, and by swallowing lots of bran, vitamins, and low-cholesterol margarine, keep our arteries as clean as new copper pipes, our hearts, lungs, kidneys, livers, and bowels vigorously pumping, breathing, flushing, and eliminating well into our sixties and beyond, but there is no known remedy for the awareness that we are going to die no matter what, or for the melancholy that comes with it.

Having confronted so much violent death early in life, it was perhaps logical that I began brooding about natural mortality a few years earlier than most people. It started with the untimely end of Bill Jones, my boss and mentor on the *Tribune's* investigative team. Six feet tall, handsome in a blue-eyed, square-jawed American way, he had won a Pulitzer before he was thirty-five, had been named managing editor before forty, and was considered next in line for the big job, editor in chief, when he was struck with leukemia. He was brought to a cancer research hospital in Houston for a bone-marrow transplant. I telephoned him from Key West when I heard the news. He described his room—not exactly a room but some kind of glass-walled compartment, hermetically sealed because the leukemia had destroyed his immune system, making him vulnerable to any kind of germ. A cold could kill him. When his wife and children visited, they had to speak to him through an intercom, and everything brought to him, his food, fresh linens, even the newspapers, had to be sterilized in infrared before he could touch them. I could not imagine anything more ghastly, but Jones was facing it with a quiet courage. "I hope this marrow thing works, Philly Beans, but if it doesn't, I'm ready." He had a newspaperman's cynical sense of humor and cracked a few jokes about his situation. "Christ, I feel like some kind of rare orchid in this damn thing they've got me in."

A few weeks later, he was dead.

I could hardly believe it. He had seemed a favorite of the gods. How could he be dead so soon, and not from bullets or shrapnel? The rebellious cells in his own body had killed him. Forty-two, only four years older than I. Prowling the house one insomnia-ridden night, in those early-morning hours when illusions whither and the most appalling truths open like night-blooming cereus, the reality struck me. *I* could be dead in four years, or four months, or four weeks. A blocked artery, an uprising of destructive corpuscles—and then, no more, no more. Natural causes: as quotidian as Monday's wash, yet awful.

Facing it was more difficult than facing the chance of a fiery extinction on the battlefield, which creates a thrilling, visceral terror that passes when the danger passes, leaving a weird exhilaration in its wake. There is nothing more exciting, Churchill once wrote, than to be shot at without effect. There was nothing at all exciting about confronting whatever doom nature had in store. I sought to offer a front to it. I had had a front as a war correspondent—a certain don't-give-a-damn dash leavened with gallows humor—but what style to adopt in the face of this new, gray menace?

Religious faith was the most obvious answer, the kind of faith Jill possessed. She believed without the slightest doubt that Bill Jones's soul had flown its corporeal cage like a splendid toucan and lived on, as hers and mine would. For all my many foxhole conversions, I could not imagine anything of the sort; maybe I had seen too many mangled corpses to believe the body harbored anything more than guts, brains, and bones.

I turned then to the pre-Christians, specifically to Marcus Aurelius. He had written his *Meditations* in a legionary camp in some gloomy northern forest, and they struck the right note for me: resignation without despair. There was a quality in his writing that had the cold, stark beauty of an Ionic column. In one of the Meditations, Aurelius said that men should not fear death, whether there is an afterlife or not; if there is, then we should be joyful to leave this flawed world for a better one; if not, then all we do is pass into a nothingness in which we would be free from all pain and anxiety. That wisdom from the noble Roman worked as a talisman in daylight, but it seemed to lose its powers in those postmidnight hours, when the cereus's pale petals spread. Courage in the face of death, that's what I sought, but not the warrior's courage, which is probably a lot of adrenaline anyway. I needed to find a different kind of bravery for a different manner of death, the kind Jones had shown: a calm, enduring valor.

Instead, I went into Afghanistan.

From Shinqaluq, we traveled to the foot of a dark mountain, where we rested in the house of a gray-bearded elder and ate, once again, flat, pie-size loaves of bread washed down with goat's milk. It was a killing six-hour climb up the eight-thousand-foot mountain. Through mulberry trees on the lower slopes, through walnut and hazel higher up, we hiked a trail steep enough in places to make our thighs quiver from strain. When we reached the pine-tree line, a thunderstorm rolled down on us. The rain turned to hail, then to snow, and the cold wind, roaring through the trees, froze our sweat. Mahmud found an overhang on the leeward side of a boulder that was as big as a garage. It wasn't much shelter, but it blunted the knifing wind. Wrapped in our blankets, we waited out the storm, then continued the climb. The last thousand feet seemed to take forever. I had put my sweater on, but the wind cut through it as if it wasn't there. Reaching the summit at sunset, too drugged with fatigue to appreciate the view, we slogged down a short distance to a miserable little village of pine-log huts.

Our night camp was in a drafty shack: an open doorway, no shutters on the paneless windows. Johnny and another guerrilla built a fire beside which we warmed ourselves and dried our clothes. Steve and I stretched out, shuddering under our *chogas*. Mahmud and the others sat around the fire, talking and singing with a few local mujahadin, men whose faces had the color and texture of the worn leather bandoliers crossed over their chests. The guerrillas seemed indefatigable. My day pack weighed a few pounds and I was exhausted; they humped packs ten times as heavy and they were talking and singing and chopping firewood. The Russians were smart to fight the war with helicopters; the best infantry in the world would have been no match for the Afghans on their own terrain.

In the morning, scratching tick bites, we started down. Gunships sent us scampering across a meadow into the concealment of a pine and cedar forest. A few miles ahead more gunships circled and strafed. The trail through the woods was slippery from the previous day's storm. Another file of refugees came up it, plodding, stumbling. One very old man hopped along like a crippled bird on crutches made of tree branches. The kettledrum of bombs kept echoing through the mountains.

"*Khali*—empty," Mahmud said. "*Majer, majer,* Pakistan."

And that take-no-prisoners look was in his eye again, a look in which the tension between sorrow and fury created an intensity that could burn holes through your shirt.

The village of Kattar hugged a hillside a thousand feet above a river valley. Its only occupants, a few bedraggled guerrillas, told us Sher Rahman had fled to Nuristan, over a mountain with the forbidding name of Nungalam Tangasaar. It rose in the distance, all twelve thousand feet of it, its peak shining above the timberline. I didn't know how Steve felt, but the thought of climbing that mountain made me want to quit. I was halfway to done in, but Mahmud wasn't ready to give up the chase. On we went, plunging down a gorge and across a thundering river, then up a narrow track with cliffs sheering away for hundreds of feet.

Bands of mujahadin passed us along the way, armed with everything from muzzle-loading shotguns to Czech machine guns. They fed us a mishmash of contradictory information. Sher Rahman had been killed; no, he lived. He had gone to Nuristan; no, to Kabul. No, he was still in Kunar Province, on this side of the mountain, in a village called Gumbier. He was leading an army of four thousand mujahadin.

We found not four thousand but four. They were sitting outside the house of a local commander, a proud, dignified man with a thick black mustache, a brass-handled knife, and bad news. Sher Rahman had definitely gone into Nuristan and had established a new sangar at Amirat, a village in the distant Weygul River valley. To reach it we would have to scale the pass over Nungalam Tangasaar. We could make the pass by the next afternoon, Amirat the day after, Allah willing.

The chieftain put us up for the night. Worn out to the point we could not sleep, Bent and I lay on our tick-infested beds and listened to the mujahadin talking. We understood nothing, but words like "helicopter," "tank," "bomb," "America," and "Roos" sprinkled the conversation. Not long ago, those isolated Afghans had been discussing bride payments, tribal disputes, crops, and livestock; now it was "helicopter," "tank," "bomb."

Mahmud roused me at some ghastly hour. "Yusef! Stand! March now!"

"Stand! March! Sit! Sleep! Shit!" Steve mimicked as we packed up. "Fucking bah-stahd talks to us like we're bloody fucking dogs."

Full of doubts and aches, I shouldered my day pack. My bad leg felt like frozen mutton. I did a few toe raises to loosen it up, looking across the dark, ridged land toward the great mountain. Its summit showed as a pale patch in the sky, like a dense but distant galaxy. We started off. My watch read four-thirty.

We reached the top of the pass a little after noon, Steve and I puffing steam and struggling to suck oxygen from the stingy air. Endless winds had blown the snow clear, exposing grasses that had a mossy, prehistoric look, the grass speckled with blue-and-yellow blossoms. The mountain's summit, looming fifteen hundred feet above, was as white and curved as a tiger's fang. Below, the meadow dropped to the timberline, black with pine, the pine lightening into hardwoods farther down, those tumbling between two buttressing spurs of the mountain into the Weygul valley. Beyond the valley, twenty or thirty miles from where we stood, mountains higher than the one we'd climbed ascended toward ranges higher still, so faint with distance we could not see each peak, but only a white line drawn straight across the sky—the frozen roof of the world.

Mahmud told us we could rest in the shelter of some rocks. He opened his pack and, as a reward for making the climb, passed around chunks of cold goat meat given to him by the chieftain at Gumbier. As we ate, four women and two men dressed in furs and hides filed out of the timber below: the men carried bolt-action rifles, the women had conical baskets of firewood strapped to their backs. They climbed toward us: Kafirs, the pale-skinned pagans, the legendary descendants of Alexander's lost legion. Steve was already shooting. I fumbled in my pack for my camera and saw that I had exposed the last frame and had not reloaded. Cursing my laziness, I started to rewind the film. Only a handful of explorers and adventurers, like Wilfred Thesiger, had ever seen those mysterious people. If I could get just one exposure of their faces ... I was too late. They were already walking past, not five yards away. I made a mental snapshot instead and was glad that was the only picture I could take; a camera would have spoiled the moment when the young woman bringing up the rear turned to give Steve a blue-eyed stare. Her hands, clutching the rope straps of her basket, were as white as his, her hair as light. With a stretch of the imagination, I could picture it spilling over a blouse or cocktail dress; instead, it fell on the bristling shoulders of the wolfskin that covered her to the tops of her boots, sewn from the hide of a mountain sheep and bound by leather thongs. Steve kept shooting. As she looked at him with her cold northern eyes, it would not have surprised me to hear her utter, in some proto-Aryan tongue, a greeting that acknowledged a racial kinship, for she looked like a woman who had stepped into the present out of Ice Age Europe. I felt a momentary completeness; she embodied the beauty and mystery I had been chasing for so long; she held the secret that lay beyond the horizon. If I'd had the nerve, and the language, I would have stopped her and asked her to reveal it. Then she turned her head and with the others trudged over the pass and was gone.

Mahmud licked his fingers clean, walked over to Steve and me.

"Yeah, yeah, we know," said Steve, standing up.

MI-24s began to strafe and bomb the Weygul. The attack went on all afternoon. The valley was fogged in smoke. Around four, after we'd trekked through forests that looked a thousand years old, we started down a steep hillside toward Klaigul, a Nuristani village. A mountain stream, which fed the Weygul River, rushed beneath us. Ahead, the gunships hovered and circled over the valley, diving into the smoke to strafe, climbing out to circle again. Sometimes a guerrilla machine gun fired a few rounds at them, which told me that the mujahadin either had great fire discipline or, as was more likely, did not have enough ammunition. Even with all the bullets in the world, their small arms would have been useless against the MI-24s, one of the marvels of late-twentieth-century death engineering. The plane's armor plate made it invulnerable to all but the heaviest antiaircraft guns; each one was armed with a conventional machine gun in the nose, an undernose minigun that fired six-thousand rounds a minute, one hundred twenty-eight rockets, eight bombs, and four air-to-ground missiles. Electronic sensor packs aided the crew in weapons control and in flying in bad weather. Watching those things flying at speeds and altitudes no American pilot would have dared in Vietnam, unless he had a death wish, listening to the pathetically brief bursts from the mujahadin's guns, I thought: *This isn't a war, it's a training exercise.*

We did not see them at first; we did not even hear them. Lazing along almost at treetop level above the stream, rising as it rose up the mountainside, the two gunships appeared suddenly, eye level with us and about half a mile off.

"*Kena!*" Mahmud shouted. It either meant "Get down" or "Take cover." I did not wait for the correct translation. The mujahadin, Steve with them, ducked into a mulberry grove a hundred feet downslope, but Mahmud and I were exposed on a patch of open ground, with only a few low bushes to hide under. We snaked into them as the helicopters climbed toward the pass. They hung in the air a moment, then—and I swear this happened, though I know it could not have—the lead chopper shuddered in the excited way a man-of-war bird does just before it swoops on a school of fish. All right, I was probably hallucinating—stress can do funny things to the brain chemistry—but I can still see a tremor pass through the steel body of the helicopter the instant before it banked sharply and came toward us, the second following, rotors flashing in the sun.

Mahmud started to pray. "*Bismillah, ar-rahman, ar-rahim!*" I pulled my sleeve over my watch but otherwise did not move and never took my eyes off the gunships, straight overhead now. They could have dropped a plumb bob and hit my nose. I concentrated, trying to project my thoughts through the choppers' plated skins and steel hydraulic veins, into their microcircuit navigational systems. *Fly away.* That was my way of seizing control from the pilots, a kind of mystical hijacking. *Go on now, fly away.*

"*Bismillah, ar-rahman, ar-rahim!*" Mahmud's praying became frantic, a garble of words in which I could only make out "Allah." Allah, Allah, Allah. The gunships hovered roughly three or four hundred feet above us—miniguns, rocket racks, bomb racks, and sensor packs, the whole nine yards of high-tech doom. Six thousand rounds a minute. A half-second burst would turn a human being into something resembling dog food. If it had to happen, then I hoped it would happen that way. The only thing I wanted to do less than die instantly in Afghanistan was to die slowly in Afghanistan.

Mahmud continued to send up his prayers: theological antiaircraft fire. The helicopters suddenly made tight turns and flew off, and I recalled the propaganda posters I'd seen in Peshawar. Whatever works, man. Go with the flow. I made the sign of the cross.

Despite the close call, Mahmud remained faithful to his mission and led us into Klaigul. The village resembled a swallow's roost. Its flat houses, resting on stilts, climbed the mountainside, which was sheer enough in places to allow a man in one house to step out his door onto his neighbor's roof. Mahmud stopped at the local mosque for the sunset prayer. Bone-tired, Steve and I were grateful for the break. We were overjoyed when, just before he started his prayers, Mahmud announced: "Here … Sleep."

We two infidels sat by the trailside, watching the war in the valley. A couple of village women, so fair and freckled their names might have been Bridget and Maureen, stood watching us from a few yards away. One of them bent down, picked up a stone, and lobbed it at Steve.

"What the hell …"

The second woman threw a rock. It landed at Steve's feet. A third missile arced in. Steve jumped to his feet.

"What the fuckin' hell are they doing?"

"I think they're stoning you …"

"*Stoning?*"

A man leapt out from behind a tree. Wiry and short, he had a reddish-brown mustache and green eyes fixed malevolently on Steve.

"Roos!" he yelled, and drew a knife.

I jumped between him and Steve.

"Nay Roos! English!"

The man feinted, tried to circle around me and get at Bent.

"Roosie!"

"Nay Roosie!"

Mahmud and the others came out of the mosque at that moment, shouting at the man, who stopped and turned with his blade poised in the air. He sheathed it after Mahmud explained Steve's fair hair and complexion. Apologizing profusely, he invited us to his house for dinner. Eating chicken that had the consistency of a hockey puck, we had a good laugh over the misunderstanding. The man was all smiles and hospitality, but I could not forget the look of concentrated malice in his eyes when his hand had gone for the knife.

We were joined by the local commander, one Gulam Saie, a twenty-two-year-old former schoolteacher garbed untraditionally in sneakers and a blue jogging jacket. He spoke passable English. When he found out I was an American, he voiced a complaint:

"I need help. Why doesn't the United States send us help to fight those helicopters?" He slapped the stock of his Lee-Enfield. "These are useless. My need is heavy machine guns and antiaircraft rockets."

I promised to quote him, and once again, saw my piece being passed around in cabinet meetings and congressional committee debates. *Did you see Caputo's story, Mister President?*

Gulam Saie told us to get a good night's rest. The next morning, inshallah, he and twenty men were going to try to make it to Sher Rahman's sangar.

Mahmud did not have to wake us up. The Russians did, with an august predawn artillery bombardment on the Weygul. At first light, gunships joined in. I counted two dozen of them and heard the terse crack of tank cannon. It was an awesome display of firepower. Gulam Saie mustered his men, reinforced by Mahmud's squad of teenagers. They had weapons now. Johnny, the would-be medical student at Harvardyale, proudly showed off his Czech machine gun.

"No more Pakistan. Now jihad," he said.

We started down the trail, toward the battle. Trudging at the rear, swallowing painkillers like M&Ms, I felt a paralysis creeping into my legs that had nothing to do with my old aching wounds. It was either cowardice or extreme prudence. In any case, I did not want to go into *that*. There is fire and there is heavy fire, and there is fire that cannot be qualified by adjectives.

We hadn't gone too far when we met three dusty mujahadin who had come from Amirat. They, Gulam Saie, and Mahmud powwowed for several minutes. Saie passed the news: Amirat had been obliterated, Soviet paratroopers had landed, and Sher Rahman had fled again, deeper into Nuristan. Big Russian columns were moving down the Weygul, toward its confluence with the Konhara; another column was sweeping through the Pech River valley, to join up with the first. The situation was clear enough: if the Russians got to the Konhara, our line of retreat to Pakistan would be blocked. As far as I was concerned, that was it. We had chased the phantom Sher Rahman for five days, often marching twelve hours a day. That was far enough. Using Saie as an interpreter, I told Mahmud I was going back, with or without him. Then I turned to Steve, telling him that I knew he hadn't gotten the pictures he was after, but if he elected to stay, he would be on his own. He mused for a minute or two, possibly wondering what his hero would have done. I didn't think even daredevil Page would have gone into that *Scheiss Stürm,* but you never could tell. The Russians ended our temporizing. A mortar barrage crunched somewhere ahead, not more than a mile off from the sound of it. Mahmud looked, and I knew what he was thinking: they were light mortars, the kind carried by infantry. The paratroopers were not far away. He got to his feet and slung his rifle, an Enfield with its fore grip tightly bound in strips of bright cloth. Handing the sealed message to Gulam Saie, he turned to me and said:

"Yusef! Stand! March now! Pakistan."

Four days later, Steve and I sat wrapped in our *chogas* against the cold and watched a column of refugees struggling up a trail toward the crest of a mountain called Pandasaar. The men were carrying bundles that looked big enough to crumple a mule, bundles of mattresses and sheepskins and whatever else was portable, bound with ropes looped into shoulder straps. The women, silver amulets and bracelets jingling, shambled along with infants tied papoose-style on their backs. Those children old enough to walk walked, as they had been walking since fleeing Nuristan. Through the mud, through the slabs of old snow lying in the lee of boulders, they were all going up the mountain, more than a thousand people.

Steve and I were awed by the Afghans' toughness and endurance. During the march, we had seen a young man carry his arthritic mother on his back up the steepest ridges. When they reached the top he would set her on her feet and she would go down on her own, using a pair of bent umbrellas for crutches; then he would lift her onto his back again and start up the next slope. I had carried a ten-year-old boy across a log bridge spanning a mountain torrent. The soles of his feet were shredded, and I was sure he could not have held his balance on the single log. When I got to the other side, his father yanked him from my arms, slapped his face, and then punched me in the chest. I thought that a peculiar way of showing gratitude, but, Mahmud signed, I had to understand: the boy had to learn to survive on his own. Because of my kindness, he would now expect a stranger to help him whenever things got tough. More than anything else, that convinced me the Russians could do everything to the Afghans except beat them.

The exodus now moving over Pandasaar mountain had begun the day we three left Klaigul. We had come to a village of about a hundred people, abandoning their homes as the advancing paratroopers mortared the valley below and the gunships strafed anything moving. Later, the one hundred became three hundred, then five. The evacuation was not planned; it seemed as spontaneous as a flash flood, refugees pouring in from the regions of the Pech and Weygul. About a fifth of the column were mujahadin, men designated to guard their families and fellow villagers on the long march to Pakistan. The presence of so many guerrillas made the flight look like a retreat. Guerrilla or civilian, everyone suffered alike, sleeping wherever they could find shelter, in the open if they could not. Mahmud, Steve, and I spent one wretched night in a dripping cave, our only protection against a fierce storm. The floor of the cave was a bed of stones that made sleep impossible. We stayed up and watched the clouds, stitched by lightning, sweep down the mountain and drench the refugees. I had been vomiting half the day, either from altitude sickness or the half-cooked chicken we'd eaten in the knife wielder's house; Steve had dysentery. Our miseries, though, were minor inconveniences compared to what the refugees had to endure. Did I want a mission? There it was. To bear witness to what was happening to them. A decision had been made far away in Moscow by warm, well-fed generals, and what was the result? A thousand people driven into exile, a crippled old woman descending mountains with umbrellas for crutches.

We ran from the Russians and then, as we neared Pandasaar, almost ran into them. They opened an attack on the crossing point on the Konhara River. Later, a mujahadin patrol gave us the worst possible news: two Russian garrisons on the Konhara had been reinforced, a force of twenty tanks and armored personnel carriers blocked the crossing point, and the rafts had been sunk. The door out had been closed. We were cut off.

Refugees and guerrillas then spread out across the mountain's slope, hiding in caves and under overhangs. Steve and I had been put up in a stable, after the cow was evicted and her shit raked out. Not two miles away, a pair of gunships circled a cone-shaped hill, dipping their noses now and then to fire rockets or machine guns. Round and round they went, like cars on some deadly carnival ride. Would they spot us eventually? Another thunderstorm blew up, mixed rain and hail pelting the stable's flimsy roof. I sunk into the deepest funk I'd ever known. "Funk" isn't the word for it; nor is "depression." It was a feeling of abandonment, of a loss of grace. Even when bleeding and crawling down that street in Beirut, I'd known I would survive. I had never lost faith in my luck, in my ability to escape, in my special destiny, but I lost it on that alien mountain. I *felt* it slip out of me and opened my wallet and looked at the charm. Maybe its breaking had been an omen after all.

An old man hauled me out of that well of gloom. Mahmud brought him in that evening; an old shrapnel wound in his ankle had festered. Could I heal him with my first-aid kit? I empathized with the old man's injury and, glad to have something useful to do, took out my Swiss army knife, a tweezers, and a bottle of hydrogen peroxide. The old man was a tough bird who barely flinched when the abscess was lanced and drained. He made a little groan as I probed for the shrapnel, but that was all. I doused his wound with antiseptic, gave him four tetracycline and a few Motrin, and bandaged him up. He expressed his thanks by offering to slaughter a goat for us.

Mahmud drew his knife and, intoning *"Bismillah, ar-rahman, ar-rahim,"* slit the kid's throat to the bone. A fire was built, the carcass strung up on a tripod of poles, and then was bled and gutted by two young girls. One of them made a smaller fire inside the stable, over which she set a big pot of rice. Mahmud invited half a dozen mujahadin to the feast. They dipped their fingers into the rice and began to eat, the coals giving their skin the color of old rosewood. I dug in and, looking outside, watched one of the girls scraping the inside of the cavity, it and the entrails steaming in the cold night air. The other girl knelt by the fire, frying the guts and organs in an iron skillet. As still as a figure in a photograph, a young mujahid nearby leaned on his Enfield and stared at her face with what seemed like longing. For a moment, the war stopped, the centuries peeled away. I was on a younger earth where pastoral tribes wandered and warriors gathered to feast by fires, an earth where no gunships flew.

The girl came in with the skillet, heaped with chunks of meat, with liver, lungs, kidney, and heart. She laid it over the coals and added a little water and salt. The smell drove us half crazy. Five minutes later, we were devouring a goat stew. When the meal was done, finished off with heavily sugared tea, Mahmud and the other mujahadin started to swap stories and sing. I lit a cigarette, full-bellied and content, my despair gone. I guessed it had been caused by nothing more than an empty stomach.

In the middle of the next morning, a mujahid walked into the stable and squatted beside the fire to warm his hands. He and Mahmud got into a long conversation, which ended with Mahmud looking toward heaven and muttering *"Alhamduillah!"* Communicating in the usual way—pidgin, sign language, pictographs in the dirt—he explained that the Russian blocking force had withdrawn. New launches had been brought up. The plan was to ferry everyone across the Konhara under cover of darkness. It would have to be completed by dawn to avoid being spotted by gunships or patrols from the Russian garrisons on the river. The gap between them, judging from the mud map Mahmud had drawn, was three miles wide, at best.

While Steve and I celebrated with a smoke and more tea, Mahmud went outside. He was back in a few minutes, carrying a shotgun in addition to his bandaged Enfield, which he handed to me. I looked at him, asking with my eyes what I was supposed to do with it. He answered with his hands: moving a thousand people across a wild river and through Russian lines at night would be a tricky business; he could not guarantee our safety or his own survival. If the worst happened, we would have to look out for ourselves. I nodded and slung the rifle, convinced it would blow up in my face if I fired it. I hoped I would not have to; it wasn't my war, though Mahmud seemed to think it had become that.

"Mujahid," he said, clapping my shoulder and smiling. It was the only time I'd seen him smile.

"Well, now," Steve said, "looks like you been knighted."

Then it was evening, and Steve and I, wrapped in our *chogas*, were watching the people toil up Pandasaar mountain as we waited our turn to move. The column was more or less organized into clans and villages. We and Mahmud had been informally adopted by the family of a dark-bearded mullah named Gulzada, whose wife and daughters huddled nearby, veiling their faces with their shawls. Finally, Mahmud turned to me.

"Yusef ..."

But I was already on my feet.

Single file, a thousand people moved down a streambed with hardly a sound. Even the infants were quiet, as if they, too, understood the danger of making noise. We were toward the rear. Though we could see only half a dozen people in front of us, we were aware of the whole column creeping in the dark like a huge millipede, huge yet weak, vulnerable, and afraid. It crawled out of the streambed and wound in segments across a bouldered field. The long creature stopped, frozen in its tracks by the blued whiteness of two illumination flares shining in the distance, evil stars. Mortars thudded somewhere, a machine gun beat a nervous tattoo. The flares fell and the creature crept cautiously forward again, across a patch of hard, flat ground to a bluff's edge. There, it ceased to be one thing, breaking up into pieces.

In tens and twenties, twos and threes, people were climbing down to the riverbanks to board the rafts. The Konhara crashed below, curls phosphorescent in the moonlight. A raft was sailing swiftly downstream, a kerosene lamp held by a boatman in the bow half revealing the passengers riding atop heaped belongings. The pontoons of inner tubes and inflated goatskins barely kept the vessel afloat under such weight, and the oarsmen fought to maneuver it cross-current to the far side. In a moment, raft and passengers could not be seen, only the bobbing bow lamp. We knew they had made it when the lantern stopped moving and the boatman, leaping ashore, swung it to signal the next craft to make its attempt. When it shoved off, the multitude on the near side stood up, hands toward the heavens, and shouted with one voice: "*Allahu akhbar!*"

We clambered down the bluff and joined our fellow refugees. Hundreds were crammed on a stony bank between the bluff and the water's edge. Mahmud told us to park wherever we could find room. There wasn't much, but we managed to squeeze between two bundles of carpet and mattresses, each big as a hay bale.

There was another great shout of "*Allahu akhbar!*" as the third raft shoved off and careened downstream, the bowman with the lantern like a lighted figurehead. Hands uplifted, the people chorused once more when the raft landed safely. "*Allahu akhbar!*" I didn't doubt the same words would have been flung at the heavens had the raft overturned and all aboard perished; for that, too, would have been God's will. The stern, simple faith of those people was moving, the sound of their prayers rising above the river's roar not without grandeur.

The ferrying went on all night. The rocks cold beneath us, Steve and I dozed and shivered on the bank, hoping we would cross before daylight. Something called "adventure travel" is in vogue these days. Entire magazines are devoted to the subject, but the fact is, pony treks and rubber raft trips are only ersatz adventure, exotic forms of tourism that are not much more arduous or dangerous than ordinary modes of travel a century ago. The unknown is the fundamental element of real adventure, dread its fundamental emotion. You will know you are on an authentic adventure when your sole desire is not to return to the comforts of the fireside but to live through the next ten minutes.

A little after five, one of the rafts was towed up. We climbed on, sitting on a pile of bedding. The boatmen shoved us off, then rowed for all they were worth, human muscle against the Konhara's greater muscle, the raft bouncing and the river blasting spray through the deck. Everyone on board was chanting Allah's name, praying for deliverance from drowning and from the Russians; it was fully light and the wind carried the faint throb of approaching gunships. As I sat, cradling my Gunga Din rifle, an old feeling crept into me: that quickening of the senses and perceptions created by a synthesis of fear,

excitement, and hope. I saw then, in one burst of insight, the fundamental reason why I had come so far at such great risk. I was still the
escape artist, a kind of Houdini. I was not a fugitive from ordinary life
on this journey but from ordinary death. With no knowledge of how
to face it or how to live with the awareness of it, I had fled its dreary
angst for the thrill of the close call and the near miss, the cleansing,
cathartic terror of being shot at without effect. Who knows, maybe I
was trying to preserve some illusion that violent death was the only
kind; if I could evade it, then I would live forever. But come which
way it would, by bullet, disease, or old age, there wasn't a soul with
the velocity to escape it.

The raft bumped against the shore. We jumped off. I threw my
arms around Mahmud and thanked him. He, of course, thanked
Allah.

We started down the trail to Pakistan. Half an hour later, gunships were pounding the crossing site.

The river crossing had broken the column into small groups.
The one we were with, about a hundred and fifty refugees and guerrillas altogether, had covered five or six miles when it was waylaid by
bandits. If courage, faith, and endurance are the Pathan's principal
virtues, greed is their principal vice, and the banditos were a mean
example of it. There were only three, led by a vicious character armed
with a Russian machine gun. They were levying a toll on everyone
passing through their territory. The leader, looking very much the role
of the wild Afghan as he stood atop a boulder with his machinegun
leveled, ordered us to move off the road and get down. The armed
men among us outnumbered the gang ten to one but didn't raise a
rifle. They moved off to the roadside with everyone else and sat
down. Two of the bandits went along the row of people, collecting
money and jewelry while the leader posed above, snarling *"Kena"* to
anyone he saw standing. Mahmud was the only one to ignore the
order. Cool-headedly, he kept walking, signaling Steve and me to follow him. We hugged an embankment to stay out of the chieftain's line
of sight and, what was more important, line of fire. After we rounded
a sharp bend, Mahmud took off at a trot. We ran behind and did not
stop until we'd put a ridge between us and the outlaws.

Mahmud flopped down and, fluttering his fingers over his chest, said his heart was pounding. I waved my hands this way and that, asking why thirty guerrillas had given in to a mere three. Mahmud swept his arms across the surrounding hills and held up ten fingers several times. We understood: there were three that we could see; hidden in the hills were dozens more of their clansmen. Shoot one and you'd have the whole crowd coming down on you. Why had Mahmud defied the leader's orders? He pointed at our faces, then crossed his wrists behind his back and said, "Rupee, rupee, rupee, rupee." And again we understood: if we had stopped, the bandits would have discovered we were foreigners, captured us, and held us for ransom.

I thanked Mahmud for pulling us out of another one. I was relieved, grateful, disgusted. The resistance had enough strikes against it, but it seemed hopeless if some Afghans were going to find in the war opportunities to rob and plunder other Afghans. No, there were no good wars. The last good war had been the one between Micheal and Lucifer, and that only because angels and devils do not bleed.

In another two days we reached the border. The march, through hot, brushy country, was hard but happily uneventful. Everyone who'd crossed the Konhara made it into Pakistan. The mujahadin would go back to fight another day. The civilians would be safe, if miserable, in the refugee camps, but a lot of them would be leaving the terrors of the war for those of a new and alien world. I recall Gulzada's youngest daughter letting out a scream as we filed down a road toward the Afghan camp at Bejauer. A pickup truck was coming toward us. That was what had frightened her. She had never seen one before.

We left them at the camp. Mahmud walked on, leading us somewhere. It was a very hot day. I was out of Motrin, out of the enteroviaform that had kept Steve's dysentery under control. It had gotten worse. He fell farther and farther behind. When I looked back, he was stumbling like a drunk.

"Goddamn you, Mahmud, where the hell are you going!" he shouted.

That seemed to take all the strength out of him. He dropped and sat in the dust, his head on his knees. I went to him.

"C'mon, Steve. It can't be much farther."

"The hell with that bah-stahd and his 'March now.' I've had it."

Mahmud came up and pointed at a walled house about a quarter of a mile off.

I put my hands under Steve's arms and pulled him to his feet.

"That's it over there," I said. "Ten more minutes."

Steve started walking again, and I want to say that the sight of him staggering across the fields showed me something about myself, but that would not be the truth. I did not experience any epiphanies then, but I do now. The Philip Caputo I see through the temporal telescope was—is—driven by pride. He stayed on his feet while Steve Bent collapsed. He, with his bum leg, outlasted someone seventeen years younger, and his pride in that tells me he'd invited Steve to join him because he wanted to test himself against a younger man and prove he was still the man he'd been. Was he? I don't know. He seems to feel, as he walks that last, flat quarter of a mile, every one of the two hundred up-and-down miles he's traveled; feeling them, he realizes that the Great Game is a young man's game and he is no longer young enough for it. It's an appealing image—the man on the frontier of middle age at last finding his limits—but because the memoirist often says more about who he is than who he was, I cannot be sure if I am endowing that past self with the perceptions, and the bodily aches, of my present self. I am sure that Afghanistan ended my years of living dangerously.

After I came back from there, various publications asked me to go to places like El Salvador and Nicaragua. I turned them down. Recently, I was offered an assignment to cover the Persian Gulf War, but I turned that down, too. Ever seeking a drama and intensity of emotion not found in life's quiet back pages, where people talk over backyard fences and ride to offices on the train, I knew I had lived too much of my life as if it were a front-page story under a headline set in war type. I had never been a Tim Page of Hunter Thompson but a child of my times nonetheless, prodded by my own particular devils to see it all, do it all, and take it to the limit every time in my own particular way. I got sick of it, which, possibly, was the state I'd sought all along; the romantic's appetite for extreme experiences is often a disguised longing for their opposite, a hunger he kills by feeding it to excess so he can, at last, find peace in a room.

°   °   °

There is peace in this room, where I write and look out from time to time on a salt marsh that fills, empties, and fills again in obedience to the mandate of the moon.

The peace is not easily kept; Wordsworth could not have imagined how much too much the world would be with us in the age of cable news, beaming the world's alarms into our living rooms even as they're sounded. As I write this, the news is of yet another war. It seems strange that only a year ago we were toasting the end of one, the cold war, and scholars were proclaiming the end of history. Then history came howling back, in the form of a mustached despot born in the Mesopotamian valley, near the gardens of Babylon, the place our geography teachers taught us to call the cradle of civilization.

The marsh is always the same yet ever changing, painting across my windows a scene constant without monotony, variable without unpredictability: a pleasing balance. As the tide fills, the marsh becomes a saltwater lake whose contours, shaped by the tidal fluctuations of the sound that feeds and drains it, are a little different each day. Black ducks, mallards, and mergansers ride the rising waters, and in autumn and spring, Canada geese, wings cupped, come in to rest from their long migrations. The radio and television speak of laser-guided bombs. The evening news shows pictures of them, snapped by the infrared gun cameras of Stealth fighters, blowing up bridges, bunkers, and power stations in the cradle of civilization.

The despot calls this struggle "the mother of battles." The American president says our triumph in it will be the advent of a new world order. Outside my window, I see the tide is running out. A pair of black ducks sail the swift ebb toward the sound. The falling water transforms the marsh's landscape. Archipelagoes of cord grass appear, sere brown on this winter day, but they'll be bright green come spring. Patches of mud are exposed, creased by meandering channels dug by hidden currents; and as the water drops farther, the patches become levees, rising above a tidal river that makes an oxbow bend around a peninsula of hardwoods jutting from the marsh's far shore. The afternoon sun, turning the cord grass a deep golden color, shines on colonies of oysters, clams, and mussels with shells ribbed like fans.

Downstairs, on the coffee table, newspapers and news magazines shout: ALLIED PLANES POUND IRAQI TROOPS ... IRAQ SETS OIL REFINERIES AFIRE, SPILLS OIL INTO PERSIAN GULF ... U.S. AND ALLIES

BOMB BAGHDAD TARGETS ... AMERICA AT WAR ... SADDAM'S WEIRD WAR ... WAR ... WAR ... WAR ... Snow geese sometimes fly over the marsh in winter. Mute swans cruise in on the tide, all in a line. Only a few days ago, while in the world too much with us tank cannons fired across a desert border, two huge tundra swans flew in with high, fluting cries. Their necks were like white arrows. IRAQI MISSILE PIERCES TEL AVIV SHIELD ... Stay tuned to "News Eighty-Eight" for up-to-the-minute coverage of the Persian Gulf ... RAIDS, ON HUGE SCALE, SEEK TO DESTROY MISSILE SITES ...

Some birds make their home in the marsh all year; others stay for a season. In the summer, herons keep their graceful vigil, waiting for the water to fall far enough to allow them to wade the shallows in patient hunts for killifish or fiddler crabs. Egrets stand sentry by the banks, their snowy feathers beautiful against the green of the full-leafed hardwoods. Once, not long after the despot seized and raped a neighboring country, I watched a harrier—a hawk whose name has been given to a carrier plane now bombing the cradle of civilization—soar from its perch in an oak and pluck a field mouse from a tussock of black grass.

The peace in this room is hard to keep: a tense truce between the part of me drawn to history and the part drawn to what is truly enduring and worthwhile. It's difficult not to tune the radio to the all-news station, the television to CNN; difficult to keep my eyes off the newspapers and on the salt marsh where, now, the tide has ebbed past midtide, and the river, giving itself to the sound as the sound gives itself to the sea, has narrowed to a creek. I suppose the despot born between the Tigris and Euphrates is the apotheosis of the Age of Terrorism. Not the child of the Beast, he is the Beast incarnate. We should have expected him. His coming was not without annunciation. He had his prophets. We brought him gifts, without which he would now be a petty menace, dispatching disciples with suitcases of plastic explosive to place in airliners or delivery vans. Now the heavens above the cradle of civilization flash and rumble—we have to kill him whose birth we midwifed; now the cable news brings images from the world too much with us of missiles shooting down other missiles, as it speaks a new language PATRIOTS BLAST SCUDS for a new war sanitized of pain and death by censors but also cleansed by its technological nature of the human valor and endurance that are war's only redemptive virtues. The clashes in the cradle of civilization are not of men at arms but of bloodless projectiles guided by electronic circuits.

I can appreciate the calculus that sends one ultrasonic missile to intersect the path of another, but there is a greater precision in my marsh when the crabs emerge from their primordial burrows at the moment when nature's clock strikes low tide, then scurry back at the second when the diurnal inundation begins again. One day this summer, I stood on our floating dock and watched hundreds of them crawl across the mud flats in exactly the same direction, as if they were following an azimuth. When I raised my hand to swat a mosquito, the crabs, mistaking the shadow of my arm for the shadow of a hunting gull or crow, turned around all together all at once and scuttled back, as precisely as a crack drill team. No electronics guided them, only the compasses God put into their heads. PATRIOTS BLAST SCUDS.

I would rather listen to the language of the Canada geese, to the sometimes comical discourses of the ducks, the noisy squabbling of the gulls, the sharp, terse warnings of osprey and harrier hawk, *kee-kee-kee-kee,* the haunting wanderer's call of the tundra swans and the wise silence of their mute cousins.

There is peace in this room. The radio and TV are off, the newspapers stacked in a recycling bin in the garage. I look out my window, which is my new means of escape. Without leaving my desk, I flee the world too much with us for the world of the salt marsh, where a more enduring, more truthful history is written, erased, and rewritten each day. The tidal creek is a brackish brook now, very still as it mirrors houses, trees, and the gulls that wheel above it or wade its mussel-shelled banks. The tide's run out; in a moment it will begin to flood again.